NEW DIRECTIONS IN GERMAN STUDIES
Vol. 40

Series Editor:

IMKE MEYER

Professor of Germanic Studies, University of Illinois at Chicago

Editorial Board:

KATHERINE ARENS

Professor of Germanic Studies, University of Texas at Austin

ROSWITHA BURWICK

Distinguished Chair of Modern Foreign Languages Emerita, Scripps College

RICHARD ELDRIDGE

Charles and Harriett Cox McDowell Professor of Philosophy, Swarthmore College

ERIKA FISCHER-LICHTE

Professor Emerita of Theater Studies, Freie Universität Berlin

CATRIONA MACLEOD

Frank Curtis Springer and Gertrude Melcher Springer Professor in the College and the Department of Germanic Studies, University of Chicago

STEPHAN SCHINDLER

Professor of German and Chair, University of South Florida

HEIDI SCHLIPPHACKE

Professor of Germanic Studies, University of Illinois at Chicago

ANDREW J. WEBBER

Professor of Modern German and Comparative Culture, Cambridge University

SILKE-MARIA WEINECK

Grace Lee Boggs Collegiate Professor of Comparative Literature and German Studies, University of Michigan

DAVID WELLBERY
LeRoy T. and Margaret Deffenbaugh Carlson University Professor,
University of Chicago

SABINE WILKE
Joff Hanauer Distinguished Professor for Western Civilization and
Professor of German, University of Washington

JOHN ZILCOSKY
Professor of German and Comparative Literature,
University of Toronto

A list of volumes in the series appears at the end of this book.

The "German Illusion"

Germany and Jewish-German Motifs in Hélène Cixous's Late Work

Olivier Morel

BLOOMSBURY ACADEMIC
NEW YORK • LONDON • OXFORD • NEW DELHI • SYDNEY

BLOOMSBURY ACADEMIC
Bloomsbury Publishing Inc, 1385 Broadway, New York, NY 10018, USA
Bloomsbury Publishing Plc, 50 Bedford Square, London, WC1B 3DP, UK
Bloomsbury Publishing Ireland, 29 Earlsfort Terrace, Dublin 2, D02 AY28, Ireland

BLOOMSBURY, BLOOMSBURY ACADEMIC and the Diana logo are trademarks of
Bloomsbury Publishing Plc

First published in the United States of America 2023
This paperback edition published 2025

Copyright © Olivier Morel, 2024

For legal purposes the List of Figures and Gratitude on pp. 251–252
constitute an extension of this copyright page.

Cover design: Andrea F. Busci
Cover image © Olivier Morel

All rights reserved. No part of this publication may be: i) reproduced or transmitted in any form, electronic or mechanical, including photocopying, recording or by means of any information storage or retrieval system without prior permission in writing from the publishers; or ii) used or reproduced in any way for the training, development or operation of artificial intelligence (AI) technologies, including generative AI technologies. The rights holders expressly reserve this publication from the text and data mining exception as per Article 4(3) of the Digital Single Market Directive (EU) 2019/790.

Bloomsbury Publishing Inc does not have any control over, or responsibility for, any third-party websites referred to or in this book. All internet addresses given in this book were correct at the time of going to press. The author and publisher regret any inconvenience caused if addresses have changed or sites have ceased to exist, but can accept no responsibility for any such changes.

Library of Congress Cataloging-in-Publication Data
Names: Morel, Olivier, 1969- author.
Title: The "German illusion" : Germany and Jewish-German motifs in Hélène Cixous's late work / Olivier Morel.
Description: New York : Bloomsbury Academic, [2024] | Series: New directions in German studies ; vol. 40 | Includes bibliographical references and index. | Summary: "Examines Jewish-German "tropes" in Hélène Cixous's oeuvre and life and their impact on her work as a feminist, poet, and playwright"– Provided by publisher.
Identifiers: LCCN 2023015211 (print) | LCCN 2023015212 (ebook) | ISBN 9798765107379 (hardback) | ISBN 9798765107386 (paperback) | ISBN 9798765107416 (pdf) | ISBN 9798765107393 (epub) | ISBN 9798765107409 (ebook other)
Subjects: LCSH: Cixous, Hélène, 1937–Criticism and interpretation. | Germany–In literature. | Jews, German, in literature. | LCGFT: Literary criticism.
Classification: LCC PQ2663.I9 Z758 2024 (print) | LCC PQ2663.I9 (ebook) | DDC 848/.91409–dc23/eng/20230718
LC record available at https://lccn.loc.gov/2023015211
LC ebook record available at https://lccn.loc.gov/2023015212

ISBN:		
	HB:	979-8-7651-0737-9
	PB:	979-8-7651-0738-6
	ePDF:	979-8-7651-0741-6
	eBook:	979-8-7651-0739-3

Series: New Directions in German Studies

Typeset by Integra Software Services Pvt. Ltd.

For product safety related questions contact productsafety@bloomsbury.com.

To find out more about our authors and books visit www.bloomsbury.com
and sign up for our newsletters.

*To Professor Jim Collins,
initiator, mentor, friend.*

Contents

List of Figures ix
List of Abbreviations xi

Introduction: "An Originary Exile" 1

I GERMANY IS CALLING: THE LANDLINE (1916–2016) 17

1 The first telephone 19

2 The dream call 31

3 The last phone call 42

II "OS, NA, BRÜCK": THE CAPITAL OF
MEMORY (1933–1935) 53

4 Ruins and remembrance: from "Os, na, brück" to "Rom'" 57

5 Osnabrück the instrument of peace: "*Recorder*," recorder 74

6 *Remembrer*-remember: A detour to Montaigne's Tower ... and its ruins (image) 89

7 "I am, we are October 23, 1935": The October 23, 1935, picture 120

8 N'ai-je pas vu (Have I not seen ...), *la neige pas vue* (... the snow not seen)? 137

III AN ORIGINARY MOVE: THE MOVE
OF THE ORIGIN (1938) 151

9 Omi was in Osnabrück ... 153

10 "Bericht" 172

viii Contents

11 "Etwas" 184
12 Epilog 188
IV ZUGEHÖR: THE JEWISH-GERMAN PSYCHE 193
13 "Envoûté," delirium 195
14 "We" 213
15 Epilog: Zugehör 221
Conclusion: *Frauenprotest* 222

*Afterword: A filmed-interrupted interview
with Hélène Cixous* 227
Gratitude 251
Bibliography 253
Index 259

List of Figures

All photographs were taken by the author.

    The city of Osnabrück, Germany, at dawn on
October 23, 2019   xiv

1   Hélène Cixous in the Hexengasse, Osnabrück,
October 25, 2019   2

2   On October 25, 2019, Wolfgang Griesert, the City Mayor of Osnabrück, and Hélène Cixous hand sweet pretzels to children outside of Osnabrück City Hall in commemoration of the Treaty of Osnabrück   60

3   The Treaty of Osnabrück was signed on October 24, 1648, as a part of the general peace negotiations known as the Peace of Westphalia to end the Thirty Years' War   60

4   The great room of the city hall in Osnabrück, October 24, 2019   62

5   Remains of the Synagogue in Osnabrück, October 23, 2019   65

6   The chandelier under which the Treaty of Osnabrück was sealed in the great room of Osnabrück City Hall, October 24, 2019   82

7   "C'est la prison, celle dont je parle tout le temps." Hélène Cixous faces the Roman Charity in the winter closet of the *librerie*, in Montaigne, on July 4, 2016 (screen capture)   103

8, 9, 10   Montaigne's winter closet ("cabinet d'hiver"), July 2, 2022   119

11   The train station, Osnabrück, October 25, 2019   123

x   List of Figures

12   Osnabrück train station, October 25, 2019   130

13   Hélène Cixous, the Hase river, Osnabrück,
     October 25, 2019   142

14   The Hase river in Osnabrück, October 25, 2019   143

15   Hélène Cixous and Karin Jabs-Kiesler on the site of the
     "well kept," "dead Synagogue" ("la Synagogue morte […]
     bien soignée" [RB, 74]) of Osnabrück, October 23, 2019   149

16   Andreas Jonas and Else Jonas's stolpersteine, Osnabrück,
     Germany, October 23, 2019   162

17   Friedrichstraße, where Else and Andreas Jonas lived
     until 1942   167

18   Friedrichstraße 25, Else and Andreas Jonas's residence,
     Osnabrück, October 23, 2019   167

19   Touching Else and Andreas Jonas's stolpersteine, Osnabrück,
     October 23, 2019   168

20   Hélène Cixous in front of Else and Andreas Jonas's residence,
     Osnabrück, October 23, 2019   168

21, 22, 23   "Ruines bien rangées": the "well-arranged," "well
     ordered" ruins of the Osnabrück Synagogue
     (Memorial), October 23, 2019   169–170

24, 25   Nikolaiort, October 23, 2019   173–174

26   Hélène Cixous on her way to Osnabrück, October 22, 2019   225

27   Celebration of the *Instrumentum Pacis Osnabrugensis*,
     the Treaty of Osnabrück (Peace of Westphalia), signed
     in October of 1648   226

28   The Book of Prayers of Abraham Meir Klein (1844–1924),
     Hélène Cixous's grandfather   232

29   Filmed interview with Hélène Cixous, Paris, June 17, 2012   233

30   Filmed interview with Hélène Cixous, Paris, June 17, 2012   245

31   Filmed interview with Hélène Cixous, Paris, June 17, 2012   246

32   Filmed interview with Hélène Cixous, Paris, June 17, 2012   250

List of Abbreviations

Abbreviations for Citations of Hélène Cixous's Texts

A	*Angst*, Paris: Des Femmes, [1977] 1998.
AA	Cécile Wajsbrot, *Une autobiographie allemande*, Paris: Bourgois, 2016.
BM	*Benjamin à Montaigne, Il ne faut pas le dire*, Paris: Galilée, 2001.
CM	*Correspondance avec le mur, Accompagné de cinq dessins à la pierre noire d'Adel Abdessemed*, Paris: Galilée, 2017.
D	*Dedans*, Paris: Des Femmes, 1969.
EES	*Eve Escapes, Ruins and Life*, trans. by Peggy Kamuf, Cambridge, UK: Polity, 2012.
EEV	*Ève s'évade, La Ruine et la Vie*, Paris: Galilée, 2009.
FJ	*La Fiancée juive de la tentation*, Paris: Des Femmes, 1995.
GO	*Gare d'Osnabrück à Jérusalem*, Accompagné de sept substantifs dessinés par Pierre Alechinsky, Paris: Galilée, 2016.
HM	*Homère est morte …*, Paris: Galilée, 2014.
N	*1938, nuits*, Paris: Galilée, 2019.
NC	*Nacres, Accompagné de dessins à la pierre noire d'Adel Abdessemed*, Paris: Galilée 2019.
OS	*Osnabrück*, Paris: Éditions des Femmes Antoinette Fouque, 1999.
OSJ	*Osnabrück Station to Jerusalem*, with seven words drawn by Pierre Alechinsky, trans. by Peggy Kamuf, New York: Fordham University Press, 2020.
PR	Mireille Calle-Gruber, *Photos de Racines*, Paris: Des Femmes, 1994.
R	with Mireille Calle-Gruber, *Rootprints, Memory and Life Writing*, trans. by Eric Prenowitz, New York: Routledge, 1997.
RB	*Ruines bien rangées*, Paris: Gallimard, 2020.

RM	*Le Rire de la Méduse et autres ironies*, "Un effet d'épine de rose," Paris: Galilée, [1975] 2010.
RT	Frédéric-Yves Jeannet, *Rencontre terrestre*, Paris: Galilée, 2005.
RV	*Revirements dans l'antarctique du cœur*, Paris: Galilée, 2011.
SC	*So Close*, trans. by Peggy Kamuf, Cambridge, UK: Polity, 2009.
SP	*Si près*, Frontispice et culispice de Pierre Alechinsky, Paris: Galilée, 2007.
TP	*Tours promises*, Paris: Galilée, 2004.
TT	*Twists and Turns in the Heart's Antarctic*, trans. by Beverley Bie Brahic, Cambridge, UK: Polity, 2014.
V	with Jacques Derrida, *Voiles*, Accompagné de six dessins d'Ernest Pignon-Ernest, Paris: Galilée, 1998.
VL	with Jacques Derrida, *Veils*, trans. by Geoffrey Bennington, artwork by Ernest Pignon-Ernest, Redwood City, CA: Stanford University Press, 2002.

La plus grande illusion est de penser que ce qui est passé est fini, me dis-je.

(SP, 98)

"The greatest illusion is to think that what is passed is finished, I say to myself" (*SC*, 70).

The city of Osnabrück, Germany, at dawn on October 23, 2019.

Introduction "An Originary Exile"

Cixous c'est quoi comme pays? Je réponds: c'est allemand. Quand j'étais jeune je disais naïvement c'est juifkabyle.

(SP, 105)[1]

In 1975, the German literary scholar and writer Hans Mayer published one of his most influential books, a work titled *Outsiders*. A politically engaged intellectual whose parents were murdered at Auschwitz, Mayer had been forced to flee Nazi Germany in 1933 under racial persecutions banning him from the workplace. Through its undeniable autobiographical dimension, the collection of essays that make up *Outsiders* has had a lasting impact on the history of the study of literature and beyond. In one famous chapter Mayer defines the long tradition of what he calls a "suffering for Germany":

> [T]here is in German literature and intellectual development the phenomenon of a suffering for Germany at the hands of Germany that has no counterpart in other peoples and cultures. It is to be found in Hölderlin and Goethe, Platen and Nietzsche. "How am I sick because of my fatherland," wrote Platen the outsider. Thomas Mann quoted the verse in his journals covering the period of exile, under the heading "Leiden an Deutschland."[2]

Mayer highlights that the phenomenon has been analyzed "as early as Heine." And he adds that Heinrich Heine had seen "the historical parallelism between the behavior of the Jews and the Germans in modern

---

1 "Cixous what kind of country is that? I answer: it's German. When I was young I used to say naïvely: it's Kabyle-Jewish" (SC, 75).
2 Hans Mayer, *Outsiders: A Study in Life and Letters*, trans. Denis M. Sweet (Cambridge, MA: MIT Press, [1975] 1982), 362.

Figure 1 Hélène Cixous in the Hexengasse, Osnabrück, on October 25, 2019.

European history."³ Drawing on the concept of German "suffering" that he helped identify, Mayer shows how the persecutions, the genocide, and the diaspora took place through what he calls the "failure" of the Jewish integration in Germany:

> A people like the Germans cannot become outsiders, because they have a language, history, and land that can act toward integration. Jewish integration in Europe proceeded from the assumption that Jewish language and history were to be sacrificed, just as Moses Mendelssohn taught; that there would be no Jewish nation. Everything was to be "adopted" from the host country and people: language, culture, region. That failed. Suffering at the hands of Germany was never anything more than the reaction of German outsiders to German rules and regularity.⁴

Hélène Cixous visited Osnabrück for the first time in 2015. In the months following this first trip to the city of the Jonas family, her German family, Cixous wrote *Gare d'Osnabrück à Jérusalem*. Published in early 2016, the book contains the following sentence that could serve as the ultimate horizon of this whole book:

> Mais ce livre n'est pas un roman fiction, il est l'hématome causé par le choc qui s'est produit entre la Ville et le moi indéfini avec tous mes livres à ses côtés et soixante-dix ans de récits homériques proférés par ma mère.
>
> (*GO*, 139)⁵

Cixous recounts the bruise, the shock, and seventy years of tales ("récits") told by her mother, Ève, Eva Cixous née Klein, who grew

---

3 Mayer, *Outsiders*, 362.
4 Mayer, *Outsiders*, 363.
5 "But this book is not a fictional novel, it is the bruise caused by the shock produced between the City and the indefinite self, with all my books by its side and seventy years of Homeric stories proffered by my mother" (*OSJ*, 109). This passage will reappear in our reflection in Part IV. It was also in 2016 that I worked at Hélène Cixous's side for more than six months while I was directing the feature-length film that I devoted to her creative life. The making of *Ever, Rêve, Hélène Cixous* (Dir. Olivier Morel, 118 minutes, Zadig Productions, France, USA, 2018) involved countless filming sessions with Hélène Cixous that started as early as June of 2012. In this context, I followed the publication of *Gare d'Osnabrück à Jérusalem* (the book was released in early 2016) and of most of the books that succeeded. Along with the lengthy dialogues that I had with Hélène

up in Strasbourg[6] and Osnabrück before leaving Germany as soon as Nazism began to rise. Through her exile, Ève, Hélène Cixous's diasporic mother, is more than Cixous's distant "link" to Germany. Ève's fate cannot be separated from Cixous's literary bruise and shock, from her literal suffering of Osnabrück, of Germany, from a certain "Germanalgia" that barred Ève Cixous from returning to Germany for a very, very long time. Ève Cixous did not set foot on German soil from 1936, when she made an attempt to convince her own mother to flee, until 1985, when she reluctantly came "back" to Osnabrück. "Elle [Ève] est contre le couteau dans la plaie," "she [Ève] is against the knife in the wound" (*N*, 79), writes Hélène Cixous about a pain also called the "maladie de l'Allemagne" (*BM*, 152) by Ève Cixous in *Benjamin à Montaigne*, the "malady of Germany from which it is impossible to cure yourself" ("La maladie de l'Allemagne on ne sait plus comment s'en débarrasser" [*BM*, 152]).

Of course, one might say that Hélène Cixous was not born in Germany and that she did not physically grow up in Germany. But in many ways such an affirmation should be tempered by the fact that she grew up *with* Germany. Cixous was surrounded by powerful German figures, notably her mother and her grandmother Rosalie Klein (called Omi), who reunited with the Cixous family in Oran toward the end of 1938 when Cixous was an infant. Hélène Cixous grew up with figures that incarnated the political and racial persecutions perpetrated by Nazi Germany—with German Jews who had fled Germany. An intriguing dimension of this background is that she grew up in a country, Algeria, where she *always* knew that she was an outsider in terms very close to those defined by Mayer. She grew up in a colonial Algeria at war with itself and from which it was clear she would have to escape. Her flight was as determined as the event of her birth. It was already set in stone that the colonial Algeria of her birth would never be "her" country. This structure might have created a unique configuration in which she was particularly receptive and formed by her Algerian upbringing, that which Mayer calls the "suffering for Germany, at the hands of Germany." Because of this German suffering, Ève Cixous was in Oran, far from Germany. The German suffering as a syndrome of estrange-

---

Cixous, I traveled with her to Berlin, in Germany (May 2016), to Montaigne (early July 2016), as well as to Osnabrück (October 2019), where our film premiered at the Osnabrück Theater on October 24, 2019. This sequence of events explains why I employ the first person on more than one occasion throughout the following pages. The majority of the sources quoted in those circumstances can be found in the film. But there are few exceptions, and I will provide enough context when that is the case.

6   Under the German Empire, namely, before the end of the Great War (1914–1918).

ment that marked Cixous's German relatives and ancestors could have been reinforced, even hyperbolically activated, by the surrounding asymmetrical, inequal, discriminatory social interactions upon which the French constructed colonial Algeria. The German suffering that had "no counterpart in other peoples and cultures" converged, for Cixous, in an Algeria that also prolonged the impossible relationship to the native land for the German exiles in Algeria. It could also be that the acuity that Hélène Cixous developed vis-à-vis the German suffering and trauma made her especially aware of the colonial *impossibility* to be "Algerian." Could her colonial impossibility to be Algerian be of a German nature? And the reverse? Perhaps the deep roots of this double bind, that of "belonging" to two estranged countries, will remain the mystery at the core of "Cixous" as one of the most energetic forces of her œuvre ... from Germany to Algeria, a malady of Germany mixed with the malady of Algeria, a "Germanalgia" that could be named her "GermanAlgeria." This double rejection, this dual ban of Cixous's so-called origin, her "c'est allemand, [...] c'est juifkabyle," is unavoidable to understand her habitus and œuvre:

> Je vois bien que mes parents ont pu croire être en Algérie, surtout mon père qui y était vraiment né et qui depuis 1908 n'avait pas cessé de progresser dans ce croire être-de et -en, s'élevant par degrés, dans une de ces courbes scolaires et universitaires ascendantes et harmonieuses qui font croire que l'on va vers la Rose Universelle et qu'elle existe. Surtout Ève ma mère qui s'étant tirée elle-même de l'enfer allemand a pu croire en se retrouvant jeune et forte à Oran en être. Tandis que moi dès le début j'ai vu qu'ils étaient poussière et je les ai vus retourner à la poussière, foulés aux semelles de ce surpays où mon père avait cru avoir une place réservée. Tandis que moi j'ai toujours su que j'avais pour toit la voûte d'une cave ou d'un escalier.
>
> (*SP*, 69)[7]

---

[7] "I realize quite well that my parents were able to believe they were in Algeria, especially my father who was really born there and who since 1908 had not ceased to progress in this belief of being-of and -in, raising himself by degrees, in one of those ascending and harmonious academic arcs that makes one believe one is going toward the Universal Rose and that it exists. Especially Ève my mother who having gotten herself out of the German hell was able to believe she was part of it upon finding herself young and strong again in Oran. Whereas I from the beginning I saw that they were dust and I saw them return to dust, trodden beneath the soles of this supercountry where my father thought he had a place set aside. Whereas I always knew that for roof I had the vault of a cellar or a stairway" (*SC*, 47).

In the introduction of her exchange of letters with Cécile Wajsbrot, *Une autobiographie Allemande*, Cixous refines this complex structure and chiasm in which the intertwining of Germany and Algeria makes her the "only survivor" of a major historical and cultural moment:

> Je suis le résultat de plus d'un pays natal. Le trait étrange, et désormais presque inimaginable, de mes conjonctions inaugurales, c'est que, par suite des guerres, violences, massacres, de façon imprévue dans la chronique humaine, il fut un temps, celui de mon enfance à Oran, où une Allemagne demeura en Algérie: l'Allemagne des fugitifs, des réfugiés. Pendant quelques années, on pouvait entendre, au jardin public d'Oran, voleter d'un banc à l'autre des phrases en allemand. Ces ans—cruels et poétiques—ont totalement disparu. Je suis peut-être la seule survivante de cette halte africaine dans l'odyssée judéo-allemande.
>
> (*AA*, 16–17)[8]

---

[8] "I am the result of more than one country of birth. The strange trait of my inaugural conjunctions, henceforth almost unimaginable, is that, as a result of the wars, violence, massacres—in an unforeseen way in the chronicle of humanity—there was a time, that of my childhood in Oran, where a Germany resided in Algeria: the Germany of fugitives, of refugees. For a few years, one could hear sentences in German flutter from one bench to another at the public garden of Oran. These years, cruel and poetic, have completely disappeared. I am perhaps the last survivor of this African stop in the Jewish-German Odyssey." All translations that do not carry a reference are mine. I have tried to render Hélène Cixous's style while giving space to her unique approaches to rhythm in French, namely, her highly creative, unconventional use of punctuation in French. Cixous's punctuation is significant because it often operates as a marker of her mother's discourse as it is embedded in her texts, including most of the texts quoted in the present work. I cannot expand on this observation here, but I merely suggest that it would be fruitful to consider Cixous's creative use of punctuation in light of how her mother intersects, interrupts, inserts herself, telephones, and sometimes also perverts, subverts, converts, and hijacks Cixous's poetic prose throughout her works of the past years. Along those lines, I wonder if Cixous's punctuation could function as a vehicle that diffuses and infuses something of the *German language* in her writing; such a study would require a meticulous linguistic analysis that I cannot conduct here, even though I am very sensitive to its texture in Cixous's audible forms of writing-voicing-breathing, full of German structures and accentuations. This dimension is also revealed, as we will discuss later, by the occurrences of German terms and syntagms in Cixous's work in general, both in original German and in French. "Osnabrück in Oran und Umgekehrt" is the title of the fourth and last chapter of the book of conversations that Hélène Cixous had with Peter Engelmann. Peter Engelmann, *Aus Montaignes Koffer, Hélène Cixous im Gespräch mit Peter Engelmann, Passagen Gespräche 7* (Vienna: Passagen Verlag, 2017), 133–77.

Not "German" figures and refugees in Algeria, but "une Allemagne qui demeura en Algérie," that is, a "Germany [that] resided in Algeria," marked by a history of war, violence, and massacre. The fact that Cixous grew up *in Germany in Algeria* justifies her inclusion in the long German history described and embodied by Mayer.

The Algerian dimension of Cixous's life and work has been well documented and studied within the broader field of postcolonial studies, more specifically after Cixous began to write about Algeria and around the time when Algeria entered in the tumultuous phase of its history with the civil war of the early 1990s. The German dimension, and precisely what Cixous calls the "Jewish-German odyssey" of her family, has been much less explored. Until the mid-1990s and the publication of *Photos de racines* in 1994, Cixous had never truly confronted herself directly in writing with what I call a German and a Jewish-German "trope" in her œuvre. In line with Hans Mayer's seminal work, studying this trope would investigate the forms of a "Leiden an Deutschland," something "cruel," "crual," as Cixous puts it. Her writing of the "hématome," of her "bruise," is sublimated into a powerful poetic horizon, an odyssey with a "Germany" that she has always cherished ... however ... "J'ai toujours aimé l'Allemagne," she writes, and she immediately adds "Et pourtant—" "however—" (*AA*, 15). Cherished ... however. This could have been the title of the present book.

This work attempts to trace the contours of Cixous's "mysterious originary exile" ("un mystérieux exil originaire" [*AA*, 15]) from Germany. I would argue that this powerful notion, the *exil originaire*, makes her the epitome of the figure of the "suffering for Germany at the hands of Germany," traced by Mayer. She is the epitome of the German wound, even, perhaps, of the "German malady" named by Ève Cixous. Cixous would become the incarnation of the emblematic "German" creation identified by Mayer in a long tradition that runs from the German romantics, to Nietzsche, Mann and himself—that is, Mayer's generation of exiles to which Ève Cixous belongs;[9] simultaneously Hélène Cixous would be the culmination of this long tradition, from which Germany is now distant. She would be an essential German creation; though she is no longer immersed in this German universe, she is an emblematic and paradigmatic historical "product" of its most defining wound, of the endemic rejection for which being

---

9   Hans Mayer was born in 1907. Ève Cixous was born in 1910.

8   The "German Illusion"

Jewish *and* German is a name in our time.¹⁰ She is the insider-outsider, born in/from the most intimate version of a Germany whose

---

10   "Vous avez déjà compris que ce qui m'intéresse dans ce séminaire, et déjà depuis l'an dernier, c'est la modernité, le passé et l'avenir d'un certain couple, du couple judéo-allemand que je crois tout à fait unique, unique en son genre, et *sans lequel il est impossible de comprendre quelque chose à l'histoire de l'Allemagne, à l'histoire du nazisme, à l'histoire du sionisme, de qui s'y s'y* [sic] *produit, de ce qui s'y rapporte par inclusion ou par exclusion, donc d'un assez grand nombre de choses dans l'histoire de notre temps,* dans notre temps et dans notre histoire [sic] ce temps. Et quand je dis 'notre', je me fie à la grammaire et à la sémantique d'un 'nous' qui ne se réduit ni à un 'nous' les Allemands, 'nous' les Juifs, nous les judéo-allemands, ni même nous les Européens. Je n'imagine pas aujourd'hui de région géo-politique de l'humanité, je n'imagine rien d'humain aujourd'hui qui ne soit concerné ou touché, directement ou indirectement, de près ou de loin par l'histoire de cette ressemblance et de ce couple judéo-allemand. Je ne suis même pas sûr que 'humanité géo-politique' soit encore une circonscription assez large ou compréhensive du phénomène. On pourrait montrer, mais je n'en ai pas le temps, qu'il va maintenant au-delà du politique et de la terre (du géo-politique), et qu'il concerne aussi la nature animale, ou non" ("You have already understood that what interests me in this seminar—and already since last year—is the modernity, the past and the future of a certain couple, of the Jewish-German couple that I believe to be completely unique, unique in its kind, *and without which it is impossible to understand something about the history of Germany, about the history of Nazism, about the history of Zionism,* [to the history] *of what takes place in* [Germany, Nazism, Zionism], [about the history] *of what relates to* [Germany, Nazism, Zionism] *through inclusion and exclusion, therefore,* [about the history] *of a large number of things in the history of our time,* in our time and in our history of this time. And when I say 'our,' I trust the grammar and semantic of a 'we' that is not reduced to a 'we' the Germans, 'we' the Jews, we the Jewish-Germans, not even we the Europeans. I cannot think of a geopolitical region of humanity, I cannot think of anything human today that is not concerned with or is not touched—directly or indirectly, from near or far—by the history of this resemblance and of this Jewish-German couple. I am not even sure that 'geopolitical humanity' is a broad or comprehensive enough perimeter for this phenomenon. We could show, but I don't have the time, that this now goes beyond the political and the earth [the geopolitical], and that it deals with the animal nature, or not") (my emphases). This quote from Jacques Derrida can be consulted in the Derrida archives of the Langson Library of the University of California Irvine (USA). Jacques Derrida, tapuscripts/notes of the seminar taught at the École des Hautes Études en Sciences Sociales, second session, 1987–1988 consulted on July 26–30, 2019, Derrida MS-C01, box 19 folder 17, Langson Library, Special Collections (archives), University of California Irvine, 8–9. We will come back to this subject in Part IV. It could be that Derrida's constant acuity and research on the subject was also generated by his long, close friendship with Hélène Cixous and her mother. His own "Algerian" habitus—the one thematized here about Cixous—also plays a critical part in his interest for the "Jewish-German couple"—as his published work on the philosopher Hermann Cohen attests. In *Ruines bien rangées,* Cixous refers to what it meant to be "French" for the Jews of Algeria in light of what it meant to be "German" for the Jews in Germany.

logic ultimately pushed outside and forced into exile those who are to this day attached to the long German tradition of outsider-poets, outsider-writers, outsider-thinkers who write in, and beyond, the German language of the figures who marked the "Jewish-German odyssey" of the *Mitteleuropa*. These span from Franz Kafka to Elias Canetti, from Rosa Luxemburg to Walter Benjamin to Hannah Arendt, from Sigmund Freud to Else Lasker-Schüler to Paul Celan, as well as the authors named by Mayer: Moses Mendelssohn in the eighteenth century, Heinrich Heine in the nineteenth century. To these figures, highly influential female writers and intellectuals should be added, such as the illustrious animators of the vibrant, enlightened, late eighteenth-century Berlin: Dorothea von Schlegel (Moses Mendelssohn's oldest daughter), Rahel Levin Varnhagen and Henriette Herz. Through this idea of an attachment to a universe that operates as within an inaugural detachment, the "exil originaire" is also the breach of origin, the "originary" breach, the wound of the origin that defines literature. For Mayer, and for Cixous, such a phenomenon is singularly a *literary phenomenon*. It is not only a phenomenon that has provoked the Jewish diaspora, as well as the anti-Nazi political exile, but it is a major literary and intellectual movement which might also explain why Cixous calls it a "Jewish-German odyssey" made of cruelty and poetry.

As of November 2022, Hélène Cixous has published at least 1,287 pages of texts *related to* "Germany," and this figure does not even include Cixous's theater play *Oy!*. These texts are written, in one way or another, *under the name, under the signs* or *under the influence* of "Germany," "German," "Osnabrück ...." "Related to Germany" is

---

She renders this sense of "being" French or German with the word "illusion": "ne-plus-être-français ça ne veut rien dire si on ne l'est plus c'est qu'on ne l'a jamais été l'illusion a quand même bien résisté depuis 1867 c'est plus long que l'illusion allemande des Jonas, mon père allait justement finir par ne plus douter mais l'indicible de la douleur c'est le coup de l'annulation du sujet, ne plus pouvoir se trouver inscrit dans la liste des vivants, être renvoyé du monde, même pas exilé, décrété non-existant, c'est une maladie brutale qui prend au cerveau" (*RB*, 64–5) ("not-being-French-anymore this doesn't mean anything, if one no longer is it means that one never was, however the illusion still has resisted since 1867, it has lasted longer than the German illusion of the Jonas family, my father was just about to end up not doubting anymore but the unspeakable of pain is the blow of cancelation of the subject, of not being able to find oneself recorded on the list of the living, of being expelled from the world, not even exiled but declared nonexistent, this is a brutal malady that takes over the brain"). This notion of illusion will persist as we progress, constituting a central topic of Part IV.

10   The "German Illusion"

a very vague notion. And "Germany" is in quotation marks, with no possessive. It is not about "her" Germany. It might not even be *about* Germany. It is about the sign, about how it is invented by Cixous, about how the signifier *takes place*, about its prevalence, its space, about the ways it spreads and informs her creative life, about the way poetry and writing define her life in and around "Osnabrück," "Germany."[11] About how "Osnabrück," "Germany," encrypts the enigma of Hélène Cixous's "place."[12] It is about how this sign, these signs, occur in writing in her

---

11   A fruitful reference in developing our research on how Cixous articulates the interactions between space and poetry—between "place" and literature throughout her œuvre—is Bertrand Westphal's highly Deleuzian essay titled *La géocritique, réel, fiction, espace*; his work is especially relevant when he stresses that literature practices the "circulation between worlds": "[la littérature] est garante de la compossibilité des univers, de la circulation entre les mondes." Bertrand Westphal, *La géocritique, réel, fiction, espace* (Paris: éditions de Minuit, 2007), 236. In translation: "[literature] guarantees the compossibility of the universe, the movement between worlds [...]" Bertrand Westphal, *Geocriticism: Real and Fictional Spaces*, trans. Robert T. Tally Jr. (London: Palgrave Macmillan, 2011), 145.

12   In his introduction to the collection of essays and texts on Cixous that he edited in 2006, Eric Prenowitz writes about what it means to "take place" in light of Cixous's œuvre. Eric Prenowitz, ed., "Cracking the Book-Readings of Hélène Cixous," *New Literary History*, vol. 37, no. 1 (Johns Hopkins University Press, winter 2006), R9–R27. This question appears in Prenowitz's text within a reflection on translation, on how "a non-French-reader necessarily comes at Hélène Cixous from light years away" (*ibid.*, xx), within an "extraterrestrial" (*ibid.*, xx) condition: "we do not know how to read—if knowing means having assurance or insurance, being certain one possesses a set of hermeneutic keys with which to unlock the text" (*ibid.*, xx). While expanding on this notion of "knowing-not knowing how to read [Cixous]," Prenowitz finds himself on the footsteps of a claim by Jacques Derrida that he quotes; Derrida writes: "To learn how to know how to read, how to read [Cixous]: I believe that this has not yet taken place [*eu lieu*], except for rare exceptions" (Jacques Derrida, *Genèse, généalogie, genres et le génie* [Paris: Galilée,] 2003, 65); Prenowitz continues: "Will it ever *take place*? Will it ever have a place (*avoir lieu*)? What is reading, after all, and where? Who? What does it mean to know or to learn how to read? Can we, will we ever learn how to know how to read Hélène Cixous?" (*ibid.*, xx). Through this powerful reflection on the notion of *avoir lieu* as "take place" and "have a place," Prenowitz, who has translated many of Hélène Cixous's texts, perhaps suggests that if Cixous's texts "have a place," if they "take place," it is precisely where the very notion of "place" is at stake. And what it means to read a place, what it means to read a place when such a thing as "reading" takes place, when reading is highly dependent on the "place." I would suggest that Cixous's texts *take place* precisely where the place is fundamentally unknown, where it is tied to their translative nature, where the "place" is in motion, in question, where it defies any form of genetic appropriation, namely, where the place defies any notion of "taking" or "having." We cannot deny the fact that we could, we should, hear Derrida's lament that reading Cixous has (still) not taken place (in 2003). But this lament

œuvre, about the way it is a part of her upbringing, about everything that attracts her to "Germany," and what interrogates forms of belonging to a certain "Germany." It is both "Germany" the signifier as well as the multiple occurrences and derivations of the German signifier, of the German trope. Of the German language(s).

Two directions could be taken from there. One is that Germany is a category, a region of Cixous's *writing* in general, which means that it is tied to an essential otherness to the extent that there is no writing—and this is especially true for Cixous—without dealing with an essential alterity that we will explore, for example, with Omi, her *alter ego* Omi, and the countless voices, many familiar, family voices, that Cixous incarnates and channels in her writing. The second is that in such an understanding of writing, the proper name "Germany" is *improper* in the sense that it cannot be owned, it cannot be reduced, exhausted, or explained; it resists theory and the logos. It resists possession as well as conceptual assignations, which could also be a marker of essential literary otherness. In other words, it is the opposite of natural and genetic and thereby opens the avenue for the idea that there is a *German psyche*, that what we are thematizing here is the German psyche in Cixous's œuvre, the psyche of Cixous's German family, of Cixous's "German" psyche. Psyche also means energy; we follow the stream of a creative drive. At the core of the German trope and psyche in Cixous's œuvre is the vertiginous complexity that puts the word "German" in the orbit of the word "Jewish." "Jewish" being both a component of "German" in the Jonas family and the name of an alterity; "Germany" is the antagonist within the "Jewish-German," within the association of the two terms. This continent of a psyche, of a psyche at work (writing) renders the great schism that divides "Germany" and "Nazi," Germany as a product of its originary suffering, the one that ultimately will be

---

allows Prenowitz (and perhaps Derrida too) to argue that it is precisely at the core of Cixous's texts that "knowing" and, more importantly, "knowing how to read" is deconstructed, especially when it operates as an authoritarian form (of "having assurance or insurance"). He pleads for an essential vulnerability in the fact that *not-knowing how* to read Cixous occurs at the core of her "place" (*lieu, avoir lieu*) in our time. In countless ways in the present study, "Osnabrück" (as well as "Germany") belongs to this critical experience of the place as an art of reading/not-knowing how to read, of reading the unknown place analyzed by Prenowitz. "Unknown," in this sense, is not necessarily opposed to "familiar," as we will see. What *takes place* in our study—if, indeed, it ever does—is a "not-knowing how to read" Cixous's *Osnabrück*(s) (the city, the book titled *Osnabrück*, the books, etc.), Cixous's Germany(ies). Prenowitz hears and reads Cixous in more than one language. As a translator of Cixous's poetic texts, his work abides by Cixous's idea that "la traduction a toujours déjà commencé" (*RT*, 31) ("The translation has always already started").

the "failure" (Mayer)—the irreducible, destructive fault within the Jewish-German couple. It is the chronicle of a "Jewish-German psyche," as Derrida defines it in an essay to be discussed in Part IV.

This framework provides the space in which we will approach the highly diverse, sprawling, and complex corpus of texts by Cixous. This complexity is not only intrinsic to these texts, with their highly amphibological nature. Such a complexity is also inherent to the nature of the trope "Germany." It bears witness to this trope. Although it could certainly be possible to show that many "German" themes have always explicitly informed Cixous's texts and work[13] (on top of the fact that Cixous's productive work is ongoing), we limit our focus to eight books that explicitly address German themes, notions, and figures: *Photos de racines* (1994), *Osnabrück* (1999), *Benjamin à Montaigne* (2001), *Gare d'Osnabrück à Jérusalem* (2016), *Ève s'évade* (2009), *Correspondance avec le Mur* (2017), *1938, nuits* (2019) and *Ruines bien rangées* (2020). In addition, *Tours promises* (2004), *Si près* (2007), *Revirements* (2011), *Une autobiographie allemande* (2016) and *Nacres* (2019) will be referred to frequently.

Our trajectory in the reading of these texts revolves around four questions.

The first part refines a notion of *telephony* that aims to analyze the ways in which Hélène Cixous's texts are "called" by Germany but also how they are "calling" a certain Germany. What is the meaning of this call? What kind of response, of responsibility, does such a call carry? In other words, what does it mean for Cixous, and in Cixous's texts, to be on the line with Germany, to carry the cryptic inscription (number) of a certain German lineage that calls Cixous in her dreams and on all kinds of telephones? There is an abundance of telephones, of coded calls, and of unanswered questions in her poetry. This exploration will have three dimensions. It begins with the historical event of Osnabrück's first telephone acquired by the Jonas family in the time of the First World War. It then moves to the territories of the dream, of the dream call, and of a call to dream within Cixous's literary telephony. This reflection ends with a last phone call that took place in March of 2016, on the first day of spring, when Hélène Cixous talked for the last time to the last remaining member of the Jonas family of the Osnabrück region. Marga Carlebach née Löwenstein was 105 years old at the time. She was born in 1910, the same year as her cousin Ève Cixous. An underlying motif of this part revolves around the way by which a country, the legal fiction named "Germany," can operate the call. The call of the fatherland was answered by Cixous's own grandfather, Michael Klein, who enlisted

---

13 *Angst* is a good, obvious example. Hélène Cixous, *Angst* (Paris: Des Femmes, [1977] 1998).

Introduction   13

in the German army in 1914 and was killed in 1916. The years 1916 to 2016: those two dates could be the temporal segment on which Part I is conceived.

The years 1933 to 1935: a photograph of Andreas Jonas, Hélène Cixous's great uncle, taken in the train station of Osnabrück on October 23, 1935, will be a central reference of Part II. This part offers a study of the status of memory, and more specifically, the dynamic process of remembrance as it is endured and engaged in Cixous's creative writing. The fact that "remembering" is tied to destructions, to a radical effacement of memory—the murdering of so many members of Cixous's German family—raises critical questions on what it means to write for Cixous and how writing is inseparable from the way her inspiration operates when it comes to Germany. Along those lines, we will pay special attention to the fact that Cixous's writing of the remembrance is an operation that both re-members and writes the memory in lieu of an impossible remembrance. What does it mean to remember in this context? This confrontation with memory as both a subject and process engaged by the act of writing operates through Cixous's relationship to Osnabrück—Osnabrück, a trope within the German trope—to the ruins and to the complex "presence" of Germany in Oran, Algeria, when she was growing up. In this context, we will analyze the considerable role played by the visual arts, by painting and photography, within Cixous's creative strategies of remembering and recording as they occur in her works. A central figure and location will arise in this itinerary: Montaigne, the writer, the tower, and specifically one room of his "librerie" that has had a critical importance in Cixous's life, especially in light of her writing of the books studied in this volume.

Among the figures designed by Cixous's œuvre is her *alter ego* Omi. Hélène Cixous's grandmother had been her muse in Oran. It is with her that Cixous sang Goethe and Heine's *Lieder* when she was a child. Omi lies at the core of the "mystery" of Germany; she could be the heart of Cixous's *exil originaire*. How is her move from Germany in November of 1938 such a revelatory moment for everything that makes Cixous who she is? For the meaning of "German" in the Jonas family? The question "Omi était à Osnabrück le 9 novembre 1938?" (*GO*, 53),[14] during the Kristallnacht, is central to two of Cixous's books, *Gare d'Osnabrück à Jérusalem* and *1938, nuits*. What kind of a breaking point is this date as a divider within the universe in which her texts evolve, within the broader Jewish-German world? This will be our third question, our third part. We will retrace the history of a nagging silence, the ellipsis that surrounds the exact timeline and

---

14 "Omi was in Osnabrück on November 9, 1938?" (*OSJ*, 37).

circumstances of Omi's flight from Germany. The subject was never directly addressed about why it took a long time for Omi to come to terms with the need to flee, and why many members of the family never did, such as Andreas Jonas, Omi's oldest brother. He left Osnabrück for Palestine in 1935 only to come back in 1938 to be arrested and deported to Theresienstadt along with his wife Else. Both were murdered there.

The last question reinstates all the questions raised in the book. It is subsumed in a word used by Ève Cixous, a German word that means "belonging" that Cixous could have translated as "appartenance," for example. *Zugehör*. It is neither *belonging* nor *appartenance*. This untranslatable remains in German; it is obstinately and idiomatically German and captures the fate of the Jonas family in Cixous's writing in German, of the German suffering that arrives only *in* German and *to* the German language. What does it mean to "belong" to Germany for the Jonas family? What was the sense of "belonging" for "Jewish-German" subjects of the empire like Omi or her husband Michael Klein, before and during the Great War? How far and to what extent was this sense of belonging, this "*Zugehör,*" a part of the impossibility to be German? How is the possibility of this impossibility tied to a point of destruction of the mind that is both a symptom and the consequence of what Derrida calls the "Jewish-German psyche"?[15]

This ultimately could address a question that remains open: that of the German language, of the possibility that the German language itself could have been Cixous's secret grandmaternal and maternal language used as a vehicle for emancipation *from the German language*. Writing, especially Cixous's invention of an idiom, that is, the appearance of the "Cixous language" on the world scene as an idiosyncratic tongue, could have been a liberation from all the barriers associated to the great schism that divides Cixous's intimate German tongue. Writing *within* the intimacy of her divisive German heritage is an explanation engaged

---

15 Christa Stevens offers a solid comprehensive analysis of "several signifiers on which or against which the author [Cixous] expresses her Jewish identity," in "Judéités, à lire dans l'œuvre d'Hélène Cixous," *International Journal of Francophone Studies*, vol. 7, no. 1–2 (Intellect, 2004), 81. While it mainly focuses on those specific signifiers, the approach does not develop the Jewish-German theme that had already started to explicitly appear in Cixous's publications at the time (*Osnabrück, Benjamin à Montaigne*). Although it more specifically addresses Cixous's "Ashkenazi" through a reading of her "Sephardic, Ashkenazi, Algerian, German and French legacy" (80), the perspective of a comprehensive approach to the "Jewish identities" (78) of Cixous remains the main focus of Maxime Decout's 2013 article. See Maxime Decout, "Standing apart/being a part: Cixous's fictional Jewish identities," *Jewish Culture and History*, vol. 14, no. 2–3 (Taylor and Francis, 2013), 78–86.

Introduction 15

by Cixous and her own self at the core of "Germany."¹⁶ Cixous decisively composes her entire œuvre in French. But in French she writes in German: "*Ich denke was ich will und was mich beglücket,*" which is a verse from the song she quotes in *Angst* from a German *Lied* that can only be written and sung in German—in French, untranslated: "Die Gedanken sind frei" (*A*, 189).¹⁷ Is it French, is it German? It is the language of all languages, that of thoughts. Music of the thoughts is the untranslatable "Die Gedanken sind frei." What remains is the musicality of German and its secret insurrection in French when "all the links are broken" ("tu as rompu tous les liens"), writes Cixous in the following passage of *Angst* that sings this German song, *Die Gedanken sind frei*. *Die Gedanken sind frei* is all that remains. It contains the untranslatable freedom of her untranslatable poetic idiom, the "Freedom," if it exists, of Cixous's worlds.¹⁸ She writes:

16 One reason why German as a language is only obliquely approached in our work is that several scholarly works offer substantial analyses on this theme, even though Cixous's relationship to Germany has generally been little studied. See Annelies Schulte Nordholt, "Osnabrück, Berlin: 'villes promises' et villes vécues. Les dessous du dialogue d'Hélène Cixous et Cécile Wajsbrot dans *Une autobiographie allemande*," in Kathleen Gyssels and Christa Stevens (eds.), *Écriture des Origines, Origine de l'écriture Hélène Cixous* (Leiden: Brill Rodopi, 2019), 124–40. Carola Hilfrich proposes a sharp interpretation the German language as a "soundscape" in her article "The Depository of *Zugehör: Ail!* and the soundscape of Belonging," in Carola Hilfrich, Natasha Gordinsky and Susanne Zepp (eds.), *Passages of Belonging Interpreting Jewish Literatures*, Perspectives on Jewish Texts and Contexts, no. 7 (Berlin: De Gruyter, 2019), 48–53. Brigitte Heymann offers an analysis of Cixous's poetic "German tongue" in "La langue véhiculaire, die deutsche Sprache in Hélène Cixous' Poet(h)ik," in Andrea Grewe and Susanne Schlünder (eds.), "Die 'deutsche Seite' von Hélène Cixous," special issue, *Lendemains*, vol. 42, no. 166/67 (Narr Francke Attempto Verlag GmbH + Co. KG, 2017), 56–70. In the same volume, Isabella von Treskow proposes a reflection on Cixous's "mother tongue," "Le fleuve sonore, les ouïes extravagantes et le sillon sensuel. Langue, *Muttersprache* et pensée dans *Osnabrück* et *Gare d'Osnabrück à Jérusalem* d'Hélène Cixous," in Andrea Grewe and Susanne Schlünder (eds.), "Die 'deutsche Seite' von Hélène Cixous," special issue, *Lendemains*, vol. 42, no. 166/67 (Narr Francke Attempto Verlag GmbH + Co. KG, 2017), 71–84.
17 *Die Gedanken sind frei* is a German song whose original lyricist and composer are unknown. The earliest occurrences of the theme seem to appear on leaflets around 1780. The most popular version was rendered by Hoffmann von Fallersleben in 1842.
18 "In the spirit of Freedom-*Freiheit* ... if it exists!" were Hélène Cixous's words when she expressed her gratitude to her hosts at the beginning of the Hegel Lecture she held in Berlin at the Freie Universität (Free University of Berlin), on May 11, 2016, available online: https://www.fu-berlin.de/en/sites/dhc/zVideothek/950hegel-lecture-mit-helene-cixous/index.html (accessed July 27, 2020).

16 The "German Illusion"

> Quand tu t'es enfermée dans la chambre, plus profondément que les morts dans leur séjour, tu as rompu tous les liens, *die Gedanken sind frei*, et des mirages te présentent les visions les plus lointaines, tes pensées t'entraînent dans des contrées oubliées depuis longtemps, te voilà dans ton pays natal, de l'autre côté du monde, te voilà descendant aux suds, par des pistes désertiques cherchant rien dans des espaces insignifiants, comme si l'extérieur se déchaînait en images les plus extérieures possibles pour affirmer jusqu'à l'absurdité son extériorité.
>
> (*A*, 191–92)[19]

"*die Gedanken sind frei*" thoughts are free. So is Cixous.

---

19 "When you locked yourself in your room, more deeply than the dead in their sojourn, you cut all ties, *die Gedanken sind frei*, and mirages offer you the most distant visions, your thoughts drag you off to long forgotten lands, you find yourself in your native country on the other side of the world, here you are, going down to the southern places through arid paths, looking for nothing in insignificant spaces, as if the exterior unleashed itself into the most external images possible in order to affirm its exteriority to the point of absurdity."

Part I

Germany is calling
The landline (1916–2016)

Que ferais-je si on n'avait pas inventé le téléphone? C'est-à-dire Dieu.

Encore faut-il qu'Il ne soit pas coupé par la tempête.

(TP, 81)[1]

---

1 "What would I do if they hadn't invented the telephone? That is, God. But let's hope that He's not cut by the storm."

One The first telephone

À la fin, *on regardait le plan du Zentrum d'Osnabrück, et on ne savait plus qui avait connu n'avait pas connu qui, tout le monde avait connu, on avait connu qui on n'avait pas connu, tout le monde était passé, s'était promené, était entré, avait acheté, avait vu, avait parlé, avait appris, avait nagé, avait été en excursion dans la forêt, avait passé l'Abitur, avait mangé, avait eu ses secrets, était mort.*

(GO, 74; *my emphasis*)[1]

"In the end" ("*À la fin*"), when everything is fading, everything is tangible but structurally uncertain. This seems to seal the "end." "[O]ne no longer knew who had known had no known whom," "who had made an excursion to the forest, had passed the Abitur," "[i]n the end, one was looking at the map of the Zentrum of Osnabrück" (*OSJ*, 55; in German). There are untranslated German words for this "end"; "Zentrum" (center, downtown), "Abitur," words that the author did not highlight. The end speaks German, one last time. This quote from a book published in 2016, seems to depict the extremity of a time line inaugurated with this one that takes us to the "*Wohnzimmer*," in German, the living room:

Tout commence par le tramway d'Osnabrück. Autour on doit imaginer la ville petite mais ville, là-dessus les lourds jours de pluie, au milieu, sur la place Nicolas, *Nikolaïort, la maison agrandissait, en bas on a une Wohnzimmer*, à l'étage ajouter une grande salle à manger quand il y avait tout le monde c'est-à-dire sept fois une famille de cinq à six en moyenne pour les fêtes quarante-cinq la bonne goy mange dans la cuisine, la grand-mère principale a eu un ascenseur et *à la fin* un téléphone dont on ne

---

[1] "In the end, one was looking at the map of the Zentrum of Osnabrück, and one no longer knew who had known had no known whom, everyone passed by, had strolled, had entered, had bought, had seen, had spoken, had learned, had swum, had made an excursion to the forest, had passed the Abitur, had eaten, had had secrets, was dead" (*OSJ*, 55).

se servit pas car il n'y en avait qu'un dans Osnabrück et c'était le nôtre mais c'était pour la suite.

(*OS*, 131–32; my emphases)[2]

"Everything begins with" ("*Tout commence* par") .... This is 1999, Hélène Cixous's first "book of Germany," as we might call it. "[A]nd in the end a telephone that was never used" ("[E]t *à la fin* un téléphone dont on ne se servit pas" [*OS*, 132]). The beginning and the end occur in the same breath, the same paragraph. A fraction of time is encapsulated at the beginning of Cixous's German history story, in German—the end in the beginning, at the beginning. The word "end" appears again in a similar way seventeen years later ("*À la fin*") in another book of Germany, at a time of Hélène Cixous's life when the last protagonist of her German family, a centenarian, is about to leave the scene shortly after that last phone call in March of 2016.

This is the end of a family history and of a world history that dates, metaphorically and literally in Cixous's œuvre, from the first telephone at the beginning. This first telephone, one that might have been acquired by the Jonas family around the time of the Great War, is the beginning of Hélène Cixous's history. This telephone, which interestingly also erupts after the locution "in the end" in Cixous's text, is telling her history. One extremity of time (it could be 1916[3]) is reaching out to the opposite one—2016. The beginning is told from the end, and the calls sound German.[4] It is as if the actual telephone was already announcing

---

2   "Everything begins with the tramway of Osnabrück. All around, one has to imagine the city, small, but still a city, under the heavy days of rains, in the middle, on Nicolas square, *Nikolaiort*, the house was growing in size, downstairs we have a *Wohnzimmer*, upstairs, add a large dining room when everyone was present, that is, seven times a family of five to six on average for parties, that's forty-five, the goy servant eats in the kitchen, the head grandmother got an elevator and at the end, a telephone that was never used because there was only one in Osnabrück and it was ours, but it was for what follows."
3   We will keep this hypothetical date of the acquisition of the first telephone, 1916, as our reference in future developments. One reason is that 1916 is the date when Cixous's grandfather Michael was killed in the war. We will often mention this event, especially in Parts III and IV, because this event is critically important to Cixous's relationship to her German "background."
4   We will devote further developments to this subject of the German language in Part III after having paid attention to Cixous's art of the sound-image in her works around Germany. In her essay titled "The Depository of *Zugehör: Ail!* and the Soundscape of Belonging," Carola Hilfrich highlights the importance of Cixous's "field of sound" as a marker of what she characterizes as Cixous's "idiom." Hilfrich, "The Depository of *Zugehör: Ail!* and the Soundscape of Belonging," 48–53.

a catastrophe, *the end at the beginning*, the beginning of the end, the anticipated end calling within the inaugural opening of a line that Cixous's books will now metaphorically call in 1999 (*Osnabrück*)—2016 (*Gare d'Osnabrück à Jérusalem*, and after). The year 2016 fictionally calls the telephone set of the beginning—1916—whose line is cut from the inside: no one called this "first" telephone.[5] This rhetorical game with the "end" and the "beginning" might secretly capture what happens within a radical gap, an abyss, that of the extermination, "Shoah" as it is named in Europe. This abyss, a radical cut of the line, could be the "téléphone dont on ne se servit pas," the telephone that one did not use, the impossibility of the call at the core of the history of this first German

---

5   It is indeed a "beginning" ("commencement") of Hélène Cixous. It is the absolute telephone of the beginning; at the beginning of Cixous's publications, as Derrida recalls, is *Les Commencements* (literally "The Beginnings") in 1970 (three years after Hélène Cixous's first published book). Jacques Derrida quotes Cixous: "Une voix met une majuscule à cette Histoire: 'Je pourrais aussi écrire l'Histoire du téléphone et comment nous l'avons dompté ...'," in "H.C. pour la vie c'est à dire," *Hélène Cixous croisées d'une œuvre*, ed. Mireille Calle-Gruber (Paris: Galilée, 2000), 26; translation: "A voice writes this History with a capital: 'I could also write the History of the telephone and how we tamed it ...'." Jacques Derrida, *H.C. for Life, That is to Say* ..., trans. Laurent Milesi and Stefan Herbrechter, ed. Mireille Calle-Gruber (Stanford, CA: Stanford University Press, 2006), 17. The quote of Cixous by Derrida appears in Hélène Cixous, *Les Commencements* (Paris: Grasset, 1970), 177, and in Hélène Cixous, *Les Commencements* (Paris: Des Femmes, 1999), 160. Derrida underscores the omnipresence of motif of the telephone in Hélène Cixous's œuvre: "cette situation partagée nous met sur la ligne sans ligne du téléphone, [...], et elle donne à penser ce qu'est ou n'est pas une ligne quand elle décrit une certaine ligne entre ceux qui sont voués, comme c'est le cas, à la ligne d'écriture—et même, comme c'est son cas, dans une écriture toute occupée de génération, et de filiation, à la lignée de l'écriture, voués à l'œuvre comme lignée," Derrida, "H.C. pour la vie," 26 ("this shared situation puts us on the wireless line of the telephone, [...], and it gives us to think what a line is and what it is not when it describes a certain line between those two, as is the case, are devoted to the line of writing—and even, as in her case, in a writing that is entirely occupied by generation, filiation, the lineage of writing—devoted to the work as lineage." Derrida, *H.C. for Life*, 17–18). Among countless telephones in Cixous's work, in *La Fiancée juive de la tentation* she writes: "Dieulephone garde seul le silence et la parole. Je suis sans pouvoir, lui peut me sonner" (*FJ*, 16) ("Godthephone alone keeps the silence and the speech. I am powerless, he can call me"). "Je suis bien obligée de le reconnaître, c'est en français que l'Appel m'appelle dans toutes les directions de l'Histoire. Et qui sait depuis et pour combien de temps" (*FJ*, 125) ("I am forced to recognize it, it is in French that the Call calls me in all of the directions of history. And who knows since when and for how long").

telephone.⁶ For Hélène Cixous, calling this side of her family is both the opening of a historical chapter of her œuvre *par excellence* and a confrontation to the aporia of history, to the impossibility of the book. It is an attempt to call the impossible, in 1916, 1999, 2016 and beyond. Could it be that the German "untranslatables" of these texts are incarnations of this aporia (dead-ends)? Could the texts also be the opening figures, the shibboleths (coded points of entry, the beginning)? Could they incarnate the impossibility of German, of Germany, the impossibility called *in German*, of texts in which the idiom, "German," calls and is called in a language familiar and foreign?

The year 2016 marked the hundredth anniversary of Cixous's grandfather's death at the Baranovici military hospital (in modern-day Belarus). The year 1916 is our temporal benchmark for the "beginning." A soldier of the 11th company of the light infantry regiment, Michael Klein, died at the age of 34 from wounds received on the battlefield of the Eastern front on July 27, 1916. Michael Klein, was a "Jewish German soldier," writes Cixous ("soldat allemand juif").⁷ The beginning, in the quote from 1999, refers to the early twentieth century in the bourgeois family of Osnabrück. The first telephone was probably acquired shortly before, during, or after the Great War. That would be around the time

---

6 Cixous's art of the cut—in many senses of the word—informs our reflections on her telephonies. *Hélène Cixous, Dreamer, Realist, Analyst, Writing*, by Nicholas Royle, contains a profound, poetic and philosophical exegesis of the many forms of the cuts in her œuvre. Nicholas Royle, *Hélène Cixous, Dreamer, Realist, Analyst, Writing* (Manchester: Manchester University Press, 2020).
7 "soldat allemand juif" (*PR*, 187) ("Jewish German soldier grandfather" [*R*, 185]). Born in Hungary, in the Austro-Hungarian Empire, Michael Klein had taken German citizenship in 1909 to marry Rosalie Jonas, Hélène Cixous's grandmother. "Mon grand-père est mort sur le front russe en tant que soldat allemand," writes Cixous (*PR*, 187). "Mon grand-père soldat allemand juif a été enterré en 1916 en Russie et on a dressé sur sa tombe un vrai petit monument portant une inscription en allemand et en hébreu et une étoile de David. La tombe est parmi d'autres tombes allemandes ornées de croix. Voilà l'Europe au début de ce siècle ... Étoile et croix ensemble" (*PR*, 187) ("My Jewish German soldier grandfather was buried in 1916 in Russia and on the grave they put up a true little monument carrying an inscription in German and in Hebrew and a star of David. The grave is among other German graves adorned with crosses. That was Europe of the beginning of this century ... Star and cross together" [*R*, 185]). It is highly probable that Michael Klein fell in the context of the Baranovichi offensive launched by the forces of Germany and Austro-Hungary (9th Army) in the period July 3–29. Following several attacks by the Russians, the German and Austro-Hungarian troops counterattacked on July 14 and took back all lost ground. The Russians fought back on July 25–29 but failed. The Germans and Austro-Hungarians counted an estimated 13,000 casualties and losses while the Russians had an estimate of 80,000.

The First Telephone 23

when Cixous's mother, Ève Cixous née Eva Klein, daughter of Michael and Rosalie Klein, was born in Strasbourg, a city of the German Empire, on October 14, 1910. Rosi Klein[8] and her two daughters Eva and Eri relocated to Osnabrück after the Great War, when the Alsatian city of Strasbourg returned to France. From Osnabrück, Eva emigrated to Paris in 1930, where she lived until 1933. She spent time in Brighton, England, in 1934, before moving back to Paris, where she met her future Algerian-born husband Georges Cixous. They moved to Oran, Algeria, in 1936, after Georges had completed the last portion of his doctoral degree in medicine in Paris.[9] Georges's entire family was of Jewish descent from North Africa (Morocco and Algeria). Ève died in Paris on July 1, 2013. She was 103.

The year 2016 is also when Marga passed away at the age of 105. Marga Carlebach née Löwenstein, born on December 30, 1910, was the cousin of Hélène Cixous's mother. Marga hosted Hélène Cixous in 1950, when she was sent by her mother to England from her native Algeria. It was then that Hélène Cixous, at the age of 13, set foot in Europe for the first time, several months after the death of her father from tuberculosis on February 12, 1948. Cixous spent several decisive weeks in the Jewish neighborhood of Golders Green in London, acquiring the English language (she later obtain the *agrégation* in English and completed a doctoral dissertation on Joyce) while experiencing her first exposure to a rigorous Jewish tradition. Marga was the last living memory of what Hélène Cixous once called the "grande chronique d'Osnabrück"[10] (the great chronicle of Osnabrück), which left a central mark on at least six of her books: *Osnabrück* (1999), *Benjamin à Montaigne* (2001), *Gare d'Osnabrück à Jérusalem* (2016), *Correspondance avec le Mur* (2017), *1938, nuits* (2019) and *Ruines bien rangées* (2020). In one way or another, these books are explicitly written "with" Germany in mind: with Cixous's Germany, with her family's Germany, with her German "background" in sight—which is to say, with the countless trajectories of what the word "Germany" implies for this family. These are "German" trajectories, "German" visions, references, meanings and flavors, German

---

8   "Omi" as Hélène Cixous often calls her grandmother, Rosalie, is sometimes spelled "Rosy" or "Rosi" in Cixous's texts. I kept the spelling "Rosi" as it appears in her later texts discussed in this book.
9   This account is based on an interview with Ève Cixous from 1996. David Blank and Gladys Blank, *Gladys and David Blanks Genealogy*, 2008–2022, available online: http://www.blankgenealogy.com/getperson.php?personID=I2662&tree=-Blank1 (accessed May 4, 2020).
10 *Ever, Rêve, Hélène Cixous* [nonfiction film], directed by Olivier Morel (Paris: Zadig Productions, 2016), 01:34:57.

words and tales, "German" fears and terrors, the "German" tongues, sounds and linguistic roots of Cixous's maternal family,[11] of the poet Hélène Cixous. The quotes from 1999 and 2016 evoke the same historical period, the years that precede the rise of Nazism. They share the same space: a Prussian town of the Hanover region, Westphalia, where the famous peace treaty ending the European wars of religion was signed in 1648.[12] In many ways, through the complex configurations of the beginning and the end in Cixous's œuvre, Germany is what appears within the cognitive confrontation of the long history of her ancestors' life in Germany and the short time of the persecutions that injured and destroyed Cixous's family members. She has known them. She has spent her life with the survivors and the memory of the dead. Their stories of Germany were alive. Around 2013 to 2016, something happened in Cixous's life and work when the last living relatives of this period disappeared. In this context we could distinguish two moments in Cixous's writings: one goes from 1999 to 2014, that is, from *Osnabrück* (1999) to *Homère est morte* ... (2014), which marks the death of Ève Cixous in Cixous's works; the other one starts with the publication of *Gare d'Osnabrück à Jérusalem* in 2016, around the time when Cixous first traveled to Osnabrück.

Although the last relatives of Cixous's German family have passed away, they keep manifesting themselves. Writing, poetry and literature as an activity is not the evocation of those figures for Cixous. It is the consistency, the art of their enduring presence with no end, an existence that obeys the rule of a general "telephony" in/of Cixous's œuvre, precisely because in Cixous's œuvre the "call" is what brings them to life in poetry. The call is what resurrects, redeems and retrieves the poetry of life. They appear in the quotation from *Osnabrück* as "seven times a family of five to six on average for parties" ("sept fois une famille de cinq à six en moyenne pour les fêtes" [*OS*, 131]). They call. Although the telephone from Osnabrück remains unused, they keep calling

---

11 This inner landscape of hers is the main focus of a text published in 2016 with the writer Cécile Wajsbrot. In the opening of this book, as already mentioned in the introduction, Cixous writes: "J'ai toujours aimé l'Allemagne
Et pourtant—
Je l'ai tenue en respect, en estime, au-dessus au-delà du Nazisme
Et pourtant—" (*AA*, 15). ("I have always loved Germany / However— / I held her in respect, in esteem, above beyond Nazism / However—").
12 All those details are provided at the very beginning of *Osnabrück*, in a long quote taken from the *Grand Dictionnaire Universel* by Pierre Larousse (*OS*, 7–8). We will come back to this in Part III.

Cixous-the-poet in her life and dreams. This real telephone of Osnabrück holds the secrets of an infinity of imaginary calls. The call also occurs through discoveries. Such discoveries are, by nature, unpredictable and unexpected. They are as eventful as a phone call can be. This is *Nacres*, published in the fall of 2019, a collection of excerpts from Cixous's "cahiers," the notebooks in which she writes all year long and that she carries with her, especially when she "retires" every summer to her writing residence:

NOVEMBRE 2018
Excavation, fouilles, chez Ève, col du Saint-Gothard
In memoriam novembre 1938, Kristallnacht, enfin Omi se rend à Oran, reddition, et reddition des clés d'Osnabrück! 80 ans. C'est alors que commence l'écheveau de mon histoire.

(*NC*, 126)[13]

The trajectory of Ève's documents leads to Cixous's 2019 book, *1938, nuits*, a work that finds its origin in the following discovery:

Et parfois Fouilles récompensées: quand le Fouilleur Chef de Saint-Gothard c'est Pif. (Chez Kafka, ça s'appellerait: Un Fils. Pieux, scientifique, stratège, un fils-de-mère, bien entendu.)
Pif ramène du fond de la mer:
1. Lettres de Fred (Note: Docteur Fred Katzman [sic], jadis né nommé Siegfried), toutes premières lettres de 1985, à Ève. Fred pas encore entré avec Ève dans leur ultime roman. Juste après leur retour imprévu et totalement distinct de la fameuse invitation à Osnabrück. *Note*: Une fois encore les dates authentiques n'ont rien à voir avec mes dates de fantaisie. Donc Fred entre en 1985. Ève, belle jeune femme de 75 ans.
Il lui demande (d'Iowa à Paris) de lui parler d'elle, d'Osnabrück, d'Alger etc. Curiosités nombreuses, ordonnées.
[…]
Il lui demande si ça l'intéresserait de lire son récit.
L'a écrit en allemand, avec difficulté, premier jet 1941, version ultime 1985. Histoire d'un Récit: elle ne le lit pas.

---

13 "NOVEMBER 2018 / Excavation, searches, at Ève's, pass of the Saint-Gothard / *In memoriam* November 1938, Kristallnacht, at last Omi gives herself to Oran, surrender, and surrender of the keys of Osnabrück! 80 years. It is then that the skein of my history begins." This book is made of Cixous's "cahiers" (notebooks) from January 1, 2017, to May 14, 2019.

> Le folio reste coincé sur une étagère du Couloir Saint-Gothard
> jusqu'en l'an 2018.
> Le roman archéologique.
>
> (NC, 127)[14]

German language, German names and dates unexpectedly arise from the dust of Ève Cixous's apartment after her death. Germany is calling. Sometimes loudly, when it erupts with a poisonous word, "Kristallnacht" (NC, 126), November 1938 to November 2018—a deadly event for the Jews all across Germany—that will cause Omi's "rendition" ("reddition") and her emigration to Oran, Algeria in late 1938, when she reunites with her daughter Ève and her family, including Hélène Cixous, who was born in 1937. It coincides with Cixous's "histoire," her interwoven story, the skein of her history, as she interprets it: "C'est alors que commence l'écheveau de mon histoire" (NC, 126) ("It is then that the skein of my history begins"). "Kristallnacht" designates the infamous night of November 9, 1938, when the Nazis destroyed Jewish stores, belongings, cemeteries and synagogues, a date when arbitrary arrests took place, and when the worst massive persecutions began. Germany manifests itself through the brutalities of Kristallnacht and everything that this moment symbolizes, but sometimes, like in the case of the "Fouilles" (searches) engaged by "Pif," Cixous's son, it seems that the call is surreptitious, soft and almost graceful. It culminates in the adventurous explorations of a diver who brings treasures up to the surface of the deep matrixial sea (the signifier "mer"). The document found by Pif is a jewel sent from darkness. It is about the persecutions of the Jews, in Germany, and more specifically in Osnabrück, that Fred personally endured in November of 1938.

---

14 "And sometimes the Searches are rewarded: when the chief Searcher of Saint-Gothard is Pif. (At Kafka's it would be called: A Son. Pious, scientist, strategist, a son-of-mother, of course.) / Pif drags up from the bottom of the sea: / 1. Letter from Fred (Note: Doctor Fred Katzman, formerly born named Siegfried), very first letters from 1985 to Ève. Fred not yet entered with Ève into their final novel. Right after their unexpected return and totally distinct from the famous invitation to Osnabrück. *Note*: Once again the authentic dates have nothing to do with my imaginary ones. So Fred makes his entry in 1985. Ève, young handsome woman of 75 years old / He asks her (from Iowa to Paris) to tell him about herself, about Osnabrück, Algiers, etc. / Countless curiosities, organized. [...] / He asks her if she would be interested to read his tale. / Wrote it in German, with difficulty, first draft 1941, final version 1985. / Story of a Tale: she doesn't read it. / The folio remains stuck on a shelf of the Saint-Gothard hallway until the year 2018. / The archeological novel." Saint-Gothard is the name of the street of the 14th arrondissement of Paris where Ève Cixous had her apartment. It is named after a German Monk of the eleventh century.

The discovery of Fred's letters and folio by Cixous's son in 2018 reflects a central structure of Cixous's entire œuvre, a structure that the phone call shares with the dreams. We never know when it will ring or when we will dream and who will be called by/in the dream. This discovery in Ève Cixous's apartment will resurface in Cixous's œuvre under the title *1938, nuits*. Literally, "1938, nights." In *1938, nuits*, the double dimension of this discovery, made of dream and call, says something of the "folio" from Fred (born Siegfried) and what it contains. The very existence of the folio is that of something both indispensable and repressed, preserved and buried. Although Ève never read it, she never threw it away. It was kept in the dark (that could be one of the "nights" of the title), "coincé sur une étagère," stuck on a shelf. This is also what hits Cixous when she starts emptying Ève's apartment: "drôle d'opération," writes Cixous, "où garder et engloutir sont indissociables," "strange operation where keeping and engulfing are inseparable" (*NC*, 127). Ève's belongings, like this folio, are engulfed in the night that *keeps them* in sight. The folio is also written in the night. It is the writing of the night. November 9, 1938, is a night in Germany, in the world (in Part III we will explore some aspects of this moment) and in Osnabrück. Siegfried Katzmann, we will learn in *1938, nuits*, is a young man from Osnabrück who witnesses the burning of the Synagogue of Osnabrück that takes place overnight. He gets arrested by the Gestapo and is sent to the concentration camp of Buchenwald near Weimar, one of the first and largest in Germany, that opened in July of 1937. That is what the folio contains. In a way, the "folio" already *contains* a certain dream, or rather a nightmare, of Germany: it is written in German with the uncanny synchrony that, apparently, Pif discovers the document exactly eighty years after the Kristallnacht. In *1938, nuits*, this "folio" is given to the reader through a dream in a dream-like opening sequence, in the middle "of the night of July," "Vers 2 heures de la nuit de juillet" (*N*, 26) ("Around 2 in the night of July"). This is the first page of the book. The folio re-enters through the doors of the dream, in writing, and what delivers this dream is Ève's *call*:

Un petit livre dort dans la nuit
Vers 2 heures de la nuit de juillet, *maman m'appelle* d'en haut. Je me lève. Elle, de sa voix, me prévient qu'elle me jette par la fenêtre en urgence un petit paquet précieux.

(*N*, 9; my emphasis)[15]

---

15 "A little book sleeps in the night / Around 2 in the night of July, mom calls me from above. I wake up. She, in her voice, warns me that she is urgently throwing a small precious parcel through the window."

28   The "German Illusion"

"She," Ève, is the *prénom de Dieu*, God's first name, who calls from above. "Maman m'appelle d'en haut," translated "Mom is calling me from above." The call from above allows the "book"—the book that is asleep in the night—to make its entrance. *Petit livre* (little book)-*petit paquet* (little parcel), Fred's German folio is calling the book in the book named *1938, nuits*. This call arrives in German. We will comment further on the language of this document in Part III.

There are many calls and dreams in Cixous's books. Could it be that they all recall the "beginning" of the Osnabrück chronicle, the one that starts with a phone call that never took place: "Tout commence ..." everything begins with a telephone so unique, in Osnabrück, that it remained unused. Cixous is composing all the numbers on a telephone that no one called to decipher a crypted Jewish-German chronicle ("et *à la fin* un téléphone dont on ne se servit pas car il n'y en avait qu'un dans Osnabrück et c'était le nôtre" [*OS*, 132], "and *at the end*, a telephone that was never used because there was only one in Osnabrück and it was ours"). She is calling this single telephone line, this landline of Germany, in her dreams and in her writing—which, in Cixous's œuvre and life, might be the same. This is a literal-literary phone. This is one of Cixous's totems. In Cixous's childhood this telephone rings in Algeria. Osnabrück rings in Oran:

> Le charme singulier d'Osnabrück réside selon moi dans son nom si obstinément sonore. C'est la sonnerie de téléphone dans les récits de ma mère lors de notre enfance à Oran. Tout a commencé par cette sonnerie. OS NA BRÜCK, c'est le premier téléphone et son fil. Au moment où cette sonnerie si antique et si familière retentit, je voyage instantanément dans les temps du temps. Le secret est dans ces syllabes.
>
> (*RB*, 32)[16]

Called by Osnabrück, Germany in Oran, her texts call Germany. She is calling Germany and Germany is calling. But what does that mean? Germany is a threat and a dream in Cixous's life, and we will have many occasions to develop this notion. The call takes place in more than one book and in more than one form. It is in notebooks (the "cahiers" of *Nacres*), in dreams, within the act of writing as an art to invoke in

---

16 "The unique charm of Osnabrück resides, according to me, in its obstinately sonorous name. It is the ringtone of the telephone in my mother's tales during our childhood in Oran. Everything has started with this ringtone. OS NA BRÜCK, it is the first telephone and its cord. At the time when this ringtone so ancient and familiar resounded, I instantly traveled in the times of time. The secret is in these syllables."

order to call, or to be available for the call—to have the *power* to do so, to be both the caller and the called in this general telephony. There would be no call without vulnerability, without deficiency, without a gap. The call exerts a sovereign power that, because of the nature of the call, is always threatened in its own sovereignty. The call has the power to *cut*—which might be the definition of power in general. Literature, as Cixous understands it, is entirely ingrained in the intrinsic precarity when facing the possibility of the call and the sovereign threat that the call imposes on its receivers. In her books, Cixous is called through the literary telephony of "Germany is calling." "Germany," in Cixous's childhood, is another name for the great historic cut of Nazism, for what cuts the family in parts. Germany is calling because it is cutting: disarming the call at the core of the power to call and to be called.

Such a "call" encrypts the impossibility of the call when there are no more living members of the "German" family to call. But this could also very much be the structural impossibility of the call embodied by the first, unique telephone of Cixous's family in Osnabrück at the beginning of the twentieth century. Ultimately, this impossibility of the call might also highlight a metaphysical structure. The disruption of presence is essential to *the act of calling*; in fact, the reason why the call takes place is the disruptive authority of a separation. An irreducible impossibility is in the call. There is no call without an irreducible distance, without the essential uncertainty of the fact that even the closest, intimate callers, even lovers, or members of the same family—Cixous and her mother, or son, or daughter, for example—are never entirely assured that they share the same world ... even when the call takes place, something remains unreachable. This disruption can never be fully reduced. Although the intrusion is what defines the concept of telephony, the call takes place on the grounds that the worlds are essentially out of tune, out of joint and discordant. There would be no call without what Derrida calls an "espacement," or an irreducible spacing at the core of every communication. No call would exist without a *différance*,[17] even within the most "fusional" accord. No call is conceivable without an

---

17   Jacques Derrida, "Signature, Événement, Contexte," in *Limited Inc.* (Paris: Galilée, 1990), 46–7 (Jacques Derrida, "Signature, Event, Context," in *Limited Inc.*, trans. Samuel Weber and Jeffrey Mehlman [Evanston, IL: Northwestern University Press, 1988], 18). "La différance, l'absence irréductible de l'intention ou de l'assistance à l'énoncé performatif, l'énoncé le plus 'événementiel' qui soit, c'est ce qui m'autorise, [...], à poser la structure graphématique générale de toute 'communication.'" Derrida, "Signature, Événement, Contexte," 46–7. ("*Différance*, the irreducible absence of intention or attendance to the performative utterance, the most 'event-ridden' utterance there is, is what authorizes me [...] to posit the general graphematic structure of every 'communication.'" Derrida, "Signature, Event, Context," 18–19).

irreducible absence, without interference, corruption, disturbance, intrusion and invasion. The call implies the intrinsic non-presence of the protagonists. Furthermore, it is about Germany. A loaded "presence." Presence of the impossible in the most intimate life of Cixous's family, an impossible presence that erupts through familiar German words, often the most toxic ones on earth such as "Kristallnacht," a presence of Germany that, in essence, again, disrupts, breaks, destroys, alienates, affects every ability to think, to dream ... to call. But this presence gives its necessity and structure to the call. In some ways, this structure is also at stake in what we call a dream, when a dream calls. And especially in Cixous's "German dreams," as we might call them.

Two   The dream call

The dream of a phone call, the phone call in/as a dream, is what the composer and musician Jean-Jacques Lemêtre places at the core of his audio creation titled "Ceci est un exercice de rêve":[1]

[*Telephone ringing*]
[*Talking on the phone, Hélène Cixous's voice*]
—Allô?

[*On the phone. Eve Cixous, Hélène's Cixous's mother*]
—Quelques fois je rêve que, que j'attends le bus et quand je finis par l'avoir, il m'emmène très loin et je ne sais plus où je me trouve. Et alors je peux pas revenir parce que y'a pas de taxi, rien du tout, c'est tout... Eh ben, je sais pas, je me réveille. Non, non, je suis embêtée...

[*Hélène Cixous*]
—Oui... Maman? Maman?

[...]

[*Ève Cixous*]
—Je sais pas pourquoi je fais ça. Ah oui, je sais toujours un peu ce qui m'amène quelque part, oui. Mais... justement, je vais, je crois aller en ville et après je me trouve tout à fait ailleurs. Je sais pas où je suis et personne sais que... y'a pas de taxi, rien pour revenir, enfin, je suis embêtée...

[*Hélène Cixous*]
—Comme s'il n'y avait, comme s'il n'y avait qu'une seule mère. Maman? Maman? Elle n'entend pas.[2]

---

1   Jean-Jacques Lemêtre, *Ceci est un exercice de rêve*, "Ateliers de création radiophonique," Paris: France Culture-Radio France (first broadcast November 20, 2005).
2   "[*Telephone ringing*] / [*Talking on the phone, Hélène Cixous's voice*] / —Hello? / — Sometimes I dream that, that I am waiting for the bus and when I end up in it,

32   The "German Illusion"

In this audio creation made for the legendary "workshops of creation radio" (ateliers de création radiophonique) of the French public "cultural" radio station France Culture, Ève Cixous recounts on the phone how she often has this same dream in which she goes "somewhere" to a "town" by bus, a town she obviously knows. Then she gets off the bus only to find herself "elsewhere" ("ailleurs"), not knowing where she is ("Je sais pas où je suis") and unable to find her way back. The trip has a goal, the city is known, but when the bus arrives, the city is not recognizable anymore, and she does not know her way around. Ève is lost going to a city she thought she knew that turns out to be an unknown place. It is a place she initially found familiar that became unknown, a city with no boundaries, it seems, where the gestures that can save her are not distinct from the ones that get her lost. In this work by Jean-Jacques Lemêtre, the phone call and the dream are inseparable.

Could Ève's dream be a dream of Germany? It would be conceivable to show how this mix of familiarity and estrangement has common themes with a certain dream of Germany analyzed above. While it is a part of the uncanniness of Ève's dream/call not to know where the city of her dream could be, it is impossible to avoid the vertigo of what happens to her going to this city precisely *because* it is familiar, *because it is a familiar city*. Because the city might already be a "home," she loses her ability to find her way ... back home. Something has turned home into an "unhomely" home.[3] What does this recurring dream by Ève say about her familiar cities? About Osnabrück, the city of her

---

it takes me very far away and I no longer know where I find myself. And then I can't come back because there is no taxi, nothing at all, that's it ... I don't know, I wake up. No, no, I'm worried. / [*Hélène Cixous*] / —Yes ... Mom? Mom? [...] [*Ève Cixous*] / —I don't know why I'm doing that. Right, yes, I always know a bit what brings me somewhere, yes. But ... precisely, I go, I believe that I am going to town and later on I find myself absolutely elsewhere. I don't know where I am and nobody knows that ... there is no taxi, nothing to get back, anyway, I'm worried ... [*Hélène Cixous*] / —As if there weren't, as if there were only one mother. Mom? Mom? She doesn't hear." Lemêtre, *Ceci est un exercice*, 00:02:14 and 00:03:04.

3   Freud's daughter, Anna Freud, is a part of a team of translators of the English edition of her father's texts; the other translators are James Strachey, Alix Strachey and Alan Tyson. To render Freud's use of the German "unheimlich" in Freud's text *Das Unheimliche*, the translators choose "uncanny." On page 219 of this translation, the translators explain: "The German word, translated throughout this paper by the English 'uncanny,' is 'unheimlich,' literally 'unhomely.' The English term is not, of course, an equivalent of the German one." *Das Unheimliche*, was first published in the autumn of 1919. Sigmund Freud, *The Standard Edition of the Complete Psychological Works of Sigmund Freud*, vol. 17, "The 'Uncanny'," trans. from the German by James Strachey, in collaboration with Anna Freud assisted by Alix Strachey and Alan Tyson (London: The Hogarth Press and the Institute of Psycho-analysis, 1917–1919), 218–53.

childhood? It is as if the familiar has become radically unfamiliar from the inside. This precisely defines the *Unheimlichkeit*. Osnabrück, in Cixous's œuvre could be the capital of her *Unheimlichkeit*, of her mom's *Unheimlichkeit*, of the *Unheimlichkeit* that marks her family's relationship to Osnabrück, Germany, the *Unheimlichkeit* of the "great chronicle of Osnabrück." Osnabrück, a city so *unheimlich*, that it is no longer named "Osnabrück" in Ève's dreams ... the ghost of an unnamed ghost town in her dreams. Ghost of a name. It is as if the etymology of Ève's dream was the *Unheimlichkeit* as it is defined by Freud, the eeriness of a strangely familiar town, "das Unheimliche sei jene Art des Schreckehaften, welche auf das Altbekannte, Längstvertraute zurückgeht" ('l'inquiétante étrangeté est cette variété particulière de l'effrayant qui remonte au depuis longtemps connu, depuis longtemps familier'[4]), "the uncanny is that class of a frightening which leads back to what is known of old and long familiar," states the English translation of the Standard edition of Freud's works.[5] "Old and long familiar" turned into "frightening," Ève says of her dream, over the phone. It is what Cixous writes of/with Osnabrück in her books of Germany. "Kristallnacht," among countless poisonous German-Nazi words that appear in Cixous's works of Germany, Kristallnacht encrypts this *Unheimlichkeit* inseparable from the long familiar city/name "Osnabrück" as it is *effaced* by Kristallnacht.[6] Osnabrück. Could it be that the structure of Ève's recurring dream carries out a certain "Osnabrück?"

After indicating that the familiar can become uncanny (*unheimlich*), Freud stipulates that the *Unheimliche* (the uncanny) would always be something in which one finds oneself *disoriented*. "Disoriented," "désorienté," is the word chosen by the French translators Fernand Cambon and Jean-Bertrand Pontalis when Freud writes: 'Das Unheimliche wäre eigentlich immer etwas, worin man sich sozusagen nicht *auskennt*'[7] (my emphasis); the English translation reads: "so that the uncanny would always, as it were, be something one does not *know one's way about in*."[8] "Sich auskennen" means "be familiar with," more specifically, "to know your way around" or "to know your way about,"

---

4 Sigmund Freud, *Das Unheimliche* (Paris: Gallimard, 2001), 30.
5 Freud, "The 'Uncanny'," 220.
6 Hélène Cixous's, *Gare d'Osnabrück à Jérusalem* is punctuated by those poisonous words. Those were drawn by the artist Pierre Alechinsky as "sept substantifs dessinés" ("seven drawn substantives"), Galilée, 2016. We will comment this aspect in Part II.
7 Freud, *Das Unheimliche*, 32. "À proprement parler, l'étrangement inquiétant serait toujours quelque chose dans quoi, pour ainsi dire, on se trouve tout désorienté," write the French translators of this bilingual edition: Sigmund Freud *L'inquiétante étrangeté*, trans. Fernand Cambon and J.-B. Pontalis (Paris: Gallimard, 2001), 33.
8 Freud, "The 'Uncanny'," 221.

namely, having the required knowledge (facts, procedures) to find the right direction. While it contains the possibility of the orientation, the translators are not translating from "sich orientieren," as it exists in German. "Sich auskennen" contains a notion of orientation, but it adds a dimension of knowledge (*kennen*) to the concept, which also implies power and expertise. Ève's itinerary, her life, her extraordinary ability to find her way in life, could also be what is at stake in her dream. Ève left her familiar city of Osnabrück as soon as Nazism started to rise. She knew. She found the right direction. And she never came back until Osnabrück called her, as well as her sister Éri, in 1985, in the scene described by Cixous above. This scene reinstates all of Ève's knowledge of Osnabrück and Germany, one that puts Fred and Ève in contact and triggers Fred's writing of the "folio" as a sum of the *knowledge* of the time ... "toutes premières lettres de 1985, à Ève. [...] Juste après leur retour imprévu et totalement distinct de la fameuse invitation à Osnabrück" (*NC*, 127),[9] an unexpected return that redirected the vehicles of the dreams. This ambivalent, tormenting "return" to Osnabrück is one of the leading narrative vehicles of *Osnabrück*. It is also the theme of Cixous's theatre play *Oy!* and a recurring subject of her "books of Germany."[10] In *Benjamin à Montaigne*, published in 2001, an estranged Osnabrück that could very much resemble the estranged city of Ève's dream is the topic of Ève and Éri's comedic quarrels on why they decided to accept the invitation of the City of Osnabrück to return as official guests invited by the city. They return to Osnabrück in their quality of former Jewish residents of Osnabrück (we will elaborate on this complexity later), along with the very few individuals of Jewish descent spread around the world that had escaped and survived the persecutions. Fred was one of the few:[11]

> Je ne sais pas pourquoi nous sommes allées. Si je craignais de mourir à Osnabrück je ne serais pas allée, Fred non plus Jennie non plus. Et pourtant nous avons été à Osnabrück comme des

---

9 "[V]ery first letters from 1985 to Ève. [...] Right after their unexpected return and totally distinct from the famous invitation to Osnabrück."
10 Directed by Georges Bigot, *Oy!*'s American premiere took place at Tim Robbins's theatre, the Actor's Gang Theatre, in Los Angeles, in June of 2012. It featured actresses Mary Eileen O'Donnell (Selma) and Jeanette Horn (Jenny). The play premiered in French under the title *Ail!* in June of 2000 at the Théâtre de la Tempête in Vincennes. A radio version was broadcast on France Culture (Radio France) on December 17, 2000.
11 Hélène Cixous's *Benjamin à Montaigne* indicates that they were seven: "Les sept Juifs d'Osnabrück, dont l'un à Des Moines Iowa USA deux à Sydney Australie

morts. Les deux sœurs Jonas qui les connaît à Osnabrück, notre époque a totalement disparu.

(*BM*, 135)[12]

Not only is it presumptuous to think that they are still "from Osnabrück" after having been absent from Osnabrück for over fifty years, in the case of Éri and Ève, and forty-six years in the case of Fred, but it is also one of an infinite number of reasons that Osnabrück is no longer the town they had known. It is something like "Osnabrück," as in Ève's dream. The war and the trauma of persecution have turned it into an *uncanny*, unfamiliar city precisely at the core, where the estrangement of the persecution took place, which culminates in this idea that they are "in Osnabrück like dead people" ("à Osnabrück comme des morts"), that "[their] time has totally disappeared" ("notre époque a totalement disparu") and that they are asked to belong to a belonging that is estranged in itself. Although it sounds extremely familiar, the name "Osnabrück" seems to be written in a radically foreign language.

In a rather literal way, what is cut, in this uncanniness, is the telephone. In the phone conversation played in Jean-Jacques Lemêtre's œuvre, the communication is cut: "Elle n'entend pas," "she doesn't hear," says Hélène Cixous while attempting to talk to her mother. During the call, she calls her. There is an essential cruelty of the cut. This

---

12 un à Paris Ohio USA un à Paris France qui est ma mère un à Birmingham Angleterre qui est ma tante un à Montevideo Uruguay ont ainsi appris qu'ils n'étaient pas morts par la mairie d'Osnabrück. Ils les ont invités tous les sept dont l'un celui de Montevideo avait donc quand même survécu à Auschwitz et celui de Des Moines aussi mais autrement et c'était Fred Katzmann. Fred était déjà en pyjama et la tête rasée en 1939 quand ses parents lui ont envoyé son visa suédois dans le camp de concentration dont il est sorti tout à fait légalement et de là il est allé aux États-Unis pour arriver avec seulement vingt dollars en poche. On sort vivant de la mort avec vingt dollars en poche et on s'installe à Des Moines Iowa définitivement" (*BM*, 129–30) ("The seven Jews of Osnabrück, including one in Des Moins Iowa USA two in Sydney Australia one in Paris Ohio USA one in Paris France that's my mother one in Birmingham England who is my aunt one in Montevideo Uruguay were thus informed by the City of Osnabrück that they were not dead. They invited them all seven including one the one from Montevideo had even survived Auschwitz and the one from Des Moines too but differently and it was Fred Katzmann. Fred was already in pajamas and had a shaved head in 1939 when his parents sent him a Swedish visa in the concentration camp from which he left entirely legally and from there he went to live in the United States to arrive with only twenty dollars in his pocket. One exits alive from death with twenty dollars in pocket and settles in Des Moines Iowa definitively").

12 "I don't know why we went. If I was afraid of dying in Osnabrück, I would not have gone, Fred neither, Jennie neither. And yet, we went to Osnabrück like dead people. The two Jonas sisters, who knows them in Osnabrück? Our time has totally disappeared."

same cruelty suddenly reunites Ève and Éri when Osnabrück calls in 1985. They are reunited by this sovereign cruelty of the persecution, attached to what separates them from "~~Osnabrück~~." The landline was cut forever and there is no "Wiedergutmachung" (*BM*, 130). "Wiedergutmachung" is a German word related to this 1985 event, directly brought by Ève Cixous to her daughter, and introduced in a passage from *Benjamin à Montaigne, Il ne faut pas le dire* that we will quote in a moment. While the goodwill behind the invitation is undeniable, the idea that there would be a "Gutmachung," an art of doing some "good," cannot be other than a fallacious one that turns the good will into toxicity. A bad dream. Uncanny. The uncanniness is unavoidable, no matter what. Which might also define it. The fact that this hospitable gesture comes through an idiomatic German concept, and a word that appears as such, *in German*, in Hélène Cixous's book, is a part of the call received by the two sisters. They receive a hospitable gesture full of hostile adversities in the language that used to be their vernacular when they still lived in Osnabrück. The wound received, its scar, is reopened by the call in an attempt to heal led by the authorities of Osnabrück. In German comes the word that at once estranges them and includes them as their own. What should be underscored here is the fact that this invitation is highlighted as a phonetic one in Cixous's text. *Widergutmachung* awakens the German language, its pronunciation, its resonance, in Cixous's household when her mom and aunt are together cooking or arguing. In Cixous's prose, the word has all the flavors of love, the love Cixous had for her grandmother Omi, for her mom, for Éri her aunt. The phonology of her poetry is full of this love for a certain German language. It is a phonetic of love, the word *Wiedergutmachung* also echoes this phonic presence of her loved-ones. There is a German call for love in Cixous's texts, but the phonemes are often loaded with pain. "Wierdergutmachung," the word-wound is a phoneme sent from the distance, a telephoneme that forms a law of Cixous's books of Germany, of words sent from the inside, the intimacy of the German language spoken by Ève and Éri in the kitchen of Cixous's home, and sent from Germany to Paris (and Des Moines, Birmingham, Montevideo …), through a language that the family always recognizes as its own maternal language— one that, at the same time, could not be more estranged:

> [C]'était un geste de *Wiedergutmachung*, de bonne volonté, de refaire du bien, un concept allemand pensais-je, un concept allemand intéressant, avec le vif accent phonique du *Wieder* et l'énergie de la *Machung*, une rebonnefaisance.
>
> (*BM*, 130)[13]

---

13 "It was a gesture of *Wiedergutmachung*, of good will, to redo some good, a German concept I thought, an interesting German concept with the lively phonic accent on *Wieder* and the energy of the *Machung*, a redoingbenefaction."

It is not incidental that the word that does good is also the one that hurts the most and causes sickness. The pain is reactivated by the word that is meant to restore and do some good. *Wiedergutmachung* brings the sisters back "home" to an estranged home from where they are absent; the "good"-sickening word and trip have much in common with Ève's travel on the bus to a town she knows and no longer recognizes: "je suis embêtée," "I am bothered," says Ève. This idea is the crypt of *Unheimlichkeit*, of Ève's *unheimlich* dream and call. This uncanniness called "German," the uncanniness that calls the German language into Cixous's texts and into the lives of her mother and aunt, obeys the strange structure of restoring the landline that connects the two ends of the telephone of Germany in the Cixous family, while making the cut of the landline explicit, present, cruel, full of misunderstandings and of the impossibilities of understanding each other.[14] No matter how much they try, on both ends, in Osnabrück and Paris, in 1916 (the family's first telephone) and 2016 (the date of Cixous's last phone call to Marga), the cut exerts its cruel law. What the call to *"Wiedergutmachung"* achieves is the reactivation of the line that cuts the line. The line begins to exist; it is restored as a severed one. It could even be that it is only restored *to be* severed. This is the ultimate cruelty of the *Gutmachung*. At the core of the most generous and, undoubtedly, "good" gesture engaged by the authorities of Osnabrück in 1985, the wound has the last word. The possibility of a landline is what would connect Ève, her sister Éri, and Fred to an estranged, uncanny city, a city that is certainly familiar, but is also turned into a monstrous impossibility inside. While facing the call to return to Osnabrück, the two sisters face the impossibility of *the call* to return to Osnabrück. They feel the cut in the call, the nightmare of Germany, the German nightmare.[15] While returning to be honored as former residents from the heartland of the persecutions, Ève ends up spelling out the cry that might summarize

---

14 It is worth noting that there is no easy translation of *Unheimlichkeit* into French. The idea that *Unheimlichkeit*—a word often used by Cixous—is a typical German call of hers might be in line with the fact that there is an essential *Unheimlichkeit* within the structure of the call.
15 In her article titled "Birthmarks (Given Names)," Elissa Marder explores the attributes of what she calls the "cixousian" "dialect" in its untranslatability (Elissa Marder, "Birthmarks [Given Names]," *Parallax*, vol. 13, no. 3 [Routlege, 2007], 49–61). Marder stresses the importance of the "inimitable 'foreign,' tongue" ("Birthmarks," 53) at the core of Cixous's language. Although not addressed in her article, in many ways some structures of the deconstructive nature of the German language infuse in Cixous's œuvre as an essential dimension of her whole experience of writing. In the footsteps of Elissa Marder's reflections, I would add that this inimitability, this "foreignness" of Cixous's "dialect" align with some essential characteristics of the German language that have always had a decisive impact on Cixous's way of writing.

her impossible decision of whether to go or not: "À qui vais-je téléphoner? Personne n'a plus le téléphone à Osnabrück" (*BM*, 134).[16] The landline was cut, meaning that the entire story of the two sisters and Osnabrück has to constantly be re-read in its entirety and in infinite repetition and dissemination of the pain. It must be re-read, reinterpreted, and reshaped while going in every possible direction with no end like in Ève's dream. This is what Hélène Cixous does in her œuvre. Ève knows where she's going. It is not that she strictly gets lost; it's more that the loss corrupts the internal structure of the trip to a point that the familiar city is disfigured. The loss is already there, like an asymptomatic disease that gets actualized as the trip goes on as soon as there is a call to go.

"Wiedergutmachung" is commonly translated into "remediation," "reparation," "compensation." In Cixous's *Benjamin à Montaigne* "Wiedergutmachung" could be an emblematic example of her relationship to German—that is, Cixous's relationship to her mother's relationship to German. "Wiedergutmachung" offers a typical case of what the German language enables; this word is a compound of several words for which Cixous invents a poetic language, in "French," that for her bears witness to the uncanniness of the German language and to the untranslatable uniqueness of the moment when "Wiedergutmachung" erupts in German for Ève and Éri: "Wiedergutmachung," a familiar German term, is defamiliarized, sublimated, both deconstructed and redeemed into "rebonnefaisance." The word "rebonnefaisance" highlights the irony, the impossibility, indeed, the stubborn *idiosyncrasy* of any "rebonnefaisance" *for Ève and Éri*, as soon as the word appears on the scene, given the context, the past, the protagonists ... and more. *Wiedergutmachung*, in German, in context, attests to the impossibility of any *Wiedergutmachung*, however performative, through the French translation-invention, this vicious word become "legible" when it enters through another magical door that drives Cixous's poetic language-dialect: that of the dream, of the dream-word in which the resistance against German, against a certain Germany, the inconceivability of any "Wiedergutmachung," is sublimated and turned into a literary, meaningful form. Cixous writes in a language marked, "birthmarked" as Elissa Marder beautifully suggests, by her immediate social environment, that of her mother Ève and of her grandmother Omi. As already noted, Cixous grows up with a mother and a grandmother who speak in German, she is "birthmarked" by German Lieder and poems, and by a father who used to play with the German words heard in the household. This playful, joyful and poetic structure is in sharp contrast with the world history during her childhood (and beyond), and how it personally affects her family. With this background in mind, Cixous's creative use of the "German" language within the "French" language contains the marks of both the inevitability and the impossibility of the German language for which the invention of a Cixousian idiom has become an inner necessity in Cixous's life. It is worth noting that Cixous's work in French—as a work that occurs between the German and the French language—applies to her creative work with the German language itself. One example is her word *"Hauptbahnhoffnung"* that combines *Hautpbahnhof* and *Hoffnung*: "central train station" and "hope" (*GO*, 113).

16 "Who am I going to call? No one anymore has the telephone in Osnabrück."

The question of where to cut, what to cut, and when, is both a moral question (should Ève and Éri cut their relationship to Osnabrück forever and decide not to go?) and a historical one. But it is also a genuinely narrative one. "When, where, what?" ... The art of cutting defines the art of writing, of filming, of photographing. After all, this question also occurs within the experience of the call, which would indicate that there is an essential telephony in the art of writing—that Cixous performs in all of her writings. "When to cut, where, what?" on the axis of time, on the long timeline of the Great Chronicle of Osnabrück. When, where, what? This is what the call from 1985 raises as a question. It is a question precisely because the German cut, the German historical breach, is what led the sisters to leave, and Fred, and ... (cut). The two sisters, and Cixous herself, have to replay the entire history all over again at this moment ... but the question of "what to replay and how" is when the notion of "cut" and cutting comes into play. It is, after all, a matter of narration. Among the graceful, yet impossible, solutions that the two sisters will find is one that Cixous uses often in *Osnabrück* and in *Benjamin à Montaigne*, as well as in the play she wrote: humor. *Oy!*, Cixous's theatre play of the "return" to Osnabrück, is full of comedic tricks, absurd humor and sarcasm. Ultimately, what made the two sisters determine to go boiled down to trivial yet deciding features offered during the trip, such as the existence of a "large" breakfast buffet in Hotel Nikolai where the sisters were invited to stay in Osnabrück.[17]

"Was there a time before the cut?" is a necessary question to answer in this context. In *Gare d'Osnabrück à Jérusalem*, it takes the form of the reminiscence of the figure of "Helene Jonas geboren Meyer," as Cixous phrases it in *Osnabrück* while using another German term "geboren" (*OS*, 131–32). Rosalie Klein's mother Helene Jonas née Meyer is Hélène Cixous's great-grandmother who gave her name to "Hélène":[18]

> Quelle belle vie elle a eue, c'est-à-dire quelle belle mort, la dernière belle mort d'Osnabrück, le savait-elle, il y avait le Docteur Pelz

---

17 "J'ai adoré leur façon d'y aller" ("I adored their way of going there"), says Hélène Cixous to Karin Jabs-Kiesler in *Ever*, 01:07:19. "Et l'hôtel tu m'as écrit c'est le meilleur, il y a un grand buffet pour le petit déjeuner" (*BM*, 135) ("And the hotel you wrote me, is the best, it has a large buffet for breakfast"). The two sisters will, of course, always argue and disagree about what brought them to Osnabrück.

18 In Cixous's play *Oy!*—that, in some ways, is a companion piece to *Benjamin à Montaigne*—the two sisters, Selma and Jenny, carry the last name "Meyer." In *Ruines bien rangées*, Hélène Cixous writes, "Hélène c'est le nom de mon arrière-grand-mère d'Osnabrück, Helene Jonas née Meyer il y a près de deux cents ans, vu du livre le temps n'a pas d'heure pas de temps" (*RB*, 11) ("Hélène is the name of my great-grandmother from Osnabrück, Helene Jonas born Meyer about two hundred years ago, seen from the book time has no hour no time").

qui conduisait l'orchestre recueilli des huit enfants fils et filles, et le docteur Pelz était encore l'honneur et le serviteur des malades et donc des bien portants de toute la ville, le patron de l'hôpital et le protecteur des pauvres, et tout de suite après l'enterrement (il y avait encore le cimetière) la mort violente et hideuse a commencé, mais on n'avait pas encore égorgé le temps juif et peint en sang juif le joyeux couteau allemand, on ne chantait pas la chanson du couteau content. Chacun a été assassiné. *Ermordet.* Que le meurtre vole la mort à ses fils et ses filles, l'aura-t-elle appris, quand? Certaines bonnes choses échappent à l'anéantissement. —Par exemple? dit mon fils. Je cherche. Je trouve: le photographe.

(*GO*, 31)[19]

Helene Jonas née Meyer was born and died "une belle mort," "a beautiful death," at the time of the first telephone that no one could use. She died before the line was cut, before the death threats that broke the *lignée*[20] of the family, the family lineage, before "the Jewish time painted in Jewish blood" was exerting its cuts under the law of the "happy German knife" in the midst of the tempest of history (*TP*, 81), before the "violent and hideous death began" (*OSJ*, 18) ("la mort violente et hideuse" [*GO*, 31]) and exterminated most of the Jonas family. What remains is the telephone, an absolute telephone, Hélène's legacy is Helene's telephone:

Ce téléphone absolu est mon legs. Je le tiens de Helene Jonas geboren Meyer mon ancêtre me dis-je. Je suis le résultat du téléphone d'Helene geb. Meyer personne d'autre que mon arrière-grand-mère n'ayant le téléphone à Osnabrück elle ne pouvait téléphoner qu'à Dieu en attendant.

(*OS*, 131–32)[21]

---

19 "What a beautiful life she had, that is to say, a beautiful death, the last beautiful death in Osnabrück, did she know that, there was Doctor Pelz who conducted the gathered orchestra of the eight children sons and daughters, and Doctor Pelz was still the honor and the servant of the sick people and thus of the healthy people in the whole city, the head of the hospital and the protector of the poor, and right away after the burial (there was still a cemetery) violent and hideous death began, but no one had yet slit the throat of Jewish time and painted in Jewish blood the joyous German knife, no one sang the song of the contented knife. One still died well. Soon after, dying disappeared. Each one was assassinated. Ermordet. The fact that murder is going to steal the death of her sons and daughters, will she have learned that, when? Certain good things escape annihilation.—For example? says my son. I seek. I find: the photographer" (*OSJ*, 18).
20 Derrida, "H.C. pour la vie," 26.
21 "This telephone is my legacy. I take it from Helene Jonas geboren Meyer my ancestor I said to myself. I am the result of Helene geb. Meyer's telephone no one other than my great-grandmother having the telephone in Osnabrück she could only call God in the meantime."

From Helene to Hélène, the landline is cut, a cut marked by a German name, another toxic German word that will never be translated, turning the event of the cut into a first hideous name: "Ermordet." This is the time of *Ermordet*. *Ermordet* is the Leviathan that destroys the Great Chronicle, *Ermordet* is the "maladie de l'Allemagne" (*BM*, 152), the malady of Germany. The "beautiful life" ("la belle vie") of Helene is her "beautiful death" ("la belle mort") before everything gets cut by the tempest of history, which also marks the death of God: "Que ferais-je si on n'avait pas inventé le téléphone? C'est-à-dire Dieu./Encore faut-il qu'Il ne soit pas coupé par la tempête" (*TP*, 81).[22]

God, the God that Helene could still call before the hideous death in *Osnabrück*, is cut in *Tours promises*. The etymology of this telephony in all of Cixous's books is what she calls "God" (*Le Prénom de Dieu*[23] is the title of her first book published in 1967), a literary divinity that is radically "cut" in the tempest of history.

The landline of the first telephone that was cut in advance by its own solitude is the telephone that Ève can no longer use because she has no more connections in Osnabrück. God-the-telephone is a telephone from Germany whose first name is Helene Jonas geboren Meyer, who died before the violent and hideous death. God, a German telephone, is dead. But its telephony absolutely remains. This impossible then severed landline is a metaphor of Germany in the Jonas-Klein family. Something is saved. There is a line that never endures the rigors and the storms of the historical cuts, a line that still endures the cut as a law of its existence, the one that narrates the stories of the possibilities and impossibilities opened-closed by the cuts of history in Cixous's German books. Ève's telephoned dream and the way that *something calls* in the dream, including the dream itself as a Call, is something that Cixous calls "mon téléphone absolu," my "absolute telephone," ("ce téléphone absolu" [*OS*, 131]) a dream-line whose name is poetry, literature, theatre, creation as an art of cultivating the uncanniness of dreams ... everything that has called Hélène Cixous from the moment she was born. She was born to receive the call from the absolute telephone of literature, her only land, as she often recalls.

---

22 "What would I do if they hadn't invented the telephone? That is, God. / But let's hope that He's not cut by the storm."
23 Hélène Cixous, *Le Prénom de Dieu* (Paris: éditions Grasset, 1967).

Three The last phone call

The jubilee marking the fiftieth anniversary of the creation of the State of Israel occurred in May of 1998, the year before *Osnabrück* was released. Ève Cixous went there. Her arrival in Jerusalem, intriguingly, appears to have common features with her recurring dream of going to the uncanny city, as told by telephone in Jean-Jacques Lemêtre's audio creation:

> —Les cinquante ans d'Israël, dit ma mère, tu ne peux pas imaginer, dit ma mère qui rentrait du cinquantenaire, où elle s'était rendue toute seule, avec la simplicité du prophète qui ne sait pas qu'il est prophète. [...] Avec la simplicité du soldat qui revient de mission, les cinquante ans d'Israël, disait-elle, c'était un traquenard. D'abord il y avait ces couloirs, c'était long, j'ai marché sous la ville pendant deux heures. Ensuite il y avait la foule. A force de chercher ma cousine je ne pouvais plus trouver de place, dit ma mère. Alors cessant de chercher ma cousine dans la foule je m'assieds sur une chaise que j'ai pu trouver. Une dame s'est jetée sur moi dit ma mère et me dit dites donc, c'est la chaise que j'ai gardée pour ma cousine, mais dit ma mère je lui ai répondu ma cousine a aussi gardé une chaise pour moi mais dans la foule on ne se trouve pas. [...]
> Pour finir, j'ajouterai que chaque fois que ma mère a rendez-vous avec Jeanne la dernière cousine qui lui reste d'Allemagne, elle la perd, c'est une relation très antique entièrement composée depuis plus de quatre-vingts ans de rencontres manquées. Selon ma mère malgré tous les efforts des cousines elles s'attendent chaque fois mutuellement à un autre endroit et s'il n'y avait pas le téléphone sauf le samedi auquel les deux cousines se retrouvent pour recommencer, cette histoire de cinquantenaire n'aurait pu avoir lieu.
>
> (*OS*, 176–77)[1]

---

1 "—The 50th anniversary of Israel, said my mother, you cannot imagine, said my mother who was coming back from the fiftieth, where she had gone all by herself, with the simplicity of the prophet who doesn't know he's a prophet.

"Je ne pouvais plus trouver de place" ("I could no longer find a place"), says Ève of her impossible, never-ending arrival in the city that appears to only be accessible through the infinite underground tunnels of a fever dream. She will, it seems, never get to see the doors of ... Jerusalem? The name never appears in this passage of *Osnabrück*. Jerusalem will enter Cixous's texts of Germany later; Jerusalem is where Ève's cousin lives. The cousins of Germany try to find each other in vain in the city of no-name that could secretly be Jerusalem. As if it was a forgone conclusion that the line that connects them was still cut. As if the discordance was what they have in common, which brings them together. Ève is lost in this missed appointment in the not-named city with her cousin from Germany "since 80 years." Eighty years of disconnects that reunite them regularly, "80 years" brings them back to their childhood in Osnabrück, and more precisely Gemen near Osnabrück[2] in the case of "Jeanne the last cousin left to her from Germany" ("Jeanne la dernière cousine qui lui reste d'Allemagne"). Every single time Ève goes to meet with her cousin, she loses her. And like in her telephoned dream, Ève does not know where she is ("je ne sais plus où je me trouve")[3] in a city without a name. In this 80-year relationship made of continual loss, what saves the two lost relatives is God-the-telephone: "malgré tous les efforts des cousines elles s'attendent chaque fois mutuellement à un autre endroit et s'il n'y avait pas le téléphone sauf le samedi auquel les deux cousines

---

[...] With the simplicity of the soldier who comes back from his mission, the 50th anniversary of Israel, she said, was a trap. First of all, there were hallways, it was long, I walked underneath the city for two hours. Then, there was the crowd. By dint of looking for my cousin I could not find a place, said my mother. Ceasing to look for my cousin in the crowd I sat on a chair that I was able to find. A lady jumped on me, said my mother, and said to me hey you, it's the chair I'm keeping for my cousin, but, said my mother, I replied, my cousin too has kept a chair for me but in the crowd we are unable to find each other. [...] / To conclude, I will add that every time that my mother has an appointment with Jeanne her last remaining cousin from Germany, she loses her, it is a very ancient relationship entirely composed of eighty years of missed reunions. According to my mother, in spite of all the efforts of the cousins, they always mutually await each other at another place and if there was no telephone except on Saturday when the two cousins reconvene in order to start over, this story of the 50th anniversary would not have taken place."

2 "Alors ce tramway est aussi le premier pour les cousins de Gemen" (*OS*, 131–32) ("Therefore this tramway is also the first one for the cousins of Gemen"). Gemen is today a part of the city of Borken in the district of the same name, in North-Rhine Westphalia, situated at approximately 130 kilometers (80 miles) southwest of Osnabrück.

3 Lemêtre, *Ceci est un exercice*, 00:02:14 and 00:03:04.

se retrouvent pour recommencer, cette histoire de cinquantenaire n'aurait pu avoir lieu" (OS, 177). Eighty years bring them back to 1918, the end of the war, the year when Ève settled in Osnabrück with her sister and her mom, a year that could be the one when Helene Jonas geboren Meyer got the first telephone in town. At the time, Ève and Jeanne, later known as Marga, were both 8 years old.

The discordance between the two cousins of Osnabrück in Jerusalem and elsewhere is addressed in a more historical way as a general structure of what affects the members of the same family line after the hideous death, after 1933, in 1938:

> Quel rapport y-a-t-il entre quelqu'un qui part d'Osnabrück-sous-Weimar en 1929, animée par l'exaltante et familière *Wanderlust*, et quelqu'un qui sort du Reich par le souterrain rayé de barbelés de Buchenwald en 1939? On ne se comprend pas bien.
>
> (N, 93)[4]

One might well be on the same family line, one no longer shares the same experiences, and each experience is unbearably untranslatable from one segment of time to another and from one language to another, since the members of the family were spread around the world. France, then Algeria, for Ève; England, then Israel, in the case of Marga. Leaving the German Republic of Weimar out of a true *Wanderlust*, like Ève and her sister Éri, is not comparable to being persecuted and pushed out of the German Third Reich like Fred, after he had witnessed the burning of the Synagogue of Osnabrück, after he had been arrested, and after he had experienced the tortures of his detention in the camp of Buchenwald in 1938 to 1939. One no longer speaks the same language in every possible sense of the word. This telephone, the one that saves the two cousins in Jerusalem, is this babelian miracle that always restarts the cousins' history anew, that keeps them together in this phenomenological discordance that speaks more than one language inside the language of their 80-year-old German childhood:

—As-tu téléphoné à Marga?
Marga a téléphoné à Ève le 14 Octobre, elles ont fait la course Jérusalem Osnabrück Paris, chaque année depuis cent ans on vérifie, comme d'habitude, Ève commence. Cette année on va fêter mon anniversaire pour quoi faire je ne sais même pas quel âge j'ai,

---

4 "What is the relationship between someone who leaves Osnabrück-under-Weimar in 1929, animated by the exhilarating and familiar *Wanderlust*, and someone who exits the Reich through the tunnel striped by the barbed wires of Buchenwald in 1939? Each does not understand the other well."

moi je sais dit Marga, le même que le mien, alles gut wünsche ich dir, mir geht es gut und meine Tochter pflegt mich gut moi aussi, ich war sehr krank, meine Gesundheit, moi je mange bien à midi du couscous des saucisses et comme dessert, du bist aber nicht mehr in deiner Wohnung, I cook for myself es müsste besser gehen, Ich war im Krankenhaus ein paar Wochen, mir geht alles gut, moi je vais très bien, je suis éphémère, toi aussi, was sollen wir mehr wünschen, c'est drôle que la vie est si courte, et toi?

(CM, 27–8)[5]

Marga Carlebach geboren Löwenstein is with Ève Cixous, the last of Cixous's relatives from Osnabrück-Gemen, from before the tempest that cuts the telephone. They were born in 1910.[6] This fragment of conversation starts with a question by Hélène Cixous to her mother and is followed by a paragraph that mixes the voices of the two cousins talking on the phone. The discussion between the cousins takes place in three languages with no real sense of interruption between them

---

5 "—Have you called Marga? / Marga called Ève on October 14, they ran the race Jerusalem Osnabrück Paris, every year for the past hundred years one checks, as usual, Ève begins. This year my birthday will be celebrated for what I don't even know how old I am, me, I know says Marga, the same as mine, alles gut wünsche ich dir, mir geht es gut und meine Tochter pflegt mich gut so do I, ich war sehr krank, meine Gesundheit, me, I eat well for lunch couscous sausages and for dessert, du bist aber nicht mehr in deiner Wohnung, I cook for myself es müsste besser gehen, Ich war im Krankenhaus ein paar Wochen, mir geht alles gut, me, I am doing very well, I am ephemeral, you too, was sollen wir mehr wünschen, it's funny that life is so short, and you?"

6 As already indicated, Marga (née Marga Löwenstein) was born in Gemen, Germany, on December 30, 1910, and Ève (née Eva Klein) was born in Strasbourg, Germany, on October 14, 1910. Helene Jonas geboren Meyer, Hélène Cixous's great-grandmother is Omi's mother, she is Ève Cixous's grandmother. She is also Marga's grandmother. I have not been able to identify Helene's date of birth. Here are a few indications provided to me by Hélène Cixous during a conversation on May 29, 2019: (1) Hélène Cixous thinks that Helene Jonas geb. Meyer has died in her eighties; she could have died "at the age of 82," said Hélène Cixous, although she cannot confirm the fact with certainty. She is sure that her death took place before November 1938 (and especially before Kristallnacht). With this date in mind, it is highly probable that Helene was born in or before 1856. She had eight children and Omi was the second youngest, born in 1882. These dates also corroborate the fact that she could reasonably have been born somewhere between 1851 (18 years old when Andreas was born in 1869, 31 when Rosi was born in 1882) and 1856 (23 years old when Andreas was born in 1869, 36 when Rosi was born in 1882), assuming it is accurate that she died around the age of 82 before 1938. (2) Marga: "Marga Carlebach née Löwenstein, daughter of Paula Löwenstein née Jonas, was married to Oskar Löwenstein. Paula is a sister of Omi," Hélène Cixous told me.

(via Cixous's typography), as if they were speaking the same savory, utopian language across French, German and English. The fact that it is not translated in Cixous's poem adds to the casualness of the exchange, and while there are many untranslated German and sometimes English words in Cixous's books, it is rare to see long sentences such as "alles gut wünsche ich dir, mir geht es gut und meine Tochter pflegt mich gut" ("I wish you the best, I am doing well and my daughter takes good care of me") or "du bist aber [28] nicht mehr in deiner Wohnung, I cook for myself es müsste besser gehen, Ich war im Krankenhaus ein paar Wochen, mir geht alles gut, moi je vais très bien," "although, you are no longer in your apartment [German], I cook for myself [English] it should get better, I was in the hospital for a few weeks, I am doing very well [German], I'm doing very well [French]." The two voices are blended in the same sentences as if the two cousins had spoken the same language from the same double-consciousness that creates this paragraph of mixed voices. What turns the scene into a comedy is that the rivalry between the two athletes of time—they are both over 100 years old—concerns who is more adept than the other, who does better, who is more savvy and healthy and well cared for, as if they were still teenagers competing in middle school sports.

Could it be that the absolute telephone that constitutes Hélène Cixous's legacy ("ce téléphone absolu est mon legs") is exemplified in this babelian single block of bicephalous conversation? In which the discordance would embody the utopian capacity to understand and speak all languages on a line that joins "Jérusalem Osnabrück Paris" in a continuity of discordant spaces, times and voices? This is what keeps and what *guards* Osnabrück in Jerusalem; Cixous's book title, the signifier, seems to indicate that *Gare d'Osnabrück à Jérusalem*, literally "Osnabrück station in Jerusalem," could be read as the imperative, the injunction "*Garde* Osnabrück à Jérusalem," "keep Osnabrück in Jerusalem!" This is what Marga, Ève and Hélène Cixous herself are embodying with this sequence of publications by Cixous. This raises countless questions on the different levels of experience mentioned above but also concerning what it means to be in a city, to be from a city, and especially, when it comes to Jerusalem, Osnabrück and Paris in Marga, Ève and Hélène Cixous's lifetimes. In our time. As the comedic rivalry between Marga and Ève keeps going, what seems to lead is the cities, the German cities of the cousins' childhoods:

—Gestern war ich in Osnabrück. —You were in Osnabrück?
—Google. Kennst du das nicht? Elle connaît pas! Cette Marga elle fait tout mieux que moi, mais ça elle a pas fait, aller à Osnabrück sans y aller, dit Ève elle parle sans arrêt et n'écoute pas, ça elle fait mieux que Marga, Marga marche mieux, Marga

aus Gemen dit ma mère. [...] On a toujours le même âge depuis cent ans, dit Ève. Parfois on parle anglais pour allemand, on ne sait pas pourquoi, ça change.

(CM, 28)[7]

After Ève leaves the scene in July of 2013, Hélène Cixous becomes Marga's interlocutor on the line. Could it be that, suddenly, the spectrum of the first, unique telephone line of Osnabrück reappears? Could Marga be the last potential interlocutor on the sole landline of Osnabrück, "at the end a telephone that was never used because there was only one in Osnabrück,"[8] in a structure that was already made explicit by Ève ("À qui vais-je téléphoner? Personne n'a plus le téléphone à Osnabrück" [*BM*, 134][9])? In 2013, Marga calls Hélène Cixous "for the first time": "La première fois que Marga m'a téléphoné, c'était le jour où j'avais dû laisser partir ma mère. Un instant j'ai cru entendre la voix d'Éri, la sœur de ma mère" (*GO*, 74).[10]

Ève is gone and while Marga is given to Hélène, Marga redeems Éri's voice for Hélène Cixous. This time, Cixous is no longer Ève's silent daughter in the shadow of Ève and Marga's phone calls. It could be that Cixous is installed by Marga, on the phone, by the phone, on the day when Ève was gone, that Cixous too becomes a part of the history of Osnabrück. "For the first time" Hélène Cixous is introduced, by Marga, as one of the protagonists of the Great Chronicle of Osnabrück.[11] This designation, a kind of dignification, opens something

---

7 "—Gestern war ich in Osnabrück.—You were in Osnabrück? / —Google. Kennst du das nicht? She doesn't know! This Marga she does everything better than me, but this she hasn't done, go to Osnabrück without going there, says Ève she speaks without ceasing and doesn't listen, this she does better than Marga, Marga walks better, Marga aus Gemen says my mother [...] We've always been the same age for one hundred years, says Ève. Sometimes we speak English for German, we don't know why it changes."
8 "à la fin un téléphone dont on ne se servit pas car il n'y en avait qu'un dans Osnabrück" (*OS*, 132).
9 "Who am I going to call? No one has the telephone anymore in Osnabrück."
10 "The first time Marga telephoned me, it was the day that I had had to let my mother depart. For a moment I thought I was hearing the voice of Éri, my mother's sister" (*OSJ*, 55).
11 For Marga, Hélène Cixous herself belongs to the Great Chronicle of Osnabrück. Although ... it depends on how we read Marga's letter, her words. In her March 17, 2016, card to Hélène Cixous, Marga writes, "We two are the only one [*sic*] still alive" (*CM*, 157). Cixous adds the "*sic*" of course. *We* are the *one*. We is one. Two is one. The *only* one. In a way Marga keeps the notion that she is the one, the only one, while including also Hélène Cixous in this "one": "we" ... Can "one" be both the unique, the only "one," and be counted as a "we"? There is more

that has always been there. Hélène Cixous has always been an actress of this epic legend of Osnabrück, as well as its messenger, throughout a life of writing.[12] Hélène Cixous's book of 1937 plus X-years is a book of Osnabrück. Once again, the telephone, "Dieulephone" (FJ, 16) (Godthephone), saves everyone. The telephone-literature and its infinite switchboard, which draws its lines and plugs to Helene of Troy, is ringing. The entire line of the Jonas family tree, now the tree of *Homère est morte* ..., is calling, starting with Erika Jonas (Éri), Rosi Klein's daughter, daughter of Helene Jonas geboren Meyer. Hélène-Helene on the line: "J'ai dit—Marga? Alors elle a dit: Hélène! Or, nous n'avions pas entendu notre voix depuis des dizaines d'années" (GO, 74).[13]

During the winter of 2016, while reading *Gare d'Osnabrück à Jérusalem*, which Cixous had written during the summer of 2015, I found out that Marga was still alive:

> Marga est toujours encore vivante. Ayant passé la cent-cinquième année, elle est maintenant la seule à garder pouvoir sur le domaine disparu, elle seule peut m'aider. Tous les personnages de nos

---

than one in "one." "One" is we and we is "one"; "one" is Hélène-Marga, the only one. There are countless ways of reading this apparent, possible slip of the tongue ... if it is a slip of the tongue. This grammatical mystery is in line with an undecided, unresolved question about what makes Hélène Cixous's "physical" trip to Osnabrück possible. The fact that Cixous might have "decided" to actually *go to Osnabrück*, does not remove the undecisive dynamic of the move—a structural, indelible, lasting non-decision is at stake in what decided Ève and Éri to go in 1985, an event which constitutes a key to Cixous's œuvre of Germany. We are reflecting on the ways by which Cixous has always been in, been from Osnabrück. In their article titled "Hélène Cixous's Imaginary Cities: Oran-Osnabrück-Manhattan: Places of Fascination, Places of Fiction," Mireille Calle-Gruber and Sarah-Anaïs Crevier write that "Osnabrück gives the narratives of a city-fiction, a fiction told by the mother." Mireille Calle-Gruber and Sarah-Anaïs Crevier Goulet, "Hélène Cixous's Imaginary Cities: Oran-Osnabrück-Manhattan: Places of Fascination, Places of Fiction," *New Literary History*, "Hélène Cixous: When the Word Is a Stage," vol. 37, no. 1 (Johns Hopkins University Press, winter 2006): 140. One reason why there is no way to trace a strict line to distinguish the "city-fiction" and the "city" where Hélène Cixous travels in 2015, and later, in 2019, is the fact that the line that separates the fiction of Osnabrück and the tangible city is essentially, necessarily, decisively blurry.

12 Which, in more than one way, is formulated as follows in *Ruines bien rangées*: "Osnabrück est une fiction" (RB, 13) ("Osnabrück is a fiction").

13 "I said—Marga? Then she said: Hélène! Now we had not heard each other's voices for decades" (OSJ, 55–6).

livres sont sous la terre. On pourrait croire qu'elle approche du silence, mais pas du tout. On peut tout à fait lui téléphoner. J'ai son numéro à Jérusalem.

(GO, 75)¹⁴

It is late March of 2016. I called Hélène Cixous, asking her if we could call Marga. It was a Friday. Hélène Cixous told me to come the next day. It was Saturday, March 19. This attempt to call Marga failed. On a Saturday she was not available: "the telephone except on Saturday" ("le téléphone sauf le samedi") ... it felt like being in *Osnabrück* in 1999, when Cixous recalls the discordant relationships between Ève and Marga (Jeanne in *Osnabrück*):

Selon ma mère malgré tous les efforts des cousines elles s'attendent chaque fois mutuellement à un autre endroit et s'il n'y avait pas le téléphone sauf le samedi auquel les deux cousines se retrouvent pour recommencer.

(OS, 176–77)¹⁵

The story starts over, thanks to "the telephone except on Saturday." On Sunday, March 20, Hélène Cixous was able to reach Marga while I was filming the call:

Ce qui se dessine dans ces derniers jours de mars [2016]: la fin d'Ève, mon personnage irremplaçable, mon immense modeste, c'est pour moi la fin du monde.

(CM, 152)¹⁶

When the phone call takes place in Hélène Cixous's apartment in Paris on that first day of spring, and in Jerusalem on the other end of the line, the two protagonists talk about *Gare d'Osnabrück à Jérsualem*, which Marga had just read. Marga does not mention the fact, but she had just sent a letter to Hélène Cixous about her reading of the book. With Marga, the entire world of Osnabrück, of the Great Chronicle

---

14 "Marga is still alive. Having passed her 105th year, she is now the only one to have power still over the disappeared domain, she alone can help me. All the characters in our books are below ground. One might think she's approaching silence but not at all. Certainly one can telephone her. I have her number in Jerusalem" (*OSJ*, 56).
15 "According to my mother, in spite of all the efforts of the cousins, they always mutually await each other at another place and if there was no telephone except on Saturday through which the cousins reconvene in order to start over."
16 "What materializes in those last days of March [2016]: the end of Ève, my irreplaceable character, my immense modest, it is, for me, the end of the world."

of Osnabrück, was present on the line. So was Homère-Ève. Once again, over the phone, Marga invited Hélène Cixous to come visit her in Jerusalem. Marga, Cixous indicates, is the one who ultimately occupies her thoughts when she "thinks about Jerusalem" from now on ("finalement quand je pense à Jérusalem dorénavant c'est Marga qui occupe tout le cadre de ma pensée" [*CM*, 24][17]). It is in Osnabrück that Cixous receives the incentive, the "push" ("poussée"), to leave "Osnabrück Ville-de-la-paix" (*GO*, 153) ("Osnabrück the City-of-Peace" [*OSJ*, 123]) to go to Jerusalem. This constitutes the main drive of *Gare d'Osnabrück à Jérusalem*. Cixous, the narrator, goes to Jerusalem to meet Marga-Osnabrück. Marga is Marga-in-Jerusalem, who keeps Osnabrück in, or as, Jerusalem. The narrator has gone through Osnabrück the City-of-Peace; she had to go through the Kristall-door of Osnabrück to be able to enter Jerusalem. This is a luminous, nearly invisible door of crystal, held in the City-of-Peace, the door of crystal that defies *Kristallnacht*:

> Il me vient à l'idée que peut-être je devais partir d'Osnabrück pour aller à Jérusalem, peut-être que la Ville est la porte de Kristall par laquelle je dois passer pour aller à Jérusalem. Il me semble que c'est d'Osnabrück que me vint l'ordre d'aller à Jérusalem où je ne voulais pas aller, il me semble que c'est sous le coup d'Osnabrück Ville-de-la-paix qu'il m'est devenu obligatoire et fatidique d'aller là-bas. Mais j'eu peur de prendre mon sentiment pour un événement vrai.
> —Ai-je été poussée, obscurément bien sûr, vers Jérusalem, par l'idée que Marga reste.
>
> (*GO*, 153)[18]

The book becomes a caller-receiver device. Cixous's books also become the witness, the messenger and the actor with which she dials all the

---

17 "Finally, from now on, when I think about Jerusalem, it is Marga that occupies the full scope of my thought."
18 "It occurs to me that perhaps I had to leave Osnabrück in order to go to Jerusalem, perhaps the City is the Kristall door through which I must pass in order to go to Jerusalem. It seems to me that it's from Osnabrück that came the order for me to go to Jerusalem where I didn't want to go, it seems to me that it's under the sway of Osnabrück City-of-Peace that it became obligatory and fated for me to go there. But I'm afraid of mistaking my feeling for a true event. / —Was I pushed, obscurely of course, toward Jerusalem by the idea that Marga is left" (*OSJ*, 123).

The Last Phone Call 51

phone numbers of the absolute telephone of Helene Jonas geboren Meyer:

> [P]eut-être Marga n'y est pas encore morte, […] peut-être elle vit encore, parle encore, ce qui est improbable, objectivement, puisqu'elle a l'âge d'Ève, et à cent cinq ans ma mère ne me parle plus qu'intérieurement? me demandai-je.
> —Absolument pas, dit le livre. Je suis témoin.
>
> (GO, 153)[19]

The book becomes the book of all telephones and telephone calls. The book is the absolute telephone that contains the world. It is the absolute telephone book of salvation in which everyone is saved. After the call, Hélène Cixous receives the letter sent by Marga before her March 20, 2016, telephone conversation. At about the time when Marga's letter had arrived, and after Hélène Cixous had replied to this letter with many questions about and around the Great Chronicle of Osnabrück, all of them addressed to Marga the last figure of the Great Chronicle,[20] Hélène Cixous is dialing Marga's phone number to reach her:

> Mais aujourd'hui, jeudi 31 mars 2016, tandis que je fais le 02.569.8825, comme promis, entre un mail disant: Marga died at age 105. Inutile de laisser sonner.
> On m'arrache la langue, douleur tenaillante comme si le reste de maman m'était arraché de la bouche.

---

19 "perhaps Marga has not yet died there, […] perhaps she is still alive, still speaks, which is impossible, objectively, because she is as old as Ève, and at one hundred and five years old my mother speaks to me only internally now? I wondered. / —Absolutely not, says the book. I am witness" (OSJ, 123).
20 "Jeanne la dernière cousine qui lui reste d'Allemagne" of Osnabrück (OS, 177). "Ah! Nous avons commencé une correspondance extraordinaire" (CM, 153) ("Jeanne, the last cousin that remains from Germany"; "Ah! We have started an extraordinary correspondence"). "C'est une lettre stupéfiante que je reçois le 26 Mars 2016, elle est partie de Jérusalem le 17 Mars à 16h32 et ce n'est pas parce que Marga meurt tranquillement tandis que je la lis, que je la lis avec une émotion extraordinaire, car tandis que je note l'intensité de mes sentiments mélangés, elle est vivante puisque je n'en doute pas un millième de seconde" (CM, 151) ("It is a stupefying letter that I receive on this day of March 26, 2016, a letter that left Jerusalem on March 17 at 4:32pm and it is not because Marga dies peacefully as I read it, that I read with an extraordinary emotion, because as I note the intensity of my mixed feelings, she is alive since I have no doubt of the fact for a millisecond").

> Toutes les questions se pressent autour du lit de Marga désormais éternellement sans réponse, elle [sic] soupirent, elle n'entend plus? alors elles se tournent vers le mur et s'éteignent une à une dans son silence.
>
> (*CM*, 157)[21]

---

21 "But today, Thursday March 31, 2016, as I am dialing 02.569.8825, as promised, an email arrives stating: Marga died at age 105. No need to let it ring. My tongue is being torn off, gnawing pain as if the remainder of mom was torn from my mouth. / All the questions squeeze against Marga's bed henceforth eternally without response, they sigh, she doesn't hear anymore? they then turn to the wall and are extinguished one by one in her silence."

Part II

"Os, na, brück"
The capital of Memory (1933–1935)

Osnabrück nous a complètement faussés.

(BM, 149)¹

On trouvera les cent autres questions dans le livre. Elles se sont posées sur le mur. Au mur. Dans le mur.
Je suis assise au pied du Mur des Lamentations.

Je cherche Andreas, Hans Günther, Irmgard, Else, Paula, Hete, Greta ... comme si je voulais les rencontrer après leur mort, vivant après leur mort, je reconnais avec surprise que je les aime, je passe des mois dans un monde étrangement familier, qui me diffère du monde ordinaire que parce qu'il n'y a pas de temps, au reste il est comme une grande ville cosmopolite, c'est la capitale de la Mémoire, les métros et les rues passent d'une langue à l'autre, sinon c'est pareil, les magasins s'imitent d'un continent à l'autre, du Nord au Sud des oncles ouvrent des usines, d'autres seulement des livres, je suis en général très bien reçue par les femmes, malgré ou à cause de ou après, leur mort, parce que c'est de leur santé c'est-à-dire de leur mort que je veux avoir des nouvelles.

Je passe mon temps à ouvrir des tombeaux, à téléphoner aux morts à vouloir faire parler les cendres à sonder les murs, j'attends des chameaux et des vaches qu'ils me confient leurs tourments
Et je ne sais même pas pourquoi
Que veulent les morts?

(CM, "Prière d'insérer")²

She calls them. For Hélène Cixous, writing means wandering in a timeless, nonspatial city, the extraordinary capital of Memory ("capitale de

---

1 "Osnabrück completely sabotaged us."
2 "We will find the remaining hundred questions in the book. They are posed on the wall. To the wall. In the wall. / I stand at the foot of the Wailing Wall. / I search for Andreas, Hans Günther, Irmgard, Else, Paula, Hete, Greta ... as if I wanted to meet them after their death, alive after their death, I recognize, to my surprise, that I love them, I spend months in a strangely familiar world that for me differs from the ordinary world that, because there is no time, is in fact like a large cosmopolitan city, this is the capital of Memory, the metros and the streets pass from one language to another, otherwise it is the same, the stores replicate from one continent to another, from the North to the South, uncles open factories, others only open books, I am, in general, very well received by women, despite, or because of, or after their death, because it is from their health that is from their death that I want to receive some news. / I spend my time opening graves, telephoning the dead wanting to make the ashes speak probing the walls, I wait for camels and cows who confess their torments to me / And I don't even know why / What do the dead want?"

la Mémoire"), in search for "Andreas, Hans Günther, Irmgard, Else, Paula, Hete, Greta ..." It is a way to spend "months" in a strangely familiar world ("étrangement familier," *unheimlich*, uncanny) in which she calls the dead, she makes the ashes speak ("faire parler les cendres"), she probes the walls ("sonder les murs").

In Jerusalem she sits at the bottom of the Western Wall, also called the Wailing Wall, the *Mur des Lamentations* (literally, the "Wall of Lamentations") in French. Andreas, Hans Günther, Irmgard, Else, Paula, Hete, Greta, all figures of the Jonas family from Osnabrück that she invokes here as residents of a "great cosmopolitan city" ("une grande ville cosmopolite") that could evoke Ève Cixous's dream of a city familiar and strange that could very much be the city of all "great cities" of the world, a city that has no name, no boundary and no specific geolocation, that easily speaks every language and moves from one to another location like in a dream. The *unheimlich* capital of Memory carries no specific address on the map. It reunites the disseminated, as well as the destroyed figures of the hideous death of a dislocated family. A dismembered family. This description of Cixous's city of Memory where she names the German members of the Jonas family of Osnabrück, could be a Jerusalem of the spirit in a vision that comes to her at the *Mur des Lamentations*. This kind of "Jerusalem" gathers the disseminated members of Cixous's German family after their deaths; and Andreas, Hans Günther, Irmgard, Else, Paula, Hete, Greta ... provide news about their lives, which means about their deaths. The site of this imaginary capital literally re-members the missing members. This is another intriguing echo of Ève Cixous's dream of urban disorientation (Part I). Cixous's lamentation is the re-membrance that acknowledges the "dis-membrance" of all memory as a memory of ashes ("faire parler les cendres"). This is the origin of the call.

In *Benjamin à Montaigne* (2001), the traces of a destroyed, reduced-to-ashes Osnabrück appear with the traits of Montaigne's Rome. The traits of Rome seem to also match the description of the capital of Memory in the quote from *Correspondance avec le Mur* (2017). The intriguing insistence of Montaigne in Cixous's texts is a remarkable aspect of all of Cixous's books that take her to Germany. This insistence is tied to a form of figuration in which the complex articulation between *writing and imaging*, between *composing a text and painting*, erupt in Cixous's œuvre when she pictures herself as a descendant of German relatives. In a way, we will show that there is no possibility for Cixous to enter into a dialogue with her German psyche, no possibility of entering in Germany and of actually *traveling to Germany* without *being called by Montaigne* and without calling Montaigne. Which means that she cannot "go to Germany" (symbolically and practically) without articulating the text and the art of painting as a critical mode of what Cixous

56   The "German Illusion"

calls "Memory" with a capital "M" when Germany is in sight. She cannot go without contemplating Montaigne's relationship to the ruin, to La Boétie, and to a certain art of envisioning, of painting as *a form of re-membrance*. One theoretical hypothesis would be that there is no memory without figuration, image or painting. What is at stake, here, in Cixous's relationship to acts of recording, writing and painting?[3] How does that define Cixous's Germany?

Germany's call, for Cixous, always begins with a city. A city that also appears as a dis-membered one: Osnabrück.[4]

---

3   "Acts of …" and not just "recording, writing and painting." The notion of performance is critical in Cixous's œuvre and I will come back to this notion later.
4   In an interview about her book *Ruines bien rangées* published in *Libération* on December 18, 2020, Hélène Cixous indicates that "[she] does not think" that she will continue writing about Osnabrück, which suggests that she is closing the series of her books around Osnabrück opened with the publication of *Osnabrück* (Des Femmes) in 1999: "Vous continuerez à écrire sur Osnabrück? / Je ne pense pas." Frédérique Roussel, "La maison d'écriture d'Hélène Cixous," *Libération* (Paris), December 18, 2020, available online: https://next.liberation.fr/livres/2020/12/18/la-maison-d-ecriture-d-helene-cixous-parution-de-seminaire-et-ruines-bien-rangees_1809068 (accessed December 31, 2020). Of course, this does not necessarily mean that she will no longer write "with" Osnabrück in one way or another.

Four Ruins and remembrance: from "Os, na, brück" to "Rom'"

Osnabrück nous a complètement faussés.

(BM, 149)[1]

---

1 "Osnabrück completely sabotaged us." "Corrupted," "compromised," "disguised," "failed," "sabotaged"? "Fausser" is difficult to render in English especially in the way Hélène Cixous uses the term here. Cixous creatively uses this verb, "fausser," which carries, among others, two potential meanings relevant for us. One relates to what is broken in a system or mechanism, in any manufactured object and, by extension, in a living organism or soul. "Fausser" refers to what compromises the system's mechanical functions, and, metaphorically, to what invalidates, corrupts, leads astray, subverts or perverts a system or an organized structure whether it is material, social or psychological. While the device, the mechanism, the institution, the apparatus (including the psyche) or the organism is damaged, the malfunction occurs through a perturbation that is not always flagrant and easily identifiable, or visible. "Fausser," in this sense, refers to some adverse event that breaks a complex system, but the emphasis is less on the event itself or on what is broken than on how a potentially insignificant or insidious malfunction can lead to a major crisis to the point that it destroys the system entirely. A common example of the use of "fausser"— instead of simply "casser" (to "break")—is for a lock ("serrure"). When the wrong key is mistakenly or intentionally used or forced into a lock, the mechanism can be altered from the inside to the point of breaking everything. This example suggests that the invisible corruption of the inside of the mechanism has in fact invalidated its basic functionalities. Which leads to the meaning of "fausser" as is relevant for us here. "Fausser" would indicate that some alteration, at first not always evident and obvious, leads to a serious, exponential and debilitating ongoing "deformation" that becomes a dysfunctional and permanent alteration of the system, instills an insidious toxicity, corrupts a system of values, and so on. This deformation takes place through an internal twist that surreptitiously changes the *nature* of the structure (of the reasoning, of the spirit, of someone's discourse, thought, philosophy, speech, for example, or of the organism of a living body, etc.). What significantly complicates the matter, in our reading of Cixous, is that she is also pointing out the fact that the "faux" of "fausser" was in fact always, already there and is perhaps not the result of a sudden event, but it was a part of the system, of the structure as soon as the system was set up. It was a culture. Cixous's use of "fausser" here is of the highest

58   The "German Illusion"

On October 25, 2019, 1,400 pupils from Osnabrück wandered across the city, heading to the city hall with their "Steckenpferde," their "horses

---

importance and significance. Not only does the word carry the meanings highlighted but also it shows that a *fault*, a *flaw* and a *perversion* of the self (and of the body) was *always* at work. It is actualized, reactivated and to an extent also revealed by the invitation of the two sisters—Ève, Cixous's mother, and Éri, her aunt—to go to Osnabrück. Something apparently generous or innocent, or incidental, majorly transformed—through deformation and falsification—the whole scene. But the fact that this scene is a primitive one is key to the entire body of work that Cixous creates around the texts of our study. The intemporal nature of the quote "Osnabrück nous a complètement faussés" is essential: it is written in the past and in the context of publication, nothing indicates that it started on the day when the sisters were invited or visited the city. An essential dimension is that the falsification occurs through the mask of sincerity—hence the notion of "false" contained in "fausser." An always-already false. A generous scene of hospitality is in fact *also*—or, maybe even entirely, viciously—a scene of hyperbolic, disguised hostility in what is here revealed, unveiled, as the hostile, adverse nature of hospitality, of what Derrida called "hostipitality": hospitality, like any gift, is always *faussée*. Key is that this adversity or perversity of the invitation and of what ensues, were not evident (and even conscious) in the first place, that there is a sense of vice within the apparent expression of good of the gesture. Any restorative, reconciliatory process is affected by the structure of the "faussé." Any scene of forgiveness—if it exists—is *faussée*. Something *sonne faux*, is out of tune. "Fausser" comes from "faux"—false, wrong, untrue—a "faux" that falsifies the apparent truth and sincerity while turning truth and sincerity into raw falseness and evilness. Other possible translations of "fausser" could have been: to corrupt, to compromise, to deform, to disguise, to fail, to upset, to unhinge, to insidiously unsettle, to subvert … Cixous's highly poetic and amphibological use of "fausser" involves something of a power relation. "Fausser," through the various meanings developed above, is also what involves a *force at work*, an ongoing labor. It is active, permanent and never stops to hyperbolically *fausse* the dynamics at play through the constant metamorphoses of the vice. Something that metaphorically forces a lock occurs through the powerful sovereign power of the authority that forces and that fails those under authoritarian oppression, that leads to intoxication, that corrupts the cells of the bodies and the integrity of the soul far beyond the event of the supposed initial shock. "Fausser" inevitably evokes, semantically and phonetically, the manipulative authority of the "faux" (false) and of the "faute" (mistake), the powers of the false ("puissances du faux," as Gilles Deleuze puts it in *Cinéma 2, L'image-temps* [Paris: Minuit, 1985], 165–202; Gilles Deleuze, *Cinema 2, The Image-Time*, trans. Hugh Tomlison and Robert Galeta [Minneapolis: University of Minnesota Press, 1989], 126–55), of the *fauteur* (one who makes mistakes but also pushes others to make mistakes in French, the troublemaker) and of the *faussaire* (the deceiver, the counterfeiter, the falsifier, the liar, etc.). Littré distinguishes no more than six different meanings of "fausser": (1) creating the false, intentionally turning the true into its contrary; (2) destroying the accuracy, the exactitude; (3) an old, medieval, legal meaning of "fausser" refers to the action of contesting the authority of a court, the authority of a sentence; (4) twisting a solid material; (5) singing out of tune; and (6) the reflexive form of "se on a stick," their hobby horses.[2] This "Steckenpferdreiten," literally the "hobby horse riding" feast and celebration, has taken place in Osnabrück every year since October of 1953. The event originates in the year 1650 and commemorates the peace agreement signed in the cities of Münster and Osnabrück on October 24, 1648. This annual peace festival marks the anniversary of the Treaty of Westphalia. After a procession across the city, through Nikolaiort square and other locations, the children climb up the stairs of the fifteenth-century city hall with their hobby horses to receive a warm sweet pretzel from the hands of the city Mayor and a distinguished guest. On that day of 2019, it was Hélène Cixous who spent over two hours handing pretzels to the 1,400 children with the Mayor of Osnabrück Wolfgang Griesert (see Figure 2). The song of the "hobby horse riding," music, fireworks and dancing are a part of the celebration, as well as evening religious services in the city churches.

Osnabrück, as Cixous recalls in her book *Osnabrück* and elsewhere, plays a central role in the history of Europe as a site where the idea of a Europe unified around a notion of peace was forged through the invention of the art of diplomatic deliberations. In Osnabrück and Münster in 1648, after years of intense negotiations, the Catholics and the Protestants reached an agreement that ended the European wars of religion, more specifically the Thirty Years' War (1618–1648). The peace treaty known as *Instrumentum Pacis Osnabrugensis*, the Treaty of Osnabrück, was a critical part of the set of agreements called the "Peace of Westphalia" (see Figure 3). In both its methodology and final form, this treaty still serves as a model for all "peace treaties." It was sealed in the great room of the city hall of Osnabrück on October 24, 1648. When I visited Osnabrück with Hélène Cixous in October of 2019, paying a visit to this great room of the city hall was a priority. Osnabrück, in this context, is a capital city of memory *as* a capital of peace, the memory

---

fausser" refers to the violation of a pact, of an agreement, the betrayal of moral, explicit or implicit rules. Émile Littré, *Dictionnaire de la langue française*, vol. 3 (Paris: Pauvert-Gallimard-Hachette, 1969), 1438–439. Jacques Derrida's concept of "hostipitality" appears in Jacques Derrida, *Hospitalité*, vol. 1, *Séminaire (1995–1996)* (Paris: Seuil, 2021), and elsewhere, including Anne Dufourmantelle and Jacques Derrida, *De l'hospitalité, Anne Dufourmantelle invite Jacques Derrida à répondre* (Paris: Calmann-Lévy, 1997); Jacques Derrida and Anne Dufourmantelle, *Of Hospitality, Anne Dufourmantelle invites Jacques Derrida to respond*, trans. Rachel Bowly (Stanford, CA: Stanford University Press, 2000).

2   Staff writer, "1400 Schüler erwartet Am 25. Oktober ziehen wieder Steckenpferdreiter durch Osnabrück," *Neue Osnabrücker Zeitung*, October 19, 2019, available online: https://www.noz.de/lokales/osnabrueck/artikel/1909922/am-25-oktober-ziehen-wieder-steckenpferdreiter-durch-osnabrueck (accessed June 28, 2020).

60   The "German Illusion"

Figure 2 On October 25, 2019, Wolfgang Griesert, the City Mayor of Osnabrück, and Hélène Cixous hand sweet pretzels to children outside of the Osnabrück City Hall in commemoration of the Treaty of Osnabrück.

Figure 3 The Treaty of Osnabrück was signed on October 24, 1648, as a part of the general peace negotiations known as the Peace of Westphalia to end the Thirty Years' War.

of a possible accord between antagonist factions and religions that had triggered religious persecutions and caused the death of millions for more than a century. The very idea that *peace could be represented and remembered* is a crucial concept in a universe where war predominantly takes center stage.³ In a way, Cixous's œuvre of Germany turns her into a very rare master of the deconstruction of the theater of war to render a picture of peace; it is no accident that *Osnabrück*, Cixous's first book of Germany, opens Cixous's "German turn" with a two-page description of the city of Osnabrück taken from the "*Grand Dictionnaire universel par Pierre Larrousse*." In this description, placed before Cixous's "Prologue" to *Osnabrück*, Cixous highlights this critical phrase: "l'église Saint-Jean et l'hôtel de ville où fut signé le fameux traité de Westphalie. La salle où la paix fut conclue est ornée des portraits des ambassadeurs de 1648" (*OS*, 8).⁴ This typographic indication is enormous. Having lived with Omi and Ève's Osnabrück since she was born, it could very much be that the gate that allowed Cixous to enter Germany *physically*, both *"literarily" and literally*, is this city hall, is this famous *Instrumentum Pacis Osnabrugensis*, the peace treaty of Osnabrück (see Figure 4).

Cixous visited Osnabrück in 2015 for the "first time."⁵

The history of Europe and the wars of religion are the origins of Montaigne's œuvre. Montaigne traveled across Europe between 1580 and 1581 on a voyage that included Germany, Switzerland and Italy. The trip was profoundly informed by the historical context of "nos Guerres civiles" (our Civil wars) as Montaigne qualifies them, from a divided Guyenne (Montaigne's region) to Protestant and Catholic regions and countries of Europe. This tour took Montaigne to Rome; while *Benjamin à Montaigne*, by Cixous, is haunted by the figure of an

---

3   The renowned German filmmaker Wim Wenders co-authored a book titled *Inventing Peace, A Dialogue on Perception* with the Australian philosopher Mary Zournazi. Wenders states baldly that "peace is largely invisible" while "war always demands centre stage." Wim Wenders and Mary Zournazi, *Inventing Peace, A Dialogue on Perception* (London: I.B. Tauris, 2013), 147. "War must have been utterly successful! It has formed into a solid notion, the sum of all its images, the BIG PICTURE OF WAR! 'Peace', however, somehow doesn't amount to a sum! 'There's no BIG PICTURE OF PEACE'." Wenders and Zournazi, *Inventing Peace*, 64.
4   "[T]he Saint-John church *and the city hall where the famous Westphalia treaty was signed*. The room where the peace agreement was signed is adorned by portraits of the ambassadors of 1648."
5   The "first time," as a concept, translates as follows into Cixous's poetry: "Voilà une ville où tu n'arrêtes pas de venir-pour-la-première-fois, me dis-je, et il n'y en a pas d'autre. Autrefois c'était la ville-où-je-n'irai-jamais" (*RB*, 28).

62   The "German Illusion"

Figure 4 The great room of the city hall in Osnabrück, October 24, 2019.

ostracized member of the Osnabrück family named Benjamin, the book invokes Rome through Montaigne's vision. Here Cixous is thinking within Montaigne's thoughts of Rome as if she were Montaigne, as if she had the ability to slip inside Montaigne's "inner," or secret, thinking of Rome, as if Cixous had the capacity to embody what Montaigne cannot say in his writing; this might also be characterized through a general notion of ventriloquism by which Montaigne is embodied in Cixous's body of text:

> Ce que je pense de <u>Rom'</u> pensait-il [Montaigne] est si violent qu'il ne faut pas le dire, il ne faut pas cracher dans la soupe du pape, tout <u>Rom'</u> n'est que <u>mort</u> et sépulcre, je garde cela pour moi, je n'ai pas exploré un cimetière pensait-il, mais plutôt le cimetière d'un tombeau et les ruines d'une ruine, le monde ennemi de sa grandeur et de sa longue domination ayant premièrement brisé et fracassé toutes les pièces de ce corps admirable et parce qu'encore tout <u>mort</u> renversé et défiguré le corps faisait horreur au monde il en avait enseveli la ruine même j'ai visité le tombeau d'une ruine criait-il *mais je ne dois pas le dire*, il ne restait plus rien de cette ville d'Osnabrück défaite et mise en pièces criait ma mère, rien que des bâtiments nouveaux dévisagés qu'on devait admirer, ça me faisait penser aux nids que les corneilles ont suspendus au reste du pilier de la vieille synagogue brûlée, au lieu des juifs les corneilles, mais

dit ma tante dans la nouvelle synagogue il n'y en a pas, ça ne m'a pas du tout intéressée de voir des choses pareilles dit ma mère.

(*BM*, 41; my underlining)[6]

Benjamin à Montaigne, "Il ne faut pas le dire": "It must not be said," is the motto of this book, and, according to Cixous's reading in *Benjamin à Montaigne*, it is also what Montaigne "thinks" of Rome in Montaigne's famous *Voyage en Italie*. There are many occurrences of "Il ne faut pas le dire" ("It must not be said") in *Benjamin à Montaigne*, including the fact that Benjamin, the younger brother of Omi, Cixous's grandmother, was expelled from Osnabrück by Ève's relatives.[7] Benjamin was a "stain" ("une tache") on the "impeccable German soul of the family."[8] While slipping inside of Montaigne's body of text, or while allowing Montaigne to be "ventroliqued" in her body of words, the maternal trope never leaves this text by Cixous. "It must not be said" is a sentence that Cixous quotes from her mother in this book that ruminates on all the reasons why it is so difficult to envisage the relationship to Germany, to Osnabrück, a relationship that is actualized by the Invitation to go to Osnabrück sent to Ève and Eri in 1985; according to Ève, they were invited to a "cérémonie de ruines" (*BM*, 152–53), a "*ceremony of ruins*."[9] Ruins. The two sisters are invited to see only ruins in Osnabrück. Like

---

6   "What I think of Rom', he [Montaigne] thought is so violent that it must not be said, it is forbidden to spit in the Pope's soup, all of Rom' is nothing but death and sepulcher, I keep this for myself, I have not explored a cemetery, he thought, but rather the cemetery of a grave and the ruins of a ruin, the world enemy of its greatness and of its long dominance having firstly broken and smashed all the pieces of this admirable body and because it was still all dead rolled over and disfigured, the body inspired horror to the world and it entombed the ruin itself, I even visited the grave of a ruin he shouted *but I must not say it*, there was nothing remaining of this city of Osnabrück, stripped and pulled to pieces shouted my mother, nothing but new disfigured buildings that we were asked to admire, that reminded me of the nests that the crows had hanged of what remained of the pilar of the old burned synagogue, instead of the Jews, the crows, but, my aunt said, in the new synagogue there were none, it hasn't interested me at all to see such things says my mother."

7   *Benjamin à Montaigne* indicates that he was born on February 1, 1883, and died in Cincinnati on February 1, 1901: "Benjamin est toujours resté une abstraction de deux lignes dans la Bible d'Abraham Jonas (je traduis): Aujourd'hui le 1er février 1883 est né notre bien-aimé fils Benjamin—le 1er février 1901 est décédé à Cincinnati notre bienheureux Benjamin" (*BM*, 142) ("Benjamin has always remained an abstraction of two lines in the Bible of Abraham Jonas (I translate): today on the 1st of February 1883 our beloved son Benjamin was born—on the 1st of February 1901 our blessed Benjamin has died in Cincinnati").

8   This passage appears on the back cover of *Benjamin à Montaigne*: "l'impeccable âme allemande de la famille."

9   Hélène Cixous's emphasis.

the ruins of the synagogue destroyed by Nazi flames during the night of November 9, 1938 (see Figure 5).[10] Ruins in and ruins of the city that transforms Ève and Éri into pieces of décor and celebration of ruins themselves. It is not by accident that Rome's ruins contain Osnabrück's, and the other way around. Rome contains Osnabrück that contains Rome. In the traces of a devastated Osnabrück, Rome appears in Montaigne's vision in Cixous's text—the vision of a city that does not seem to resemble what Montaigne knew before seeing it.

This cognitive dissonance and sensory discordance are central to the history of the texts, *Voyage en Italie* and *Benjamin à Montaigne*, and to what it means to write. The modus operandi of the writing process is relevant in this context. What Montaigne's secretary notes of Montaigne's initial perception of Rome is his bad mood from coming across too many French fellows in Rome.[11] Later, when Montaigne begins to

---

10 A dominant theme of Hélène Cixous's book *Ruines bien rangées* is the ruin, the ruins of the synagogue of Osnabrück, and how a monument erected in 1994 remembers the burning that took place during the night of November 9, 1938. I took pictures of this monument when we visited Osnabrück on October 23, 2019. A picture of the site is reproduced in *Ruines bien rangées*: "Un espace rasé entre deux demeures. Derrière les grilles une haute collection de grosses pierres prisonnières. Ce sont les os de la Synagogue qui restent éparpillés sur le sol après l'incinération. Os bien rangés. Comme des poules les ruines bien rangées dans leur cage à moellons. / Astiquées / C'est donc ça, la troisième synagogue, un poulailler calcifié, ou bien une version expressionniste des larmes de Niobé?" (*RB*, 73–4) ("A razed-to-the-ground space between two buildings. Behind the grid a high accumulation of large imprisoned stones. These are the bones of the Synagogue that remain spread on the ground after the incineration. Well managed bones. Like chickens the well-arranged ruins in their cinderblock cages. / Polished / This is it, the third synagogue, a calcified henhouse, or else an expressionist version of Niobe's tears?").

11 Montaigne's bad mood is made more explicit in the *Essays*: "Au rebours je pérégrine très saoul de nos façons: non pour chercher des gascons en Sicile, j'en ai assez au logis: je cherche des Grecs plustost, et des Persans, j'accointe ceux-là, je les considère: c'est où je me preste, et où je m'employe." Michel de Montaigne, "De la vanité," in *Essais*, l. 3, ch. 9 (Paris: Abel L'Angelier, 1604), 902. The text of this edition of the *Essays* is similar to the one established in 1595 by Marie de Gournay after Montaigne's death. In the following pages, I quote the Gournay edition published by L'Angelier in 1604, followed by the André Lanly edition in modern French from 2009: "Au rebours [de nos compatriotes], je voyage fatigué de nos façons de vivre, non pour chercher des Gascons en Sicile (j'en ai laissé assez au pays); je cherche plutôt des Grecs et des Persans: c'est ceux-là que j'aborde, que j'observe; c'est à cela que je me prête et que je m'emploie." Montaigne, "Sur la vanité," in *Les Essais*, l. 3, ch. 9, adapted in modern French by André Lanly (Paris: Gallimard Quarto, 2009), 1192. A recent English translation

Figure 5 Remains of the Synagogue in Osnabrück, October 23, 2019.

get to know the city physically, when he confronts his knowledge of the city and the actual locations, Montaigne shares the same frustration that Hélène Cixous identifies in the way Ève Cixous reports her perception of Osnabrück in 1985. "He said," Montaigne's secretary writes (another ventriloquy):

> Il disait qu'on ne voyait rien de <u>Rome</u> que le ciel sous lequel elle avait été assise et le plan de son gîte; que cette science qu'il en avait était une science abstraite et contemplative, de laquelle il n'y avait rien qui tombât sous les sens; que ceux qui disaient qu'on y voyait au moins les ruines de <u>Rome</u> en disaient trop; car les ruines d'une si épouvantable machine rapporteraient plus d'honneur et de révérence à sa mémoire; ce n'était rien que son sépulcre. Le monde, ennemi de sa longue domination, avait premièrement brisé et fracassé toutes les pièces de ce corps admirable; et, parce qu'encore <u>mort</u>, renversé et défiguré, il lui faisait horreur, il en avait enseveli la ruine même. Que ces petites montres de sa ruine

---

of this passage reads as such: "I on the contrary, as one who has had his fill of our customs, do not go looking for Gascons in Sicily—I have left enough of them at home. I look for Greeks, rather, or Persians. I make their acquaintance and study them. That is what I devote myself to and work on." Michel de Montaigne, "Of Vanity," in *The Complete Essays*, l. 3, ch. 9, trans. M.A. Screech (London: Penguin Books, 2003), 1115.

qui paraissent encore au-dessus de la bière, c'était la fortune qui les avait conservées pour le témoignage de cette grandeur infinie que tant de siècles, tant de feux, la conjuration du monde réitérée à tant de fois à sa ruine, n'avaient pu universellement éteindre. Mais qu'il était vraisemblable que ces membres dévisagés qui en restaient, c'était les moins dignes, et que la furie des ennemis de cette gloire im<u>mor</u>telle les avait portés premièrement à ruiner ce qu'il y avait de plus beau et de plus digne; que les bâtiments de cette <u>Rome</u> bâtarde qu'on allait asteure attachant à ces masures antiques, quoi qu'ils eussent de quoi ravir en admiration nos siècles présents, lui faisaient ressouvenir proprement des nids que les moineaux et les corneilles vont suspendant en France aux voûtes et parois des églises que les huguenots viennent d'y démolir.

(my underlining)[12]

Juxtaposing the text published under Cixous's name, *Benjamin à Montaigne*, and the one published under Montaigne's name as a *Journal de*

---

12 Michel de Montaigne, *Journal de voyage*, ed. Fausta Garavini, (Paris: Gallimard, 1983), 200–01. This passage appears on pages 114–16 of the first edition (Paris: Le Jay, 1774). Originally found in a chest in Montaigne's Château by Prunis, *Chanoine régulier de Chancelade en Périgord*, this 178 in-folio was authenticated and published in 1774 by Le Jay. "M. de Montaigne affirmed that he could now see nothing more of Rome than the sky under which it lay and the area of its site; that all the knowledge he possessed thereof was of an abstract and contemplative nature, a knowledge in no way to be apprehended by the operation of the senses; that those who affirmed that they might at least behold the ruins of Rome, affirmed too much. The ruins of a mechanism of such terrible power suggested to his own mind reverence and respect rather than comprehension. What he saw was naught but a sepulchre. The world, resentful at her long domination, first broke and shattered all the portions of this marvellous whole, and then, horror-stricken at this spectacle of death, ruin, and disfigurement, entombed the ruins themselves. As to these minor indications of her overthrow which yet lie upon her bier, they have been preserved by fate as a testimony to that immeasurable greatness which all these centuries, all these conflagrations, all these repeated alliances of the powers of the world, have failed to destroy entirely. But it was almost certain that these defaced fragments which survived were those of the least merit, for the rage of the enemies of this immortal renown would surely have prompted them to destroy in the first instance all that was most lovely and most noble. He declared that the buildings of this bastard Rome, which were now being joined on to the ancient masonry (what though they sufficed to kindle the admiration of the present age), reminded him exactly of the nests the martins and crows were building in the roofs and on the walls of the French churches which the Huguenots had destroyed." Michel de Montaigne, *The Journal of Montaigne's Travels in Italy by Way of Switzerland and Germany*, vol. 2, trans. W.G. Water (London: John Murray, 1903), 95–7.

voyage across Europe to Italy opens infinite avenues of critique. One essential aspect is that although those texts carry the names of "Cixous" and "Montaigne," the two authors have multiple voices, and the multiplicity of voices finds more than one path into Cixous's text. In the passage from *Benjamin à Montaigne*, in one single shot and just one breathless sentence, "je" is Montaigne's voice heard by his secretary and transcribed by Cixous in the form of what Montaigne is secretly saying-without-saying that Cixous gives voice to with the words: "Ce que *je* pense de Rom' pensait-*il*" (my emphases), writes Cixous (*BM*, 41).[13] "Je" is "il"—it is her, Cixous, saying what he says without saying it aloud. Then, suddenly, without a period, without quotation marks, the text articulates Ève's voice embodied by Cixous's already complex network of ventriloquial enunciations in the text (from Montaigne's secretary, to Cixous, to Ève ... and reverse): "il ne restait plus rien de cette ville d'Osnabrück défaite et mise en pièces criait ma mère" (*BM*, 41).[14] Such a structure of intermingled voices insists itself in Cixous's œuvre as it is also often interwoven in Montaigne's texts. It is especially the case in Cixous's work around and with Germany where Ève's voice is omnipresent, interruptive—like the ringing of a telephone, the slip of the tongue, the voice of the subconscious-it-must-not-be-said—often in a comedic and sarcastic way, and often the vehicle for all kinds of other voices.[15] Ève is the voice of the members of the Jonas family, of Montaigne, of Homère ... Ève is Homère-mère, Homer-mother. The general (and often ventriloquial) telephony of Cixous's œuvre is here at stake with more than one person on the line, n+1 voice rising from the inside, shared and divided at the same time, a *rhapsody* that Jean-Luc Nancy

---

13 "What I think of Rom', he thought."
14 "there was nothing remaining of this city of Osnabrück, stripped and pulled to pieces."
15 *Homère est morte ...* being probably the most radical form of this deconstruction of authorship through a written expression in which Ève is the origin—for the lack of a better word. Here are the first lines of *Homère est morte ...* : "Prologue / Ce livre a déjà été écrit par ma mère jusqu'à la dernière ligne. Tandis que je recopie voilà qu'il s'écrit autrement, s'éloigne malgré moi de la nudité maternelle, perd de sa sainteté, et nous n'y pouvons rien" (*HM*, 9) ("Prolog / This book has already been written by my mother up to the last line. As I recopy, there it writes itself differently, moves away despite myself from the maternal nudity, loses its sanctity, and there's nothing we can do about it"). Interestingly for us, on the first page of this prologue Cixous writes, "Le livre par excellence serait plein de livres et de ces photos magiques que l'on voit s'animer sous le regard d'un lecteur passionné, il s'ouvrirait sur des villes qui donneraient sur d'autres villes où ma mère aura séjourné" (*HM*, 9) ("The *par excellence* book would be full of books and of those magical photos that we see animated under the gaze of a passionate reader; it would open itself on cities that would overlook other cities where my mother would have sojourned").

called once the "partage des voix" on the same line.[16] Montaigne's Rome voiced by his secretary, Montaigne's secretary's voice voiced by Cixous is Ève's voice regarding Osnabrück. This is also the circulation of the secret, the "secretary" being originally one who administers "secrets," and Cixous's text addresses Montaigne's undisclosed, secret thoughts about Rome (to which we could add the fact that Montaigne never published the *Journal*[17]).[18] Secret: it must not be said. These are thoughts that Montaigne cannot truly share without being at odds with the pope, indicates Cixous.

There is no economy of secrecy without a multiplication of voices, of parasites, without ghostly interruptions and involuntary perturbations, without all kinds of repressions. The history of repression, of censorship, of self-repression and of self-censorship is crucial in these passages.[19] This is the history of being internally divided, of keeping thoughts for self, of allowing a dismembered self—a self in ruin—to persevere in writing. This dislocation of the voices, the assembly of interlocked secrets, this chorus of disjointed voices converges in Cixous's text in the description of the body of a city "broken and shattered in pieces" ("brisé et fracassé toutes les pièces de ce corps admirable"). It is disfigured ("défiguré"), writes Cixous. "Tout Rom' n'est que mort et sépulcre" (*BM*, 41), "all of Rom' is death and sepulcher," she says. If we take a close look at the passage of Montaigne's *Voyage*, the expressions are very similar: "ce n'était rien que son sépulcre,"[20] "brisé et fracassé toutes les pièces de ce corps,"[21] "mort, renversé et défiguré."[22] What are Ève-Hélène Cixous

---

16 Jean-Luc Nancy, *Le Partage des* voix (Paris: Galilée, 1982). In French, "partage" carries the double meaning of what is being shared, the idea of the shared parts, and of what divides, the idea of what separates. This law is present in Cixous and Montaigne's passages analyzed here.
17 To this day, it is still difficult to decipher the reasons why Montaigne kept this journal.
18 Circulation of the secret, secrecy, secretary. Secretion. The secretive nature of the ventriloquial and telephonic circulation and the sharing of voices also signals a fluidity (secretions) that, again, never truly leave the theme of maternity, and the womb, very far ... "comme s'il n'y avait qu'une seule mère." ("—[...] as if there were only one mother." Lemêtre, *Ceci est un exercice*, 00:02:14 and 00:03:04.).
19 One of Montaigne's necessary steps in Rome will be a meeting and evaluation by the pope's censors who received a copy of his first edition of the *Essays* (by Simon Millanges, 1580); and made requests on what they considered points that Montaigne would have to address and modify due to their content with regard to the doctrine of the Catholic Church. Montaigne took note and the changes were not implemented in the following edition of the *Essays* in 1582 and later.
20 "What he saw was naught but a sepulchre." Montaigne, *Journal*, 95–7.
21 "[B]roke and shattered all the portions of this marvellous whole." Montaigne, *Journal*, 95–7.
22 "[D]eath, ruin, and disfigurement." Montaigne, *Journal*, 95–7.

with the secretary-Montaigne saying when their heterogeneous voices converge in *Benjamin à Montaigne*? They are saying what cannot be said in a somewhat divided state of mind. Divided by the ruins. They are the ruins. They are voicing what divides their selves. In a way, they are already saying that their voices are not theirs, that they are not unveiling the secrets that they ultimately disrobe through Cixous's writing. They say, "It must not be said" ("Il ne faut pas le dire"), they ask for forgiveness for saying *and* for not saying, for unveiling everything while keeping everything secret—the definition of literature according to Derrida.[23] One reason it cannot be said is that "ceux qui disaient qu'on y voyait au moins les ruines de Rome en disaient trop," writes Montaigne.[24] Either too much or not enough, that is the crazy, unintelligible logic of ruins. This logic is not affecting their voices at the periphery of the logic of ruins. It is the logic of ruins in themselves. Montaigne wanders a step further: "il en avait enseveli la ruine même."[25] The world had buried its own ruin. Literature unveils this secret of the secret, which Cixous also

---

23 "Le lecteur alors sent venir la littérature pui là voie secrète de ce secret, un secret à la fois gardé et exposé, jalousement scellé et ouvert comme une lettre volée." Jacques Derrida, *Donner la mort* (Paris: Galilée, 1995), 175 ("The reader therefore senses literature coming down the secret path, a secret that is at the same time kept and exposed, jealously sealed and open like a purloined letter." Jacques Derrida, *The Gift of Death & Literature in Secret*, trans. David Wills [Chicago: University of Chicago Press, 2008], 131). "Pardon de garder le secret, et le secret d'un secret, le secret d'un énigmatique 'ne pas vouloir dire', d'un ne-pas-vouloir-dire-tel-ou-tel-secret, d'un ne-pas-vouloir-dire-ce-que-je-veux-dire—ou de ne pas vouloir dire du tout, point. Double secret, à la fois public et privé, manifeste dans le retrait, aussi phénoménal que nocturne." Derrida, *Donner*, 176 ("Pardon for keeping the secret, and the secret of a secret, the secret of an enigmatic 'not meaning (to say),' of a not-meaning-to-say-such-and-such a secret, of a not-meaning-to-say-what-I-mean-to-say—or of not meaning at all, no way. A double secret both public and private, manifest in its withdrawal, as phenomenal as it is nocturnal." Derrida, *Gift*, 131–32). "Secret *de* la littérature, littérature *et* secret auxquels semble alors s'ajouter, de façon encore peu intelligible mais sans doute non fortuite, une scène de pardon." Derrida, *Donner*, 176 ("This is the secret of literature, the literature *and* secrecy to which a scene of forgiveness seems now to be added, in a still scarcely intelligible but probably not fortuitous manner." Derrida, *Gift*, 132).
24 Montaigne, *Voyage*, 200–201. "[T]hat those who affirmed that they might at least behold the ruins of Rome, affirmed too much." Montaigne, *Journal*, 95.
25 "[E]ntombed the ruins themselves." Montaigne, *Journal*, 95. Several other sentences by Montaigne in this passage, are extremely similar in Cixous's text: "*il en avait enseveli la ruine même*" (*BM*, 41, my emphasis). Here is the longer version: "qu'encore mort, renversé et défiguré, il lui faisait horreur, *il en avait enseveli la ruine même*," writes Montaigne, Montaigne, *Voyage*, 200–201, my emphasis. ("and then, horror-stricken at this spectacle of death, ruin, and disfigurement, entombed the ruins themselves." Montaigne, *Journal*, 95–7); Cixous: "qu'encore tout *mort renversé et défiguré* le corps faisait horreur au monde *il en avait enseveli la ruine même*" (*BM*, 41, my emphases).

named "ashes." In Cixous-Ève's language it is also what Cixous-Ève calls, and what secretary-Montaigne calls it secretly, the "ruins of a ruin": "all Rom' is nothing but sepulcher, I keep it for myself, I have not explored a cemetery, he thought, but rather the cemetery of a tomb and the ruins of a ruin" ("tout Rom' n'est que mort et sépulcre, je garde cela pour moi, je n'ai pas exploré un cimetière pensait-il, mais plutôt le cimetière d'un tombeau et les ruines d'une ruine" [*BM*, 41]). The ruins of a ruin. Ruins of a ruin is what cannot be said. This is "Rom,'" says Montaigne-Cixous, which is Osnabrück, says secretary-Ève through Hélène Cixous's poem.

Not "Rome" but "Rom'." "Rom'" is a dismembered name. "Defaced members," "dismembered faces," "membres dévisagés" of Rome, writes Montaigne. "All Rom' is anything but *mort*, death," writes Cixous while *almost* quoting Montaigne, Montaigne himself being quoted by his secretary: "tout Rom' n'est que mort," writes Cixous (*BM*, 41); "one does not see anything of Rome [...] that is still dead," "on ne voyait rien de Rome [...] qu'encore mort," writes secretary-Montaigne.[26] The anagram of *Rom'*, as it is written by Cixous, is already present as *mort* in Montaigne's text. *Rome-mort*. Literally: "Rome-Death." That is the secret encrypted in Montaigne's writing reported by his scribe-secretary. And, of course, the secretary of all secrets is writing itself, the signifier. He writes Rom'. What significantly appears as a salient secret in this intertextual circulation of secrets between the secretaries—everyone being the secretary of the other in one way or another—is ashes. Ashes, ruin of ruins: "the old burnt synagogue" ("la vieille synagogue brûlée" [*BM*, 41]), writes Cixous-Montaigne-Ève-secretary. Secret ashes, this must not be said. And that is when, in the two texts, birds, and not just any birds, make their appearances: "Corneilles." Cixous: "qu'on devait admirer, ça me faisait penser aux nids que les corneilles ont suspendus au reste du pilier de la vieille synagogue brûlée, au lieu des juifs les corneilles" (*BM*, 41). Montaigne: "les bâtiments de cette Rome bâtarde qu'on allait asteure attachant à ces masures antiques, quoi qu'ils eussent de quoi ravir en admiration nos siècles présents, lui faisaient ressouvenir proprement des nids que les moineaux et les corneilles vont suspendant en France aux voûtes et parois des églises que les huguenots viennent d'y démolir."[27] The *corneille*, known as corvus, the crow, is often depicted as one who foretells storms, calamities and catastrophes. In antiquity,

---

26 Montaigne, *Voyage*, 200–201.
27 "[T]he buildings of this bastard Rome, which were now being joined on to the ancient masonry (what though they sufficed to kindle the admiration of the present age), reminded him exactly of the nests the martins and crows were building in the roofs and on the walls of the French churches which the Huguenots had destroyed." Montaigne, *Journal*, 95–7.

the *corneilles* were known as the messengers of omens, and crows appear as such in Aesop. In Montaigne's passage, the catastrophes are the destruction of *places of worship*, destruction of churches during the wars of religion, specifically the destruction of Catholic churches by the Huguenots.[28] In Cixous's texts, the catastrophes are the destruction of synagogues in Germany by the Nazis. For this reason, this text carries more than just a "convergence" of voices. Montaigne's self-censorship, heard by Cixous with an infinite number of voices, operates as a way of breathing together with the dead of destructions; this is why Cixous's sentence is breathless, why it never stops breathing, why its breath is the breath of a wave of silenced victims. Breathing together: in Montaigne or Cixous, this n+1 voice is a *conspiration* of peace, reflecting the etymological root of *conspiration* as "breathing together." The crows are not just flying around this scene of ruins, in Montaigne and Cixous the crows have a special way of voicing, a highly recognizable way of singing whose almost-human sounds belong to the tragic soundtrack Rom'-Osnabrück. No wonder this scene is also a highly cinematic one.

While Montaigne's crows recall the fact that we are always contemplating ruins of ruins, that we are not seeing Rome but a truncated Rom', Rom'-mort, that we are witnessing human destruction motivated by persecutions, the question of what remains is at stake. Montaigne's Rome was that of his readings, of books; that of Virgil, of Horace, of Ovid, of Catullus, of Seneca the Younger and beyond.[29] The quoted text from the *Voyage* provides a description of a certain Rome marked by

---

28 The *Voyage* is full of ethnographic records and observations by Montaigne about the way the Reformation is shaping Europe in his time. It is established that Montaigne's choice of going to Italy while not taking the shortest route had one goal, that of documenting the state of the Reformation in the parts of Germany and Switzerland that he crossed. Philippe Desan shows that Montaigne always had Rome in his mind when he was traveling across the east part of France and Germany in the early stage of his journey, which makes clear that Montaigne knew exactly why he was taking this long route. Philippe Desan, *Montaigne, une biographie politique* (Paris: Odile Jacob, 2014), 317–94.

29 In her article titled "Contradictory impulses in Montaigne's vision of Rome," Margaret McGowan highlights the fact that Montaigne had gone to Rome after having studied a variety of books and other popular guides; she lists several works: "Lucio Mauro's, *Le Antichita de la città di Roma* (Venice, 1558), which took the reader through the city hill by hill and palace by palace, each object of interest being briefly indicated. The specialist information which Montaigne found there was less secure, however, than in the works he purchased in Venice: Onufrius Panvinius' *Principum et eorum quarum maxima in Italia imperia fuerunt* (Basle, 1558) provided a convenient source of reference, listing dates, titles and genealogies of all the emperors from Augustus to Charles V; while the same author's compendious *Republicae Romae commentarium* (Venice, 1558) furnished descriptions of Rome (1–195), its principal civic offices (296–645), causes of decline (646–57), organization of Empire (658–807), and activities of the Roman

the actual decay but also provides access to Montaigne's inner Rome, a Rome existing before a long line of sacks occurring from 390 (Brennus) to 410 (Alaric), 455 (Genseric), 546, 549–550 (Totila), up until 1527, a bit less than six years before Montaigne's birth, when Rome was sacked by the mercenary troops of the German emperor Charles V.[30] The occurrence of Osnabrück in Cixous's œuvre arrives through the generation of her mother, of Éri and Marga; similar to Montaigne's Rome, Osnabrück traces the story of a city marked by intense physical destructions. The city is still alive in its pre-destructive form through the voices of Cixous's ancestors. Here, again, Osnabrück is a Roman city for Cixous:

> Osnabrück évoque plutôt une Pompéi d'avant 79, une ville juvénile, européenne, jouisseuse, un coffret plein d'êtres doués pour la vie, on nage, on va au théâtre, on fait du sport, et un matin on est frappé de guerre. Foudroyé. Os, na, brück.
>
> (*AA*, 23)[31]

"Os, na, brück" is marked by what Rome is going through when Cixous's Montaigne discovers "Rom'." This is the Osnabrück we know, the one from before the hideous death, its dislocations and other dismembered pieces. Rom', Os':

> Le visage navré qui échappe à ma mère lorsqu'elle dit le nom d'O̲s̲nabrück, comme sur le rivage de l'O̲céan on découvre un o̲s̲ laissé par un cétacé disparu, admirable féro̲cité.
>
> (*OS*, 128; my underlining)[32]

"[U]n os": a bone. The "Os" of Osnabrück, of the Ocean (pronounced O[s]éan in French), an "os" abandoned on the shore, remains of limbs discovered long after the enormous animal died and was washed off, a long gone "ferocious"—another "oc" (similarly pronounced

---

legions (808–66). Additionally, Montaigne had a copy of Guillaume du Choul's *Discours de la religion des Romains* (Lyon, 1556)." Margaret McGowan, "Contradictory impulses in Montaigne's vision of Rome," *Renaissance Studies*, vol. 4, no. 4 (Wiley, December 1990), 392–409.

30 Montaigne was born on February 28, 1533. The sack of Rome by Charles V took place on May 6, 1527.

31 "Osnabrück evokes rather a Pompeii before 79, a juvenile city, European, pleasure-seeking, a case full of gifted-for-life beings, one swims, one goes to the theatre, one plays sports, and, one morning, one is hit by war. Blitzed. Os, na, brück."

32 "The air of sadness that drops from my mother's face when she utters the name of 'Osnabrück,' like on the shore of the Ocean one discovers a bone left by an extinct cetacean of admirable ferocity."

"os")—"cetacé," cetacea. "Cetacé" in French is the phonetic equivalent of "C'est assez!" meaning "That's enough!"

Montaigne's internal division, the schism between the "abstract," the "contemplative" Rome and the destroyed one—this is Ève's experience of Osnabrück. What Montaigne and Ève have in common here is the secret, the fact that they have to mourn in secrecy, the ruined Rome-Osnabrück that also ruins their contemplation: "cette science qu'il en avait était une science abstraite et contemplative, de laquelle il n'y avait rien qui tombât sous les sens,"[33] writes secretary-Montaigne. The impossible reconciliation between this "corps admirable" of Rome and what their senses, their feelings, tell them of the ruins before their eyes is not only a *dislocation of their contemplative vision* of the admirable body of Rome-Osnabrück, but it is also *a dislocation of memory*, which means a dislocation of the subject of writing that I would like to call a "textual dis-membrance." In other words, the "admirable" Rome (Montaigne), the "ville juvénile, européenne, jouisseuse, un coffret plein d'êtres doués pour la vie, on nage, on va au théâtre, on fait du sport" (*AA*, 23),[34] which is Ève's Osnabrück ... all that beauty no longer exists. It is alive in books, revived in writing, and lives through a performative *and* deconstructive literary gesture. Books offer, as Montaigne indicates, what "*fortune*" has accidentally kept as a "témoignage de cette grandeur infinie," "a testimony of its infinite greatness." What allows this fortune to exist is the capacity to read the ruins, that is, to remember that they bear witness. Montaigne is in Rome with his books on Rome to remember in writing, to paint the insurrectional discrepancy that he cannot say when he sees Rom' for the "first" time. So does Hélène Cixous, the secretary of Ève (and reverse), with Os, na, brück. There is no peace, *if it exists*, which means there is no justice without facing the sum of impossibilities erected by ruins, without facing the wound that hinders and requires the performance of writing, an act whose name can be "peace treaty." The *Essays*, the *Voyage en Italie*, Cixous's books of Germany: if they are readings of ruins, treaties of ruins, peace treaties, it is through a divided state of mind that intrinsically owes its division to the ruins. Which is why Ève is not just "seeing" the ruins: she is forced to be part of them ... *it must not be* ...

---

33 "That all the knowledge he possessed thereof was of an abstract and contemplative nature, a knowledge in no way to be apprehended by the operation of the senses." Montaigne, *Journal*, 95.
34 "[J]uvenile city, European, pleasure-seeking, a case full of gifted-for-life beings, one swims, one goes to the theatre, one plays sports."

Five Osnabrück the instrument of peace: "*Recorder*," recorder

The chiasmus between the act of writing as an art of contemplating ruins, on the one hand, and the art of allowing an n+1 voice in the text, on the other hand, is highly dependent on the idea that Hélène Cixous is built on a ruined ground that she calls a "chain of abysses and moving sands" in the passage below ("une chaîne d'abîmes et de sables mouvants"). "Germany," her mother's Germany, stands at the crossing. Germany is "rooted" in this crumbly ground. Writing, in the way it is practiced by Cixous, is made more explicit as *Benjamin à Montaigne* progresses:

> La nuit me montre mes ruines et comme je suis bâtie sur une chaîne d'abîmes et de sables mouvants.—Tu ne vois pas que je suis ethnologue? Je voudrais expliquer à mon frère que je ne suis pas ramasseuse de déchets et conservatrice de délires. J'ai un métier lui dirai-je s'il ouvre soudain la porte dans mon dos et brandit son épieu en carton. Heureusement le magnétophone tournait lorsque la peur d'être prise en état de péché arrêtait ma main au-dessus du papier.
>
> (*BM*, 76)[1]

This passage provides another name for writing in this context. This is also what she calls the "night," what calls in the middle of the night, a texture of the night that we will unfold in more detail in Part III when we consider Kristallnacht, the night of November 9, 1938, when the synagogues were burned in the midst of other horrific persecutions.

---

1 "The night shows me my ruins and how I am built on a chain of abysses and quicksand.—Don't you see that I am an ethnologist? I would like to explain to my brother that I am not a garbage collector and a keeper of deliria. I have an occupation I would tell him if he suddenly opened the door in my back while brandishing his cardboard pike. Thankfully the tape recorder was rolling when the fear of being caught in a state of sin stopped my hand above the paper."

Writing the night, writing in the night, writing in the night of flames, ruins and ashes, the ashes of Germany, becomes an art of collecting, now with a technological secretary. With a recording device ("magnétophone"), she records:

> J'enregistre sans arrêt je dépose les instants, je m'épuise à *recorder*, j'appuie sur la touche mentale chaque minute, je suis constamment à côté de moi, de ma mère.
>
> (*BM*, 185)[2]

The eruption of the word "recorder" here is another crucial moment in which Cixous's relationship to Montaigne as a relationship to her mother Germany develops into a form of ethnographic research similar to the one that Montaigne is engaging throughout his 1580 to 1581 *Voyage*. After all, Montaigne also records and archives "instants" during the many months of his trip, offering a very detailed account, not only of the physical curiosities of his multiple stations along the way (landscapes, architecture, etc.), but also of the way people speak, worship, cook and feed themselves, on the habits and customs and all kinds of details, including incongruities, that are very typical of any ethnographic work. How people eat, greet, assemble, their clothing, their sexuality, the quality of their beds and sheets, of their culinary specialties, of their bread and wine, of their fruit and meat, the way they celebrate and pray ... on prices, on habits and so on. Much like the *Essays*, the *Voyage* does not seem to follow strict rules of exposing a fully coherent and logical, hierarchical thinking. However, what organizes them meticulously is a very subtly crafted poetic way of writing and wandering. The ruins of Rome are a part of this overall activity that consists of gleaning observations in a decisively poetic way. The ephemeral trace that people, actions and locations leave on the author's mind and his culture meets the inner imaginary landscapes of the writer-poet Montaigne. Montaigne confronts himself with strangeness, which makes him an ethnographer through a contemplative, non-judgmental attitude. He constantly seeks the perspective of the other, of the stranger, as a way to interrogate his own strangeness—something that is, of course, a major, notorious dimension of his *Essays*. He even writes in the language of the other, in a philosophical and practical sense, starting in May of 1581, when during his *voyage*,

---

2 "I incessantly record, I deposit the moments, I exhaust myself recording, I push the mental button every minute, I am constantly next to myself, to my mother."

Montaigne writes his diary directly in Italian.[3] This defines literature and philosophy for him, as well as for Cixous and Derrida.[4]

The resulting attention to such details makes him especially aware of what usually seems insignificant or irrelevant. With his ethnographic-poetic mindset, it could very much be that, to a certain extent, Montaigne's mind operates like a technical device—his secretary, the pen and, later, himself, being the technology utilized in the process. Cixous's use of the *magnétophone* evokes this ability to capture, to glean and to document what appear to be the minor events, attitudes, accents and formulations with which Cixous has portrayed her mother and her aunt in her books of Germany. The recording device is here to capture small grains of meaning and other micro-events. This approach also implies an ethnographic attitude that regards Cixous's closest relatives like strangers. Whether it is the tape recorder (magnétophone) or what she calls her "mental" recorder—the mental button that she presses as soon as she is in the presence of her mother—Hélène Cixous functions like the secretary in Montaigne's *Voyage*. Later, Montaigne himself will write his *Journal* in the same state of mind.

In a way, ruins and ashes are often barely visible. In the middle of the night, they present themselves in the form of illegible grains, of microscopic eruptions of meaning that serve as a point of entry for enigmatic dreams and precarious visions. Montaigne and Cixous pay attention to these pieces of sand, pieces such as the slightly audible German accentuation in Ève's use of a French word, pieces of *il ne faut pas le dire*, of it-must-not-be-said underneath the surface of the ruin (assuming that any ruin is the result of a negation), of a denial of meaning, of a repression, of a destruction, of a forced conversion or of a forced change of language. Ruins are phantoms of destruction, and the writing-recording device operates like a magical vehicle to seize them. For Montaigne-Cixous, who allows the ghosts of history to come in and find

---

3   "Assagiamo di parlar un poco questa altra lingua massime essendo in queste contrade dove mi pare sentire il piu perfeto favellare della Toscana." Montaigne, *Voyage*, 460–500. "Essayons de parler un peu cette langue, me trouvant surtout dans cette contrée où il me paraît qu'on parle le langage le plus pur de la Toscane." Montaigne, *Voyage*, 279–369. The original edition of the *Voyage* presents a double-page printing of the French translation (right-hand pages) and of the Italian (left-hand pages) texts. See Michel de Montaigne, *Journal du Voyage de Michel de Montaigne en Italie, par la Suisse et l'Allemagne en 1580 et 1581*, with notes from M. de Querlon, vol. 3 (Paris: Chez Le Jay, 1774). ("Let me now try to discourse a little in another language, especially as I am now in that district where meseems I may listen to the most refined Tuscan accent." Montaigne, *Journal*, 56.)

4   Derrida will always defend the idea that one *always* thinks in the language of the other against Heidegger.

their way into the recording device, ruins arrive as negations. Ruins, in the sense established here with Montaigne and Cixous, are negations of justice. History is spectral. Historical events arrive to us through ghostly eruptions and returns. Ghostly interruptions. Phone calls that trigger answering machines and other recording devices. One reason why recording devices are especially designed to capture the ghosts of history who have been negated by its injustice is that those devices allow for careful rereading of the historical sequences. They allow for a translation to take place, a decoding of the enigmatic form that the ruin contains—they know that historical events are mostly written in a foreign language. This is a way to highlight that, for Cixous, the writing process invokes the ghosts. Montaigne-Cixous invites the ghosts of history in writing, through writing. Writing is the *Schibboleth* of ruins. *Schibboleth*: "Os, na, brück" says Cixous; she says "Rom'" in Montaigne's footsteps—Cixous's books of Germany are the *Schibboleth* of Rom'-mort. She awakens Montaigne's dead, her dead, "Andreas, Hans Günther, Irmgard, Else, Paula, Hete, Greta ..." (*CM*, "Prière d'insérer"). In Rome, in Rom', Montaigne is in search of the ghosts of the beloved ancient writers and philosophers who populate his *Essays*, his being, his flesh, his childhood that he retrieves in writing in the *librerie*, in the midst of "nos guerres," in his region of Guyenne torn by the European wars of religion. Ruins carefully allow the margins of consciousness to trace their fragile tracks.

It is undeniable that this act of recording is pleasurable in the way it redeems or compensates for an immeasurable loss. The fact that in writing Cixous revives her German relatives is not a metaphoric notion. Montaigne in his own way also "revives" the figure of his dear friend, Étienne de la Boétie. Montaigne always has the victims of the various cruelties of his time, namely, the religious persecutions, in mind when he travels and when he writes. It is what Cixous-Montaigne, what *Hélène Cixous de Montaigne*, enjoys as a writer. Cixous-Montaigne practices the pleasure of recording, of writing as a form capturing the insignificant repressed, of keeping the irrelevant, the powerless, of archiving the grains of meaning left by the tortured and the dying, beneath the heavy surface of the wars. The action of collecting and tracing in general could be a form of conjuring the ruin, a protest against the pain of destruction, an insurrection against the scandalous erasures of justice (which defines "insurrections"). The grains of near-insignificance that the ruins manifest are *spectral manifestations*.

This historic materialism of the ruins is not turned into poetry merely for the sake of writing poetry, for the sake of creating the Apollonian beauty of harmony and peace. Poetry, here, is the prophetic revolt of the specters. This transforms the text into a point of entry for a future that would be liberated from the heaviness of the present: it is no accident that Montaigne has the cruelties of the wars of religion (among others) in sight when he visits the ruins of "Rom'." The pleasure of recording is not motivated by an aesthetic inclination nor a contemplative attitude; it is a practice in which the concept of time is prophetic and spectral. It announces a possible liberation. It is seeking the liberation that the ruins bring to the present in the form of destroyed, unrealized, unaccomplished *moments of emancipation*. Cixous is a rag-picker, and the tape-recorder is her tool.[5] The ruin revives the dream of justice in the midst of a heavy, foggy, destructive and cruel time. Such an art of writing, in this sense, participates in a re-collection that redeems "Andreas, Hans Günther, Irmgard, Else, Paula, Hete, Greta ..." from underneath the petrified surface of oppression, to "meet them after their death, alive after their death, I recognize with surprise that I love them" ("les rencontrer après leur mort, vivant après leur mort, je reconnais avec surprise que je les aime"), Cixous writes (*CM*, "Prière d'insérer"). This is Cixous's relationship to her German demonstrators "Andreas, Hans Günther, Irmgard, Else, Paula, Hete, Greta ..."; their resurgence in writing proclaims that they are alive because their cause is to be heard. They are alive in writing through the process of a recording whose future is the justice to come. Writing is an act of reviving the dead *as a form of liberation*, of returning the call (of the ghosts)—it is activism as an art of reviving the specters to hear their call for justice. Cixous's absolute telephone of the previous Part is the apparatus of this "call." Her œuvre is the complex answering machine that picks up the call for the future justice. Her physical and mental tape-recorder captures the calls. She writes as an exclamation-redemption of all the possibilities that their deaths annihilated. In writing—and perhaps in general—time does not pass, does not flee, does not escape: it returns. Time is revenant.

The ruin revives the dead as an unaccomplished possibility in an act of justice that also turns the act of writing into an art of building scar tissue at the places of traumatic events such as the ones that burned the Synagogue-Os, na, brück-Rom'. In the peace treaty known as *Instrumentum Pacis Osnabrugensis*—literally "the instrument, the record of the peace of Osnabrück"[6]—peace is an event, symmetrical to the theater of war marked by destruction and death. Peace is a form of theatre that

---

[5] In a sense, Montaigne could be seen as a rag-picker due to the way he describes his reading and writing habits (and through what we know of his use of books).

[6] Émile Littré recalls that "instrument" is also a term in use in liturgy: "Instruments de paix, reliquaire, image, anneau, patène, etc. que l'on baise." Littré, *Dictionnaire*, vol. 4, 1057. "Lord, make me an instrument of your Peace," "Instrument de paix," in French, starts the Peace Prayer of Saint Francis. The last verse contains this sentence: "c'est en pardonnant qu'on est pardonné," "it is in pardoning that we are pardoned."

also occurs *in writing*, which is far from incidental. Writing, after all, could always be a way of writing a peace treaty, at least it is the way Montaigne and Cixous write while building scar tissue on the ruins of Rom', of Os, na, brück. The "crazy, unintelligible logic of ruins," as we called it earlier, invokes a *writing performance*. The October celebration that takes place in Osnabrück every year reenacts the difficult writing of the book of peace when negotiators had recourse to messengers, who, during many years of negotiations between the Protestants and the Catholics, traveled on horses between the antagonist parts.

What remains salient here is that while it brings pleasure, this activity of writing does not provide any narcissistic satisfaction. For Cixous, like Montaigne, rebelling against the injustice of destruction that comes to her as "ruins" is marked by a certain level of self-censorship, repression and guilt. It is as if the repressive nature of the ruin made its way into the minds of the writers—as if writing is an activity that participates in what could be called a culture of the ruin, even though *it conjures the ruins*. Writing is a constitutive element of what makes the ruin a ruin, writing is inseparable from what makes the ashes ashes. And the sadness always remains. The frustration that only the act of writing dissipates also reinstates the traumatic nature of ruins. It is impossible to delineate those effects. In Cixous's account, the pleasurable use of the tape recorder is always entangled in a pattern of guilt:

> Le téléphone sonne.
> À ce moment-là je donnai moi-même un grand coup de pied dans le magnétophone. Je l'avais posé au milieu de la marche tourné vers la cuisine ce que je n'aurais pas dû faire. Je me levai vite et je marchai moi-même sur la machine une petite Sony. J'entendis nettement le petit craquement d'une pièce de l'engin qui s'écrasait au sous-sol. J'étais surprise: pourquoi avais-je fait tout ce que je n'aurais pas dû faire? […] J'utilisais pour enregistrer les deux sœurs à la dérobée "les cassettes du dalaï-lama," il faut dire que c'est tout ce que j'avais trouvé dans la maison: douze cassettes de quatre-vingt-dix minutes (qu'une amie tibétaine m'avait données) sur lesquelles étaient gravées des journées entières d'orations du Dalaï-Lama en anglais et en tibétain, en vérité une série d'Essais sur les questions De la vanité, Que philosopher c'est apprendre à mourir, […] de toute évidence un usage-remake tibétain assez exact de la pensée de mon Montaigne, usage que certains pourraient réprouver, mais d'un autre côté enregistrer Selma et Jennie par-dessus le Dalaï-Lama avais-je répondu à la voix de la réprobation est un acte qui ne manque ni de sens ni d'audace ni de calcul inconscient, car c'est là le signe d'un hommage que certains pourraient contester

à la dignité et à la sagesse des deux vieilles. D'un autre côté il faut dire que dans l'obscurité de mes pensées magiques, l'idée d'un mélange de Selma avec le Dalaï-Lama d'une mystérieuse chimie magnétophonique m'avait effleurée. Il n'y a rien de mal me disais-je. Je mets ma mère au-dessus du Dalaï-Lama très exactement sur les mêmes sillons. Là-dessus le grand coup de pied que je me suis donné à moi-même demande plus d'une explication. La machine avait produit un petit craquement. Tout petit, net. L'image sonore de la fatalité: comme le passage de vie à trépas se fait avec une discrétion tragique. Crac.

(BM, 87–8)[7]

Here again, we have a subtle crossing that intermingles the "two sisters" from Germany with Montaigne in a passage triggered by a telephonic interruption. The presence of the word "recorder" in the previous citation, as well as the recording device of this scene, is what should arrest us here. "Recorder" is no longer in use in French today. It is highlighted in Cixous's text of *Benjamin à Montaigne* on page 185 ("je m'épuise à *recorder*") for the reason that is provided in the quotation from pages 87–8 above. While it is very much possible that "recorder" is a reference to the English verb (which would explain why the word is written in italics by Cixous)—"to record," and the use of a "tape recorder" in this text—in Cixous's writing "recorder" is also calling to an old French verb

---

7   "The telephone rings. / At this moment I abruptly kick the tape recorder. I had set it in the middle of the step, turned towards the kitchen, something I should not have done. I quickly stood and myself walked on the device, a little Sony. I distinctly heard the little crack of a piece of the machine as it crashed in the basement. I was surprised: why is it that I had done all that I was not supposed to do? [...] I used to record the two sisters surreptitiously using 'the tapes of the Dalaï-Lama'; I have to say it's the only thing I had found in the house: twelve 90-minutes tapes (that a Tibetan friend had given to me) on which entire days of orations of the Dalaï-Lama in English and Tibetan were etched, in truth, a series of Essays on the subjects Of vanity, That to philosophize is to learn to die, [...] evidently a rather exact ready-to-use Tibetan remake of the thinking of my Montaigne, a usage that some could reprove, but on the other hand recording Selma and Jennie on top of the Dalaï-Lama, I said to the disapproving voice [in my head], is an act that is neither lacking meaning and audacity, nor missing unconscious calculations, because it is there, the sign of a tribute that some might dispute to the dignity and wisdom of the two old ladies. On the other hand, it must be said that in the obscurity of my magical thoughts, the idea of blending Selma and the Dalaï-Lama, the idea of a mysterious tape-recording chemistry had crossed my mind. There is nothing wrong, I told myself. I put my mother above the Dalaï-Lama, precisely, in the exact same grooves. With that the great kick that I gave to myself requires more than one explanation. The device had produced a little crack. Very little. Clean. The sonorous image of fatality: like the passage from life to demise occurs with a tragic discretion. *Crac*."

for "enregistrer" that she reinstates. From the Latin "recordor," the verb "recorder" carries the double meaning of bearing witness and memorizing, which is ultimately what Cixous-Montaigne is doing when writing in the aforementioned texts: bearing witness and memorizing, bearing witness to memorize and the reverse. This essence of writing as an action of *recorder* in French has a legal etymology; Littré indicates that a synonym for "witness," "témoin," is "recors."[8] It is an act of memorization and conservation, and a relational concept; the action of "recorder" also means "conciliation" ("concertation"), "accordance," finding the right "accord" with someone, *recorder* being the act of *raccorder*, passing the cord to tie the protagonists and the antagonists.[9] In other words, it is highly codified as a technical and normative activity that involves the acts of archiving, of witnessing and of reconciling the dispersed, the opposed figures and entities. Peace building, the fight for justice and recording have more than one feature in common. After all, the cult around Osnabrück City Hall, where the peace agreement was signed and sealed, is a form of totemic *cult of the recording* and, maybe, of the recorder. The recorder being both the machine, that is, the technical operation of recording (secretary, scribe), and the subject who records (notary, writer). History is recording this moment—the peace treaty—and the location—the room, the city hall— with its witnesses and seals (see Figure 6). All these elements (treaty, room, witnesses, seal, etc.) *are* the recorder. The recorder (both human subject and machine) is what brings the group together around the *īnstrūmentum* of peace, the treaty is an *Instrumentum Pacis Osnabrugensis*, namely, a technical device that ties together (accords) the discordant entities. There is no peace without *īnstrūmentum*, without a recording device, a recorder.[10] *The recorder is a totem*. The totem is *Gare d'Osnabrück à*

---

8 Littré, *Dictionnaire*, vol. 6, 1012.
9 Recorder as an act of "raccorder" of establishing the "raccord," in French, is also a notion used in telephony ("raccorder au réseau téléphonique," "connecting to the telephone network"). To a certain extent, the friendship between Hélène Cixous and Jacques Derrida is recorded in *Voiles*, the "first" book that they wrote together—the "first" publication that explicitly associates their names: they have written more than one book "together." *Voiles* is inscribed in this history of the *recorded* texts; their texts in *Voiles*—and elsewhere—are interwoven, and they are also about this fact, about what it means to weave together, to sew, to mend, to pass the yarn, the string, the cord, from one text to another, from one body of texts to another, what it means, in French, to *raccorde* (join, put together, connect), to *raccommode* (mend). (*V*); (*VL*).
10 In Latin, *īnstrūmentum* means four things: (1) the instrument, the tool, the utensil; (2) the supply, the provision; (3) the equipment; and (4) the records, the documents.

Figure 6 The chandelier under which the Treaty of Osnabrück was sealed in the great room of Osnabrück City Hall, October 24, 2019.

Jérusalem, Osnabrück, Correspondance avec le Mur, Benjamin à Montaigne, 1938, nuits … The totem is literature.

What triggers the use of "recorder" in Cixous's text here is similar to Montaigne's *need to record*. Montaigne cultivates the act of writing in front of the discordance produced by his discovery of the ruin of ruins.[11] It is something that both Cixous and Montaigne are facing. A technical difficulty motivates the intertextuality between Montaigne and Cixous. They are both attempting to record what dramatically resists, what exhausts the possibilities of recording. There would be no recording without resistance, including a powerful resistance to recording, to the recorder. Without the discordance of an "it must not be said." Recording, Montaigne-Cixous would argue, implies a pre-accord on what is there to be recorded and on the *tékhnē* (recorder). And when facing ruins, ashes, this accord is uncertain, compromised, corrupted and inaccessible. It is repressed in its very existence. The insignificance of most ruins is a symptom of how a warped network of repressions are always at stake in our relationships to ruins—ruins of the destructions of Rom', ruins of a synagogue in Germany—that always remain difficult and

---

11 Among many interpretations, Montaigne is also the "recorder" as a "raccordeur" (and "raccommodeur") of the antagonists who are opposed in the wars of religion (this element also appears in the account of the secretary in Rome).

confrontational. Ruins are like scars that are always open in one way or another, a constant reminder of the existing wound. They defy justice and reconciliation. Ruins are, by definition, remnants of destruction, abandonment, famine, traumatic social changes, wars, genocides, pandemics, displacements, repressions and exhaustion ... all this is exhausting. This also exhausts the possibilities of recording, of writing. Guilt might be the symptom associated with the possible impossibility of the recording, a certain *acedia* that Walter Benjamin circumscribes in his "Thèses sur le concept d'histoire" when he famously describes Paul Klee's angel as it appears on his painting titled *Angelus Novus*:

> Là où nous apparaît une chaîne d'événements, [l'ange] ne voit, lui, qu'une seule et unique catastrophe, qui sans cesse amoncelle ruines sur ruines et les précipite à ses pieds. Il voudrait bien s'attarder, réveiller les morts et rassembler ce qui a été démembré. Mais du paradis souffle une tempête qui s'est prise dans ses ailes, si violemment que l'ange ne peut plus les refermer.[12]

Cixous's "je m'épuise à *recorder*" (*BM*, 185), literally, "I am *exhausting myself* recording" (my emphasis) is the fatigue of the angel. But the angel knows that this exhausting battle is also what opens the road to freedom. The guilty use of the tape recorder, which leads to the failure of the recording and ends in the tragic and sacrilegious destruction of the recorder in Cixous's text, is a reiteration of the essential non-redeemable, irreducible tragedy of ruins. It is as if the synagogue was burning again. In reality, it is an actualization of the fact that the synagogue's fire *was never extinguished*. *Recorder* (the verb, in French) the ruins, ashes of a synagogue, for example, means *recorder*, to record the impossibility to record, it means bearing witness to the impossibility of bearing witness. The tale of the recording device in Cixous's aforementioned text offers access to the impossibility of the attempt. She bears witness to this impossibility. The impossibility to record is recorded: the synagogue is (still) burning.

---

12 Walter Benjamin, "Sur le concept d'histoire," in *Œuvres*, vol. 3, trans. Maurice de Gandillac, Rainer Rochlitz and Pierre Rusch (Paris: Gallimard, 2000), 434. I chose to use the French version of this text that Benjamin composed in French during the first months of 1940. "Where a chain of events appears before us, he sees one single catastrophe, which keeps piling wreckage upon wreckage and hurls it at his feet. The angel would like to stay, awaken the dead, and make whole what has been smashed. But a storm is blowing from Paradise and has got caught in his wings; it is so strong that the angel can no longer close them." Walter Benjamin, *Selected Writings*, vol. 4, *1938–1940*, ed. Howard Eiland and Michael W. Jennings, trans. Edmund Jephcott et al. (Cambridge, MA: Harvard University Press, 2006), 392.

Which is why Cixous *has to record Ève and Éri (Jenny and Selma in the text) secretly*; which leads to the hastily and somewhat inadvertent destruction of the device: "Là-dessus le grand coup de pied que je me suis donné à moi-même demande plus d'une explication. La machine avait produit un petit craquement. Tout petit, net. L'image sonore de la fatalité: comme le passage de vie à trépas se fait avec une discrétion tragique. Crac" (*BM*, 88).[13] Which is why Montaigne secretly holds his thoughts on Rom' to himself. The thoughts that save can be destructive. At least they are, he knows, she knows, subversive. After clandestinely recording Ève and Éri, Hélène Cixous surmounts her guilt and tries to obtain the sisters' permission to record them. The two sisters, who constantly used to disagree and argue about anything and everything, often about the most trivial things, answer without even a hint of hesitation:

> Alors j'ai dit que j'aimerais les enregistrer. Cette fois les deux vieilles ont été d'accord. Elles ont refusé d'une seule voix. Non, non, et *nein*. Tout d'un coup elles se sont regardées et elles se sont entendues entendues.
>
> (*BM*, 70)[14]

"Non, non, et *nein*": no recording allowed! There is a peace accord on not recording. Archiving, witnessing and reconciling cannot be achieved. The synagogue is still burning. No recording is what Benjamin's angel faces, who might well record, but the wind blows from paradise and the angel-sisters' wings are already opened by the wind; there is no way they would close them and record, no matter the language (French, German ...). The comedic and sudden agreement of the two oldies only increases the impression that there is something somewhat obscene and indiscreet, something that presents a form of absolute (angelic) nudity that resists the act of recording. Peace, reconciliation, would never fully dissipate the obscenity of acceptance of the crime that any peace treaty implies. Which is why, in highly complex and subtle ways, Cixous's œuvre both archives (records) the impossibility of any telling of the history of the genocide and, at the same time,

---

13 "With that, the great kick that I gave to myself requires more than one explanation. The machine had produced a small crack. Very little. Clean. The sonorous image of fatality: as if the little passage from life to demise was performed through a tragic discretion. Crac."
14 "That's when I told them that I would like to record them. This time, the two old ladies agreed with each other. They refused in one single voice. No, no, and *nein*. All of a sudden, they looked at each other and heard themselves agree with each other."

might offer the ultimate archive of this destruction, of this ruin, of this ash, that was *ever* conceived. This is an archive that confronts the an-archival, the radical anarchic nature of the crime: "Non, non, et *nein.*" Which would also offer, in this sense, an immensely powerful deconstruction of the concept of peace as it was established in the previous chapter. From this deconstruction, Cixous is the secretary (Plato?). Ève and Éri are the philosophers (Socrates?).

The idea that the recording would disrobe, that it would present someone's absolute nudity, that it would steal the core of its own subject, is, after all, the act of birth of literature as it is understood today; "je t'assure que je m'y fusse très-volontiers peint tout entier & tout nud,"[15] writes Montaigne in his famous address "To the Reader" at the opening of his *Essays*.[16] "I assure you," I swear, that I can conjure the impossibility of the recording, the impossible archive, that I can defy the "Non, non, et *nein.*" Literature's original guilt is *literature itself*, its malady is the malady of (non)recording. The malady of injustice contaminates the entire scene but nonetheless allows the ghosts of justice to enter, to sneak in, in a split second. In a tension that drives the writing of the *Essays*, the attempt to "disrobe" *in writing* (recording) would always be loaded by a "Non, non, et *nein*" so that the naked self-portrait would always be differed, denied, disjointed and marked by denials such as "It must not be said" and "Il ne faut pas le dire." What must not be said is what literature says. It is literature's outcry, its cry. It records the non-recordable. Again, this structure molds Cixous's writing on/with Germany. It is a ruined archive at work, an archive of the impossible archiving.

Again, this foundational moment of literature has roots in Montaigne. "Recorder," "recordation," is a locution that Montaigne uses in "De l'exercitation,"[17] an essay very close to the one mentioned by Hélène Cixous in this excerpt, titled "Que philosopher c'est apprendre à mourir."[18] While "Que philosopher c'est apprendre à mourir," written at the end of the winter of 1572, revolves around how "study and contemplation draw our souls [...] which forms a kind of apprenticeship of [death]" or how "wisdom and argument [...] teach us not to be

---

15 Montaigne, "Au lecteur," in *Essais* [1604], [4]. "Je t'assure que je me serais peint tout entier dans mon livre et tout nu." Montaigne, *Les Essais* [2009], 9.
16 Montaigne, "To the Reader," in *The Complete Essays*, lxiii.
17 Montaigne, "Sur l'exercice," in *Les Essais* [2009], 2, 6, 461. Montaigne, "De l'exercitation," in *Essais* [1604], l. 2, ch. 6, 320.
18 Montaigne, "Que philosopher c'est apprendre à mourir," in *Les Essais* [2009], l. 1, ch. 20, 100. Montaigne, "Que philosopher c'est apprendre à mourir," in *Essais* [1604], l. 1, ch. 19, 47. Montaigne, "To philosophize is to learn how to die," in *The Complete Essays*, l. 1, ch. 20, 89.

afraid of dying,"[19] "De l'exercitation" makes an account of what Montaigne fantasizes as a possible death through the death-like moment of the syncope he experienced when he had a horse accident near his residence in Guyenne sometime between 1567 and 1570. The moment of "recordation" in this essay paradoxically incarnates the moment of the non-recordable, non-"conciliable" death: "Cette *recordation* que j'en ay fort empreinte en mon ame, me representat son visage & son idée si pres du naturel, me concilie aucunement à elle [la mort],"[20] writes Montaigne ("The memory of this, being deeply planted in my soul, paints for me the face of Death and her portrait so close to nature that it somewhat reconciles me to her").[21] The event takes place in the

---

19 "[L]'étude et la contemplation retirent quelque peu notre âme hors de nous et l'occupent à part du corps, ce qui est une sorte d'apprentissage et de ressemblance de la mort"; "c'est que toute la sagesse et tous les raisonnements du monde ont ce point d'aboutissement: nous apprendre à ne point craindre de mourir." Montaigne, "Que philosopher," in *Les Essais* [2009], l. 1, ch. 20, 100. "[L]'estude & la contemplation retirent aucunemet nostre ame hors de nous, & l'enbesongnent à part du corps, qui est quelque apprentissage & ressemblance de la mort"; "la sagesse & discours du monde se resolut enfin à ce poinct, de nous apprendre à ne craindre point à mourir." Montaigne, "Que philosopher," in *Essais* [1604], l. 1, ch. 19, 47. "[S]tudy and contemplation draw our souls somewhat outside ourselves, keeping them occupied away from the body, a state which both resembles death and which forms a kind of apprenticeship of it"; "it is because all the wisdom and argument in the world eventually come down to one conclusion; which is to teach us not to be afraid of dying." Montaigne, "To philosophize is to learn how to die," in *Essays*, 89.
20 Montaigne "Sur l'exercice," in *Les Essais* [2009], l. 2, ch. 6, 461. Montaigne, "De l'exercitation," in *Essais* [1604], l. 2, ch. 6, 320.
21 "Le *souvenir* que j'avais de cela, si fortement gravé dans mon âme, me représentant le visage et l'image de la mort si proches du naturel, m'accorde en quelque manière [i.e., *dans une certaine mesure*] avec elle," writes Michel de Montaigne. Montaigne, "Sur l'exercice," in *Les Essais* [2009], l. 2, ch. 6, 461, my emphasis. "Cette *recordation* que j'en ay fort empreinte en mon ame, me representat son visage & son idée si pres du naturel, me concilie aucunement à elle." Montaigne, "De l'exercitation," in *Essais* [1604], l. 2, ch. 6, 320, my emphasis. Montaigne uses "aucunement" as an equivalent for "en quelque manière" (A. Lanly), "to a certain extent," "en quelque façon," writes Littré, *Dictionnaire*, vol. 1, 710. "The memory of this, being deeply planted in my soul, paints for me the face of Death and her portrait so close to nature that it somewhat [*to a certain extent*] reconciles me to her." Montaigne, "On practice," in *The Complete Essays* [2003], bk. 2, ch. 6, 419. The word "planted," in the English translation, misses a critical part inscribed in the notion of "recordation" (Montaigne's word); the notion of "recordation" is rendered in the French adaptation as "souvenir." Montaigne implicitly plays with "concilier" and "recor*d*ation," the two terms playing with the notion of "cord" in "recordation" and the fact that passing the cord between antagonist parts ("me," Montaigne and "Death") is a "conciliation" and "accord," a peace agreement, in line with the argument developed earlier.

"moyau,"[22] the heart, the midst ("the very hub," writes the translator[23]) of the "Civil Wars" of religion, as he recalls at the beginning. This mention of the wars is nothing but crucial as if the possibility of an attempt on his life had crossed Montaigne's mind. The idea of not having the "record," what he calls the "recordation," the impression of a printed memory of the instant when he lost consciousness, is what triggers the use of the word and the act of *recordation*. Of recording-writing this essay.[24]

It could very much be that the use of the old French verb *recorder* by Cixous in the aforementioned text from *Benjamin à Montaigne* is a way to refer to this network of texts on death by Montaigne. This passage of *Benjamin à Montaigne* explicitly names "Que philosopher c'est apprendre à mourir" in a scene of destruction of her tape recorder. The destruction of the recorder is explicitly tied to what Cixous calls "the passage from life to demise" ("le passage de vie à trépas" [*BM*, 88]). After all, what Montaigne describes as "death" is the *destruction of the ability to record* as a critical experience, the experience of the destruction of experience known as "death." And "De l'exercitation" revolves more around the essential inability to record, to record the ruin of death—death being simultaneously the moment when the recorder is destroyed and what the whole experience of writing is about. As if writing reached its ultimate goal when the recorder broke for Montaigne-Cixous. The colossal, radical erasure of memory that death implies is Montaigne's subject, it is the essential texture of his writing when, at the beginning of the essay on "De l'exercitation," he recalls the story recounted by Seneca about the Roman man Canius Julius. While he is facing the moment of his own death by execution on Caligula's orders, Canius Julius informs his friends that he is going to attempt to record the moment of his death to be able to tell them what happens in that instant if he happens to come back from it. This parable shows that Montaigne himself is exploring a concept of ruin, not as a surviving trace, but as *a massive, radical, erasure of memory*. The "assassination of the Synagogue" ("l'assassinat de la

---

22 "[E]tant allé un jour me promener à une lieue de chez moi qui suis installé au milieu de tout le désordre des guerres civiles de notre France." Montaigne, "Sur l'exercice," in *Les Essais* [2009], l. 2, ch. 6, 460. "[M]'etat allé un jour promener à une lieuë de chez moy qui suis assis dans le moyau de tout le trouble des guerres civiles de France." Montaigne, "De l'exercitation," in *Essais* [1604], l. 2, ch. 6, 319. "I went riding one day about one league away from my home, which is situated at the very hub of the disturbances in our French Civil Wars." Montaigne, "On practice," in *The Complete Essays*, bk. 2, ch. 6, 418.
23 Montaigne, "On practice," in *The Complete Essays*, bk. 2, ch. 6, 418.
24 Montaigne, "Sur l'exercice," in *Les Essais* [2009], l. II, ch. 6, 457. Montaigne, "De l'exercitation," in *Essais* [1604], l. 2, ch. 6, 316 sq. Montaigne, "On practice," in *The Complete Essays*, bk. 2, ch. 6, 416.

Synagogue" [*N*, 56]) is of a similar nature, something that takes place in Os, na, brück. The deconstruction of presence as the core of any writing process is another word for this erasure. This structure is not present by accident in Cixous's texts of Germany at the boundaries of documenting and fictionalizing, of testimony and fiction. Of course, death will occur, and, of course, no one comes back from it to recount it. But still, this fiction of coming back, of talking from the side of death (the side where "Andreas Jenny Paula Moritz Hete Zalo Zophi Michael Benjamin" [*OS*, 129] and Canius Julius are to be found) is what any mortal bears witness of while contemplating his/her own death. It transforms into writing for Montaigne and Cixous when this structure is tied to persecutions, torture and cruelty. To injustice. Montaigne: Canius Julius is a political prisoner awaiting his execution by "ce marault de Caligula," by that "blackguard Caligula," "ce fripon de Caligula."[25] Cixous: the Nazi persecution.

Such an accident—the destruction of the "recorder"—is a catastrophe. The destruction of the recorder wards off *and* replays the primitive scene of the persecution. The catastrophe is not meant to happen, and it happens—it happens precisely as a "catastrophe" because *nothing predicts* that it should take place, even when the mortal is condemned to death, structurally. It is precisely this notion of accident, of catastrophe, that organizes a discourse around the possibility and impossibility of memorizing the erasure, the fact that when facing this destruction by persecution, we are *absolutely* naked, *radically* vulnerable, skinless, in all kinds of ways and languages: "Non, non et *nein.*" *Non, non et* nein says the ruin, the ashes, the burned synagogue. *Non, non et* nein is what Hélène Cixous faces when she attempts to ask the family archives, especially photographs, why they do not record (witness, memorize, reconcile), why they do not carry *any* recollection, *any* trace, *any* sign and figurations of the destruction of her German family: "il n'y a pas d'album des ruines et des supplices" (*GO*, 58).[26]

---

25 Montaigne, "Sur l'exercice," in *Les Essais* [2009], l. 2, ch. 6, 458. Montaigne, "De l'exercitation," in *Essais* [1604], l. 2, ch. 6, 317. "[T]hat *monster* Caligula," writes Lucretius, as the translator recalls. Montaigne, "On practice," in *The Complete Essays*, bk. 2, ch. 6, 417.
26 "[T]here is no album of the ruins and the tortures" (*OSJ*, 42).

Six *Remembrer*-remember: A detour to Montaigne's Tower ... and its ruins (image)

> *Moi aussi je passais par Krahnstrasse, des planètes ont été abattues des gouffres se sont ouverts, des bandes de démons se sont installés dans les quartiers d'Osnabrück mais j'en ai marre de répéter mon histoire et vous qui vivez après mon épopée, vous mâchez du chewing-gum et ne m'écoutez pas, ça va durer longtemps cette mélopée? pensez-vous, non, non, si si, je vous entends, alors je m'arrête et je résume mon Iliade en onze mots, et, philosophe, je n'ai que deux mots à vous dire:* Remember me.
>
> (GO, 100)[1]

"[L'ange] ne voit, lui, qu'une seule et unique catastrophe, qui sans cesse amoncelle ruines sur ruines [...]. Il voudrait bien s'attarder, réveiller les morts et rassembler ce qui a été *démembré*,"[2] writes Benjamin (my emphasis).

"Démembré," Benjamin writes in this text that he wrote in French in 1940. Dismembered. He had the ruins of Europe in sight. The ruins of Germany. Of German synagogues.

"Ruines sur ruines," ruins on ruins. Os, na, brück, writes Cixous. The commas mark the existence of the ruins, of the ashes, a syncope that ties the members together through their separated presence. They are tied to their separation. Os, na, brück. The dislocated name echoes Montaigne's unmentionable Rom'.

---

1 "I too used to pass by Krahnstrasse, planets were struck down gulfs opened up, gangs of demons settled into the neighborhoods of Osnabrück but I am tired of repeating my story and you who are living after my epic, you chew gum and don't listen to me, is this going to last a long time this threnody? You think, no, no, yes, I hear you, so I stop and I sum up my Iliad in eleven words, and, philosopher, I have but two words to say to you: *Remember me*" (OSJ, 76–7).
2 Walter Benjamin, "Sur le concept d'histoire," 434.

Ruins, lacerations, disfigurement, defacement. Dismemberment. This is what Montaigne-Cixous *sees* in Rom' in Os, na, brück. This is what Benjamin's angel would like to reassemble, remember and revive. The angel wants to revive the dead, the dead of injustice. This is what they see. What does it mean to see? What does it mean to have the dismembered, the ruined in sight? How can one see "what was dismembered," "ce qui a été démembré"?

The underlying theme-question of this reflection on what is there to be seen, on what can remain unseen in a given situation, the complexity of what remains unseen at the core of what is there to be seen in front of our eyes, is at the core of Cixous's œuvre, and more specifically, Cixous's œuvre of Germany. One simple way to approach this would be to reflect on why Ève Cixous escaped, on why and how she was able to flee Germany and escape the persecutions. Without this "évasion" of Ève from Germany, it could be that Hélène Cixous would not exist. This notion will be at the center of our reading of *1938, nuits* in Part III. This is not merely a historic question but a metaphysical one; for the Jews of Germany, of Austria, especially (and other countries of persecution such as France, Italy …), the question of *seeing-not seeing* what was always there—the genocidal dynamics of anti-Semitism—is a matter of life and death after 1933. Here is Ève's voice in *1938, nuits*: "Je connais quelqu'un qui est parti quand on a interdit le tennis" (*N*, 98).[3] The first aspect at stake is not "When is it time to leave?" or even "Is it necessary to leave?" It is rather: "What do I, what do we *see* that should raise the question of leaving or not?"

Around 2008, Cixous recalled something she saw. She wrote it. It became *Ève s'évade. La Ruine et la Vie*. The title, which explicitly refers to her mother Ève, links Ève to the motif of the escape (évasion, Ève-vasion …)—Ève, who found the escape on many occasions in her lifetime, including when she escaped from Germany as soon as she saw Nazism arise. Ève, who knew all too well the meaning of the ruin. The title also refers to what happens to Cixous one day when she leaves her mother at home in Arcachon to make her annual visit to Montaigne/Montaigne's Tower. This is Montaigne's *librerie*, as he called it, in Saint-Michel-de-Montaigne in the French region of Dordogne, the "Guyenne" in Montaigne's *Essays*. The *librerie* is located approximately 60 kilometers (37 miles) east of Bordeaux. Montaigne wrote his *Essays* in the Tower, and when Cixous arrived in this region of Bordeaux, she found in Montaigne (both the location and the writer) a gate that allowed her to enter into "a France that [she] could love."[4] After

---

3 "I know someone who left when tennis was banned."
4 *Ever*, 01:48:40.

having left (or escaped) Algeria, where the rebellion against the French colonial oppression had started, and considering that she had been at odds with France—to say the least!—throughout her life, Montaigne's Tower seemed to provide a psychic lodging and refuge in Cixous that she always secretly inhabited. This "country" of hers in which she finds Montaigne, was, of course, literature. The Tower is, in many senses of the word, an entry point to literature. It is another form of the totem.

The concepts of image (figuration) and vision (sight) are subtly interwoven in Cixous's relationship to the process of "remembering" throughout her œuvre of Germany. Image, vision and remembrance are impossible to conceive in this œuvre without a profound conversation, without a companionship with "Montaigne," without an art of *embodying* Montaigne, or of being embodied by Montaigne. Like the camera is innervated by the photographer's self and body, it seems that Montaigne, both the writer and the Tower, his flesh, his body, his *corpus*, innervates Cixous's own "German" *corpus*.

Let's turn to the core of this body of work, of this body at work.[5]

---

5 The pages that follow will revolve around a "Vision" that appears to Cixous after seeing an "Image" consisting of a painting (re)discovered by Cixous in Montaigne's Tower. My overall approach to this painting expands on the seminal work of Christa Stevens, who forged the fruitful notion of "écriture-peinture" ("writing-painting") in Cixous's *Portrait du Soleil* and beyond. While offering a "reading" on the ways Cixous's writing is marked by, and "reads," works of art—especially Rembrandt—Stevens opened the avenue for a reflection on what it means to write for Cixous, as an art of painting beyond the traditional notion of art understood as a "système de représentation" ("system of representation"). I am especially convinced by Stevens's argument that Cixous's writing on paintings essentially exceeds what the concept of *ekphrasis* typically allows; in Cixous's work, it is impossible to distinguish the work of art at work in her writing from what makes the substance, the texture and the subject of her texts. Christa Stevens, *L'écriture solaire d'Hélène Cixous, Travail du texte et histoire du sujet dans Portrait du Soleil* (Amsterdam: Rodopi, 1999), 220–72. Cixous's way of writing while working with the arts is also explored through the motif of "entente" (commonly translated into "understanding," "entente" has an idiomatic connotation, that of listening and/or being listened to) between the visual arts and writing in Stéphanie Boulard and Catherine Witt, *Ententes—À partir d'Hélène Cixous* (Paris: Presses Sorbonne Nouvelle, 2019). Two other sources nourish my reading of Montaigne's and Cixous's relationship to the act of "painting" and to pictorial works: one is Georges Didi-Huberman's work in general, but more specifically his chapter titled "L'image comme déchirure et la mort du Dieu incarné," in *Devant l'image* (Paris: éditions de Minuit, 1990), 169–269; the second is Louis Marin, specifically his collection of essays titled *L'écriture de soi*, and especially the texts titled "C'est moi que je peins …," "De la figurabilité du moi chez Montaigne," and "Transparence et opacité de la peinture du moi." Louis Marin, *L'écriture de soi* (Paris: Presses Universitaires de France, 1999), 113–25 and 127–36.

The vision: Montaigne's Tower

Cixous's first visit to the Tower might date from 1956, before she had published anything. It is nothing but one of Cixous's origins as a writer—an origin that, again, has always existed, as soon as she was born.[6] The Tower, we will see, is, quite literally, one of Cixous's (re)birthplaces. Cixous pays her visit to Montaigne every summer at a time of the year when she also writes most of her longer poetic texts. Here again, she answers a call:

> Le jour venu pour naître je retourne à la Tour. C'est la Loi. Je dois retourner à mon point de départ. On ne saurait le contester: je dois retourner à mon for intérieur, c'est ma force et c'est plus fort que moi, rien, sauf la mort ne pourrait m'en empêcher. Le jour venu je me rends naître à la Tour. Je me rends. On obéit à la loi aveuglément. Ni défaite ni victoire ni savoir, on rampe au nid natal. C'est parce que je me rends je rampe. C'est au fait que je me vois ramper et franchir avec peines et angoisses des distances déchirantes que je reconnais l'Autorité absolue: je suis appelée, et c'est la Vie même qui est au téléphone. La Vie sans Visage, l'Appel sans Appel. La Force à laquelle on ne dit même pas oui. Il n'est pas de non qui remue devant elle. Elle souffle.
>
> (*EEV*, 26)[7]

"L'Appel sans Appel," a "Call without Call," which Cixous also calls a "Vie sans Visage," a "Faceless Life," answers a "she" calling, meaning "*La* Tour," she-the-Tower is calling, this is the absolute telephone line[8]

---

6   "J'écris depuis que je suis" ("I have been writing since I was"), writes Hélène Cixous in *Mdeilmm, Parole de taupe* (Paris: Gallimard, 2022), 58–9.
7   "When the day to be born comes I return to the Tower. That is the Law. I have to return to my point of departure. One cannot argue with it: I must return to my heart of hearts, that is my strength and it's stronger than I am, nothing except death could keep me from it. I go, I surrender myself. One obeys the law blindly. Neither defeat nor victory nor knowledge, one crawls to the natal nest. It is because I surrender that I crawl. It is by the fact that I see myself crawling and crossing with pain and anguish excruciating distances that I recognize the absolute Authority: I am called, and it is Life itself that is on the telephone. Life without Face, Call without Call. The Force to which one does not even say yes. There is no no that stirs in front of it. It breathes" (*EES*, 14).
8   The space does not allow for a development that would probably take us too far. However, it is worth noting that Cixous's notion of "for," of "for intérieur" in this passage, is precisely what the notion of "absolute telephone" could mean. *For intérieur* means the interior law of someone, their consciousness, the authority, the power, but also the space for deliberation within someone's mind. "For" notably comes from the antique notion of "forum." The forum is a place

that, quite explicitly, binds Hélène Cixous to her mother Ève, for Cixous writes about "la Tour [...] ma mère littéraire":

> [S]'il y a un lieu auquel je suis liée comme on est lié à l'amour même, c'est-à-dire pour moi à la littérature comme vie, comme je suis liée à ma mère, la tour étant ma mère littéraire, c'est Montaigne. Je ne pouvais pas m'ôter la littérature du cœur.
> (*RV*, 172)[9]

"The Tower being my literary mother," Montaigne-Mother-Tower-Literature also calls in *Revirements* in 2011. Three years earlier, in *Ève s'évade*. *La Ruine et la Vie*, Cixous writes that "la nostalgie que j'ai de la Tour dès que je m'y retrouve tourne en nostalgie de ma mère" (*EEV*, 31–2).[10] In light of Cixous's relationship to a certain Montaigne in "Rom'"

---

of deliberation, exchanges and power. It is not an accident that, when the Tower "calls" Cixous, in this passage, she refers to the Tower's law (loi), to the Tower's "force" (power, strength), to the "Absolute authority" tied to the Tower. The Tower, in other words, like the *for*, is a super-ego, a consciousness, it is the authoritative dimension of the consciousness that is calling. There is no responsibility, no capacity to answer, without engaging the "for." One should note that the semantic chain of this passage phonetically links the "for" to "Force" (with a capital "F"), to "fort" (strength, power). "[J]e dois retourner à mon for intérieur, c'est ma force et c'est plus fort que moi, rien, sauf la mort ne pourrait m'en empêcher" (*EEV*, 26) (I must return to my heart of hearts, that is my strength and it's stronger than I am, nothing except death could keep me from it [*EES*, 14]). One decisive tension Cixous highlights here is that there is, in the "for," a notion of force, of enforcement, a law that requires a response, an answer, which means, at least, a form of deliberation, of interactive thinking on the need to answer and how to respond. A complexity is tied to this "force" of the call, Cixous writes, as it does not leave *any space* for such a deliberation on the forum of the *for*: "La Force à laquelle on ne dit même pas oui. Il n'est pas de non qui remue devant elle. Elle souffle" (*EEV*, 26) ("The Force to which one does not even say yes. There is no no that stirs in front of it. It breathes" [*EES*, 14]). In this absolutism of the "for" there is no decipherable distinction between the call and the answer. At the same time, if the Tower is an absolute "for intérieur," it is because the Tower is the embodiment of the *forum* of Montaigne's self: his temple of deliberation, the infinite deliberation of the essay. It is impossible to distinguish the "for" of the Tower from the *Essays*. The fact that this powerful structure engages a figure of the *mother* is an abyssal theme of Cixous's entire œuvre.

9 "[I]f there is a place to which I am attached as one is attached to love itself, I mean, for me literature as life, the way I am attached to my mother, the tower being my literary mother, that place is Montaigne. I couldn't excise literature from my heart" (*TT*, 124).

10 "[T]he nostalgia I have for the Tower as soon as I am there turns into a nostalgia for my mother" (*EES*, 21).

being a relationship to "Os, na, brück," returning to the Tower, to her mother-Tower, to her mother-Osnabrück, to her mother, to literature, all this also leads to the particular attention to ruins that she inscribed in her relationship to Osnabrück: "car c'est ici, ici, le cœur même de sa bibliothèque, ils ne nous ont laissé qu'un débris ruiné" (*EEV*, 39).[11]

We have a network of themes circulating from Ève, to Montaigne (the Tower), to the cities of Rome and Osnabrück. This circulation always goes back to the Tower through literature, through Montaigne the writer. The heart of Montaigne's *librerie* is a debris in decay, a debris in ruin. Montaigne-mother, mother-Montaigne, literature, these are all tied to what remains, "un debris ruiné," "debris in decay." It is intriguing that the more she writes about her Germany, and about her mother especially, the more Montaigne becomes an explicit, insistent, recurring theme. There are many references to Montaigne and to the trip to Montaigne (the Tower) in Cixous's books after 2001. The year 2001 is not just any date in the history of towers. The year 2001 is when *Benjamin à Montaigne* was published (in June):

> Ce n'est pas que j'aime retourner au Château de Montaigne, c'est que j'en ai vitalement besoin. Je ne suis jamais *allée* chez Montaigne, dès la première fois, il y a des dizaines d'années, j'y suis retournée. On n'y arrive pas. On s'y trouve depuis toujours ou jamais. Dès qu'on entre dans la tour on reconnaît Montaigne, sa respiration, sa taille, sa pierre. Au monde il n'y a qu'une tour. C'est avec sa tour que Montaigne a fait le tour de l'Italie. L'Italie était sa tour. Il la notait pas à pas, pierre à pierre, mille à mille, il la citait et la gravait sur le vif. Il l'a vue en double, quand il était dans la tour il était en Italie, quand en Italie, dans la tour. Quand je suis dans la tour, je me retrouve. Chaque fois. Comme l'odeur du Poivron Grillé toute-puissante ainsi l'odeur psychique physique de la chair de Montaigne de ses proportions, de sa voix, du torrent de ses pensées, inextinguible. J'ouvre les *Essais*, la porte, son chien de joie aboie, le grand chat noir sur pattes blanches s'appelle maintenant Balzac, la Tour est construite comme un Essai et vice versa, Montaigne reçoit, la Tour, le Livre, tout nous dit ouvrez. De la Tour se voit le monde entier. La Tour voit le Monde.
>
> (*BM*, 186)[12]

---

11   "[F]or it is here, here, the very heart of his library, they have left us but the ruined debris" (*EES*, 26).

12   "It is not that I like to return to the Château of Montaigne, it is that I vitally need it. I never *went to* Montaigne; as soon as I went for the first time, dozens of years ago, I was returning. One does not arrive there. One finds oneself ever since or never. As soon as one enters the tower one recognizes Montaigne, his breath,

While Cixous knows the Tower like she knows Montaigne and points out that the Tower and the *Essays* are inseparable in more ways than one, the Tower is Montaigne's stone(s) and a part of the *Essays*, the *Essays* are the Tower under the form of the return. The Tower is also Montaigne's body. Cixous is habituated to come back to Montaigne *for the first time* each time; she returns "for the first time," she rediscovers anew him-her (*lui* Montaigne, him, *la* Tower, her) every year. She writes that the entire world is in sight from the Tower, that the Tower *sees* the world. The Tower is a machine of vision. The Tower is an optical apparatus and a recorder that has the form of a cylinder. The Tower is an *īnstrūmentum*. The Tower sees and turns, it is rolling like a camera. Twists, spins and turns occur in the Tower as soon as we climb the spiral of its stairs. This renewed *return to the Tower* could very much have become a pilgrimage for Cixous, a routine over several decades of returns. But, again, one day, something happens that renews the nature of the return to the Tower as an eternal return of the Other. The return to the Tower is an event, forever and always. On that day ... within this intimacy and repetitive structure of what turns around the Tower and makes the Tower turn on itself, *Ève s'évade* bears witness of the sudden, *considerable shock* that she calls a "Vision" as reported in this passage:

> C'est alors que je vois apparaître devant moi, au-dessus des touffes de cœurs-de-marie, la Vision que je reconnais comme à moi destinée depuis toujours, et qui pendant quarante ans m'était restée inaperçue, toute proche, et maintenue invisible pendant toute la durée de mon aveuglement. Et par les lois étranges de l'optique de l'âme, c'est une fois sortie de la Tour, séparée de l'image par l'épaisseur des murs auxquels je m'appuie, que soudain je la vois après coup et pour la première fois. Je me vois appuyée à la Tour comme au corps le plus maternel du monde, saisie par cette double révélation, celle de l'Image, dans laquelle

---

his size, his stone. In the world, there is only one tower. It is with his tower that Montaigne made the tour around Italy. Italy was his tower. He noted the tower step by step, stone by stone, mile after mile, he quoted and etched the tower on the spot. He saw it in double, when he was in the tower he was in Italy, while in Italy, [he was] in the tower. When I am in the tower, I meet myself again. Every time. Like the all-powerful smell of Grilled Bell Pepper, so the psychic and physical smell of Montaigne's flesh, his proportions, his voice, the torrent of his inextinguishable thoughts. I open the *Essays*, the door: his dog barks with joy, the big white-legged black cat's name is now Balzac, the Tower is built like an Essay and vice versa, Montaigne hosts, the Tower, the Book, everything says 'open.' From the Tower, the entire world is to be seen. The Tower sees the World."

je reconnais le portrait de mon destin, et celle de cette longue nuit inerte qui m'a gardée pendant quarante ans dans sa caverne. Je vois que je n'ai pas encore décrit cette image.

(*EEV*, 34–5)[13]

Something monumental happens here. Both an event and a repetition. Before even addressing the content of the "image," the complex structure of the Vision participates in the profound meaning of *what is to be seen* in the image itself. It has at least five characteristics (and certainly more):

1. A "first time" within what has already taken place within the return. An event that matches something that has always been in Cixous: her essence. She has been lodged in this structure without knowing or recognizing. She now seems to recognize something that she perceives as an event. This informs the notion of "Vision," as it is written, in French by Cixous, with a capital "V."
2. Vision is also "l'Image" with a capital "I." Although it arrives within the structure of an event, *the Vision is an Image that she recognizes*. Although she had been blind to this Image for forty years, although it has been here for centuries, it is brand new.
3. This novelty has another remarkable quality in that *such an Image was not an Image until the Vision occurred*. It is the Vision that creates its Image. The Vision carries out an Image that was kept "invisible": "la Vision que je reconnais comme à moi destinée depuis toujours, et qui pendant quarante ans m'était restée inaperçue, toute proche, et maintenue invisible pendant toute la durée de mon aveuglement" (*EEV*, 34).[14] Always destined for her, it was here all along, for all those years, and on this day she recognizes an Image carried out

---

13 "That is when I see appear before me, above some tufts of bleeding hearts, the Vision that I recognize as destined for me since forever, and that for forty years had remained unnoticed very close, and kept invisible, for the whole duration of my blindness. And by the strange laws of the soul's optics, it is once I exit the Tower, separated from the image by the thickness of the walls against which I am leaning, that suddenly I see it after the fact and for the first time. Which means that perhaps up close, without anything separating us, I would not have withstood receiving its truth without the mantle in which already I cloak it. I see myself leaning against the Tower as against the most maternal body in the world, gripped by this double revelation, that of the Image, in which I recognize the portrait of my destiny, and that of this long inert night that for forty years has kept me in its cave. I that I have not yet described this image" (*EES*, 23).
14 "The Vision that I recognize as destined for me since forever, and that for forty years had remained unnoticed very close, and kept invisible, for the whole duration of my blindness" (*EES*, 23).

to her through a "Vision," meaning that it was always meant to be seen. It was there, but it remained unseen, blinded, veiled, precisely where everything in Cixous predisposed her to recognize herself in this "Image."

4. The Image-Vision is a reflection. She recognizes that she is also herself an Image of/in this Image. That *this Image is an image of the self*. Which self? She is an image in this Image-mirror, which is key to any "reflection" as she practices it in her texts.

5. This Image is both her own self and the *alter ego*: Montaigne, La Boétie, her mother ...

Everything in this complex structure is of the highest importance. It is only when she exits the Tower while holding on to the walls of the "cave," when she is *separated and freed*, that the Image-reflection becomes such. *She figures*. She remembers for the first time what she has never thought while having been a member, a part of the scene that she uncannily re-members. She seems to have seen without seeing. She is like Plato's prisoner (she references the "cave," Plato's "caverne") who sees the shades while not recognizing them as shades, she begins to see what she has not seen for forty years. When she exits the Tower she begins to see what was in front of her eyes, what is revealed to her by the mysterious "optique de l'âme," the "optic of the soul." This ultimately means that she sees with the shock of "the first time" ("pour la première fois") what was always there to be seen but that she had not seen until around 2008 to 2009,[15] although she had compulsively returned to the Tower. This Vision appears to her for the first time but within the uncanny structure of the eternal return of the same/of the

---

15 It is intriguing that Cixous has been to Montaigne before 1968–1969, which could be the date of her "first" visit to Montaigne according to this text. There are only hypotheses on this subject matter, since Cixous arrived in the Bordeaux region as early as 1956 when she studied at the university of Bordeaux and later began her career as a teacher in Arcachon in 1958–1959. The year 1968, needless to say, is a crucial date in Cixous's life. At the time she was a professor at Nanterre University where she had been nominated in 1967 and saw the rise of the student movement of 1968. The year 1967 is a central date for Cixous the writer, as it is the date when she published her first volume of short stories, *Le Prénom de Dieu*, at the Grasset publishing house. First book. Whether it is factual or fictious-poetic, I would be tempted to interpret the "forty years" benchmark inscribed in *Ève s'évade* (1968–2008) as a poetic reference to this moment, around 1967 to 1968 when Cixous was born as a published poet and a writer, her date of entry in the Tower of Literature. Of course, Cixous's role in the movement of 1968 is central. In a certain way, the structure shown in her passage of the discovery of the Image in the Tower, here, is the one that also applies to the historical sequence 1956–1968–2008: she might have been in the Tower in the 1950s, but she truly entered the Tower when she became a published poet.

other. As if she had been imprisoned in this image that she only began to "see" when she freed herself from its shade, from the cave in which it was given to her. As if the image had been a screen blocking her from being able to see it, although the Image was always here. This screen is both the bars of the prison and the door to free herself *from* the prison.

What is the screen, which she also calls a "wall," that prevented her from seeing, that separated her? That separated her from herself? That revealed to her the prison in which she was kept without seeing? What is this quasi-cinematic structure in which the power of illusions is intermingled with the contemplative form that both trumps and enlightens her? That is awakening her while it is also entrenched in a loss of consciousness that blocks her ability to see the Image, the Image that occupies the entire field of view and her psychic stream? An image that blindfolds her and opens her field of view? This highly cinematic structure in which the screen blocks what it allows to see is structured like Plato's cave.[16] The subconscious of a Vision, of any vision, is always structured like Plato's cave. It offers a complex mix of imprisonment, illusion and reflection at the core of what it means to "see" when seeing is profoundly tied to the possibility of emancipation in its revelation of the contours of oppression.[17] It leads to a liberation process in which the Image, the reflection, will be revealed as such. What liberates the prisoner, like in Plato's cave, is that his/her vague, confusing, troubled memory is revealed by a strange *malaise*, an uncanny feeling, a dizzy and risky endeavor that leads to freedom but comes with a profound threat whose name can be light, a fragile and uncertain knowledge, but still, the memory of a native land that is not comparable to a legal birthplace. The Vision is a birth.

A few pages later, the scene is reiterated in what begins to appear as an eternal return of the Vision—as already mentioned, the Vision is, in

---

16 In his *Montaigne*, one of the very last texts he wrote while in exile in Brazil before taking his own life in February 1942, Stefan Zweig uses a (pre-)photographic metaphor to present Montaigne's retreat in the Tower, "Er will die Welt nicht mehr sehen, er will nur wie in einer camera obscura [Lochkamera] in seiner Studierstube sich spiegeln lassen." Stefan Zweig, *Montaigne* (Frankfurt: Fisher Verlag, 2012), 68 ("Il ne veut plus voir le monde, il veut juste observer son propre reflet dans sa pièce d'étude comme dans une *camera obscura*." Stefan Zweig, *Montaigne* [Paris: Librairie Générale Française-Le livre de poche, 2019], 110; "He no longer wishes to see the world; he only wants to reflect on his own self in his study room, as if in a camera obscura." Stefan Zweig, *Montaigne*, trans. Will Stone [London: Pushkin Press, 2015], 118).

17 As indicated earlier, this will be at the center of our reading of Cixous's *1938, nuits*. More specifically when Cixous interrogates, in this book, the complex reasons why Omi stayed in Germany (Osnabrück in the book) in spite of what she "saw" in Germany until November 1938's Kristallnacht while "seeing" what she saw ... Or not.

essence, a *return*, but it is the return of a non-present present; it is a reminiscence, a *remembrance*, it is the memory of something that might never have had the texture of the present, of a presence. A phantom. There is no Vision without this strange form of re-membrance: a sort of déjà-vu in which no Vision occurs without a remembrance of the unseen, without specters, without the memory of something that has never been or the first eruption of something that has always been. This scene of the "first time" when she saw it is always entangled in this déjà-vu that Montaigne himself experiences in his writing. This dimension is critical for any understanding of what it means to read, and especially to read Montaigne for Cixous: she reads Montaigne in herself. What is at stake here is nothing less than the essence of reading-writing. Hélène Cixous is *in*, she *is* Montaigne's heart. Montaigne appears in Cixous's œuvre within the complex structure of the Vision as a dialogue in Montaigne's heart, with Montaigne himself as if she had been pregnant with him or the reverse, as if she had been lodged in his-her chest. Montaigne contains Cixous, and vice versa:

> Qui? À qui seul parlait Montaigne seul, dans son cœur? De liberté et de mort? Quelles paroles, quelles pensées, misères et commisérations, quelles luttes de lumières et de ténèbres? Auprès d'un jardin ou peut-être au sein, la visière d'un caveau. Il vit avec cette scène creusée dans sa poitrine, il porte une cruauté au côté de la route parfumée de livres et du ciel labouré des sentences qui lui apprennent inlassablement à vivre inlassablement, ça souffre côte à côte, la liberté qu'est-ce, le corps ou la prison?
>
> (*EEV*, 39)[18]

Is it possible to have a reminiscence of something one sees for the first time? Or to see for the first time something that has always been here? The "scene" that Cixous sees in her Vision of the Tower has always been in Montaigne's chest, "Il vit avec cette scène creusée dans sa poitrine" (*EEV*, 39).[19] The scene, the Image digs a gap, a hole in Montaigne's chest. In other words, if the viewer has already dealt with the Image in one way or another, it is less with its "presence" than with the "caveau" that

---

18 "Who? To whom alone did Montaigne speak alone, in his heart? Of freedom and death? Which words, which thoughts, miseries and commiserations, which struggles between lights and shadows? Near a garden or perhaps in its center, the visor of a vaulted cell. He lives with this scene carved in his chest, he bears a cruelty alongside the road scented with books and the sky plowed with sentences that teach him tirelessly to live tirelessly, it suffers side by side, what is freedom, the body in prison?" (*EES*, 26-7).
19 "He lives with this scene carved in his chest" (*EES*, 27).

it carves; "caveau" is a word that reminds of the cavity of the "cave," a semantic reminiscent of the reference to Plato's "caverne." "Caveau" is the French word for "vault," indicating that it is less about a presence than about a *void*, the fact that the "scene" opens an abyss that encrypts the secret of the Vision. Cixous calls this void, this hole, a "cruauté," a cruelty, recalling that the theme of cruelty is omnipresent in the *Essays* and in Montaigne's writing in general, and reflecting Montaigne's life in the midst of the Guyenne region during the wars of religion. It is at the core of the whole enterprise known as the *Essays*. Cruelty, torture, the injustice endured by the prisoners (and the prisoner par excellence, Socrates)—these are also fundamental to Plato's allegory. The Image must be experienced with the flesh; it must be seen and embodied to operate as a Vision. If Montaigne-Cixous is haunted, it is by Visions of injustice, of torture. Cixous always *incarnates* her description of the Vision in Montaigne's flesh. The presence of Montaigne's body is a powerful underlying theme of this text. Cixous recalls that the "Vision" is what has already been read in and through Montaigne, in his body and in his body of works, meaning that the scene has spread in the *Essays*, in the *Voyage*, but also in Montaigne-the-Tower on the walls, on the beams (to which Cixous refers as the "ciel labouré des sentences," "the plowed sky of the maxims," that Montaigne had inscribed on the beams of his *librerie*—we will get back to this in a moment).[20] This scene, the void in this scene, cruelty, has always been at work. Cruelty is what is at stake in Rom' and Os, Na, Brück. For Cixous, this is an Image that literally resides in Montaigne's chest, Montaigne's body and flesh, Montaigne's "heart," and turns any inscription into a writing on the skin and underneath the skin in a form that could take the metaphor of the tattoo, the scar or the bruise. To a certain extent, no inscription would be possible without being something like a tattoo, a scar, a bruise, traces of a burn or of a knock.[21] The Tower *is* Montaigne's body for Cixous. What is at

---

20 Alain Legros's work offers a comprehensive study of Montaigne's paratextual writings and paintings, the marks left by Montaigne in his Tower, that Legros proposes to call Montaigne's "Essays on the beams." Alain Legros, *Essais sur les poutres, Peintures et inscriptions chez Montaigne* (Paris: Klincksieck, 2000).
21 This will help us refine our approach to Cixous's relationship to Osnabrück. We highlighted in the introduction that the word "bruise" appears in *Gare d'Osnabrück à Jérusalem*. Cixous envisions the book that she is writing as a result of her relationship to the city of Osnabrück: "Mais ce livre n'est pas un roman fiction, il est l'hématome causé par le choc qui s'est produit entre la Ville et le moi indéfini avec tous mes livres à ses côtés et soixante-dix ans de récits homériques proférés par ma mère" (*GO*, 139) ("But this book is not a fictional novel, it is the bruise caused by the shock produced between the City and the indefinite self, with all my books by its side and seventy years of Homeric stories proffered by my mother" [*OSJ*, 109]).

stake is nothing less than "liberté" and "mort," liberty and death, *mort* and *Rom'*. The inscriptions, the books, are bruises.

What is it that Cixous sees without seeing for "forty years," what is it that she sees while exiting the Tower that suddenly becomes a Vision, what is this image that Montaigne was secretly carrying in his heart and flesh within the spatial and spiritual continuity that links the *Essays*, the *Voyage*, the "essays on the beams" (inscriptions on the roof in the Tower), the essays on the walls (inscriptions) in the Tower of Montaigne, and beyond? The Tower, Cixous recalls, *sees* the world and is the place from which the world is seen. What is there to be seen-unseen is, at first, a scene of laceration, of ruins and destruction, a scene similar to the ones Montaigne sees in Rom' that Ève Cixous sees in "Os, na, brück." It is a "débris ruiné," a ruined debris, a ruin, a decay, a destructive gesture. The Tower remembers its own decay, that is what Cixous sees for forty years and after. This is as blinding as the ashes of a synagogue or Rom'. One reason why it is a Vision is because it prosaically arrives to Cixous-the-viewer as something hardly visible:

> Et pendant quarante ans je suis passée devant la galerie d'âme de Montaigne, et *je ne voyais que les traces des griffes, les lambeaux de la peau du mur, les inguérissables lacérations du corps, les lèpres et pas les fruits*. Mais un jour où je sors précipitamment de la Tour seule à ma solitude, et tandis que je m'appuie à sa poitrine, un souvenir de soupirail me revient, d'abord vague, puis se précisant peu à peu puis foudroyant et avec un étonnement vertigineux je reconnais les barreaux de la grille, celle sur laquelle repose toute la construction de mon enfance et je me rappelle que je suis née d'une prison et d'une liberté.
>
> (*EEV*, 37; my emphasis)[22]

It arrives as something that returns, the presence of this Vision is that of the return, of the *revenance*. What she remembers is, at first, the "re" of re-members, of the re-turn; she remembers-sees through a dismemberment, that of the scratches, of the pieces of skin of the wall, the incurable lacerations of the body, of the leprosy ("traces des griffes, les

---

22 "And for forty years I passed in front of the gallery of Montaigne's soul and *I saw only the claw marks, the shreds of the wall's skin, the incurable lacerations of the body, the leprosies and not the fruits*. But one day when I hastily leave the Tower alone in my solitude, and while I am leaning against its chest, a memory of an airshaft comes back to me, vague at first, then getting more precise little by little then a thunderbolt and with dizzying amazement I recognize the bars of my grate, the one on which the whole construction of my childhood stands and I remember that I was born from a prison and a freedom" (*EES*, 25; my emphasis).

lambeaux de la peau du mur, les inguérissables lacérations du corps, les lèpres" [*EEV*, 37]).[23] It is no accident that the dominant theme is the body, a wounded one, a sick body: Montaigne's tortured body. And this remembrance of the dismemberment of the body arrives through the breath of a "soupirail," an "airshaft," through the bars. It is a memory of bars, a memory that slips through the bars in the maze of the vertigo created by this whole structure. *This*, she recognizes, is nothing less than Cixous's self: "je me rappelle que je suis née d'une prison et d'une liberté" (*EEV*, 37).[24] The Vision carries "toute la construction de mon enfance" (*EEV*, 37).[25] The memory of having been in the cruelty of the scene-Image comes and returns from very deep inside, from very far in the night of time and memory, this is a (primitive) scene of Hélène Cixous's childhood that she sees and recognizes in Montaigne's *librerie*. This is what is to be seen in the Tower of Montaigne, the most intimate location where Montaigne lived as he produced his *Essays*, a scene that has (nearly) disappeared:

> Ce qui a disparu du manteau de la cheminée c'est la scène appelée la Limite du Désespoir. Il s'agit de ce moment que nul n'eût imaginé où un amour qui n'a pas de nom prend subitement le commandement des événements humains. D'une minute à l'autre les personnages sont déplacés et emportés hors du commun par une force à laquelle aucun ne peut résister quels que soient son rôle ou sa fonction. Le personnage du Père passe dans le caractère d'un bébé. Celle qui était la fille devient sous les yeux du monde entier la mère de son père et par conséquent une incarnation de la maternité absolue et sans limites.
>
> (*EEV*, 101)[26]

She sees Montaigne who used to live "with this," "avec ça," precisely where she, Cixous, used to live with this too.

---

23 "[T]he claw marks, the shreds of the wall's skin, the incurable lacerations of the body, the leprosies" (*EES*, 25).
24 "I remember that I was born from a prison and a freedom" (*EES*, 25).
25 "[T]he whole construction of my childhood" (*EES*, 25).
26 "What has disappeared from the mantle of the fireplace is the scene called the Limit of Despair. It's about that moment no one would have imagined in which a love that has no name all of a sudden takes command of human events. From one minute to the next the characters are shifted and carried off beyond the commonplace by a force which no one can resist whatever may be his or her role or function. The character of the Father passes into the personality of a baby. The one who was the daughter becomes before the eyes of the entire world the mother of her father and consequently an incarnation of absolute and limitless maternity" (*EES*, 75–6).

When I visited Montaigne's *librerie*-Tower with Hélène Cixous, she pointed at the "manteau de la cheminée," the guard of the fireplace, on the western wall of Montaigne's winter closet (cabinet d'hiver) (see Figure 7):

> C'est comme ça que, un jour, je me suis retrouvée enfin seule, devant ça, et je me suis dit "Mais, mais c'est, c'est la prison, celle dont je parle tout le temps," et … avec ses … et qui raconte en plus cette histoire extraordinaire d'un, d'un prisonnier qui est condamné—ça c'est une histoire, c'est une fable antique, mais qui existe réellement—qui est condamné pour une offense à la cité, et dont les gardiens constatent qu'il ne meurt pas alors qu'il est condamné à mourir de faim et de soif, là. C'est parce que sa fille qui vient le visiter régulièrement l'allaite. À travers les grilles. C'est … se dire—parce que ça, ce sont des choix de Montaigne, hein—"voilà avec quoi il vivait." C'est une chose dont je me ne suis rendue compte qu'après coup, hein. On entre et ce qu'on voit d'abord, c'est la destruction: y'a plus rien. Et puis un jour je me suis dit "Mais non, y'a!" Il y a le Paradis et l'Enfer. Le Paradis … [*elle montre les ornements fleuris qui entourent l'œuvre, visibles dans le coin à gauche*] et l'Enfer [*le soupirail, les grilles du cachot*].

Figure 7 "C'est la prison, celle dont je parle tout le temps."[27] Hélène Cixous faces the Roman Charity in the winter closet of the *librerie*, in Montaigne on July 4, 2016 (screen capture).

---

27 "It is the prison, the one I speak about all the time."

Et … et finalement je crois que j'ai toujours travaillé sur … parce que le Paradis et l'Enfer sont les deux grosses entités de notre existence. Voilà. Nous sommes des êtres de Paradis et d'Enfer. C'est tout à fait mitoyen. Voilà, c'est justement l'incarcération et la libération. C'est ce que j'ai traité aussi, par exemple, dans un de mes livres qui s'appelle *Ève s'évade* et où j'ai pris cette image et d'autres images de … et où, en fait nous sommes souvent incarcérés, dans, dans l'histoire de nos vies nous connaissons des périodes d'incarcération. Alors, ce qui me touche ici, c'est bien sûr, le … ce sont les grilles. Parce que les grilles c'est tellement, justement, la frontière entre la vie et la mort que nous connaissons toujours et pour moi ça rejoignait les grilles qui ont marqué ma petite enfance, c'est-à-dire le grillage du Cercle Militaire à Oran que je longeais quand j'avais trois ans, et qui … même avant, quand j'avais deux ans, puisque ce Cercle Militaire qui était enfermé, dans des grilles qui étaient hautes comme ça, ça je l'ai vérifié, mais à travers lesquelles on voyait, on voyait un jardin, mais un jardin, justement, dans lequel on n'avait pas le droit de rentrer. Et, ce jardin s'est ouvert quand j'avais deux ans et demi puisque c'est au moment de la guerre, donc de [19]39, quand mon père a été enrégimenté comme médecin militaire, ce jardin d'Oran, central, était le jardin réservé aux officiers, et hop!, la grille s'est ouverte. Donc, j'avais deux ans et demi. Et, je suis rentrée dans le paradis. Je croyais que j'entrai dans le paradis! Puisque je désirai ce jardin depuis toujours. Et à l'intérieur, qu'est-ce que j'ai trouvé? L'Enfer! Je comprenais absolument rien. J'étais dedans, je n'avais jamais été aussi dehors. Aussi inadmissible, aussi rejetée, y'avait des enfants. Et … et voilà, et c'était la chasse! Et je comprenais absolument pas pourquoi. C'est là que j'ai fait mes premières expériences philosophiques et politiques. Que … que j'ai compris que quand on croyait entrer, [quand on croyait] être reçu, on était expulsé! Enfin, c'était mon cas. Et donc la clef que j'ai découverte, enfin, pas immédiatement, au bout de peut-être, un ou deux mois, je sais pas … parce que je cherchais comment faire pour rentrer, alors que j'étais dedans et puis non … et [la clef] c'était un mot que je ne connaissais pas et qui était le mot "juif." C'est-à-dire que tout d'un coup, les petits qui étaient plus grands que moi m'ont craché dessus en me disant "Mais toi, tu es juive," moi je ne savais pas ce que c'était ce mot-là.

Voilà.

Et finalement, la littérature c'est ça aussi, c'est le passage entre les grilles. C'est-à-dire que quand, quand on écrit aussi d'ailleurs on écrit comme ça avec des petits grillages à travers lesquels, à travers lesquels passent des souffles, sur lesquels se jouent des signifiants ... voilà. Et ... Mais alors, Montaigne, cette expérience il l'a faite de mille autres manières. Bon, lui évidemment, il était de l'autre côté de l'échelle socio-politique, mais, *ça il savait*. Et d'ailleurs, il le savait puisqu'il suffisait qu'il regarde autour de lui pour les Guerres de Religion etc., et, il voyait ça. Et il voyait aussi la cruauté, la violence."[28]

---

28 "And in this way I finally found myself alone, in front of this, and I said to myself, 'But, it's the prison, the one I talk about all the time!' with its ... and the one that, furthermore, recounts this extraordinary story of a condemned prisoner, it's a fable of Ancient Rome, of a prisoner condemned for an offense committed against the ancient city, and the prisoners' guards notice that he doesn't die, despite having been condemned to death by starvation and dehydration. It's because his daughter who comes to visit him regularly breastfeeds him. Through the bars. When you think about it, it is Montaigne's choice to live with this vision! it's something I only realized in retrospect. Because when we enter here, what we see first is disrepair. But one day ... 'No! There is something!' There is heaven [*H.C. shows the flowers of the grotesque surroundings the painting, visible in the left corner*] and hell [*H.C. shows the bars on the window of the prison*]. Heaven ... and hell. / I think that I've always worked on this ... because heaven and hell are the two overarching entities of our existence. We are beings of heaven and hell. Altogether. And it's both incarceration and liberation. This is what I addressed, in one of my books called in which I took this image, which embodies the fact that we are often incarcerated. In the course of our lives we endure periods of incarceration. So, what strikes me here are the bars. Because the bars are very much the border between life and death that we are always aware of, and for me, this brings together the bars that marked my childhood, the military fencing in Oran, Algeria, which I would walk along when I was three years old, and even before that, when I was two years old, since the Military Circle had been locked up, in bars that were tall like that, that I verified, but through which you could see, you could see a garden, but a garden, that was forbidden. This garden opened when I was two-and-a-half years old, during the war, in 1939, when my father was recruited as a military doctor. This garden of Oran was a garden exclusively reserved for officers, and suddenly the bars opened! At two and a half, I headed into heaven! I believed that I'd entered heaven since I'd always longed for this garden. And inside, what did I find? Hell! I absolutely couldn't understand! I was inside, yet I had never been so far outside. Ostracized, rejected! Surrounded by children. And ... and the hunt began! And I absolutely could not understand why. It was there that I had my first philosophical and political experiences. In which ... I realized that when we are taken in, it might mean we'll be thrown out! And thus the key I found, the one I finally came upon, after two or three months, (because I was trying to find a way in), having been inside and then not ... was a word I was not familiar with, and it was the word 'Jewish.' Because all of a sudden, the older children spat on me, saying 'you're Jewish,' and I had no idea what this word meant. / After all, literature is like that too, it's the passageway between bars. Meaning that when, when we write, we write like that, with little bars through which through which breath passes, through which signifiers are at play ... Montaigne went through this experience in a thousand different ways. He, of course, was on the other end of the social scale, but he was aware of this. He could simply look around and

The dream of the prisoner is a Roman Charity that depicts the secret passage of the milk of salvation from the daughter to her imprisoned, starved father, through the bars of the prison cell.[29] We will come to this theme of Cixous's Vision in a moment. For now, it is noteworthy that this Roman Charity has been damaged by the passage of time but probably also by the "cruelty" of vandals who, in the seventeenth century, could no longer stand the image of a woman's breast. In a way, time and vandals have also created a barrier, a set of bars, that explain why the "scene" was not evidently accessible to Cixous's view for forty years: "ce qu'on voit d'abord, c'est la destruction. Y'a plus rien," "what is here to be seen is at first destruction. There isn't anything anymore," says Cixous.

---

witness the Wars of Religion. He witnessed them personally, the cruelty, the violence." *Ever*, 01:48:40 to 01:52:52. This theme of the prison in Montaigne's Tower echoes what Cixous finds in Osnabrück when she visits the Bucksturm. Built as a watchtower in the thirteenth century, the Bucksturm was also used as a prison and a torture chamber that played a central role in the intense witch-hunting that took place in Osnabrück during the sixteenth and seventeenth centuries. In *Ruines bien rangées*, Hélène Cixous envisions the Bucksturm as a "double," a "terrible twin," the opposite of Montaigne's Tower: "—Regarde cette tour, dis-je à ma fille. / —C'est la Tour de Montaigne? En anatomie. / —C'est son double. La jumelle terrible. Son contraire. / Elles sont toujours là. Elles ont toujours le même corps depuis le quatorzième siècle. La Bocksturm [sic 'Bocksturm' with an 'o' is the ancient, medieval name of the tower], et ses trois étages, se tient sur le mur des remparts entre Heger Tor et Natruper Tor" (*RB*, 115) ("—Look at this tower, I said to my daughter. / —Is it the Tower of Montaigne? In its anatomy. / —It is its double. The terrible twin. Its contrary. / They are still standing there. They have still had the same body since the fourteenth century. The Bocksturm, and its three floors, stands against the wall of the fortifications between Heger Tor and Natruper Tor"). The prison is also Cixous's theme of her seminar taught at Paris 8 and the Collège International de Philosophie during the 2020/2021 academic year.

29 Paintings, book illuminations, drawings, prints, medals, frescoes, marble statues, even, as the historian Jutta Gisela Sperling indicates, watches and pharmaceutical bottles. There are countless artistic representations, in the European culture, of the Roman Charity, of Pero and Cimon, the breastfeeding father-daughter couple, that appears to Hélène Cixous as a Vision after a visit to Montaigne's Tower. Some of those representations have been found in the antique city of Pompeii. This scene is attested in the preoccupation of early modern audiences in Valerius Maximus' account in his *Memorable Sayings and Doings*, written 31 CE (the theme echoes the mythologic legend of Juno milking Hercules, and creating the milky way through a spill of milk; one day, when he was a child, Hercules was put on Juno's breast while she was asleep. Hercules, who still had not tamed his strength, attempted to feed himself at the Goddess' breast but he pulled it so fiercely that the milk spilled and spread in the sky). It is in the early seventeenth century, shortly after Montaigne's death, that the motif begins to be called "Roman Charity." Jutta Gisela Sperling, *Roman Charity, Queer Lactations In Early Modern Visual Culture* (Bielefeld: Transcript Verlag, 2016), 9.

"Avec l'écriture je peins," Germany, a dismembered self

In 1939, through the bars of anti-Semitism, Cixous "sees" a destruction, the ruins of a continuous oppression that ties Algeria and Germany under the sign of anti-Semitism, as soon as she is born. This dislocation, this dismemberment, is a primitive scene. The dismemberment of origin is as old as her when she is reminded of it in the form of the Vision. Its dismembered nature forges her memory. It is "remembered" because it is dismembered.

The artifact, Montaigne's Roman Charity, arrives to us as a dismembered, disfigured icon through the scheme of the return. A similar structure of the return, highlighted by Cixous in *Benjamin à Montaigne*, affects Montaigne's reflections on cruelty in a scene that enlightens our concept of remembrance. In January of 1581, Montaigne witnessed the dismemberment of a man who was sentenced to death and executed in Rome. The return, Montaigne's way of "tirelessly returning" ("revient inlassablement" [*BM*, 35]) to the scene traces the contours of a type of captivity that Cixous describes in the passage below:

> Nous non plus, pensai-je, nous ne Nous remettons pas de notre voyage à Montaigne Nous non plus nous ne sommes pas encore arrivés à en revenir, nous-mêmes nous sommes retenus dans ce voyage en captivité malgré notre retour dans nos Maisons habituelles, pensais-je en faisant le café pour les deux vieilles sœurs assises inhabituellement, il y a donc des voyages dangereux. [...] Ce ne sont là que brèves lignes de mémoire mais absolument inusables et que j'ai beau déjà avoir lues maintes fois depuis des années toujours j'y reviens. C'est qu'on n'arrive pas à retrouver la porte de la souffrance c'est-à-dire de la jouissance obscure, du jouir de souffrir, on n'arrive pas à recommencer la première scène d'amour, on se gratte l'âme jusqu'au sang. *Montaigne revient inlassablement sur cette rencontre cherchant en vain à user le point de ce point exact où on défaçonnait Catena, le changeant au-delà de la mort simple en viande de cuisine, pensais-je d'un seul coup d'œil acéré dans la cuisine.*
>
> (*BM*, 34–5; my emphasis)[30]

---

30 "Neither do we, I thought, We are unable to recover from our trip to Montaigne, neither have We we haven't been able to come to terms with the return from it, we ourselves are retained in this trip in captivity in spite of our return in our usual Homes, I thought, while making coffee for the two elderly sisters who were uncharacteristically seated, and so, there are dangerous journeys. [...] These are only brief lines of memory but absolutely indelible and that I may have already read many times for many years, I always come back to them.

Something happens at this "point exact où on défaçonnait Catena," this "exact point when one dismembered Catena" (or this "exact point where Catena was quartered") when Catena's body transitioned from his simple death inflicted by the executioners in Rome into meat, "kitchen meat," as Cixous puts it. Montaigne, Cixous recalls, comes back tirelessly to this exact moment when one "dismembered," "défaçonnait," Catena. On January 11, 1581, Montaigne's secretary notes:

> [C]omme M. de Montaigne sortait du logis à cheval pour aller *in Banchi*, il rencontra qu'on sortait de prison Catena, un fameux voleur et capitaine des bandits, qui avait tenu en crainte toute l'Italie et duquel il se contait des meurtres énormes, et notamment deux capucins auxquels il avait fait renier Dieu, promettant sur cette condition leur sauver la vie, et les avait massacrés après cela.[31]

Catena is executed in public. Montaigne observes that the act of killing Catena by strangulation does not produce much reaction among the spectators—a "simple mort," a "simple death," as Montaigne writes—the expression is used, slightly changed into "mort simple," by Cixous in *Benjamin à Montaigne* (*BM*, 35).[32] It is when the knife cuts Catena's dead flesh that the public reacts with disgust and loud emotion. Montaigne had published the first version of the *Essays* in Bordeaux in 1580, before undertaking his voyage with the idea of becoming

---

It is that one never manages to rediscover the door to suffering, that is, of the obscure enjoyment, the enjoyment of suffering, one never manages to rebegin the first love scene, one scratches its soul until it bleeds. Montaigne returns tirelessly to this meeting while searching in vain to exhaust the point of this exact point where Catena was quartered, changing him beyond his simple death into kitchen meat, I thought, with a single sharp glance in the kitchen."

31 Montaigne, *Voyage*, 197. Bartolomeo Catena is what one would name a "serial killer" today. He is believed to have had fifty-four murders to his name, as Charles Dédéyan indicates, in Michel de Montaigne, *Œuvres completes* (Paris: Les Belles Lettres, 1946), 208. "As M. de Montaigne was leaving the house on horseback to go to the bank, he met Catena, a famous robber and banditti chief, whom they were taking away from the prison. This man had raised a panic all through Italy, monstrous tales of murder being told about him; notably concerning two Capuchins, whom he forced to deny God, and promised to spare their lives on this condition. But he slew them afterward." Montaigne, *Journal*, 89.

32 "He died as criminals commonly do, without movement or cry." "It is the custom amongst these people to *kill criminals without torture*," says the English translation (my emphasis), to translate Montaigne's "Ils ne font guère mourir les hommes que d'une mort simple." The locution "mort simple" is lost to "kill without torture." Montaigne, *Voyage*, 198; Montaigne, *Journal*, 90.

an ambassador in Rome.[33] In the first edition of the *Essays* published by Montaigne upon his return from Italy in 1582, Montaigne adds a paragraph on Catena to his essay on cruelty,[34] which indicates that he writes about Catena with his reflection on cruelty in sight. In this edition, Montaigne writes "quand on en vint à *le mettre en morceaux*" (my emphasis),[35] "quand on en vint à *le mettre à quartiers*"[36] (my emphasis), and in the 1604 edition established by Marie de Gournay in 1595 he writes "on l'étrangla sans aucune émotion de l'assistance, mais quand on vint à le mettre à quartiers, le bourreau ne donnoit un coup, que le peuple ne suivit d'une voix plaintive, & d'une exclamation, comme si chacun eust presté son sentiment à cette charogne":[37] "when one came to tear him into quarters, into morsels [of flesh]"; "the crowd showed no emotion when he was strangled, but when they proceeded to quarter him the executioner never struck a blow without the people accompanying it with a plaintive cry and exclamation, as if each person had transferred his own feelings to that carcass," writes the translator.[38] In the *Journal*, it appears as: "Après qu'il fut étranglé *on le détrancha en quatre quartiers*" (my emphasis), "once he was strangled, one chopped him off in four quarters"; "ce point exact où on défaçonnait Catena,"[39] writes Cixous (*BM*, 35).

Catena is sentenced to death and executed, and from Catena's body cut into pieces Montaigne recalls the spectacular postmortem "torture" of his "défaçonnement," a word that is no longer used in French today until it is, like "recorder," revived by Cixous. The "défaçonnement" is the idea of the ripping, of the quartering, of the dismemberment that tears apart not Catena the living human being but his corpse. This operation fascinates Montaigne from the perspective of the torturer, as it is about the operation of disfiguring a figure, of dismembering a living *image*. The figure is created by the action of cutting, of dismembering; the figure becomes tangible in the act of dismembering. In other words, the act of dismembering creates a *substitutive image* of Catena's body that transforms his body into meat as Cixous indicates in the passage

---

33 In his political biography of Montaigne, Philippe Desan enlightens the conditions in which Montaigne's purpose of becoming an ambassador failed. Desan, *Montaigne*.
34 Montaigne, "Sur la cruauté," in *Les Essais* [2009], bk. 2, ch. 9, 527. Montaigne, "On cruelty," *The Complete Essays*, bk. 2, ch. 11, 484.
35 Montaigne, "Sur la cruauté," in *Les Essais* [2009], bk. 2, ch. 9, 527. Montaigne, "On cruelty," in *The Complete Essays*, bk. 2, ch. 11, 484. This is a Modern French edition of the essay.
36 Montaigne, "Sur la cruauté," in *Essais* [1604], bk. 2, ch. 11, 375.
37 Montaigne, "Sur la cruauté," in *Essais* [1604], bk. 2, ch. 11, 375–76.
38 Montaigne, "On cruelty," in *The Complete Essays*, bk. 2, ch. 11, 484.
39 "[T]his exact point where Catena was quartered" or "was dismembered."

from life to meat. This moment of the dismemberment is the image that triggers Montaigne's description and what he brings to his *Essays* in his 1582 addition. This moment of the dismemberment ends up occupying the entire field of memory when "Catena," the infamous figure of a living, legendary, spectacular face, becomes an unrecognizable piece of meat, turning the scene and the image of a dismembered Catena into *a screen-image that deconstructs the possibility of a remembrance*.

Montaigne's reflection is sequential, and Cixous highlights this salient dynamic. Montaigne's return to this scene is tireless, "inlassable," as Cixous puts it, and vain, as he cannot "picture," or "figure," the passage from life to meat. But what Montaigne does, and Cixous also does, consists in remembering—could it be that "remembering" metaphorically means "reviving" the meat that used to be the body of Catena? As a consequence Catena is figured through, or because of, the operation of dismembering, he becomes an image through the operation of dismembering. The sequence creates the remembrance, precisely where the dismemberment tends to radically erase the "membered" Catena under the screams of disgust of the spectators.

The remembrance of Catena is what prompts Montaigne to *write* about the dismemberment, if we follow Cixous's trajectory in Montaigne's text. Montaigne seems to keep Catena in this sequence when the metamorphosis operates from an image-body in flesh to dismembered pieces of meat. The arc that Montaigne highlights is what happens when one remembers, when Catena-the-remembered begins *to exist in writing*, given the fact that writing becomes an operation of figuring a dismembered amount of meat. In other words, there would be no remembrance of the cruelties of history without an act of re-membering, that is, a sequential act of remembering the dispersed pieces of a horrific *défaçonnement*. *Writing is figuring* and this operation consists of putting back together what the traumatic memory of the dismemberment has torn apart as a memory of the member of Catena the living human being who is, at first, turned into a dead body (image), and then into a dismembered body-image. Catena is alive, he is a corpse, "he" is quarters of meat (dismemberment). Montaigne puts the radically heterogeneous moments together in one single line, in one touch, on the same tableau. Through the twists and turns of the remembrance, it remains that there would probably be no mention, no memory, no remembrance of Catena without the written spectacle of his dismemberment produced by Montaigne. The *dis*memberment is the origin in its opacity (dis-); the origin cannot be distinguished from the dismembered (Rom'). Cixous reactivates this sequence, or animated tableau; we have Montaigne, in Rome, showing how the transition from Catena to meat occurs, how the change from Rome to Rom' operates, from Osnabrück to Os, na, brück. Memory, memorization and remembrance is what happens when the screen on which the remembrance projects the image of the dismembered is torn by the act of dismembering. Hence the Vision. *The Vision is a remembrance of remembrance, of the dismemberment of the origin.* The prisoners in the cave do not even remember that they are the dismembered. Their liberation will only occur once and only if they break the screen-memory fabricated by this opacified dismemberment. There is no memory of a cruelty without an act of remembering the original quartering, which is the quartering of the origin, the tear that also tore the representation. There is no action of remembering without reviving the memory of the tortures of dismembering, which implies breaking the screen-memory, the opacity that covers the whole scene in its cruelty. This opacified version of the dismemberment is what we know as "ruin." This is how Cixous remembers what "la mort violente et hideuse" (*GO*, 31), the "violent and hideous death" (*OSJ*, 18), means as a dismemberment of the Jonas family from which all she has is proper names ... and "memories." This is why Cixous gravitates toward Montaigne and his description of Catena in the same sequence of writing that puts her in dialogue with Eve's German fate and her family ... "Os, na, brück."

This defacement, or, to be more precise, *what remains of the dismemberment*, is the Image, the Vision. In a way, *everything* is in the Image. What remains is Montaigne's vision of the quartered Catena in the moment when the audience gasps in disgust. To be more specific, the Vision is a reminiscence of the substitutive image created by the writer-painter, but also by the photographer, the cinematographer, when this traumatic image of the passage from Catena to meat—Os, na, brück—replaces the face of the living subject "Catena," "Rome," "Osnabrück." The painter, the writer, produces a reiteration (and a sublimation) of the traumatic moment. As indicated earlier, the Vision, when it occurs, consists of the production of a figure. There would be no vision without going through remembering the art of disfiguring. It is now crucial to remember that the theme of Hélène Cixous's Vision in the Tower leads to the death of Catena, to cruelty, and to the ways by which Montaigne is attentive to the process of viewing, to the *spectacle* of Catena's death and dismemberment, *in public*. We have already paid attention to the fact that in some ways there is a cinematic process at stake in Cixous's description of the Platonist arrival of her Vision—the cave being a pre-cinematic device of some sort, and Montaigne's winter closet being a similar cinematic "camera" in which the mantelpiece is the screen. Cixous highlights the fact that it is Montaigne's decision to live with this depiction, with this Roman Charity, which is, like Catena's execution, a scene of torture, a scene of execution—both scenes have the death penalty in sight. She argues that one can never separate Montaigne's Tower from his *Essays*, that the *Essays* cannot be separated from the inscriptions on the beams, the walls, and the paintings. She argues that the Tower is the *Essays*, and the *Essays* the Tower. She claims that the *Voyage in Italy* is a voyage around the Tower. She asserts that there is only *one* Tower in the world. She exhibits this long series of connections between Montaigne, his wandering, his writings, and the totality of the Tower. In doing so, Cixous turns around a fundament of the *Essays*, which is the fact that the *Essays* attempt to *depict*, to *create a portrait*. To paint a figure. To figure. This is the essence of the *Essays*: "c'est moy que je peins,"[40] "it is my own self that I am painting"[41] (see Figures 8, 9 and 10). The *Essays* are a portrait of Montaigne himself, that of the self that Montaigne paints. And when Montaigne engages with this depiction, *he does it as a dismembered subject*, a subject who is grieving, who is torn apart, tortured. He is a self, his own self, as an *alter ego* of his friend, the flesh of his flesh, Étienne de la Boétie, whose death symbolically quartered Montaigne. Montaigne is the dismembered self of his dismembered *alter ego* La Boétie. Painting-writing, here again, consists of recreating this tortured self through what was once cut into pieces.

It is in Montaigne's famous essay on friendship (given to him by his missing *alter ego* La Boétie) that Montaigne explicates one origin of the *Essays*, and it is there that he offers a key to the meaning and reading of the *Essays* when he names La Boétie. Again, in an echo to *c'est moy que je peins*, *painting* appears as a central subject in the introductory lines of the essay on friendship. What is remarkable is that this essay is also the one in which Montaigne engages in a discussion on *what it means to remember*, quite literally, as an act of putting together "monstrous bodies" ("corps mostrueux" in Montaigne's words; "monstrosities" in the English translation) made of "limbs" (in French "membres") "having no defined shape," in other words, *to re-member the dismembered* elements. And this is given to Montaigne by his observation of the way by which the paintings that adorn his *librerie* are created by "a painter who is at his service":

> Considérant la conduite de la besogne d'un peintre que j'ai, il m'a pris envie de l'ensuivre. Il choisit le plus bel endroit & milieu de chaque paroy, pour y loger un tableau elabouré de toute sa suffisance; et *le vide tout autour, il le replit de crotesques: qui sont peintures fantasques, n'ayant grace qu'en la varieté & estrageté. Que sont ce ici aussi à la vérité que crotesques et corps mostrueux, rapiecez de divers membres sans certaine figure, n'ayant ordre, fuite, ni proportion*

---

40 Montaigne, "Au lecteur," in *Essais* [1604], ii.
41 Montaigne, "To the Reader," in *The Complete Essays*, lxiii.

que fortuite? [...] Je vay bien jusques à ce fecod poinct, avec mo peinture; mais je demeure court en l'autre, & meilleure partie: car ma suffisance ne va pas si avant, que d'oser entreprendre un tableau riche, poli et formé selon l'art. Je me suis advisé d'en emprunter un d'Estienne de la Boitie, qui honorera tout le reste de cette besogne.⁴²

(My emphasis)

Considérant la façon dont est conduit le travail d'un peintre que j'ai [à mon service], il m'a pris envie de l'imiter. Il choisit le plus bel endroit et le milieu de chaque mur pour y loger un tableau élaboré avec tout son talent; et le *vide, tout autour, il le remplit de grotesques, c'est-à-dire de peintures bizarres* n'ayant d'agrément que dans leur variété et leur étrangeté. *Que sont ici aussi, à la vérité,* [ces Essais] *sinon des "grotesques" et des corps monstrueux formés, pièce par pièce, de membres divers, sans forme déterminée, n'ayant ordre, de suite et de proportion que fortuits?* [...] Je vais bien jusqu'à ce second point avec mon peintre, mais je n'arrive pas à le suivre dans l'autre partie, la meilleure, car ma compétence ne va pas jusqu'à oser entreprendre un tableau riche, agréable et fait selon [les règles de] l'art. Je me suis avisé d'en emprunter un à Étienne de la Boétie: il honorera tout le reste de cet ouvrage.⁴³

(My emphasis)

---

42 Montaigne, "De l'amitié," in *Essais* [1604], bk. 1, ch. 27, 140–41 ; my emphasis.
43 Montaigne, "Sur l'amitié," in *Essais* [2009], bk. 1, ch. 28, 227. "While considering the work of an artist that I had hired I felt a desire to emulate him. He chooses the finest place and the core of each wall in order to create a painting to which he devotes his whole talent; *then he fills up the empty space all around it with* grotesques, *that is, bizarre paintings whose only pleasurable nature lies in their variety and strangeness. And in truth what are these Essays if not monstrosities and* 'grotesques' *and monstruous bodies formed, piece by piece, of various limbs having no defined design, having no other order, sequence, and proportion, than purely fortuitous?* [...] I feel until now in harmony with the work of my painter but I fall short of being able to go any further: my abilities cannot stretch so far as to venture to undertake such a rich and fine picture [in my writing], one fashioned according to the rules of art. So I decided to attempt a 'painting' of Etienne de la Boëtie: it will honor the rest of this book." Montaigne, "On affectionate relationships," in *The Complete Essays*, bk. 1, ch. 28, 205–06; translation significantly corrected and modified. The translation reads as follows in the aforementioned edition by Rev. Michael Andrew Screech: "I was watching an artist on my staff working on a painting when I felt a desire to emulate him. The finest place in the middle of a wall he selects for a picture to be executed to the best of his ability; then he fills up the empty spaces [sic] all around it with *grotesques*, which are fantastical paintings whose attractiveness consists merely in variety and novelty. And in truth what are these *Essays* if not monstrosities and grotesques botched together from a variety of limbs having no defined shape, with an order sequence and

Perhaps the contours of Cixous's Vision of the Roman Charity is what Montaigne has in mind here. The entire enterprise known as the *Essays*, as a gigantic attempt to re-member a dismembered *figure* of the self (Montaigne writes, "divers membres sans certaine figure," that can be translated into English as "various limbs having no defined design," no defined "figure," "figuration"), in his self, the dismembered figure of La Boétie who is essential to himself, to Montaigne; the self who writes-paints finds its form in the way his painter creates the iconographies seen in the Tower. "Étienne de la Boétie: il honorera tout le reste de cet ouvrage" ("Étienne de la Boétie: he will honor to the rest of this book"), the *Essays* are nothing less than a "tableau," an *attempted* painting destined to honor Étienne de la Boétie.[44] In this crucial passage, Montaigne also delivers a notion of what he means in the prologue of the *Essays*, the famous "To the reader" when he uses the word "paint." Painting, here, is no longer this classical, scholastic idea of representing traditional figures of gods and myths, of religiosity and heroism. Montaigne's idea of painting marks the entrance into modernity of a concept

---

proportion which are purely fortuitous? [...] I can manage to reach the second stage of that painter but I fall short of the first and better one: my abilities cannot stretch so far as to venture to undertake a richly ornate picture, polished and fashioned according to the rules of art. So I decided to borrow a 'painting' from Etienne de la Boëtie, which will bring honour to the rest of the job." Here the same segment in the translation offered by Donald Frame: "As I was considering the way a painter I employ went about his work, I had a mind to imitate him. He chooses the best spot, the middle of each wall, to put a picture labored over with all his skill, and the empty space all around it he fills with grotesques, which are fantastic paintings whose only charm lies in their variety and strangeness. And what are these things of mine, in truth, but grotesques and monstrous bodies, pieced together of divers [sic] members, without definite shape, having no order, sequence, or proportion other than accidental? [...] I do indeed go along with my painter in this second point, but I fall short in the first and better part; for my ability does not go far enough for me to dare to undertake a rich, polished picture, formed according to art. It has occurred to me to borrow one from Etienne de La Boétie, which will do honor to all the rest of this work." Michel de Montaigne, "Of Friendship," in *The Complete Essays of Montaigne*, Modern Languages Association 9th edition, trans. Donald Frame, 1, 28 (Redwood City, CA: Stanford University Press, 1958), 120.

44 Montaigne's inability to be as talented as his painter can be understood as an essential trait of the notion of dismemberment that lies at the core of the grotesque. This trait enlightens the nature of his writing of the *Essays* in the same way it embodies the difficulty of his mourning of La Boétie. A mourning that, ultimately, is above and beyond the ability to *figure*, to paint, to write. It is beyond the ability to ever complete the painting. The impossibility of the picture in writing is the essence of what writing stands for in the *Essays* as a necessary endurance of the dismemberment, of the necessity and the impossibility to fully "paint."

that, interestingly, discusses less the theme of Montaigne's painter's works than what his painter does *in the margins*, in the "void" ("vide"), the "empty space," around the main theme: "le *vide, tout autour, il le remplit de grotesques, c'est-à-dire de peintures bizarres* n'ayant d'agrément que dans leur variété et leur étrangeté" (Lanly modern edition)—"then he fills up the empty space all around it with *grotesques, that is bizarre paintings whose only pleasurable nature lies in their variety and strangeness.*"[45] ("[I]l le replit de crotesques qui font peintures fantasques, n'ayant grace qu'en la varieté & estrageté," writes Montaigne [Gournay-L'Angelier edition 1604].) What interests Montaigne is the *abstract dimension* of what we should interpret as a description of the dismemberment that lies at the core of the painting, of the *Essays*, nothing less: "*Que font ce ici aussi à la vérité crotesques et corps mostrueux, rapiecez de divers membres sans certaine figure, n'ayant ordre, fuite, ni proportion que fortuite?*"[46] (Gournay-L'Angelier edition), "*what are these Essays if not monstrosities and 'grotesques' and monstruous bodies formed, piece by piece, of various limbs having no defined design, having no other order, sequence, and proportion, than purely fortuitous?*" "[M]onstrous bodies" that are "*rapiecez,*" literally, "pieces put together" of "various limbs" without a "certaine figure" ("sans certaine figure," literally, "without a certain figure" that I propose to translate into "no defined design") ... the themes and lexical fields could not be closer to what we have isolated from the *Voyage* and Cixous's references to Montaigne. We have a straight line from the Roman Charity, Catena's quartering, writing as painting and friendship. Grieving, the work of mourning, is at the core of an entire process (the lost friend, painting, writing) marked by a void that cannot be dissociated from the motifs of dismemberment and disfigurement.

This is the cornerstone of the *Essays*, of Montaigne's grief of La Boétie, the dismembered figure that haunts Montaigne when he attempts to remember in writing. This network of texts, inscriptions and paintings from the *librerie*'s paintings to the *Essays*, to the *Voyage*, significantly finds its core in the grotesques that surround the painting, and the painting itself, that produces Cixous's Vision in the Tower. Interestingly, it could be that what triggers Cixous's Vision in the Tower is what Montaigne calls a "grotesque" here: the fact that the lacerations of time, the decay—"y'a plus rien"[47]—is a kind of grotesque, a dismemberment. The fact that what remains intact from the Roman Charity *is* the grotesque, the "void" surrounding the painting (according to Montaigne himself) and the grid that represents the bars of the prison. Cixous begins to see

---

45 Montaigne, "On affectionate relationships," in *The Complete Essays*, bk. 1, ch. 28, 205–06.
46 Montaigne, "De l'amitié," in *Essais* [1604], bk. 1, ch. 27, 140–41.
47 "[T]here isn't anything anymore," *Ever*, 01:48:40 to 01:52:52.

through this dismemberment when she pays attention to the grotesque that she calls "paradise." This is the point of entry in the reading of the Roman Charity: at first she sees the destruction, the decay, the ruins, *the void-ruin at work*; then she sees the flowers turned into grotesques that are still visible on the left corner of the painting, then she sees the bars of the prison; later, the Vision appears to her when she leaves the room. She remembers. The construction of her entire life, of a childhood dismembered by anti-Semitism, the war, the death of so many members of the Jonas family. The prison and the escape, which is also Ève's prison, Ève's escape, the ruin-origin of the Jonas family, *Ève s'évade, la Ruine et la vie*.[48] The keyword revealed by Cixous in front of the Roman Charity, the word that she remembers from her childhood in Oran is the word that dismembers the whole scene-sequence in Cixous's life-Jonas family: "the word 'Jew'."[49] A word also marked by the void for the child: "je ne savais pas ce que c'était ce mot-là," "I had no idea what this word meant."[50]

We could track this attempt to re-member the dis-membered in any process of remembrance, including the public scene of remembrance to which Éri and Ève are invited in Osnabrück in 1985; we could trace it in any reconciliation process, any commemoration, memorial, or other celebratory attempts to compensate for the cruel losses (voids) of history. After all, Éri and Ève are invited to go to Osnabrück under the sign of a word, the word "Jew," and the possible variations in which it is included, "Jews of Osnabrück," and so on. The word cannot be separated from the dismemberment of the Jonas family, from a profound void. Remembering consists of recomposing the figure of what was disfigured by the quartering of such a dismemberment. It is, per se, a form of painting in which the gap of horror, the void, operates as a missing experience. The void is the experience of the missing experience, it is what Montaigne heard when the executioner-butcher began to cut Catena's remains into pieces. We can trace this void in history, as ruins, griefs, wounds, ashes. History of the void: this is Rom' for Montaigne, this is Os, Na, Brück, for Cixous.

---

48 The motifs of the flight and of the prison are also at the center of Hélène Cixous's *Ruines bien rangées*: "Je comprends maintenant que l'histoire d'Ève avait pris la Hexengang dès 1928, chemin qui la mènerait en prison à Barberousse en 1962. Une histoire en alerte, sur ses gardes, toujours prête à fuir, toujours les mêmes motifs, Valises, Maison rime avec Prison, Fuites, Valises" (*RB*, 107) ("I now understand that Eve's story had taken the Hexengang as early as 1928, a path that would take her to prison in Barberousse in 1962. Story in a state of alert, on guard, always ready to flee, always with the same motifs, Suitcases, Home, this rimes with prison, Flights, Suitcases").
49 *Ever*, 01:48:40 to 01:52:52.
50 *Ever*, 01:48:40 to 01:52:52.

We can trace it in New York City, in the shadow of the missing, dismembered Twin Towers:

> Je n'ai pas encore eu *the heart* de m'approcher de ce qu'on appelle ici "Ground Zero" avec les mots qui *remember*. Tout seul ici les forces me manquent parfois. Toi qui as le monde et ses fenêtres dans ta poche, à toi la veille de nos *Twin Towers*. Souviens-toi de *Montaigne* et *La Boétie*, comme nous les avions appelées je ne sais plus quelle fois. À ton tour de nous remembrer.
>
> (*TP*, 232–33)[51]

There is no memory for the prisoner unless this memory is faced during a transformative process of liberation that will necessarily consist of two things: a process of remembering the dismembered and a reappropriation, a redemption, of the [monstrous] image created by the executioner. This transformation has another name. It is a "sublimation." For Montaigne, writing the *Essays* is painting this process as an act of liberation. "Remembrer" in French, *remembrer* Montaigne and La Boétie, writes Cixous in *Tours promises*. Montaigne re-members, he recalls, recollects the members, the pieces of meat that once were Catena the human being. This applies to what Cixous does with the ruins of the Synagogue of Osnabrück, which Cixous calls a "Carcasse" with a capital "C," the "cadavre de l'animal" whose torn body was exposed.[52]

---

51 "'I still haven't had *the heart* to approach what is called 'Ground Zero' around here with the words that *remember*. All alone here, I sometimes lack strength. You, who have the world and its windows in your pocket, for you [is] the eve of our *Twin Towers*. Remember *Montaigne* and *La Boétie*, as we had called them, I no longer remember what time. Your turn to remember [*remembrer*] us."

52 "Omi ma grand-mère est-elle venue voir la Carcasse? Je n'ai jamais pensé à lui poser cette question." "Souvent je vais voir le portrait de la Carcasse. […] en 38 ils lui ont crevé les yeux et ils l'ont arrosée d'essence, il y a des photos, on voit dans sa figure mortellement triste deux yeux éteints, la rosace a explosé, les vitraux latéraux se sont écroulés en gerbes d'éclats […]. / On a laissé le corps exposé toute une journée. Les photos qui immortalisent le cadavre de l'animal ne captent pas l'effroi que suscite la folle rapidité" (*RB*, 50–1) ("Did Omi, my grandmother, come to see the Carcass? I have never thought about asking her the question." "Often I go to see the portrait of the Carcass. […] in 38 they gouged out her eyes and sprinkled her with gasoline, there are pictures, in her fatally sad face we see two turned off eyes, the rosacea has exploded, the lateral stained-glass windows have collapsed into a spray of pieces […]. / They have left the body exposed for an entire day. Pictures immortalizing the corpse of the animal do not grasp the dread that this crazy rapidity provokes"). It is important to note that Cixous mixes this description of the Synagogue of Osnabrück with the vision of Hope, a female orangutan who was shot seventy-four times, and stabbed, on an oil palm plantation in March of 2019 in Indonesia. Hope was

It applies to "Rom'." In the first phase, we have Cixous's Vision. The second phase is writing, writing to be able to *see* the ruin, the ashes, which means to see the void of dismemberment through/within the act of painting; therefore, painting is an art of writing and there would be no writing without an art of depicting-painting:

> [E]n général je ne *raconte* pas avec l'*écriture*. [H.C.'s emphasis] Avec l'écriture, je peins,—quoi? le peuple des pensées et *des visions*, les passages, pas les pas. *L'Allemagne*—une Allemagne ou des Allemagnes—parle, passe, chante, se lève et se couche en moi, tous les jours.
>
> (*AA*, 30; my emphases)[53]

Germany is Cixous's dismembered self. That of her mother, of her aunt, of her entire "German" family. The quotation marks ("German," "Germany") that we have used on multiple occasions since the beginning are meant to mark the dismemberment at work underneath the surface of the word-ruin, of the word-Roman Charity in Montaigne's Tower, of the word-grotesque. "Germany" is not a part of Cixous but of her etymology, the construction of her childhood, a prison and a liberty from where she was born, from when she grew up surrounded by anti-Semitism, with Ève, her father Georges and Omi. *C'est Omi que je peins*, Cixous would say, to write her *C'est moi que je peins*, "moi" the *alter ego* of La Boétie, "moi" the *alter ego* of Omi my German self. From the dismembered there is no "representation," no reconciliatory, transparent rendering or even explanation. The void is always digging its abyss, its night, underneath the surface of the ruins, of the ashes. This can only be painted and thereby redeemed by the act of creating a *figure of the disfigured*: "D'un moment extranaturel on ne peut pas parler, il faut le peindre ou le filmer" (*CM*, 100), "From an extranatural moment, one cannot talk; it must be painted or filmed".

---

treated at the Sumatran Orangutan Conservation Program where she survived after a 4-hour-long surgery. Her month-old baby did not. Liam Stack, "An Orangutan Named Hope Was Repeatedly Shot With an Air Rifle. She Was Blinded but Survived," *New York Times* (New York City), March 19, 2019, available online: https://www.nytimes.com/2019/03/18/world/asia/orangutan-shot-gun.html#:~:text=the%20main%20story-,An%20Orangutan%20Named%20Hope%20Was%20Repeatedly%20Shot%20With%20an%20Air,dozens%20of%20air%20rifle%20wounds (accessed January 4, 2021).

53 "[I]n general I do not *narrate* with *writing*. With writing I paint,—What? the people of the thoughts and of the visions, the passages, not the footsteps. Germany—one Germany or some Germanies—speaks, passes, sings, awakens and goes to sleep in me, every day."

Figures 8, 9, and 10 Montaigne's winter closet ("cabinet d'hiver"), July 2, 2022. "Le travail d'un peintre que j'ai,"[54] "I was watching an artist on my staff working on a painting."[55] "C'est moy que je peins,"[56] "it is my own self that I am painting."[57] The airshaft of this Roman Charity appears on the left top of the painting that adorns the mantelpiece of Montaigne's fireplace in the winter closet of his *librerie*. The damaged portion on the right featured a daughter nursing her father who was a prisoner sentenced to death by starvation and thirst.[58]

---

54 Montaigne, "Sur l'amitié," in *Essais* [2009], bk. 1, ch. 28, 227.
55 Montaigne, "On affectionate relationships," in *The Complete Essays*, bk. 1, ch. 28, 205–06.
56 Montaigne, "Au lecteur," in *Essais* [1604], [4].
57 Montaigne, "To the Reader," in *The Complete Essays*, lxiii.
58 Winter closet ("cabinet d'hiver") of Montaigne's Tower, photographs, July 2, 2022.

Seven "I am, we are October 23, 1935": The October 23, 1935, picture

Painting is writing, and writing is painting. To see, one has to paint.

"Avec l'écriture je peins [...] l'Allemagne," "through writing I paint [...] Germany" (*AA*, 30). "Omi a traversé toute ma vie. Elle est un peu m,o,i" (*PR*, 185), "*Omi* traversed my whole life. She is a bit *m,o,i* [me]" (*R*, 183; my emphasis), writes Cixous in *Photos de racines*. *C'est moi que je peins / c'est Omi que je peins* (It is myself I paint / it is Omi I paint). Painting as a way of writing Germany, writing as a way to paint Germany, Germany as a painting of her *Omi-Moi*, her Omi-self, her *alter ego* Omi, Cixous's grandmother with whom she grew up in Algeria shortly after Cixous was born. In the history of Cixous's publications this iconography as a subject and form appears in 1994 with the publication of *Photos de racines*. It never ceased being prominent in Cixous's books, significantly, if not exclusively, when it comes to how photographs play a crucial role in most of Cixous's books on Germany.[1] Most of the photographs of *Photos de racines* come from Hélène Cixous's personal family photo albums. Those contain private images taken by family members from both sides of the family, the North African one and the German one.

The very existence of the German photo albums is tied to a historic miracle. Omi was allowed to leave Germany with them in November of 1938, as she had received a French passport after a visit from the French "Consul" (French Embassy) informing her that she was eligible. At the time, the racial laws in place in Germany blocked any Jewish-German individuals from leaving the country with their belongings, which were

---

1   Hélène Cixous's 2020 *Ruines bien rangées* contains five photographs, all related to Osnabrück, from various sources (*RB*, 12, 20, 71, 73, 83). "Plötzlich—Soudain une Photographie" is the title of the third chapter (*RB*, 81) ("Plötzlich—Suddenly a Photograph").

confiscated. This did not apply to Omi. Such a privilege is due to the fact that she had ties with the city of Strasbourg where she and her husband had settled before 1914, when Alsace was still a part of Germany (after France had lost this region in the aftermath of the 1870 French-Prussian War). Omi's address in Strasbourg implied that she was eligible for French citizenship after the First World War, therefore she was allowed to leave Germany in 1938, with a French passport. She was not only allowed to leave freely but also to exit the country while carrying her belongings with her, including the photo albums.[2] The German photo albums are a painting, in many sequences, of Omi, of her fate, of her *lignée* (lineage). But they also paint their own "being," as their existence cannot be distinguished from what they bring to our view.

Among other iconographic documents, *Gare d'Osnabrück à Jérusalem* contains three photographs taken from the albums. The first one, reproduced on a full page, features a smiley Ève with seven joyful friends at the time when they were probably in high school; the caption reads "Entre jeunes. Une soirée à Osnabrück. Ève est la deuxième jeune fille depuis la droite" (*GO*, 162).[3] The two other photographs brought from the albums constitute a sequence that features one single moment: when Omi's older brother born in 1869, Andreas Jonas, and his friend Gustav Stein say farewell on the train platform of the Osnabrück train station on October 23, 1935. The photograph on the left-hand page shows three men wearing hats and one who is wearing a cap in the foreground. The wagon of the train appears in the background; it shows

---

2 "Chose belle: comment ma grand-mère, veuve de guerre allemande est devenue veuve de guerre française. Juste avant la guerre, mon grand-père s'était installé à Strasbourg en Alsace allemande où il avait ouvert une petite fabrique de jute. Veuve, Omi est rentrée en Allemagne proprement dite, avec ses filles, à Osnabrück, où ma mère a fait ses études L'Alsace est devenue française: Omi, du fait de cette adresse alsacienne a eu droit alors à un passeport à double nationalité. Lorsqu'elle est sortie d'Allemagne en novembre 1938, de l'Allemagne nazie grâce à ce passeport, elle est partie en gardant son statut de veuve de guerre" (*PR*, 190). ("A wonderful thing: how my grandmother, a German war widow, became a French war widow. Just before the war, my grandfather moved to Strasbourg in German Alsace where he had opened a little jute factory. Widowed, Omi returned to Germany proper, with her daughters, to Osnabrück, where my mother went to school. Alsace became French: because of the Alsatian address, Omi then had the right to a double nationality passport. When she left Nazi Germany in November 1938 thanks to this passport, she went keeping her status as a war widow" [*R*, 188–89].)
3 "Young people together. An evening in Osnabrück. Ève is the second girl from the right" (*OSJ*, 134).

people cheering from the inside through the opened windows. The caption reads: "Gare d'Osnabrück le 23 octobre 1935/Andreas Jonas (premier à droite) et son ami Gustav Stein (deuxième à gauche) se disent adieu" (*GO*, 166).[4] This photograph faces one taken from the same angle, slightly closer to the train, on which one person holds the hand of a traveler through the window of the wagon. The train is about to leave. The caption reads: "Ils s'en vont pour toujours!" (*GO*, 167).[5] This series of photographs appears among other iconographic and historic documents in a special section printed on a different, white and glossy paper, at the very end of *Gare d'Osnabrück à Jérusalem*. The two photographs depicting Andreas Jonas's departure are in dialogue with Cixous's text, and they are preceded by two separate pictures featuring Andreas Jonas and his wife Else Jonas's "Stolpersteine" in Osnabrück. The latter were taken in Osnabrück by Annie-Joëlle Ripoll, and they are inserted within the main text of the book near its end, on a right-hand page (*GO*, 157; *OSJ*, 127), vis-à-vis a short, three-page chapter that is concluded, on the left-hand page, with the word "FIN," "THE END" (written in capital letters [*GO*, 156; *OSJ*, 126]). A new, two-page chapter immediately starts after "THE END," after this page with the two pictures of the Stolpersteine, and is followed by the photographic section printed on glossy paper. This montage is important as it underlines the interaction between iconography and text within the broader context of what it means to write and paint "Germany" in Cixous's œuvre. What it means to figure her Germany. We have different regimes of iconography that are organized within the text in different manners.

It is important to note that the photographs of the "Stolpersteine" in *Gare d'Osnabrück à Jérusalem* are a part of a whole sequence into which the reader stumbles after what Cixous marks as the "end" of the book and before seeing Andreas Jonas on the October 23, 1935, picture. This sequence indicates that, potentially, the addition of images builds a cinematic structure—or folioscopic—at least, a proto-cinematic form. The pictures of the Stolpersteine are strictly tied together with the main text by Cixous. This montage and text are in dialogue with the photographs reproduced in the photographic section after the book, after "THE END" and after the two-page text that follows. In this photographic section, we have the "youngsters" with Ève and friends and then the photographs of Andreas at the train station when he leaves Osnabrück. Such a sequence makes it impossible to contemplate the joyful picture of the friends, the "youngsters," without knowing that

---

4 "Osnabrück Station, October 23, 1935; Andreas Jonas (first on the right) and his friend Gustav Stein [second on the left] say farewell" (*OSJ*, 132; translation modified).
5 "They are leaving forever!" (*OSJ*, 133).

"I am, we are October 23, 1935" 123

Figure 11 The train station, Osnabrück, October 25, 2019.

the extermination took Andreas and his wife's lives. The pictures of the departure "forever" seen after the Stolpersteine, after "THE END," leaves an absent trace in the film, the blank of a syncope, *the missing picture* of a dismemberment that is inserted in the series of images. Cixous's writing finds its origin in this missing element (experience, picture, trace). This is a way to indicate that Cixous finds *her origin* in this missing element whose etymology is a certain "Germany." The text written by Cixous takes place in the void between the two sequences of images (Stolpersteine and Ève with friends, Andreas Jonas's departure). Tied to photographs, her text begins when there is no "album des ruines et des supplices" (*GO*, 58).[6]

Stolpersteine are urban writings of this missing piece across Germany. "Stolpersteine," literally a "stumbling stone" and metaphorically a "stumbling block," are cubes bearing brass square plates of 10 centimeters (3.9 inches) riveted to the ground, featuring inscriptions that state the name and dates of the life of victims of Nazi extermination or persecution. They are placed next to the domiciles of the victims, often on the sidewalks. The Stolpersteine project was initiated by the German artist Gunter Demnig in 1992. As of December 29, 2019, 75,000 Stolpersteine

---

6 Our quote from earlier reads: "il n'y a pas d'album des ruines et des supplices" ("there is no album of the ruins and the tortures" [*OSJ*, 42]).

had been laid all across Germany.⁷ The two Stolpersteine indicate that both Andreas and Else were murdered in Theresienstadt after having been deported in July of 1942, Andreas on September 6, 1942, and Else on January 25, 1944. Earlier in the text, Cixous writes:

> La rue Friedrich dort. Westerberg se lève tard. Et sur le trottoir devant le 25, deux Stolpersteine me défient avec leurs yeux de bronze qui ne se ferment jamais.
> Cit-gît le dossier Andreas Jonas enregistré dans l'archive de l'Éternité. "Ici a habité Andreas Jonas pour être déporté et assassiné le 06.09.1942
> Andreas JONAS
> Geboren am 05.02.1869 in Borken"
>
> (*GO*, 107)⁸

This is followed by an archival text that could be a basis for the shorter version of Andreas and Else's Stolpersteine.⁹ These Stolpersteine appear two times in different manners: first, on page 107, as a text that seems to be an archival document, cited and reproduced within the book's stream of writing, Cixous's writing. They then appear as photographs, taken by Annie-Joëlle Ripoll in Osnabrück, within the text on

---

7   Staff writer, "Germany: 75,000th 'Stolperstein' for Holocaust victims laid," *Deutsche Welle* (Bonn), December 29, 2019, available online: https://www.dw.com/en/germany-75000th-stolperstein-for-holocaust-victims-laid/a-51827506 (accessed May 30, 2020).
8   "Friedrich Street is sleeping. Westerberg rises late. And on the sidewalk in front of 25, two Stolpersteine defy me with their bronze eyes that never close. / Here lies the Andreas Jonas dossier recorded in the archive of Eternity. 'Here lived Andreas Jonas to be deported and killed 09/06/1942' / Andreas JONAS / Geboren am 05.02.1869 in Borken" (*OSJ*, 85).
9   Here is what the official website of the Stolpersteine indicates for Else and Andreas Jonas: "Else Andreas, geb. Cohn heiratete 1903 Andreas Jonas, Inhaber der Lederhandlung 'A. u. J. B. Jonas' am Nikolaiort 2. Vom 8. August 1934 bis zum 22. April 1941 lebte die Familie Jonas in der Friedrichstraße 25. Die Tochter Irmgard, verh. Michel, emigrierte nach Palästina, der Sohn Hans Günther nach Chile. Das Ehepaar Jonas meldete sich 1941 zur Großen Straße 44 bei Otto David um. Am 3. Februar 1942 wurde die Familie gezwungen, in das 'Judenhaus' in der Kommenderiestraße 11 zu ziehen. Von dort aus wurden sie im Juli nach Theresienstadt deportiert. Andreas Jonas starb dort am 6. September 1942, seine Frau Else am 25. Januar 1944." ("Else Andreas born Cohn married Andreas Jonas in 1903, owner of the leather company 'A. u. J.B. Jonas' on Nikolaiort 2. From August 8, 1934 until April 22, 1941, the family resided on Friedrichstrasse 25. The daughter Irmgard married Michel and emigrated to Palestine while the son

page 157.[10] These are followed by the two photographs of Andreas Jonas with the caption "Ils s'en vont pour toujours!" This complex sequence that mixes text and photographs of different regimes, distilled at different locations of Cixous's book, revolves around this central notion, written in German: "Für immer." For ever. They are leaving forever, with an exclamation point, in the final iconographic section of the book. This is an echo of the following segment on page 111:

> Dans quelques minutes le train va être parti, la vie de ce peuple d'Osnabrück va sortir du cadre pour toujours. *Für immer*. Il a fallu un artiste du *Fürimmer*, cela ne pouvait être que Felix Nussbaum, mais ce jour-là il n'était pas à Osnabrück, il était peut-être à Ostende ou à Bruxelles, alors lui aussi est dans la photo, en route pour le *Fürimmer*. Si ce n'est pas lui alors ce ne peut être qu'un autre Felix.
>
> (*GO*, 111)[11]

Pour toujours, forever, *Für immer*, and then, Cixous writes, "Fürimmer" in one single word. At this point in his life, Andreas Jonas leaves Osnabrück by train to go settle in Palestine. The many paths that photographs and documents (the considerable archival resource and research that helps create the Stolpersteine) forge in Cixous's book match the many trajectories of this fragmented display of elements. This is also a

---

Hans Günther emigrated to Chile. The Jonas couple resided in Grossen Strasse 44 in 1941 at Otto David's location. On February 3, 1942 they were imprisoned in the "House of the Jews" of the Kommenderiestrasse 11. From there, they were convoyed to the camp of Theresienstadt were Andreas Jonas died on September 6, 1942 and his wife Else died on January 25, 1944"). This information comes from the work by Martina Sellmeyer and Peter Junk, *Stationen auf dem Weg nach Auschwitz* (Bramsche: Rasch Verlag, 2000). [Martina Sellmeyer and Peter Junk], "Ehepaar Jonas," Stolpersteine Guide, Stadt Osnabrück, Büro für Friedenskultur, Osnabrück, available online: https://stolpersteine-guide.de/map/biografie/1338/ehepaar-jonas (accessed August 3, 2022).

10 Andreas and Else's Stolpersteine appear again in Cixous's *Ruines bien rangées* (*RB*, 71).
11 "In a few minutes the train will have left, the life of this people of Osnabrück is going to exit the frame forever. *Für immer*. There had to be an artist of the *Fürimmer*, it could only have been Felix Nussbaum, but that day, he was not in Osnabrück, he was perhaps in Ostend or Brussels, so he too is in the photo, en route for the *Fürimmer*. If it's not he then it can only be another Felix" (*OSJ*, 85). To which a fifth regimen of text-image will be added, that we will discover when we analyze *Correspondance avec le mur* and *1938, nuits*: the photographic facsimile. Those books present portions of manuscripts and typed archival texts. One is a card from Marga Carlebach (*Correspondance avec le mur*), the other document is made of two pages of a typed account by Fred Katzmann (*1938, nuits*).

metaphor for the profound dislocation, the literal dismemberment of the members of the Jonas family, that Cixous always has in sight in *Gare d'Osnabrück à Jérusalem*. Many trajectories, many directions are taken by the Jonas family, book after book, from Ève (*Osnabrück*) to Benjamin (*Benjamin à Montaigne*) to Marga (*Gare d'Osnabrück à Jérusalem, Correspondance avec le Mur*), through Andreas, here, and, of course, Omi. All paths on which Cixous wanders in her œuvre of Germany. In many cases, the trajectory ends in the death camps. "Fürimmer" raises the abyssal question of the departure, of exiles and arrests, of how and when they left. In Andreas's case, it is about the way he left for Palestine and later came back to Germany: "Qu'est-ce qui fait que cette année (1935), tant de gens s'en vont tandis que lui seul revient?" (*GO*, 124),[12] an event that recurs in *1938, nuits*:

> [E]t Onkel André qui ne part pas, qui ne part pas, qui part en Palestine pour revenir pour la *Kristallnacht*, qui finit par être déménagé en 1941 dans la Judenhaus de la Kommanderiestrasse, le petit ghetto forcé pour les Juifs d'Osnabrück, qui a déjà été annoncé en 1939.
>
> (*N*, 98)[13]

In the next Part, we will come back to this question of perceiving danger since one major reason why Cixous grapples with this question of the departure deals with Omi's late presence in Germany at the end of the year 1938. What we retain from this series of events, namely, Andreas's departure in 1935, is his return to Germany before November 1938, his arrest, his deportation and murder in 1942. It is the fact that a dismemberment takes place in which the murder of Andreas is preceded in Cixous's book by *a last picture*. Or to be more specific, two last images that Cixous associates with the art of painting. The immortality of testimony extends not only to the paintings of the great Osnabrückian artist Felix Nussbaum who was mentioned in the earlier quote from *Gare d'Osnabrück à Jérusalem*, but also, here, to Rembrandt:

> [E]t j'oublie totalement de dire que le petit homme à la chemise blanche est glabre, il ne lui est jamais venu à l'idée de se laisser pousser barbe ou moustache, en quoi il ne se distingue pas

---

12 "How to explain that that year (1935), so many people leave while he alone comes back" (*OSJ*, 97).
13 "[A]nd Onkel André who does not leave, who does not leave, who leaves for Palestine only to come back for Kristallnacht, who ends up being moved to the Judenhaus of the Kommanderiestrasse in 1941, the little forced-ghetto of the Jews of Osnabrück that was already announced in 1939."

tellement de ses voisins ou des miens. Sauf dans sa façon d'écouter quand l'autre parle un peu, avec sérieux et douceur. Ne pas oublier de dire: je tiens ces indications de La Photo. La Photo est une œuvre d'art. Elle a été prise le 23 Octobre 1935. Ce jour-là elle était un acte de témoignage d'une part d'amitié d'autre part de savoir-faire. Plus tard La Photo est entrée dans le patrimoine mondial. Elle vit parmi ces objets visuels qui tiennent autant de la peinture que de la photographie. En tant qu'œuvre d'art, elle passe dans un temps sans âge et sans date, comme, au premier regard, un portrait d'échevin par Rembrandt.

(*GO*, 109–10)[14]

"La Photo," *The Photo* (in capital letters), that Cixous writes is an active testimony ("acte de témoignage"), a recording, an act of friendship and the documentation of a savoir-faire. It is an essay on friendship in the way it depicts and paints the friendship that it also puts into practice. Later, this painting makes its entrance into art history. When Cixous evokes the possibility that the pictures have been taken by, or *could* have been taken by, or even, that they *are*, in fact, bearing the signature of Felix Nussbaum, it is not because Nussbaum was the one who actually took the pictures but, more importantly, because the pictures are marked by an art of the "Für immer," that becomes "Fürimmer," a concept that epitomizes Nussbaum's art. Nussbaum is an artist of the *Fürimmer*. And the *Fürimmer*, as practiced by Nussbaum, is the essence of art. What stands out in this dialogue between painting and photographing is that "Fürimmer," forever, is also a critical part of the *essence of photography*. Photographs capture the "fürimmer" of time, movement and beings, and this "fürimmer" is both friendship and savoir-faire; there is no perceptible distinction between friendship and art in this hybrid artifact that features Andreas and Gustav at the train station in Osnabrück on October 23, 1935. Similarly, there is no distinction between the art of painting the self as a dismembered (*alter*) *ego* and the act of writing for Montaigne: Montaigne paints the passage in

---

14 "[A]nd I totally forget to say that the small man in the white shirt is beardless, the idea has never occurred to him to let his beard or mustache grow, whereby he is not so different from his neighbors or mine. Except in his way of listening when the other speaks a little, with seriousness and gentleness. Don't forget to say: I take these indications from The Photo. The Photo is a work of art. It was taken on October 23, 1935. That day it was an act of witnessing on the one hand of friendship on the other of know-how. Later The Photo entered into the world's patrimony. It lives among the visual objects that draw as much from painting as from photography. As a work of art, it passes into an ageless and dateless time, like, at first glance, a portrait of magistrates by Rembrandt" (*OSJ*, 84).

its nudity. Painting the passage consists of depicting movement and time, of creating a temporal image of time-movement. What this deconstruction of the so-called boundary between painting and photography suggests is something that might also turn Montaigne into a photographer-painter, like Nussbaum. Both deconstruct the present through turning it into a temporal form of the image-movement. Cixous's use of the photographs is inseparable from her relationship to Germany. It is a movement, it is time in motion, and the temporality is not limited to the present in which she writes. This is a present that spans all kinds of temporalities and movements. History is not the past. This only exponentially enhances the hyperbolic dimension of any "last" picture, of what is called a "last" picture that both *captures and de-picts the instant of someone's deferred death, but a death that is haunting the picture and provokes its de-piction.* Something that Barthes writes about when he writes on the picture of the prisoner sentenced to death. His caption reads "Il est mort et il va mourir," "he is dead and he is going to die."[15] "Fürimmer" is the work of an infinite movement of the past.

The last picture is an arabesque (or grotesque) of all those dimensions: *painting, the uniqueness of the instant, friendship and a grief that is entrenched in the "presence" of the being (image-movement) figured on the painting-photograph.* Saying that the last picture bears witness means that it actively testifies, that it performs a never-ending testimony. In motion. Testifying means no substitute. No one can testify in lieu of the testifier, no one bears witness for the witness. This is the position of the photographer, here, including the "mental photographer-recorder" that Cixous embodies when she rediscovers-writes those pictures of Andreas Jonas's unique departure, Andreas's last departure in the *Fürimmer* of his deferred-actual death. The secret of this act of friendship and artistry is that it is taken at 11:59 p.m. in the history of the destruction of the Jews of Europe. Of Cixous's family.

To depict the event at stake, that of the persecution of Andreas, which is also the persecution of Nussbaum himself, art has to become an art to push its own boundaries, boundaries that take it to its nature as an *art of the forever, as an art of the deferred death, as an art of the impossible substitution.* This is where the boundary that traditionally divides painting and photography is blurrier than ever. Art is the testimonial apparatus of the *Fürimmer-forever*. *Fürimmer-forever* is at first a photographic concept, and it applies to the two pictures of Andreas Jonas. They are dated, "23 octobre 1935," and they incarnate the "Ça-a-été"

---

15 Roland Barthes, *La chambre claire, Notes sur la photographie* (Paris: Cahiers du Cinéma, Gallimard, Seuil, 1980), 149 (Roland Barthes, *Camera Lucida*, trans. Richard Howard [New York: Hill and Wang, 1981], 95). This caption a refers to Alexander Gardner's photograph of Lewis Payne, dated 1865.

"that-has-been"[16] of photography that Barthes also calls its "noeme" in his essay on photography, *La Chambre claire*.[17] "That-has-been" is the "einmal," the "once," "une fois," it is the essence of what photography captures as a mix of immediate reality and past. "Fürimmer" means uniqueness, it suggests that there is no repetition. This immediately contradicts the very existence of the photograph as a reproducible artifact in a machinery that also engages everything Montaigne has in mind when he publishes the *Essays*, considering that the *Essays* contain an art of exposure of the self in their uniqueness, their exhibitionist nature, their "one-time" destined to be repeated, infinitely repeated (everybody writes "essays" after Montaigne). As soon as the photograph is taken, it is reproducible in its unicity, in its irreplaceable nature.

Despite its unique and unpredictable nature, an event is never a pure eruption that takes place in a vacuum; it always carries the return of something. Such a return might be archeo-photographic in essence if we follow Cixous's relationship to what she also calls "fantôgraphie" (a compound word made of "fantôme" and "graphie," "phantomgraphy") in *Ruines bien rangées*:

> Je regarde la photo. C'est une fantôgraphie, me dis-je, toutes ces femmes sont des rescapées. Elles auraient dû être mortes.
>
> (RB, 84)[18]

This passage is tied to a photograph published in the local newspaper in Osnabrück, the *Osnabrücker Zeitung*, on June 8, 1985, featuring Ève Cixous along with a handful of other "Jews from Osnabrück" when they visited Osnabrück at the invitation of the city. On the same page, Hélène Cixous writes:

> Toutes ces femmes ont le sourire-de-circonstance. Un sourire modeste. Il n'y a pas de quoi se vanter. "Rencontre avec les

---

16 Barthes, *Camera Lucida*, 76–7.
17 "Dans la Photographie, je ne puis jamais nier *que la chose a été là*. Il y a double position conjointe: de réalité et de passé. Et puisque cette contrainte n'existe que pour elle, on doit la tenir, par réduction, pour l'essence même, le noème de la Photographie. [...] / Le nom du noème de la Photographie sera donc: 'Ça-a-été', ou encore: l'Intraitable." Barthes, *Chambre claire*, 120. ("In Photography I can never deny that *the thing has been there*. There a superimposition here: or reality and of the past. And since this constraint exists only for Photography, we must consider it, by reduction as the very essence, the *noeme* of Photography. [...] / The name of Photography's noeme will therefore b: 'That-has-been,' of again: the Intractable." Barthes, *Camera Lucida*, 76–7.)
18 "I look at the photo. It is a phantomgraph, I said to myself, all these women are survivors. They could have been dead."

Figure 12 Osnabrück train station, October 25, 2019.

Revenantes" dit le journal. Moi, ce que je regarde, ce sont les pieds.

(RB, 84)[19]

A few pages later, the word "revenant" persists:

—Et si on *revenait*? Si on n'était pas des "revenants," des invités—à être concitoyens-pour-huit-jours comme dans un rêve, des fantômes-fêtés-exorcisés?

(RB, 93)[20]

In *Ruines bien rangées* Cixous shows how the return of the past is tied to the texture of the present. The way the persecution takes place in Osnabrück after 1933 is preceded by a hunt that has ramifications in the long history of hunts, including the witch hunts in Osnabrück that haunt and populate *Ruines bien rangées*.[21] This notion of the present, and of the literary presence of the Jonas family, captures something of the essence of Cixous's relationship to Germany, to Osnabrück. "Für immer" could suggest that the entire event is forgone, but Cixous highlights the fact that "Für immer" might, on the contrary, be the mark of a *never-ending event* that is still happening and will happen forever, a traumatic moment that will *never* be fully over. Germany, Osnabrück, is *constantly*, compulsively, reinvented and redesigned, revisited and renewed by Cixous's notion of the return, of the revenant, of the *revenance*. There is no "Ça-a-été" of the "Ça-a-été." Cixous reinstates the shock to hear the never-ending shock of the *fürimmer*. This is the "one-time" of a continuous shock that keeps repeating itself through all kinds of ghostly reappearances and triggers. This is the occurrence of "Germany" in her work. She reinstates the shock's novelty and its conjured disastrous future; the photograph of a dismemberment profoundly signifies the return of an *intact, instantaneous shock*.

Given the repetitive nature of the *fürimmer*, the two pictures of Andreas Jonas found in *Gare d'Osnabrück à Jérusalem*, like the painting in Montaigne's cabinet, are always seen for the first time. The photograph, as it is conceived by Cixous, resists the risk of blindness that threatens any photographic (or cinematic) capture of an event. In doing so,

---

19 "All these women have the smile-for-the-occasion. A modest smile. No reason to boast. 'Meeting with the returned' says the newspaper. As for me, what I stare at is the feet."
20 "—What if we *returned*? If we were not some 'returned,' guests—[invited] to be citizens-for-eight-days like in a dream, to be ghosts-celebrated-exorcized?"
21 "Avant l'Osnabrück qui prend son élan européen à partir de 1881, il y avait eu un Osnabrück qui s'entredévorait et brûlait celles de ses sorcières qui n'étaient pas déjà mortes noyées" (RB, 93).

Cixous avoids the risk of turning photographs into clichés. This *return*, the essential hauntology (phantoms are timeless and tireless) that defines Cixous's relationship to the photographs, is the core of her German trope, of her approach to writing on/with Germany. The phrase that marks this literary event is sent or whispered to her through a phantasmal, ghostly, ventriloquist deep voice addressed by an estranged self inside herself, "'Je suis, nous sommes le 23 Octobre 1935'" (*GO*, 110).[22] In other words, it is impossible to surmount. There is no end to the radicality of this intact, *Fürimmer*-shock. No "Ça-a-été." Here is the passage:

> J'ai moi aussi été séduite par la perfection dans l'espace, le jeu des plans, le décalage des volumes, la puissance des personnages qui occupent l'avant-scène, le travail des temporalités qui s'inscrivent dans une condensation remarquable, le passé grandissant tandis que le futur se perd dans le clair-obscur d'un regret, si bien qu'il m'a fallu vingt ans pour me désenvoûter et me ressaisir afin de redevenir sensible au message que cette splendeur obnubile. "*Je suis, nous sommes le 23 Octobre 1935*, tu m'entends? dit le message. Il t'en a fallu du temps!"
>
> Je l'avoue. Non seulement il m'a fallu du temps, mais il m'a fallu venir à Osnabrück, apercevoir sur le quai le panneau qui confirme: *Osnabrück Hauptbahnhof*, voir les rails, j'étais énervée, en 2015, pour qu'enfin la date de La Photo de la gare m'atteigne dans le cœur et reprenne force à ma vie. Tu vois ici les dernières minutes d'un siècle, il s'agit du siècle d'Osnabrück, une ère extraordinairement profonde et brève, qui a vu la naissance, la croissance, la fleur et l'extinction d'une espèce humaine représentative du cycle de vie-mort du genre humain.
>
> (*GO*, 110; my emphasis)[23]

---

22 "'I am, we are October 23, 1935'" (*OSJ*, 84).
23 "As for me, I was also seduced by the perfection in space, the play of planes, the interval among the volumes, the power of the characters that occupy the foreground, the work of temporalities that are inscribed in a remarkable condensation, the past growing larger while the future gets lost in the light-shadow of a regret, such that it took me twenty years to break the spell and to recover myself so as to become sensitive again to the message that this splendor obscures. 'I am, we are October 23, 1935, do you hear me?' says the message. 'It took you a long time!' / I admit it. Not only did it take me a long time, but I had to come to Osnabrück, so late, so late, get off the train at the Osnabrück station, see the sign on the platform that confirms: *Osnabrück Hauptbahnhof*, see the rails, I was irritated, in 2015, for the date of The Photo of the station to reach my heart finally and regain strength from my life. You see here the last minutes of a century, I'm talking about the Jewish century of Osnabrück, an extraordinarily profound and brief era, which saw the birth, growth, flourishing, and extinction of a human species representative of the life-death cycle of humankind" (*OSJ*, 84–5).

"I am, we are October 23, 1935"   133

This insistence on the date that characterizes Montaigne's and Cixous's accounts marks the notion of non-iterability of what becomes iterable *in writing*, in painting, as a continuous, never-ending shock. This structure operates like a proper name: unique and iterable, the proper name is what Cixous has in sight here when she writes about the event "October 23, 1935." October 23, 1935, Cixous discovers, is the proper name of an event that is larger than the image, but one that the image also entirely contains. The image allows us to see through its cryptic code "October 23, 1935," precisely where a date is a proper ineffaceable name. Yet, what she sees, interestingly, is not just what is there to be seen in the image, within its own regime. What she sees is the *out-of-frame* of the continuous shock, something that she also seems to see with a difference in time, "il m'a fallu vingt ans" (*GO*, 110);[24] like she saw the painting in Montaigne's closet with an interval, a delay of forty years, as if she had been a part of this delay, of the out-of-the-frame: "Tu vois ici les dernières minutes d'un siècle, [...] siècle d'Osnabrück" (*GO*, 110).[25] Of course, anyone who sees this photograph of Andreas Jonas at the train station for the first time might not see what Cixous sees. Cixous's text-caption-book-poem allows us to see the shock. At the same time, the "that has been" of this picture is also engraving the disappearance of the protagonist: if that has been Andreas Jonas in this photograph, it is because, structurally, the photograph contains the possibility of the protagonist's disappearance as soon as the photograph is taken. What we "see" is the after-image of Andreas Jonas's never-ending disfigurement.

Through and beyond this structure, Cixous sees what the photograph does not show, what she names the "sortie du cadre" in the quote reproduced earlier: the exit from the frame (of the photograph): "Dans quelques minutes le train va être parti, *la vie de ce peuple d'Osnabrück va sortir du cadre* pour toujours. *Für immer*" (*GO*, 111; my emphasis).[26] The exit from the frame and its outside is the shock. It can never be separated from the frame itself, from what is in the frame.[27] What lies

---

24 "[I]t took me twenty years" (*OSJ*, 84).
25 "You see the last minutes of a century, [...] the century of Osnabrück" (*OSJ*, 85).
26 "In a few minutes the train will be gone, *the life of this people from Osnabrück will exit the frame* forever. *Für immer*" (*OSJ*, 85).
27 Deleuze, following André Bazin, will enlighten this dimension of cinema in his work: the fact that the "out" of the out-of-the-frame can never be "out." The "out" might not be visible but it does not mean that it is not a part of the shot—something that the sound will always highlight, and beyond (needless to say, the sound in the out-of-the-frame can play a role as important and "present" as what the frame points). This notion is especially developed by Bazin in his essay on theatre and cinema. André Bazin, *Qu'est-ce que le cinéma?* (Paris: Cerf, [1951] 2011), 129–78. André Bazin, *What Is Cinema?* vol. 1, trans. Hugh Gray (Berkeley: University of California Press, 2004), 76–124.

outside the frame is the extermination, the genocide. What is outside the frame is the possibility of this photograph being the "life of this people from Osnabrück" of whom the photograph is the last vision. Cixous's notion of the "last" puts the out-of-the-frame within the regime of the Vision contained by the photograph. Therefore, the photograph is both an encapsulation of the life of these people from Osnabrück and its destruction. Inseparably. It is not only that the photograph of October 23, 1935, records the contemporary scene of its existence at the train station at this date, it is not only that it also records what came next, as it records what happened before, before the hideous death and after, it is that such an image is a *figure* of the destruction-dismemberment that it contains. In other words, there would not be such a figure without a complex web of textualities. It is Cixous's writing as an act of producing a figure that creates the *dunamis* of her text as a force of *transformation* and *conversion* from the figurability of Andreas Jonas at the Osnabrück train station with his friend Gustav on October 23, 1935, to a *figuration of the de-figuration* (de-piction) of which the photograph bears witness. Therefore, the center of gravity of this reading of the photograph lies in how Cixous builds an *exchange* and a *crossing* between reading and seeing, between painting and figuring, between picturing and enunciating. That type of writing as a way of painting consists of a way of *figuring*. But this is not figuring in the sense of creating an image or, worse, as illustrating. The photographs in Cixous's books of Germany are no illustrations. They embody the ground, the space where this exchange between writing and figuring takes place in an economy of the shock, of the void, which, of course, fully applies to what Montaigne engages in his relationship to La Boétie, to the painting of the self and to the never-ending activity of writing the *Essays*.

For Cixous, there is no writing, defined here as a form of painting, without a profound activation of the powers, of the forces of figuring as acts of *transformations*, that engage the tear, the opacity, the void of history, the shock of a dismemberment that lies at the core of any image, of any text, of any figuration, that she actively constitutes in her literary relationship to Germany-Osnabrück-her German family. Beyond the traditional conception of the frame and the out-of-the-frame in the frame, what interests her is the gap, the void, the absence that tears the image at the core of the depiction, within the very existence of the frame. In this context, it is impossible, radically impossible, to delineate, to distinguish what belongs to the self "Hélène Cixous" from what happens through this *dunamis* of the exchange (conversion, transformation), between what is there to be seen and the unseen but figured, as a scene of the extermination. Her books of Germany build this scene of the extermination in a unique way that is not comparable to other attempts. The "sortie du cadre pour toujours," the "exiting from the frame forever" to which she refers, is something *inherent* to the photograph of Andreas Jonas. It cannot be outside—or opposed to—the photographs. The outside of the photograph *is the photograph*. There is no out-of-the-photograph while the core of the photograph lies in its exteriority. Which explains why this scene would not be intelligible without Cixous, without her text. She is this exteriority. This is "Germany" for Cixous. "Germany" is her outside-inside. She is Germany's exteriority at the core of what arrives to *us* as "Germany" today on October 23, 1935—as Germany on October 23, 1935, in *Gare d'Osnabrück à Jérusalem* today ("'Je suis, nous sommes le 23 octobre 1935'" [*GO*, 110], "'I am, we are October 23, 1935'" [*OSJ*, 84]).

This tear, this opaque and blinding dimension, this excess and this nothingness *is* writing. Writing as the place where the possibility of this impossible exchange takes place in Cixous's persona, Cixous's texts. This is what the "sortie du cadre," the exiting from the frame, means: it is happening inside the process of figuring, of painting as a way of *crossing* and of *exceeding* the narration. If we think about this logic of the excess, there is not *one book* by Cixous, especially among her books of Germany, that escapes this law of the an-archy, an-archive, in which every single of her texts is in a transformative dialogue with the primary *failure of memory* that constitutes the proper of any archive. There is no archiving, no archival photograph like the ones reproduced in Cixous's book, that is not, at the same time, a trace of the corruption of memory from which the photograph bears witness. Every memory would be the memory of a quartering, of a dismembering of Catena-Andreas Jonas. This is what "sortie du cadre" means. The photographic archives are ultimately the story of the destruction that takes place in and out of the frame that we named "opacity," "tear," "excess." What ultimately determines the unique nature of Cixous's writing, of her creative writing is this major *deconstruction of the archive*, or to be more precise, of the authority of the archive, that she engages with her œuvre.

Exteriority. We have already indicated that before 2015, Hélène Cixous had never set foot in Osnabrück. Eighty years after the 1935 photograph, almost to the day, she went. But she had already been in Osnabrück. She only got closer to what the figuration means in this reading of her books of Germany. Germany might also be this complex "figure" of an impossible journey for Cixous. She went to Osnabrück, Germany, not to picture herself, or to render a reconstructed image of "what remains," or to illustrate her thoughts and reflections, her writings ... but rather to make the disfiguration consistent. To embody the core of the opacity that ties her to "Germany." To inhabit the exteriority. Cixous's reading of October 23, 1935, is posterior to her trip to Osnabrück. Perhaps only by undertaking this historic trip she was able to come to terms with everything that her photo albums encrypt as a treasure, not as what remains, not as relics, but as a substitute for what the presence of Omi's "German" relatives meant for Omi, for what it meant in Cixous's childhood to be put in the presence of Omi's "German" relatives through Omi. This is less about the presence of the photographs, than about the present that the photographs embody for her, for us. They are her, us. Although they were not physically "present" in Oran, Omi's relatives were *here*, alive, they were *consistent*. Omi was the hyphen to the world before the hideous death. *C'est Omi que je peins*, says Cixous, and she paints with the photo albums of a Homeric poem. This is the figure. Beyond a restrictive concept of photography, the figure here is *what consists* in the sense that it allows the void of the massacre to consist. Consist: not "exist!" She makes the ashes speak, "faire parler les cendres." She builds the consistent memory of what used to be the flesh of Omi's relatives in Omi's voice and flesh, that which also lies in Cixous's *poetic voice and flesh enhanced by her physical proximity to Osnabrück today*. This consistency is crucial as it incarnates the life of Andreas Jonas at the core of the picture where Andreas's hideous death also lies. This figuration of the disfigured in the image (as a dismembered remembrance) lies in the "sortie du cadre," the exiting of the frame, as a presence of those who do not come back. Those who do not come back are alive in Omi-Hélène Cixous-writing. Cixous is in Osnabrück where those who left the Osnabrück of before the hideous death (Ève, Éri, Omi ...), meet those who did not leave (or did not come back, such as Andreas): "Mais on n'entendra jamais les réponses ou les explications de ceux-qui-ne-reviennent-pas à Osnabrück parce qu'ils ne sont pas partis" (*N*, 100).[28]

This is what Cixous's writings of Osnabrück do as performance. This is the twin of what Ève used to say: "—À la gare d'Osnabrück il y a maintenant une plaque dans la salle d'attente avec les noms des Juifs *qui sont partis* de là pour les camps de concentration enchaîne ma mère à toute vitesse" (*BM*, 147) ("In the city of Osnabrück there is now a plaque in the waiting room, with the names of Jews *who left* from there for the concentration camps my mother carries on at top speed").[29]

---

28 "But one will never hear the responses or the explanations of those-who-do-not-return to Osnabrück because they never left."
29 This is also where literature comes from and begins. I checked, I asked, I did not find the plaque at the train station when I visited Osnabrück.

Eight   N'ai-je pas vu (Have I not seen ...), la neige pas vue (... the snow not seen)?

Je ne peux pas dire que <u>je n'ai</u> pas vécu à Osnabrück, aussi longtemps et plus qu'à Oran dis-je à mon fils, j'ai toujours vécu, d'abord à Oran, avec Osnabrück, à Osnabrück sans Osnabrück, à Oran comme à Osnabrück. Je peux dire que <u>je n'ai</u> jamais vécu à Oran sans penser à Osnabrück, quand j'étais au lycée d'Oran, j'avais l'âge de ma mère au Gymnasium, je regardais pas la fenêtre, je voyais qu'il n'y avait pas de <u>neige</u>, à force de ne pas voir qu'il n'y avait pas de <u>neige</u>, à force de ne pas voir et ne pas voir la <u>neige</u> que <u>je n'ai</u> jamais vue, à force de faire fondre le mot <u>neige</u> dans ma bouche, et d'imaginer tâter son goût inconnu de crème fouettée, elle avait fini par tomber du ciel, la <u>neige</u>, et je l'ai vue, quoique je ne sois pas sûre de ne pas l'avoir fait tomber en rêve, je ne suis pas sûre, <u>n'ai-je</u> pas vu ma mère se dresser au fond de l'allée du lycée debout sur ses skis comme dans son rêve, en vérité il y avait des moments délicieux où <u>je devenais Ève</u>. Avec le temps moi aussi je courais le long de la Hase.
(GO, 28–9; *my underlining*)[1]

She sees the *neige* (snow) that she has never seen in Oran. "[N]'ai-je pas vu ma mère[?]" ("have I not seen my mother[?]") in Oran in

---

1   "I cannot say that I have not lived in Osnabrück, as long as and longer than in Oran I say to my son, I always lived, first in Oran with Osnabrück, in Osnabrück without Osnabrück, in Oran *as* in Osnabrück. I can say that I never lived in Oran without thinking of Osnabrück, when I was in high school in Oran, I was my mother's age when she was at the Gymnasium, I used to look out the window, I saw that there was no snow, by force of seeing there was no snow, by force of not seeing and not seeing snow that I had never seen, by force of making the word snow melt in my mouth, and of imagining tasting its unknown taste of whipped cream, the snow ended up falling from the sky, and I saw it, although I am not sure that I didn't make it fall in a dream, I am not sure, didn't my mother rise up at the end of the high school driveway standing on her skis as in a dream, in truth there were delectable moments when I became Ève. With time I too used to run along the Hase" (*OSJ*, 16).

Osnabrück, in her mother's dream, "I too ran alongside the Hase," writes Cixous who dreams Ève in Osnabrück, in Oran, *n'ai-je*, "n'ai-je pas vu[?]" She dreams, she pictures herself in Osnabrück in Oran during the time of the persecution, through the bars of a long litany of German words that we will analyze momentarily. "*Neige-n'ai-je*," has the same phoneme in French. It is phonetically impossible to distinguish "neige" (snow) and "n'ai-je" (Have I not). The homophony performs the tension between the visible and the invisible; it renders the invisible snow of Oran that she sees. *Neige pas vue* (snow not seen), *n'ai-je pas vu* (have I not seen). In Oran in Osnabrück, *neige-n'ai-je*. Visions. Visions are also embedded and encrypted; they are visions because they are secretly encrypted in signifiers, in dreams and in this text. Those are also reversed phonemes around "neige, n'ai-je" that turn into "je n'ai." "Je n'ai" will become, toward the end of the fragment, "je de*ve*nais Ève" (I became Ève), which associates "je n'ai" the reversed "neige-n'ai-je" and the signifier *eve* of "*deve*nais," Ève, a word with a nose, "v" and two eyes "e," "e." This face lodged in the word "Ève," Hélène Cixous's *alter ego*-portrait, in this text, is one of the poetic creations that Cixous offers when words are also figures, something that we will explore in a moment while analyzing Alechinsky's work in *Gare d'Osnabrück à Jérusalem*. *Je n'ai Ève* (I do not have Ève), *je n'ai* (I have not), *neige-Ève* (snow-Ève), *n'ai-je Ève* (Haven't I Ève), *je devenais Ève* (I became Ève) … the chain of signifiers carries out the meaning of the whole fragment on a separate line that could serve as an underlying iconographic theme for the presence of Osnabrück underneath Ève's presence in Oran.[2] This chain signifies the presence of the snow of Osnabrück in Oran, the way Hélène Cixous is becoming Ève that leads to Osnabrück in 2015, among other possibilities by which Cixous became the mother of her dying mother (*Homère est morte*). She became the daughter-nurse, the daughter who was nursing her mother (Roman Charity). *Je n'ai* is also the phoneme through which Hélène Cixous is born, through which she sees her birth as (*alter ego*) Ève, *je [d(eve)]nais Ève*, we might hear that "je nais en tant que Ève," I was born as Ève, since "je n'ai" (I don't have) and "je nais" (I am born) share the same phonetic resonance.[3] Image

---

2 In September of 2013, a few weeks after Ève's death, Cixous visited Cornell University where she gave a lecture. During this stay, she also led Professor Laurent Dubreuil's research seminar. Cixous evoked her dream from the previous night where the first name "Geneviève" appeared to her. In French, "Geneviève" sounds like "Je ne vis Ève" (I have not seen Ève).
3 Which should also recall Cixous's proximity to Derrida, in particular, the way Derrida read Genet in *Glas*, in Jacques Derrida, *Glas* (Paris: Galilée, 1974); and Cixous's own reading of Genet that will always be a close reading of Ève, in *Entretien de la blessure* in Hélène Cixous, *Entretien de la blessure* (Paris: Galilée, 2011).

and sound are here to allow us to hear, to allow us to hear what cannot be heard, to allow us to see and to allow us to see the unseen. To let the Visions enter, to invite the phantoms.

When Hélène Cixous looks backwards, she sees Osnabrück. When she looks at herself, she sees Osnabrück where she was not born (n'ai-je), where she was born (je nais), where she was the *neige* (snow) of Osnabrück. When she looks at herself in Oran, she sees that she, too, is running alongside the Hase, the little river, from Osnabrück (see Figures 13 and 14). She sees the snow that she has never seen. In Oran she is the only one, along with Omi and Ève, who sees this snow, the snow that melts like the unknown taste of the German whipped cream ("à force de faire fondre le mot neige dans ma bouche, et d'imaginer tâter son goût inconnu de crème fouettée, elle avait fini par tomber du ciel, la neige, et je l'ai vue, quoique je ne sois pas sûre de ne pas l'avoir fait tomber en rêve" [*GO*, 29]).[4] She sees through her dreams of seeing. She sees through magic words, through the magic of words. Osnabrück, Cixous often reports, is *in* her childhood in her native Algeria. "Il y a ces jours ou Osnabrück est dans mon enfance à Oran" (*GO*, 14).[5] She looks back to when the question of what was seen at the time decides who will stay and die in Germany, and who will be able to leave and survive. She has been in Osnabrück long before 2015, when she finally got to go to Osnabrück. Her life is the

---

4   "[B]y force of not seeing and not seeing snow that I had never seen, by force of making the word snow melt in my mouth, and of imagining tasting its unknown taste of whipped cream, the snow ended up falling from the sky, and I saw it, although I am not sure that I didn't make it fall in a dream" (*OSJ*, 16).
5   "There are those days when Osnabrück is in my childhood in Oran" (*OSJ*, 4). This notion is rendered with the following words by Hélène Cixous in this interview: "Vous écrivez: 'C'est le livre que ma mère m'a laissé à lire et à écrire.' / —Absolument. Quand j'étais petite, c'était un conte de fées. Sauf que je croyais qu'Osnabrück était ma ville, je considérais que l'enfance de ma mère et mon enfance, c'était une sorte d'enfance d'enfance. J'avais le sentiment que, quand je prenais l'escalier de la maison d'Oran, je prenais celui d'Osnabrück. Je savais que c'était une fiction mais c'est le charme de l'existence." ("You write: 'This is the book that my mother left for me to read and write.' / —Absolutely. When I was little, it was a fairy tale. Except that I believed that Osnabrück was my hometown, I considered that my mother's childhood combined with my childhood constituted a sort of childhood's childhood. I had the feeling that, when I was climbing the stairs of the house in Oran, I was climbing the one from Osnabrück. I knew for a fact that this was a fiction, but that's the charm of existence.") Frédérique Roussel, "La maison d'écriture d'Hélène Cixous," *Libération* (Paris), December 18, 2020, available online: https://next.liberation. fr/livres/2020/12/18/la-maison-d-ecriture-d-helene-cixous-parution-de-seminaire-et-ruines-bien-rangees_1809068<%22> (accessed December 31, 2020).

history of going to Osnabrück where she was long before she actually went to Osnabrück. She goes to Osnabrück where she has always been as soon as she was born in Oran. In Oran she is in Osnabrück where she has never been. She sees Osnabrück that she has never seen. This is a literary structure. Cixous writes that this structure is an original state of literature. This moment is the mother of literature, Ulysses's long journey, Homère-mère, it is the Homer-Cixous's mother of all literature:

> Je trouve que je suis dans l'état du chasseur Gracchus, quand il était dans l'état d'Ulysse pionnier pour la littérature, attaché à sa barque et débarquant pendant des années de toutes parts, en se disant chaque fois *faudrait qu'un jour j'arrive à mon point de départ*. Et tout s'est toujours passé comme si le voyageur s'était dit en secret: puissé-je arriver
> le plus tard possible
> C'est comme arriver à arriver à Osnabrück en arrivant à ne pas y être arrivé.
>
> (*GO*, 21)[6]

In this playful use of the idiomatic meanings of the verb "arriver," which can both mean the arrival and the capacity to achieve something, she navigates the dreams of her never-ending travels to Osnabrück where she manages to arrive while being able to not arrive. The fact that she got to go to Osnabrück is still a dream, it is in her dreams:

> Rien. En traversant la ville sans rivière, toute la ville est défaite, est-elle en destruction ou construction, je ne reconnais plus rien, je me perdrai, j'ai au fond de moi les images de mon enfance. Détruite à 60%. De 42 à 45. On me conduit. On me donne des explications. Je finis par dire: mais je suis née ici. C'est vrai, mais. Peut-être que tout a changé. Peut-être que j'ai changé. Maman m'attend. Que c'est long et étiré cette arrivée qui se dérobe!
> C'est peut-être un rêve-qui-n'arrive-pas.

---

6 "I find that I am in the state of the hunter Gracchus, when he was in the state of Ulysses, pioneer for literature, attached to his bark and disembarking for years in all sorts of places, while saying to himself each time *I should one day arrive at my point of departure*. And everything always happened as if the traveler had said to himself in secret: may I arrive / as late as possible / It's like managing to arrive in Osnabrück while managing not to have arrived there" (*OSJ*, 10).

Je finirai bien par y arriver, me dis-je, à Osnabrück, à force d'en parler, à force de l'imaginer, me dis-je, et même à force de ne pas y aller.

(GO, 15)[7]

It is as if Ève's impossibilities to go and arrive in Osnabrück had become Cixous's. In her dream of Osnabrück she often sees Omi. She is Omi-Moi. This could be Omi's voice in Hélène Cixous:

C'est avec émotion que je vole vers O.Ran. Le train survole les pays, roule au-dessus de la France et de l'Algérie. Il y a si longtemps. Je *voisdéjà* notre quartier, Nikolaiort, notre maison est toujours sur la grande place. Maman m'attend.

(GO, 15)[8]

This could be Omi's journey from Osnabrück to Oran, or Cixous's dream of Omi's journey. With Ève, Cixous's mother-Homer, with Omi when she arrives in Osnabrück in November of 1938, Osnabrück is in Oran, Oran arrives in Osnabrück; but Cixous also discovers a literary treasure in which, literally, the signifier "Oran" is anagrammatically lodged and can be seen *through* "Osnabrück": "Oran" is in "Osnabrück." Furthermore, Oran is in "Nikolaiort," the great place of Osnabrück where Omi's family used to live. This has always been here, it was always here to be seen, like Montaigne's Roman Charity, like Andreas Jonas's photograph from October 23, 1935. The signifier is already lodged, visible and hidden, within the tableau. In a way, this anagrammatic treasure that Cixous alone can *see* during her poetic research could very much be called a "Vision." A Vision is something that is already seen without being evidently figured, something that has always been seen but is transfigured by a creative act of writing as a way of reading and painting, or seeing, like a painter. Seeing through and dreaming are very close notions here for Cixous, as ways of being

---

7 "Nothing. Crossing the city without a river, the whole city is ravaged, is it in destruction or construction, I no longer recognize anything, I will get lost, deep within I have images of my childhood. Sixty percent destroyed. From '42 to '45. I am guided. I am given explanations. I end up saying: but I was born here. That's true, but. Maman is waiting for me. How long and drawn out is this arrival that slips away! / It is perhaps a dream-that-does-not-arrive. / I am going to end up arriving there, I say to myself, in Osnabrück, by force of talking about it, by force of imagining it, I say to myself, and even by force of not going there" (*OSJ*, 5–6).

8 "It is with emotion that I fly toward O.Ran. The train flies over countries, rolls above France and Algeria. It was so long ago. I *alreadysee* our neighborhood, *Nikolaiort*, our house is still on the main square. Maman is waiting for me" (*OSJ*, 5).

able to see (*arriver à voir*), and being able to dream, *réussir à rêver*, manage to dream, *arriver à rêver*, le rêve-qui-n'arrive-pas, the dream-that-does-not-manage-to, the dream-that-does-not-arrive. My hypothesis is that in its earliest forms, Cixous's capacity to *see through* words (signifiers) requires a cinematic, photographic way of watching-dreaming *like a painter*. Seeing through signifiers implies that the signs are both the eye and the screen, the sight and the bars (of the prison), the word-eye (or optical device), the prosthetic eye that allows us to see and the word that sees, which watches us at the same time.

This capacity not only to see and use words, but also to pay attention to their design, their form, their length and common features requires an ability both to turn words into images and the reverse, to see images like words. This is what is at stake in Cixous's use of "painted images" (Nussbaum, Rembrandt) in her recent books. Cixous, like Montaigne, is a painter who sees before anyone else something that has always been there. "Je *voisdéjà*" (*GO*, 15). O<u>s</u>nabrück. <u>N</u>ikol<u>ai</u>ort. "I *alreadysee*." I "alreadysee" is what painters do when they see through the void of destruction, of injustice, when they see through the tear of the visible, when they see through the bars of the prison. The prison: Osnabrück cannot be seen throughout Cixous's childhood, a period that coincides with the wartime. Later, in 1951, she goes to Germany for the first time; with Omi, she goes to "Köln" (Cologne) but is not sure whether she's set foot in Osnabrück, or not, at the time. Cixous's first Osnabrück is

Figure 13 Hélène Cixous, the Hase river, Osnabrück, October 25, 2019.

Figure 14 The Hase river in Osnabrück, October 25, 2019.

that of political refugees, Omi, Ève ... As the previous quote indicates, the reason why it is difficult to see is because trauma is a part of the picture: "toute la ville est défaite, est-elle en destruction ou construction, je ne reconnais plus rien, je me perdrai" (*GO*, 15).[9] Osnabrück is a synonym for all the reasons why Omi is in Oran, the tears of destructions, of the war, of incarcerations, of persecutions, of the genocide, of exile. In her earliest childhood memories, Cixous is in the park in Oran with her grandmother, and she hears the German language spoken. The language of political refugees, of German war resistors and of persecuted Jews. There are many German exiles in Oran at the time, during the Second World War, and most of them are on their way to safer locations.

Cixous grows up in Oran surrounded and pierced by German words that paint life, along with all its seismic forces of survival, persecutions and destruction. There is no Vision without this mix of life, trauma, cryptic signs and (dis)figuration. This structure of the Vision is as old as Cixous herself. The German words of Cixous's childhood find their trajectory as sounds and images passed through the bars of the Jonas's family persecutions. Words were also thrown out the window of a train on its way to the death camp of Theresienstadt:

---

9   "[T]he whole city is ravaged, is it in destruction or construction, I no longer recognize anything, I will get lost" (*OSJ*, 5).

[I]ls ne pouvaient pas avoir une bonne de moins de cinquante ans on leur a enlevé toute l'argenterie, et nous à Oran Omi et moi nous avons reçu une carte postale que Hete a jetée du train: "Nous partons je ne sais pas où, nous ne savons pas où nous allons" on n'a jamais su qui l'a envoyée de Theresienstadt. C'était quelqu'un.
(OS, 147)[10]

Cixous grows up with those words uttered by her mother and Omi. Sometimes they are sweet delights such as *"Torte mit Schlagsahne"* (cake and whipped cream),[11] they are night-time songs by Goethe, or they carry the darkness of the worse poisonous words. What Cixous sees, what she allows us readers to see in *Gare d'Osnabrück à Jérusalem*, is words. German words. German words spread in Cixous's writings of Germany, but they are more directly addressed in *Gare d'Osnabrück à Jérusalem*. Cixous's books have always spoken in German, but *Gare d'Osnabrück à Jérusalem* is probably the most "German" of all her books in terms of the use of the language. I counted a minimum of 242 words and occurrences in German in *Gare d'Osnabrück à Jérusalem* (this count includes words that appear more than once).[12] The vast majority of

---

10 "[A]nd they were unable to have a servant of less than fifty years of age, all the silverware had been taken from them, and the two of us in Oran, Omi and I, had received a postcard that Hete had thrown from the train: 'We are leaving for I don't know where, we don't know where we're going' we never learned who sent this card from Theresienstadt. It was someone."
11 In this passage, Cixous recounts her first visit to Germany with her grandmother Omi, in 1951: "Köln 1951 est épanouie, prospère, si si, je viens d'Alger. Et de Londres où on a faim et des tickets de rationnement. Alors qu'à Köln, enfin je rencontre pour de vrai les énormes Torte mit Schlagsahne, dont Omi a nourri mes rêves pendant toute la guerre. Délicieuses. Encore aujourd'hui pour moi, les meilleures" (*AA*, 25) ("Köln 1951 is radiant, thriving, yes yes, I'm from Algiers. And from London where people are hungry and there are ration cards. Instead of that, in Köln, at last, I experience for the first time for real the humongous Torte mit Schlagsahne, with which Omi had filled my dreams during the totality of the war. Delicious. Today still, for me, the best ones"). Cixous expands on this trip while wondering if she had visited Osnabrück at the time: "Reste le mythe d'Osnabrück: y suis-je allée avec Omi? Ou ai-je rêvé que j'y suis allée? Je m'y vois avec elle dans les rues étroites, je nous vois à Nicolaiort [sic], comme en rêve" (*AA*, 25) ("There remains the myth of Osnabrück: did I go there with Omi? Or did I dream that I went there? I see myself there with her in the narrow streets, I see us in Nicolaiort [sic], as in a dream").
12 Here is the exhaustive list of all the German occurrences in *Gare d'Osnabrück à Jérusalem* (*GO*): *"in der Hose," "in der Hase"* (13); *"der Oberbürgermeister"* (21); *"ermordet"* (24); *"Ermordet"* (31); *"deportiert," "ermordet"* (32); "Kristallnacht" (not highlighted), *"Dreck"* (37); *"Halt dein Maul"* (40); *"Judenhaus"* (twice), "Hauptbahnhof" (not highlighted) (45); *"vornehm; ermordet"* (51); *"das verstehe ich überhaupt nicht*, dit ma grand-mère, *Onkel Andre hat sich total geirrt"* (52);

those words, often in complete sentences, are not translated. This raises a host of questions. One possibility could be precisely that they highlight their visibility per se, that they occur as raw shapes and sounds, as graphic occurrences; this way of reading them aligns with Alechinsky's "reading" of Cixous that we review below. They paint a "photograph" of Germany as a written obligation to write and, at the same time, to not write in German. They are part of Cixous's mother tongue and not "foreign" entities. Those words stand up in the text as ambassadors, as witnesses, as German signifiers, *before signifying anything*. They are in German as reminders of their existence as words that have to be deciphered, therefore watched, monitored, surveilled, contemplated and de-picted. But what aggravates this "profiling" of the words-shapes is that many of them are precisely here to stress their condition as oppressing, torturing signs, as signs of the oppression that they were turned into. This is where the foreignness of those words arises. They

---

"Kristallnacht" (not highlighted), "Kristall" (twice, not highlighted) (53); "*furchtbar, ekelhaft, widerlich, dreckig, hässlich, grässlich, entsetzlich, schauderhaft und so weiter*" (54); "*Osnabrücker Judentempel fällt*" (56); "Zuckerkrönchen" (twice) (60); "*Andreas Jonas ein Vater; Stationen*," "Vater du bist alt liebes kind," "Zuckerkrönchen" (not highlighted) (61); "Zuckerkrönchen" (not highlighted) (63); "Zuckerkrönchen" (not highlighted) (66); "les mots en '*-ung*'; *-ung, -ung, -ung; -dung, -tung* (prononcer oung, guttural, comme ang, dans angoisse, ungoisse, oungoisse), *-bung, -rung*"; "*-ung;* Vertreibung. Vernichtung. Entrechtung." (not highlighted) (69); "*-ung!; Jude; sich melden*" (70); "'*Achtung! Juden!*'"; "'*Der Führer Kennt nur Kampf Arbeit und Sorge. Wir wollen Ihm den Teil abnehmen Den wir ihm abnehmen können*'"; "'*Entjudung*'" (72); "Zentrum" (not highlighted) (74); "*Liebste Helene / Nach gutter Reise kamen wir in einem netten Hotel. Wir spazierten durch schöne Strassen mit alten Prunkhäusern lauter Kaufhäusern. Leider ist es kalt: Eben kommen wir aus einem gemütlichen Restaurant wo gut und zu viel assen. Morgen ist ein busy day with the mayor, a woman. Love and kisses, your loving mother / Gruss aus Osnabrück*" (90); "*Weder oder nicht*"; "Domtorte" (not highlighted) (93); "Herr Oberbürgermeister" (not highlighted) (94); "*ein Knirps*" (95); "Ariesierung"; "Zentrum" (not highlighted) (96); "Bürgermeisterin" (not highlighted) (97); "Abmeldung nach Zukunft" (not highlighted), "Recht Friede Toleranz Wissen" (not highlighted) (98); "Stolpersteine" (not highlighted), "*Nach guter kam ich in einem netten Haus an und fand Ève, Omi, Éri und Gruppe, lauter netten Frauen von heute vor. Wir spazierten durch rauschende sprechende Strassen*" (101); "*Unheimlich*" (103); "Arierparagraph" (104); "*Osnabrück Hauptbahnhof*" (110); "*Für immer*" (111); "Hauptbahnhoffnung" (as mentioned earlier, this word combines *Hautpbahnhof* and *Hoffnung*: "central train station" and "hope") (113); "*Stationen; Für immer in Palästina*" (114); "*gemütlich*" (131); "*Wertheim Deutsche Herren Mode; Christliche Weihnacht = Jüdischer Verdienst; Lebt der schaffende Deutsche Mensch demnach in Hinterhäusern und Keller Wohnungen*" (133); "es ist Zeit." "Kann ich nicht" (not highlighted) (136); "*Stationen*," "als Lehrer" (not highlighted) (137); "Bürgermeisterin" (not highlighted), "Mitbürger" (not highlighted) (145); "*Schlimm*" (twice), "*Ekelhaft, grässlich; widerlich*" (151); "*Opfer; das ist schlimm*" (152).

mark a certain impossibility of writing German while simultaneously attesting to the fact that Cixous writes in German, that she has to write in German to be able to write. They mark without contradiction—these options are coextensive—the impossibility and the necessity to write in German. As toxic words, words that killed the Jonas family, they are the name, in German, of the impossibility of German and Germany. Some of the German words of Cixous's mother and grandmother tongue become estranged, these are the Nazi words that dig the gap of an abyssal void within the mother, within Moi-Omi. The German language is twisted from the inside; everything that is and sounds "German" in this history is twisted, poisoned. Cixous's tormented account of the void that the genocide digs in her family is what at once holds together and threatens her entire œuvre, especially books such as *Gare d'Osnabrück à Jérusalem*. Like the bars of the prison in Montaigne's Roman Charity, *Gare d'Osnabrück à Jérusalem* utters the prisons-words, poisonous substances that the Nazis made of the German language.

This aspect finds its logic in another modality of Cixous's writing-painting, with another *alter ego* that has had a considerable influence on Cixous's life and a remarkable impact on Cixous's latest publications, notably, the ones that have Germany in sight. Pierre Alechinsky offered his own "reading" of *Gare d'Osnabrück à Jérusalem* while painting, or, to be more precise, drawing. In *Chapitre Los*, in 2013, Alechinsky also painted "Was ist los?" in German, "What is going on?" He painted "Si près," "So Close" in Cixous's *Si près* in 2007, while using the "S" to draw a cypress when he reversed the design of the two words "Si près" (in French the pronunciation of "Si près" is the same as "Cyprès," phonetically). Alechinsky's reading of Cixous follows our notion of writing as painting, of painting while writing, of using the words as meaningful forms as a reminder that the signifiers of writing are intrinsically tied to figurative notions.

In *Gare d'Osnabrück à Jérusalem*, Alechinsky chose to write-paint (and draw)[13] the word "Kristall" (Crystal), on page 6; "Erinnerung" (Memory), on page 35; "Hiob" (Job), on page 57; "Ekelhaft" (Disgusting), on page 81; "Zuckerkrönchen" ("little crown sugar"), on page 105; "Ariesierung" (Aryanization), on page 127; and "Vertreibung" (Expulsion), on page 149 (*GO*).[14] The way Alechinsky graphically represented those words is such that the word sometimes does not immediately appear as legible; its morphology does not physically stand up as a

---

13 Alechinsky used charcoal to write those words. Of course, when we use the word "paint," here, it is for its generic meaning, as a way of graphically rendering or building a visual representation.
14 The drawings are reproduced in the English version; we refer to the words as translated into English by Peggy Kamuf on page 135 (*OSJ*).

word. This articulation of the shape and its meaning, or of its identification as a signifier, is a strong marker of Alechinsky's work overall. In many of Alechinsky's works, reading the shapes resembles the poetic activity that one engages while reading the shapes of clouds or stains, or the oracular procedure in Delphi. The idea that some readers would not immediately read and see the graphic forms as words was confirmed by my discussion with Hélène Cixous and Pierre Alechinsky. In this painted writing, in this textual image, we are prone to see what we do not see, or not, and this could serve as a physical depiction of a certain status of the out of the frame within the frame, within the transformative tensions that we have circumscribed when analyzing Cixous's relationship to the photograph of October 23, 1935, but also what we envisioned in Cixous readings of Montaigne, and more specifically anything in Montaigne (both the Tower, the *Essays* and the *Voyage*) that deals with the status of the figure, of the figuration, of the figurability. This defining feature of the image gives space to the void of the genocide and allows the phantoms of Germany to enter. Such a regime of transformations suggests that Alechinsky's painted words have the same properties as the ones identified in our (previous) analysis of the Vision (more specifically the Vision that Cixous had in the Tower of Montaigne).

It is notable that out of Alechinsky's "seven drawn substantives"— as they are called on the front cover of *Gare d'Osnabrück à Jérusalem*—*Erinnerung* and *Zuckerkrönchen* are not directly related to the pain of the past, to the trauma of Nazism that the others explicitly carry. There is a fine line between seemingly anodyne but loaded words, such as *Erinnerung* and other toxic Nazi words. This line traces the divide within the same language (but is it really the same language?)—between life and death.

Erinnerung (remembrance, memory) comes from the verb *erinnern*, which means the capacity to put inside, to inscribe/read the interiority and to allow it to be relived or revived. *Erinnerung* is what Cixous does in her books of Germany, between languages. It is also possible that "Erinnerung" appears in German to mark the deconstructive nature of all the ethymological differences at play: *Erinnerung*, remembrance, memory, *mémoire*—without even mentioning "souvenir"—are not the same thing. She remembers the delights uttered in German by Omi. But the act of remembering through the Vision also takes her—and us—to the heart of darkness. Then, we have the word "*Zuckerkrönchen.*" *Zuckerkrönchen*, we might say, is a sweet name, meaning "my little sugar crown," a term applied to Irmgard by her father Andreas Jonas. A fine line. The word signifies love, the love of a father for his daughter. But this is also tragic. It leads to the disastrous ending of Andreas. Irmgard is Andreas Jonas's daughter who already lived in Palestine in 1935, at the time when Andreas left Osnabrück to go settle in Palestine; Irmgard rejected her father when he arrived in Palestine, and he decided to go back to Osnabrück.[15] And there is also *Hiob*, Job, the biblical figure. Alongside *Zukerkrönchen*, *Hiob* and *Erinnerung*, Alechinsky "wrote" and "drew" poisonous words, one word expressing the disgust (*Ekelhaft*), the others being the worst markers of the Nazi persecution, *Vertreibung*, *Kristall*, *Ariesierung*. Prison-words, the words that *performed* the mass-killing. A close look at the 242 words in German in *Gare d'Osnabrück à Jérusalem* would lead to a similar conclusion: that a great schism, a cruel split has dismembered the German language in its interiority, in its intimacy, in its chest. And further, that, for Cixous, saying German words, and sentences, speaking and writing in German, can at the same time revive the delightful German tastes, the melodies and sensations of Osnabrück where she was-was not, and also signify the worst tortures. In a similar fashion to what Cixous sees through the Roman Charity in Montaigne's Tower, hell and paradise are the two overarching entities of this textuality, of these figures.

Seeing this tension with the words and images of Germany means seeing through the bars of the prison; it means that we are also asked to be seen by them, that those words judge us as contemporaries of those persecutions, that we have a relationship to the genocide today. We are seeing the persecution and we are being seen, we are taken as witnesses of its existence. This is quite literal in Alechinsky's writing-painting. One possible reason why those words are made barely legible is that they all seem to carry a face in them. There are two eyes and a mouth drawn on the letters, and depending on how we orientate the drawing on the page, we distinguish a word, or a face, or an abstract drawing. It could be that those faces are faces of the persecutors. But they could also depict the faces of pain, the torment of the quartered victims. Sad, angry, desperate faces? Dislocated, trembling words? Grotesques? Arabesques? Long after the genocide, long before it happened: "Je *voisdéjà*" (*GO*, 15) ("I *alreadysee*" [*OSJ*, 5]), *Fürimmer* (*GO*, 111; *OSJ*, 85).

---

15 *GO*, 59 *sq*; *OSJ*, 43 *sq*.

Figure 15 Hélène Cixous and Karin Jabs-Kiesler on the site of the "well kept," "dead Synagogue" ("la Synagogue morte […] bien soignée" [*RB*, 74]) of Osnabrück, October 23, 2019.

Part III

An originary move
The move of the origin (1938)

Quand ma grand-mère a obtenu son expulsion inespérée, Osnabrück est arrivé à Oran comme l'exotisme incarné. Je résume:

Ma grand-mère a obtenu son expulsion à la fin de l'an 1938. Elle n'a parlé à personne de la Kristallnacht. Le mot de Kristall est arrivé à Oran pour désigner les verres de Bohême. Ces verres étaient trop beaux pour être vrais. On n'a jamais bu dans ces verres. C'est impossible. Les verres sont toujours debout sur leur étagère. Ils sont pleins de silence. Personne n'a jamais osé avoir poussé la curiosité d'entamer le silence venu d'Osnabrück.

Omi était à Osnabrück le 9 Novembre 1938?

(GO, 53–4)[1]

---

1 "When my grandmother obtained her unhoped-for expulsion, Osnabrück arrived in Oran like exoticism incarnate. I summarize: / My grandmother obtained her expulsion at the end of the year 1938. She spoke to no one about Kristallnacht. The word Kristall arrived in Oran to designate Bohemian glassware. These glasses were too beautiful to be real. We never drank from these glasses were too beautiful to be real. We never drank from these glasses. It was impossible. The glasses are always standing on their shelf. They are full of silence. No one ever dared to push curiosity to break the silence come from Osnabrück. / Omi was in Osnabrück on November 9, 1938?" (*OSJ*, 37).

Nine Omi was in Osnabrück ...

Nous y serons dans le prochain livre, pensai-je.

Osnabrück où il n'y a plus de juifs.

—On prend le train à la gare de l'Est et on voyage toute la nuit, dit ma mère, les mots revenaient, ses morts s'apprêtaient à venir à notre rencontre, ses yeux brillaient.

J'aurais dû être heureuse.

Je ne peux pas écrire ce livre. Ni commencer ni finir. Pas encore.

Nous voilà toutes les deux dans la cuisine avec Omi notre mère dans le récit, Eve épluche les oignons et je verse un torrent de larmes.

(OS, 230)[1]

J'aurais voulu-lui-poser-des-questions, et voilà ce que souffle le fameux regret qui mordille tant de cœurs, lorsque, longtemps après que la source est tarie, ils sont pris du tourment d'une triste soif, c'est trop tard, il n'y a plus de temps, il n'y a plus d'eau, on souffre désormais de la mélancolie de saint Augustin dont se plaignait Derrida, Sero te Amaui, je t'ai aimé(e) trop tard. C'est toujours comme ça: les questions arrivent essoufflées longtemps après que les réponses se sont retirées

trop tard, le dernier des Juifs-aktionnés est mort, c'est toujours pareil les parents n'ont rien dit, ils ne parlent pas du passé, les parents sont des

---

1 "We will be there in the next book, I thought. / Osnabrück where there are no more Jews. / —One takes the train to the East train station and travels overnight, my mother said, the words were coming back, her dead were about to come to meet us, her eyes were shining. / I should have been happy. / I cannot write this book. Neither begin nor finish. Not yet. / Here we are, the two of us in the kitchen with Omi, our mother in the tale, Ève peels onions and I pour a torrent of tears."

personnes qui ne parlent pas à leurs enfants, les parents savent que leurs enfants ont tant d'autres choses en tête, ils ont l'avenir et personne ne sait ce que c'est, les enfants ne posent pas de questions aux parents, puisque les parents ne demandent pas aux enfants de leur poser des questions, le passé est le passé, parce que les enfants ne demandent pas ce qu'a été le passé, les questions mènent à d'autres questions, on n'a jamais vu de réponses répondre aux questions, c'est toujours pareil, dit ma mère, chez les anciens Allemands et chez les anciens Juifs aussi, silence,

l'être humain est anachronique, j'ai remarqué, on enterre quelqu'un et tout de suite après on se dit, ah, dommage, j'aurais dû lui demander, dit ma mère, tu ferais bien de me poser des questions avant, je ne me rappelle déjà plus le nom de ton père,

(N, 81–3)[2]

car ce fut le temps Unique dans l'Histoire, certains ont tout oublié, certains se souviennent de chaque minute de l'Unique, personne ne sait avec exactitude ce que c'est qu'oublier, ce que les souvenants oublient, ce que les oubliants n'oublient pas, combien de temps dure l'oubli, le souvenir,

l'auteur se souvient-il une fois pour toutes afin de pouvoir oublier.

(N, 33–4)[3]

---

2   "I would-have-loved-to-ask-her-questions, and that's what whispers the famous regret that chews so many hearts, when, long after the source has dried up, these [hearts] are taken by the torment of a sad thirst, it's too late, there is no more time left, no more water, one suffers from now on from saint Augustine's melancholia, the one which Derrida suffered, Sero te Amaui, I loved you when it was too late. It is always like that: the questions arrive out of breath long after the answers have receded / too late, the last of the 'aktioned'-Jews has died, it is always the same story, the parents haven't said anything, they do not talk about the past, the parents are people who do not speak to their children, the parents know that their children have so many things on their minds, that they inhabit the future and nobody knows what it carries, the children do not ask questions to their parents since the parents do not require the children to ask questions to their parents, the past is the past, since the children do not ask what the past was, the questions lead to other questions, we have never seen answers answering questions, it is always like that, my mother says, among the ancient Germans and among the ancients Jews too, silence, / the human being is anachronical, I noticed, we bury someone and as soon as it's done, one thinks, uh, what a shame, I should have asked him/her, my mother says, you should really start to ask me questions before, I can even no longer remember the name of my father."
3   "because it was the Unique time in History, some have forgotten everything, some remember every minute of the Unique, no one knows with certainty what

Les parents n'ont rien dit. Silence. The parents said nothing.
Osnabrück où il n'y a plus de juifs. Osnabrück where there are no Jews anymore.
Void. What is the history of the void? How can one archive the empty book?

> Cela fait des dizaines d'années, quarante disons, je peux dire soixante ou quatre-vingts en m'adressant au lecteur de 2020, que je n'arrête-pas-de-ne-pas-écrire le fameux livre
> J'écris toujours assise, debout, marchant sur la voûte de ce fameux livre que j'ai sous les pieds comme un tombeau vide. Le Livre Vide. Le Livre de Vie. Le Lit Vide. Tous mes livres sont des déviations du Livre Vide. Ce qui me retient c'est la peur de découvrir l'immense ignorance de mon propre secret qui me sert d'étoffe à vivre.
>
> (BM, 66–7)[4]

The empty book is sent to us from 2001, when *Benjamin à Montaigne* was written, to 2020. A book arrives in 2020 from 2001 and says to us that it is like a blank note, that this book is the Empty Book, "Livre Vide," and an empty bed, "Lit Vide." The signifier "lit vide," in French, also lets the book turn into a "pale bed," a book that would have the complexion of a corpse; the signifier "Lit Vide" can be heard as "livide," which can also be translated into "pallid," "deathly pale." The deathly pale book rests on an empty bed.[5] It arrives like an enigmatic blank piece of paper slipped into the mailbox of 2001 and sent to the 2020 recipients. Today. A postponed book, a deferred reading, a "deviation," writes Cixous, the deviation of 2001 in 2020 of the emptiness, the void, the blank, the pallid absent text on which Cixous sits, walks; she walks

---

it is to forget, what the rememberers forget, what the forgetters do not forget, how long the forgetfulness lasts, the remembrance, / the author remembers once and for all in order to be able to forget."

4   "It has been so many years, let say forty, I can say sixty or eighty while addressing the reader from 2020, that I-do-not-stop-writing the famous book / I write always while sitting, standing, walking on the vault of the famous book that lies underneath my feet like an empty tombstone. The Empty Book. The Book of Life. The Empty Bed. All of my books are deviations from the Empty Book. What holds me back is the discovery of the immense ignorance of my own secret that serves as my fine fabric in order to live."

5   This chain of signifiers that ties the bed to a death bed probably goes back to the death of Hélène Cixous's father as it appears in many of her texts, including the earliest ones like *Tombe*, in 1973; Hélène Cixous, *Tombe* (Paris: Éditions du Seuil, 1973).

on the vault of the empty tombstone that lies under her feet. All of Cixous's books ("tous mes livres") are "deviations of the empty book." The book slips. It is not the book itself that we are reading, but its deviations. And what "deviates" in an infinity of forms is the empty book of the origin, of the origins. The book does not deviate from the origin. *It is the deviation of the origin.* Cixous's origins. The missing origin. This arc is our subject.

The book is empty, and as such it encrypts a secret that remains inaccessible to its own author but without barring the route to creation. To writing. The *need to write* is even greater. This is the deviation at the origin, *the need*, it is required for the author for her to be alive and not merely "create." At the origin is the need. It occurs as a deviation. This is what life, what *pour la vie* means—"H.C. for life!" proclaimed Derrida.[6] Being alive and creating do not make any difference for the poet Hélène Cixous. The creator in Cixous is greater than she is; it is even older than she is. There is such a thing as "I write" because of the underlying structure of secrecy and emptiness that exceeds the constraining boundaries of time in 2001 to 2020 (dates are always fictitious), for Hélène Cixous wrote in 1969 that she was born in Westphalia, Germany, 200 years ago.[7] Cixous's archive of "there was nothing" spreads all over her œuvre of the past forty to eighty years. Sixteen years after *Benjamin à Montaigne*, it is reiterated in *Correspondance avec le Mur* in 2017: "La moitié du feuillet du calepin du Shelley Hotel, sur laquelle il n'y avait rien" (*CM*, 117). It was not meant to happen this way, but there was *nothing* on the piece of paper that the narrator of this book mistakenly and inadvertently slipped in the *Mur des Lamentations* (the Western Wall) in Jerusalem. In a comedic but also somewhat tragic scene, the Freudian slip of a blank paper into the Wall is one of the many occurrences of the empty document—and what a document!—at the core of Cixous's writing. In this case, it is not incidental that the scene occurs at the core of a text that associates Jerusalem and Osnabrück, a link so loaded that it also appears in another book that Cixous writes during this period of her life, *Gare d'Osnabrück à Jérusalem* (2016).

---

6   Derrida, "H.C. pour la vie" (Derrida, *H.C. for Life*).
7   "Je suis née il y a deux cents ans en Westphalie et il y a trois cents ans en Espagne, il y a six cents ans en Palestine, il y a cent ans en Afrique, et depuis une fois ou deux ici et là; le désert; autant que nécessaire; personne; aucune raison" (*D*, 149) ("I was born two hundred years ago in Westphalia and three hundred years ago in Spain, six hundred years ago in Palestine, one hundred years ago in Africa, and since then, two or three times here and there; the desert; as much as needed, nobody; no reason").

The Freudian slip of Jerusalem, which she only discovers upon her return to Paris after a trip from Osnabrück to Jerusalem, is the rediscovery of an incredible oblivion. What is not meant to happen has already happened, and it is a repetition of the same primitive scene of the book that is not written. However, the scene is always eventful and performative at the core of what it repeats, in the sense that it always takes a different, unpredictable form. Deviation. Perhaps the dream keeps awakening her, the same dream configured with different settings, different protagonists, sounds and colors, forms, times and locations. The veil of the origin—a rare word in French, "voile" can be "la voile" and "le voile," la, le, she, he ... both feminine and masculine. The origin reveals itself as an encrypted Freudian slip, which is per se, a slip of the origin. The slip operates behind a veil, a mask, and presents itself disguised in the form of the masquerade. The blank paper, as a mask, as a veil, reveals the void in a comedic-tragic masquerade.

It could also be that the veil is a screen, like a movie screen, on which the dream of writing projects itself: it reveals everything while keeping everything secret and encrypted.[8] When she realizes that she has put the wrong paper in the Wall, a blank paper, she cannot believe what she has done. She cannot believe it happened. Cannot believe it happened *again*—even though it is the "first time"—there is no such thing as the "first time," which is why it is unbelievable. Can the first time repeat itself as such, always the first time? It seems that the slip is bound to happen at another time in the future without being able to predict when and how and through which form. From archiving the empty book to archiving the oblivion, the forgetting of the blank paper in the Wall is a persistent echo in Cixous's entire œuvre, in which the oblivion is central:

> car ce fut le temps Unique dans l'Histoire, certains ont tout oublié, certains se souviennent de chaque minute de l'Unique, personne ne sait avec exactitude ce que c'est qu'oublier, ce que les souvenants oublient, ce que les oubliants n'oublient pas, combien de temps dure l'oubli, le souvenir,

---

8   This notion is in line with André Bazin's idea that the *cinematic* screen is less the frame of a picture (drawing or painting) than a "cache," a cover, a blindfold or a "mask" (this last term is what the translator Hugh Gray chose): "L'écran n'est pas un cadre comme celui du tableau [drawing or painting], mais un *cache* qui ne laisse percevoir qu'une partie de l'événement." Bazin, *Cinéma*, 160. ("The screen is not a frame like that of a picture ['tableau,' i.e., drawing or painting] but a *mask* [my emphasis] which allows only a part of the action to be seen" [Bazin, *Cinema*, 105]). Roland Barthes also comments on this aspect in *La chambre*, 90.

l'auteur se souvient-il une fois pour toutes afin de pouvoir oublier.

(N, 33–4)[9]

Writing is this operation in which the oblivion projects itself on the blank paper. *Benjamin à Montaigne* and *Correspondance avec le Mur* explore the "Unique time in history," that of the oblivion. There is a subtle network of correspondences among the empty book, the oblivion, the Freudian slips and the empty beds of memory in Cixous's books. Such an archive fever—*mal d'archive*, as Derrida puts it—is as old as the theme and act of writing in Cixous's life. As soon as she started to write, she dealt with the feeling of not-writing, that feeling that not only was writing deemed incongruous at the time when she composed her first texts but also that writing was in relation to a "right to write" in face of the multiple effacements of origin, which, in the same move, blocked *and* induced the inner necessity of writing. Among those effacements and (self)repressions is one that occurs especially at the "beginning" of her career as a writer, when she has the feeling that she is stealing a right to write that she does not have (or deserve). She feels that she has to write in secret, for herself, to hide.

From writing in secret, in hiding, to writing *the* secret, to confronting herself with essential secrets, Cixous's hauntology opens a powerful quest that has taken a remarkable turn with *Osnabrück* in 1999. Cixous's trajectory on writing has gone from the singular, "I," Cixous, "am writing in secret" in a gesture that informs her initial *venue à l'écriture* as a *woman*, to the "us," us "wom*en* writing." With the publication of her 1999 "récit" titled *Osnabrück* we see the eruption of another instance of a complex "us." The history of women (to be more precise, women in her family) is, this time, in sight. Osnabrück, Germany, is the city of her mother, Ève, the city of her aunt Éri, of her grandmother Rosi Klein, Omi. There is always more than one mother.[10] It is the city of Helene Jonas geboren Meyer, Hélène Cixous's great-grandmother, city of more than one H[e]él[e][è]ne. Osnabrück operates as a

---

9 "[B]ecause it was the Unique time in History, some have forgotten everything, some remember every minute of the Unique, no one knows with certainty what it is to forget, what the rememberers forget, what the forgetters do not forget, how long the forgetfulness lasts, the remembrance, / the author remembers once and for all in order to be able to forget."

10 This could be the meaning of the enigmatic sentence that Cixous utters in Jean-Jacques Lemêtre's audio creation: "—Comme s'il n'y avait qu'une seule mère" ("—As if there were only one mother." Lemêtre, *Ceci est un exercice*, 00:02:14 and 00:03:04). Only one mother, as if there were, only one mother. There is always more than one in the mother, more than one mother exists in the mother. Many in one.

mother-grandmother-great-grandmother-aunt-city where Cixous had never set foot before 2015, that Cixous only knew mentally, so to speak, through the ways by which it was "narrated" and quite literally "brought" to her through the lives of her female ancestors in Oran, Algeria—this marks the birth of "us." To make this clear, Cixous has always written with this "us."[11] This "us" is what-who writes with her. But as soon as she begins to write with Germany, with the complex narrated *topoï* produced by the aforementioned "us," it is "us three women plus one, the four women" from Germany, Ève, Omi, Hélène, in Oran and beyond, that takes center stage. To add a layer of complexity, this family and the history of "us-women-Jewish-German-Family," to be considered in Part IV, is the history of "us" as a void, as a "I do not know" that cannot, by definition, be written:

> En vérité je ne sais rien de Nous, je suis devant Nous comme devant l'incroyable, on ne peut pas écrire un livre sur l'incroyable, on ne peut pas écrire un livre sur l'incroyable vérité je ne Nous crois pas, le fait de notre existence se situe au-delà de l'au-delà de tout croire et de toute croyance.
>
> (*BM*, 67)[12]

She writes "us," she is "us writing," and this "us" obeys the same structure of I-do-not-stop-writing-the-book-I-am-not-writing ("je n'arrête-pas-de-ne-pas-écrire le fameux livre"), of writing the void that lies at the core of "our" history, the history of "us" that I do not know *je ne sais rien*. *Incroyable*-unbelievable. An impossible story, an impossible narration, marked by the repression of the women's voice, by the impossibility of "us," of saying, of writing "us." Writing about this impossibility: what does it mean to say "us" when "us" is a synonym with "I don't know anything" (about us)? History, for "us," is the history of the impossibility to narrate, history of the aporia at the core of "us," a blank paper slipped inadvertently in the Wall of disbelief. Yet, there is a wall. The wall could very much be the veil, the screen behind which the story of "I don't know anything" lies, but it remains the name of the

---

11 Of course, "us" can often be read as the rise of an "us women" in Cixous's public life and in her writings, in a move that informs the creation of the Centre d'Études Féminines et d'études de genre at the University of Vincennes in 1974—among many powerful political gestures. With Germany "us" becomes more personal, intimate. The fact that this intimacy is related to German figures directs our analysis.

12 "In truth I do not know anything about Us, I stand before Us as before the unbelievable, one cannot write a book about the unbelievable, one cannot write a book about the incredible truth I do not believe Us, the fact of our existence is situated beyond the beyond of believing everything and of all belief."

Impossible. The wall, the concrete wall, the concretion of the Impossible is the only thing that seems to remain. It attests to the existence of what is not accessible. The impossibility of writing "us," she tells us, is the impossibility of us. Could this be the letter that Benjamin *à Montaigne* is sending *us* from 2001 to 2020, the letter addressed to us (2001), to the future "us" (2020) today, *if "us" exists*? If we, "us," exist today, gathered around Cixous's name and œuvre to read her together, together we are posing the question with Cixous, of knowing who is "us," many "us(s)," we are asking who is with us, we are posing the abyssal question, "What kind of story am I telling you, am I telling us, today, the story of what brings us together, here and now, in 2001–2020?" This is the history of Cixous's name in our history. "Our" history is inseparable from the history that was not narrated (to us) as it is depicted here in her book *Osnabrück* in 1999. The story of what was not narrated arrives with someone. This has to be recalled to memory. This non-story has a name. This name is "Omi":

> Omi n'a pas narré. Sa fille collectionne les traces car elles sont tout l'héritage de ma mère, ses perles, ses coraux, ses tableaux ces frères et sœurs déposés en images dont Omi sa mère ne pouvait naturellement détacher le regard de ses yeux bleus anormalement bleus. Comment parler du frère qu'elle aime sans le perdre sans l'enrouler dans du papier et l'embaumer, Omi aimait faire rouler les noms des siens sur sa langue ils n'étaient pas ses éloignés sinon par les distances, ils l'habitaient présents et je les ai moi-même encore entendu nommer vivants par la voix de ma grand-mère, ils étaient dans sa chair elle faisait l'appel et ils répondaient, ceux qui étaient morts dans les camps aussi, elle leur donnait encore sa chair pour demeurer. Andreas Jenny Paula Moritz Hete Zalo Zophi Michael Benjamin
>
> Ensuite commença le conte. Et ce n'est plus du tout la même histoire ni les mêmes personnages. Ceux d'Omi étaient différents les uns plus intérieurs, plus chéris plus chauds plus sanguins parfois ils avaient des humeurs, des chagrins et jusqu'au désespoir. Ceux d'Omi encore vivants d'elle après leur mort. Les mêmes racontés par ma mère.
>
> (*OS*, 129)[13]

---

13 "Omi did not narrate. Her daughter collects the traces because they are the entire legacy of my mother, her pearls, her corals, her paintings these brothers and sisters registered in images from which Omi her mother naturally could not detach the gaze of her blue eyes, abnormally blue. How to speak about the brother that she loves without losing him without wrapping him in paper and

A possible name for the Wall is "Omi." From there, the Wall will have many names, including "Osnabrück." Starting with *Osnabrück* in 1999, Cixous writes the book of *Omi n'a pas narré* "Omi did not narrate." Ève, Rosi's daughter, Ève, Hélène Cixous's mother, collects the traces, she archives "images" from Omi's family, from her sisters and brothers. But how is it possible to talk about the brother Rosi loved without losing and "embalming" (embaumer) him? How can one narrate without extinguishing him, without accepting the idea that he is gone? His name is "Andreas." Through Omi's voice Andreas and his brothers and sisters were more cherished and warmer; they were hotheaded ("sanguins"), despondent ("chagrins"), they were still embodied by Omi-Rosi, they were housed ("ils habitaient"), they were living beings while named by Omi, housed in Omi's flesh—they all responded, those brothers and sisters of hers, they answered when she called them, even when they had died in the Nazi death camps, like Andreas. We have opened this reflection while considering the photographs of Osnabrück in Cixous's family photo albums. They have names in Omi's flesh ("chair")[14] to "demeurer," a beautiful verb in French that reminds of the "demeure"—home, residence, refuge—that has the proper meaning of what stays and remains, of the remainder and the roof, but also lets the vibration of death erupt in its signifier "demeure." "Demeure" phonetically contains "meurt" (die), and it calls out names who "demeure," who stay, remain, and reside in Omi: "Andreas Jenny Paula Moritz Hete Zalo Zophi Michael Benjamin" (*OS*, 129) ....[15] This also explains what "Omi n'a pas narré" means: there was no need to narrate because they were *demeurant*, they were still around when Omi was around, they were hosted in Omi's flesh-refuge, and they remained. Omi, who, after all, was one of them, *needless to say*, needless to narrate.

---

embalming him, Omi liked to let the names of her loved-ones roll on her tongue they were not far away in spite of the distance, they inhabited her, present, and I heard them myself being named alive through the voice of my grandmother, they were in her flesh she called them up and they responded, those who were dead in the camps too, she still gave them her flesh for a home. Andreas Jenny Paula Moritz Hete Zalo Zophi Michael Benjamin / Then the story begins. And it is no longer at all the same story nor is it the same characters. Omi's were different some most intimate, more cherished, warmer, more hotheaded, sometimes they had moods, griefs, to the point of despair. Omi's loved ones were still alive through her after their deaths. The same narrated by my mother."

14 To this notion of Omi's flesh, her *chair*, in French, we could add the importance of the body, of the feminine body in Cixous's idea of feminine writing, so essential for us in these pages "je les ai moi-même encore entendu nommer vivants par la voix de ma grand-mère, ils étaient dans sa chair" (*OS*, 129).

15 The poetic occurrence of "demeure" in Cixous's text reminds of its powerful deployment in Jacques Derrida's book, *Demeure Maurice Blanchot*; Jacques Derrida, *Demeure Maurice Blanchot* (Paris: Galilée, 1998).

Figure 16 Andreas Jonas and Else Jonas's stolpersteine, Osnabrück, Germany, October 23, 2019.

"Ensuite commença le conte." The tale started. And that is Ève's part. "Les mêmes racontés par ma mère." The same recounted by Ève, Rosi's daughter, Cixous adds. It is interesting to note that "Omi did not narrate" is a part of how Omi's characters were gone but not lost, in a sense, that Omi kept them while not "talking," but "rolling" their names on her tongue ("Omi aimait faire rouler les noms des siens sur sa langue"). In Omi's omissions they were fleshy, sensual, oral, accentuated, phonological, in her blood. Omi's characters change when they are passed to another generation. Omi, Cixous's grandmother, was born on April 24, 1882,[16] in Osnabrück and died in Paris, France, on August 2, 1977.[17] She lived with Hélène Cixous at home for a while. As indicated earlier, Ève, Hélène Cixous's mother, was born on October 14, 1910, and she passed away on July 1, 2013. With *Osnabrück* in 1999, the story of Hélène Cixous's German family makes its way through an entire book for the first time. Prior to this date, they have always been here, but less

---

16 Stephen P. Morse and Peter Landé, "German Jews," 2012, available online: https://stevemorse.org/germanjews/germanjews.php?=&offset=39551 (accessed July 20, 2020); Blank and Blank, *Genealogy*.
17 "Mort d'Omi à l'âge de 95 ans" indicates the biographical note at the end of *Photos de Racines* (*PR*, 212) ("Omi dies at the age of 95" [*R*, 211]).

explicitly, for all kinds of reasons that might align with the ways those characters were embodied by Omi until the late 1970s.[18] When Osnabrück reappears in the title of a book by Cixous in 2016 (*Gare d'Osnabrück à Jérusalem*), the scene of the blank paper slipped in the Western Wall echoes another loaded word. A word replaces the void that leads Cixous's writing and questioning and relaunches the questioning. This word is "night." The night. Night of the narration. The books see the night, and they also see *in the* night—the night that hosts, absorbs, extinguishes, captures and encrypts all questions. The question-night, "nuit de la destruction du monde-Osnabrück" (*GO*, 55),[19] "nuit fendue, violente, secouée de tremblements. On n'en parlait pas" (*GO*, 55–6; my emphasis),[20] this night precipitates all the questions. It is very late in the book when the story of not-talking-about-it appears. The delay of the deviation is infinite. This delay, the late book of the Night, is the deviation. The veils of the night have covered and silenced the entire family from Osnabrück except one single person named Marga, who lives in Jerusalem in 2016 and constitutes the pretext for Cixous's trip to Osnabrück to Jerusalem and the reverse, physically and in writing. Omi is gone, Éri and Ève are gone, and all the questions crystallize even as they remain unanswered:

> Quand ma grand-mère a obtenu son expulsion inespérée, Osnabrück est arrivé à Oran comme l'exotisme incarné. Je résume: Ma grand-mère a obtenu son expulsion à la fin de l'an 1938. Elle n'a parlé à personne de la Kristallnacht. Le mot de Kristall est arrivé à Oran pour désigner les verres de Bohême. Ces verres étaient trop beaux pour être vrais. On n'a jamais bu dans ces verres. C'est impossible. Les verres sont toujours debout sur leur étagère. Ils sont pleins de silence. Personne n'a jamais osé avoir poussé la curiosité d'entamer le silence venu d'Osnabrück.
> Omi était à Osnabrück le 9 Novembre 1938?
> Omi est composée des traits suivants: 1) les robes de soie luisante 2) le mot de Kristall qu'elle utilisait pour désigner les verres de Bohême, arrivés avec elle à Oran. Des verres élevés comme des cloches d'église, mélodieux lumineux. On les

---

18 Needless to say, this period is crucial to Cixous's literary and theoretical production. Her works on feminine writing could be reevaluated in light of the relationship that Cixous is having with her grandmother and mother as it appears later in *Osnabrück*.
19 "[Ni]ght of the destruction of the world-Osnabrück" (*OSJ*, 39).
20 "[C]loven night, violent, shaken by trembling. One didn't speak about it" (*OSJ*, 39).

regardait. On les désirait. Ils montaient hauts comme des tiges de roses métamorphosés sur leur étagère. On n'osait pas. [...]
—Omi était à Osnabrück le 9 Novembre 1938? demande ma fille.
—Sans aucun doute, dis-je. D'une manière ou d'une autre. Entre Osnabrück et Jérusalem.

(GO, 53–4)[21]

Omi was in Osnabrück on November 9, 1938? Indeed, during the deadly November night, she was in Osnabrück. Was she? No doubt. Yet the doubt persists. What kind of doubt? The repetition of the question in this fragment sets the tone. The first occurrence lets it surface from the text written by Cixous. Then it is addressed by "my daughter" ("ma fille"), echoing the chain of transmission and transformations of "Omi did not narrate" and the "same story recounted by my mother," now told by Cixous and voiced by Cixous's daughter in a question: "—Omi was in Osnabrück on November 9, 1938?" Not "—Was Omi in Osnabrück on November 9, 1938?" but rather the distorted grammar of an exclamation, of the incredible, of the unbelievable. "—*Omi was in Osnabrück on November 9, 1938?*" is a rhetorical question. The rhetoric of an exclamation, of a question-exclamation "?!" that cannot believe that it could be true.[22] This is an exclamation of incredulity, of course. Unbelievable utterance, utterance of disbelief in what could very much be in dialogue with the Freudian slip of the Western Wall, facing the wall of a rhetorical question turned into utter stupefaction. We find this

---

21 "When my grandmother obtained her unhoped-for expulsion, Osnabrück arrived in Oran like exoticism incarnate. I summarize: / My grandmother obtained her expulsion at the end of the year 1938. She spoke to no one about Kristallnacht. The word Kristall arrived in Oran to designate Bohemian glassware. These glasses were too beautiful to be real. We never drank from these glasses were too beautiful to be real. We never drank from these glasses. It was impossible. The glasses are always standing on their shelf. They are full of silence. No one ever dared to push curiosity to break the silence come from Osnabrück. / Omi was in Osnabrück on November 9, 1938? / Omi is composed of the following traits: (1) dresses of shiny silk (2) the word Kristall that she used to designate the Bohemian glassware, arrived with her in Oran. Glasses raised like church bells, melodious luminous. One looked at them. One desired them. They mounted high like rose stems metamorphosed on their shelf. One didn't dare. [...] / —Omi was in Osnabrück on November 9, 1938? asks my daughter. / —Without any doubt, I say. In one way or another. Between Osnabrück and Jerusalem" (OSJ, 37–8).
22 This interpretation is also enriched by my experience of listening to Hélène Cixous reading this text aloud. It was clearly a question-exclamation. Not a question but the sound of a stupefaction.

imaginary conversation with Ève again one page later in *Gare d'Osnabrück à Jérusalem* in 2016, three years after Ève's death:

—Qu'est-ce qui s'est passé? —C'est ancien. Je ne me rappelle pas. J'aurais tant aimé pouvoir continuer cette conversation avec ma mère. Quand je l'aurais conduite jusqu'au mystère du 9.11.38, je lui aurais dit, en observant l'effet de surprise sur son visage et dans l'espoir de recueillir une de ces phrases inimitables dont elle seule avait le secret recueillir une de ces phrases inimitables dont elle seule avait le secret.

(*GO*, 55)[23]

Nobody answers the questions:

—Omi était peut-être déjà en Algérie? dit ma fille.
Comment le savoir? Plusieurs fois, dit ma fille, j'ai eu envie de te dire, si Ève ne répond pas on n'a qu'à demander à Éri. Mais Éri aussi ne répond pas.
—Je sais qu'Omi sait, dis-je, où qu'elle soit. Andreas Jonas aussi est à Osnabrück en novembre 1938. Il regarde l'histoire de sa vie brûler. C'est lui qui fait à Rosi le récit de la nuit de feu. Je sais qu'il récite en sanglotant. Je sais qu'il ne pleure pas la synagogue, il pleure sa fille, dans l'écroulement monumental du bâtiment l'embrasement des souvenirs-images Irmgard la dernière fois c'était quand?
Il n'a peut-être rien dit.

(*GO*, 56)[24]

Rosi (Omi) and Andreas are in Osnabrück on November 9, 1938, when the Synagogue of Osnabrück goes up in flames. A narration begins. It

---

23 "—What happened? —It's a long time ago. I don't remember. / I would like so much to have been able to continue this conversation with my mother. When I would have led her to the mystery of 11/9/38, I would have told her, while observing the effect of surprise on her face and in the hopes of gathering up one of those inimitable sentences for which she alone had the secret" (*OSJ*, 38).

24 "—Omi was perhaps already in Algeria? says my daughter. How to know? Several times, says my daughter, I've wanted to tell you, if Ève doesn't answer one has only to ask Éri. But Éri too doesn't answer. / —I know that Omi knows, I say, wherever she is. Andreas Jonas is also in Osnabrück in November 1938. He watches the history of his life burn. He's the one who tells Rosi the story of the night of fire. I know he tells her while sobbing. I know he is not crying for the synagogue, he cries for his daughter, in the monumental collapse of the building the burning of the Irmgard memories-images the last time was when? / He perhaps said nothing" (*OSJ*, 39–40).

is also a narration within the narration, that of Andreas telling Rosi, his sister, the story of the fire: "C'est lui qui fait à Rosi le récit de la nuit de feu. Je sais qu'il récite en sanglotant" (*GO*, 56).[25] The repetition of "I know" in the account is the symptom of what one does not know: "He might not have said anything" to Rosi … As if he had said, in the book, what he might not have said. And at the core of this structure, Cixous herself ("dis-je") writes: "I know" ("je sais"). I know. Might. An account of the account that might not have taken place. Because Omi did not narrate, *Omi n'a pas narré*. This is what "I know." What I know has been taken by the flames, the tale has been taken over by the ashes of the synagogue. That's the story of "I know what Omi did not narrate" consumed by the fire, by the Night. This Night is in Omi's flesh that contains the flesh of "Andreas Jenny Paula Moritz Hete Zalo Zophi Michael Benjamin" (*OS*, 129).

What remains of the Synagogue of Osnabrück appears three times in Hélène Cixous's books. It appears the first time in 1994 in *Photos de Racines*, the first published confrontation that Cixous engages with her "roots"—her roots in pictures, photographs of her roots. Among those roots is the ruin of the synagogue in Osnabrück. A photograph is reproduced in a small format with a caption that reads: "La synagogue dévastée par les allemands" (*PR*, 190).[26] This same photograph appears in *1938, nuits* in full page (*N*, 171). The remains of the synagogue, the empty spot, the synagogue that no longer stands in Osnabrück—this was our second stop on the day of our arrival when I traveled with Hélène Cixous in October of 2019. In *Ruines bien rangées*, a photograph of the location of the Synagogue of Osnabrück is the memorial that gives its title to Cixous's book. The first stop upon our arrival was for Friedrichstraße 25, where Andreas Jonas and his wife Else had their last domicile.

At this location (see Figures 16, 17, 18, 19 and 20), Hélène Cixous leaned toward the ground and touched Andreas and Else's stolpersteine.[27] Then, after a short walk from Andreas's residence, we stood in silence in front of the memorial replacing the synagogue (see Figures 21, 22 and 23).

---

25 "He's the one who tells Rosi the story of the night of fire. I know he tells her while sobbing" (*OSJ*, 39).
26 "The synagogue destroyed by the Germans" (*R*, 188). This picture appears in the final section of the book, titled "Album et légendes" (*PR*, 177 sq) ("Albums and legends" [*R*, 175 sq]). The word "legend" means "caption" in French but is also used for "legend" or "tale."
27 I saw Hélène Cixous touch the Tower upon her arrival in Montaigne. She similarly touched the pink stone of the memorial of the Rosenstraße in Berlin (see the conclusion of this book).

Figure 17 Friedrichstraße, where Else and Andreas Jonas lived until 1942.

Figure 18 Friedrichstraße 25, Else and Andreas Jonas's residence, Osnabrück, October 23, 2019.

Figure 19 Touching Else and Andreas Jonas's stolpersteine, Osnabrück, October 23, 2019.

Figure 20 Hélène Cixous in front of Else and Andreas Jonas's residence, Osnabrück, October 23, 2019.

Omi was in Osnabrück 169

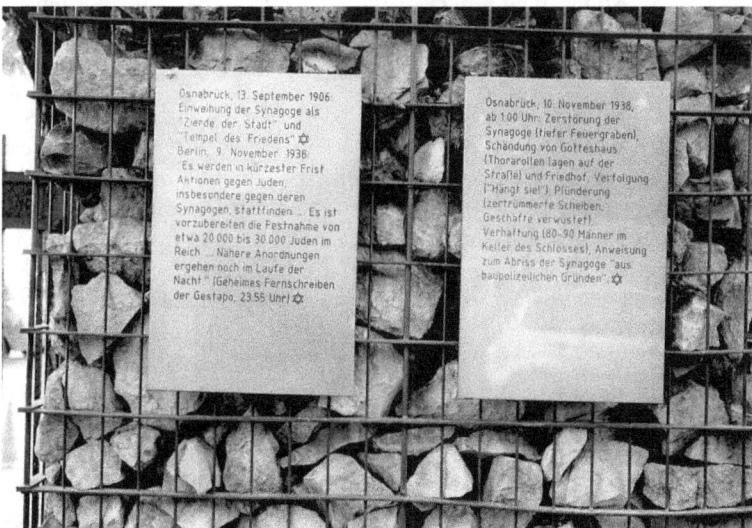

Figures 21 and 22 "Ruines bien rangées": the "well-arranged," "well ordered" ruins of the Osnabrück Synagogue (Memorial), October 23, 2019.

Figure 23 "Ruines bien rangées": the "well-arranged," "well ordered" ruins of the Osnabrück Synagogue (Memorial), October 23, 2019.

"Omi did not narrate" from *Osnabrück* in 1999 has transformed into Omi's silence about November 9, 1938, in *Gare d'Osnabrück à Jérusalem* in 2016. "Le silence venu d'Osnabrück" (*GO*, 53), ("The silence come from Osnabrück" [*OSJ*, 37]), "*come* from Osnabrück," which should also be understood in French as a "silence brought to Oran from Osnabrück, transported to Oran from Osnabrück, arrived from Osnabrück." "Ne touchons pas au silence" (*GO*, 160) ("Let us not tamper with silence" [*OSJ*, 130]) is the last sentence, after the "FIN" (*GO*, 155) ("THE END" [*OSJ*, 126]) of *Gare d'Osnabrück à Jérusalem*. Silence is, and has, the last word. It is a heady silence. A powerful one, as apparently Omi does not keep it; this silence arrives with her in Oran from Osnabrück, as if she had been kept by this silence, as if *she was* this silence. She was the silence that kept her. This is what occurs to Hélène Cixous, who is one-and-a-half-years old and in Oran in "November 1938," when Omi arrives in Algeria to live under the same roof as the Cixous family, according to Cixous in *Photos de Racines*. November 1938. But *when* in November? It all boils down to that. Was it *before* or *after* November 9? Question. Exclamation point. One could not establish the date with certainty. Is it the beginning or the end of the story? The beginning and end of "I know." The beginning of Cixous's writing of the empty book. In a sense, Omi's silence might indicate that, for her as a potential witness, the event is nonexistent; Omi might have or might not have been in Osnabrück on November 9, 1938. The event of the arrival of Omi's silence is and is not constituted as such. How can one say that the silence is an event? It will take years, decades and several layers of transmission from Omi to Ève to Cixous and her daughter, until Cixous, in 2016, asks herself the question that revolves around "Omi-n'a-pas-narré" (*OS*, 129) "Omi-did-not-narrate": "—Ne-pas-en-parler a été une des lois de cette histoire, dit ma fille" (*GO*, 150).[28]

---

28 "—Not-talking-about-it has been one of the laws of this history, says my daughter" (*OSJ*, 120).

Ten "Bericht"

Silence, night: "tout le monde se tait du coup tous ces silences font à la nuit une sorte de souffle haletant" (*N*, 19), "everyone keeps quiet so that all these silences give some sort of breathless breath to the night."

This is *1938, nuits*, published by Hélène Cixous in 2019. "One of the laws" (*OSJ*, 120) of this history-story is the silence of the night that breathes throughout the empty book. This publication attests to the insistence of the theme, of the origin of the un-narrated. The book notably revolves around the great mystery of Omi's attitude toward the event of the burning of the Synagogue of Osnabrück on November 9, 1938, *if* she was around on that night. While the subject remains an obsessive question mark, *1938, nuits* seems to be less unsure about whether she was present or not and instead focuses predominantly on what exactly happened during this night in Omi's mind. The shift from Omi's silence to the "Night" of 1938 is geared toward the fate of a man, Siegfried Katzmann, who was in Osnabrück on November 9, 1938. Siegfried Katzmann was among the Jews arrested and thrown by the Nazis into a cave in Osnabrück to be transported later to a concentration camp. The victims of these arrests are known as the "Aktionjuden":

> [C]eux qui ont comme *attendu* la *Kristallnacht* pour décider subitement de s'en aller, ceux-là qui n'ont pu vouloir partir que quand on ne pouvait plus partir, les Katzmann par exemple et Omi ma grand-mère
> sauf Siegfried qui n'a pu partir quand c'était impossible qu'en passant par Buchenwald afin d'être Aktionné.
> [...]
> Nikolaiort 2, par la fenêtre elle donnait sur l'horlogerie-bijouterie Kolkmeyer NSDAP en chef, elle ne voyait pas qu'elle

voyait la bannière du Reich pendre depuis la fenêtre jusqu'au sol, elle ne voyait pas qu'elle ne voyait pas ce qu'elle voyait, depuis 1938 elle ne voyait ni 1933 ni 1942, une femme si distinguée.

(*N*, 101)¹

This silence is not only a silence about what happened but an even more primal silence. It is a silence, for Omi, of having seen what she was not seeing, that she saw. It was right before her eyes on Nikolaiort (see Figures 24 and 25). Through the window of her bourgeois apartment in this central place in Osnabrück, she could see her neighbor and fervent Nazi supporter, the jeweler Kolkmeyer, whose Nazi banner was

Figure 24 Nikolaiort, October 23, 2019.

---

1 "[T]hose who *waited* for the Kristallnacht to decide suddenly to go away, those who were only able to want to leave when it was no longer possible to leave, the Katzmanns, for example, and Omi my grandmother / except Siegfried who was only able to leave when it was impossible by passing through Buchenwald in order to be Aktioned. / […] / Nikokailort 2, through the window she overlooked the watchmaking-jewelry store Kolkmeyer NSDAP in chief, she did not see that she saw the banner of the Third Reich hanging from the window to the ground, she did not see that she did not see what she saw, since 1938 she has not seen, neither in 1933 nor in 1942, such a distinguished woman."

Figure 25 Nikolaiort, October 23, 2019. The building where the Jonas family used to stand before the war is located on the left.

hanging on the building. She could see that. She could see that she did not see that she saw that she did not see. In 1938. *1938, nuits* allows us to see this silence of the eyes. "What does it mean to see?" asks the empty book, the book of silences that now becomes a book of blindness within what is there to be seen. It is as if Cixous was always, and throughout more than one book (and maybe throughout all of her books as the book she is not writing), attempting to *picture this enigma for herself*. The book might be an attempt to picture herself what Omi saw that she did not see. And it is compulsively inscribed in one question. Was Omi in Osnabrück in 1938? Could it be that she *saw* the Nazi banner? This apparent lack of sight is the blind origin of the book(s) relating what cannot be pictured. Could the book act or serve as a substitute photograph for what Omi saw that she did not see? The book of an impossible photograph. The book as a blindfolded camera or as a camera that photographs the blindfolded. Could the book be the *impression* of not-seeing-what-is-there-to-be-seen? What is an impression, here? The impression of what did not seem to impress Omi's internal camera. The impression of "silence"? Of "not-narrating"?

The book. Even the *form* "book" is in question. *Camera obscura* or *camera lucida*? Where to place this camera on such a photo set is a question. The form "book" is also at the core of the book *1938, nuits*. Night: *camera obscura*. The form-book is very often a question, a subject, a character in Cixous's books. Could the book be an optical device? In Cixous's first book of Germany, *Osnabrück*, the writer-operator of the camera-book thinks that she should instead drag the device from the underground to put it in the kitchen:

> Ce livre devrait commencer dans la cuisine et pas sous la terre pensai-je ce matin à sept heures ici même pendant les préparatifs orageux du petit déjeuner, l'orage de l'aube dans la cuisine devant les placards et dehors la tempête du siècle les hurlements des temps passés présents et passés passés des rafales des guerres qui ne troublent pas la pure concentration de ma mère sur les objets obéissants.
>
> (*OS*, 15)[2]

---

2 "This book should be starting in the kitchen and not underneath the earth, I thought this morning at seven even on this very spot even as the stormy preparation of breakfast was taking place, the storm of dawn in the kitchen in front of the cabinets and outside the thunderstorm of the century the screams of the past present and of the pasts passed the gusts of the wars that do not trouble the pure concentration of my mother on the obedient objects."

176   The "German Illusion"

"It looks like a book" ("on dirait un livre" [*N*, 9]), writes Cixous at the beginning of *1938, nuits*. We have already paid attention to the call (Part I), to the telephony of the dream that seems to awaken Hélène Cixous when she is called by her mother at 2:00 a.m. during a night in July: "Vers 2 heures de la nuit de juillet, maman m'appelle d'en haut. Je me lève" (*N*, 9).[3] It rings in the dark. Dawn will soon appear and she will be awakened. Is it a dream? The second paragraph of *1938, nuits* recalls that Cixous's mother had left on the night of July 1st, five years earlier, in 2013 (we are in 2018 in this scene). She left the *camera* at night. At night she calls. Cixous's mother is calling in a dream set at the first extremity of a book in a first chapter that will end with a strange text-photograph, a facsimile of what the book will soon refer to as "Bericht" in German, the "report" in English. The *Bericht* will be the book in the book, the book of the book that she is/is not writing. After having paid attention to the telephony of this passage (Part I), the form of this object—the empty book, the book-I-am-not-stopping-to-not-write?[4]—is our focus. Right now, it's a "package" thrown by her mother: "elle me jette par la fenêtre en urgence un paquet précieux" (*N*, 9).[5] Cixous's mother alerts her daughter that she is hastily throwing a small precious package through the window of a dreamlike sequence. Dawn will come soon. This "Bericht" is not coming to us, like Omi's silence, in a language that would be unattainable. The event reported by the "Bericht" is German, written in German, its nature is undefined; it looks like a book, it is and is not a book, it is a "thing," it shines (lucida) in the dark (obscura):

> Il faut sauver cette chose que ma mère m'a lancée et dont j'ignore la nature. Dans l'obscurité. Brille. Un petit paquet blanc, net, enveloppé de papier. On dirait un livre. Je le ramasse. Quel poids! Pas de doute, c'est de l'or. Je remonte avec ce trésor vêtu de papier blanc.
>
> (*N*, 9)[6]

Inside the package is a "document," a "text," a "folio," "typed with a typewriter," and its formal qualities make it look like a "report in

---

3   "At about 2 in the night of July, mom calls from above. I stand up."
4   A passage we already analyzed: "je n'arrête-pas-de-ne-pas-écrire le fameux livre […] Le Livre Vide" (*BM*, 66).
5   "[I]n a state of emergency she throws me a precious parcel through the window."
6   "This thing that my mother threw me and whose nature I ignore must be saved. In the dark. Shines. A little white parcel, neat, wrapped in paper. It looks like a book. I pick it up. How heavy! No doubt, it's gold. I climb back up with this treasure dressed in white paper."

German" ("rapport en allemand" [*N*, 14]) that is then qualified as "Fred's deposition. Full to breaking point" ("déposition de Fred. Pleine à craquer" [*N*, 14]):

> [J]auni et racorni, sans titre, sans aucun intervalle, sans alinéa, sans signature, sans couverture.
> Il y a des virgules et des points, mais pas de vide, ce texte n'a pas le temps, il roule vit lourdement, comme un bélier à épaisse toison parcourt un grand troupeau de brebis dans le rêve d'un chef de guerre, depuis la première phrase jusqu'à la dernière ligne il est sans relâche.
>
> (*N*, 10)[7]

Later in Cixous's book we learn something factual about the origin of the "document":

> Ma mère laisse traîner le rapport de Fred, c'est-à-dire de Siegfried, sur une étagère depuis l'année 1986, elle ne le lit pas. Ça ne sert à rien, elle est contre le couteau dans la plaie.
>
> (*N*, 79)[8]

We have already commented on the conditions of this discovery. It is when Hélène Cixous was moving her mother's belongings from her Parisian apartment that her son found "Fred's report" ("le rapport de Fred"). Cixous immediately makes a crucial specification: it is "Siegfried's report" ("c'est-à-dire de Siegfried"). The way in which Cixous recalls how her mother described the "report," whether it is fictionalized or not, focuses on the impossible nature of the "object" in a structure that remains in profound dialogue with Cixous's own deconstruction of the object-book-writing-text-document-empty-book:

> —Fred m'a envoyé une lettre impossible, dit ma mère. Je ne crois pas qu'il s'adressait à moi. Trop long. T'as pas besoin de lire, dit Fred.

---

[7] "[Y]ellowed and hardened, without title, without a single indentation, without paragraphs, without signature, without cover. / There are commas and points, but no spacing, this text doesn't have time, it rolls, lives heavily, like a thick-fleeced ram traveling along a great herd of ewe in the dream of a warlord, from the first to the last line, it is relentless."

[8] "My mother has left Fred's report lying around, that is, Siegfried's, on a shelf, since the year 1986, she doesn't read it. There's no point, she is against the knife in the wound."

—C'est tout Fred, dit Ève. Ce n'est peut-être pas lui qui m'a écrit, ça n'est pas signé. J'ai pas lu. Tout ça c'est du passé. Pour moi, c'est un livre que quelqu'un n'a pas écrit. Ne pensait pas écrire. Ensuite, il y a ce volume, on ne sait pas quoi en faire, alors on l'envoie. Herbert aussi m'a envoyé. Marga m'a envoyé son autobiographie, qui ça aurait intéressé? Je ne sais pas où elle est. Je me méfie de la grosse tête, tu connais cette expression en français?
C'est pas une lettre.
C'est un livre que quelqu'un n'aurait pas pu écrire. Si c'est un livre. L'auteur n'a pas d'importance. Ce qui compte ce sont les Événements.

(N, 25)[9]

"[An] impossible letter" sent by Fred; Fred, who promptly recommended that his friend Ève not read the document. "For me it's a book that someone has not written," says Ève. One does not know what to do with this "volume." Here, the notion of "empty book" is ingrained in Hélène Cixous's maternal words. It is the core of the historical experience at the core of Hélène Cixous's family. A ~~book~~, a non-book that someone would not have been able to write. The author is of no importance ... and so on. We do not know who writes. The shapeless, deformed nature of the object is sealed with the effacement of its "author." It is the letter without letter of a text without quality, density and form. Its literal absence of quality, its lightness that leaves no impression, is what makes its letter a "letter" from which Fred is effaced, absent as an "author." Although it emanates from "Fred," it is unsigned. This "thing" takes the shape of its effacement as a thing. This is the book of Fred's effacement and of Fred's "away-ness." The author is of no importance, writes Cixous, as if it was important to conceive that the author does not carry (*portance*) the book and the book does not carry an author's name. The author is of no weight, does not leave an impression in terms of pressure, press or print. It is as close as possible to ashes. The trace of the extinction of a possible trace. The ashes of the synagogue. It is infinitely light, so light that it was forgotten, nearly

---

9   "—Fred has sent me an impossible letter, says my mother. I don't believe that he was writing to me. Too long. You don't need to read, says Fred. / —That's typical of Fred, says Ève. It might not be him who wrote me, it's not signed. I haven't read. All that is the past. For me, it's a book that someone did not write. Did not think to write. Then, there's this volume, he doesn't know what to do with it, so he sends it. Herbert too, sent to me. Marga sent me her autobiography, who would be interested in that? I don't know where it wound up. I am very wary about getting a big head, do you know this expression in French? / It is not a letter. / It is a book that someone should never have been able to write. If it is a book. The author is of no importance. What counts is the Events."

lost, on a shelf in Ève Cixous's apartment since 1986. The thing emanates from Fred *in absentia*. This lightness of Fred in how he transmits the thing, the lightness of a text that is not meant to weigh in, is all the more so "important" in that it does not weigh anything at all. The thing erupts as an intruder in the night without disturbing anything, seemingly somewhere in the dead zone between absence and effacement. And *this* is what makes it spectacular. The spectacle here, if any, is what Cixous calls "the Events," "les Évènements," with a capital "É." The event is what carries weight. Not the text itself. As if the event had ignited and consumed the possibility of the text-ash. The "event" for which the text is an absent substitute arrives to us in the German language: "Die Synagogue brennt" (*N*, 23). This is the non-book of "Die Synagogue brennt." The synagogue burns. The burn burns the author and the "book." It sucks the air all around. Ève asks, "Tu as déjà vu tellement de mots sur une seule page? Bon pour le papier, oui. Pour moi, ça manque d'air" (*N*, 15).

The lack of air is the report. The report becomes a character as it talks about itself with Cixous's writing slipping into the flesh of this character:

> C'est que lorsqu'il y a imminence de feu ou d'eau de marée l'espace est brutalement retiré, il n'y a pas une ligne à perdre, chaque millimètre compte, chaque instant est du luxe, en une heure ou deux on bourre la cave d'environ cinq mètres sur deux d'à peu près vingt Juifs de la ville, [...]. Le boyau de pierre n'est pas élastique, mais la chair vivante l'est plus que ce qu'on aurait cru.
>
> Voilà à quoi fait penser la page en danger d'étouffement.
>
> (*N*, 15)[10]

It is the book imprisoned, this apnea of writing. As noted earlier, in addition to the aforementioned uncertainty regarding the author, and maybe, as a critical component of this uncertainty, the question of who writes is inscribed in the proper name of the "author." The event synagogue-brennt is the deconstructed "what" of writing. It deconstructs the "who" of writing as it cancels the author in more than one language through a variation-deviation of appellations. The language of this

---

10 "It is when there is an imminence of fire or of tide water that the space is brutally pulled out, there isn't a single line to lose, every millimeter counts, every instant is luxury, in one hour or two, one crams the basement of five by two meters with about twenty Jews of the town, [...]. The narrow passage of stone is not flexible, but the living flesh is, more than one would think. / That's what the page in danger of suffocation brings to mind."

cancelation of the "what" and of the "who" is inscribed in the ways that Cixous's appellations of the object vary from "small book" ("un petit livre" [(*N*, 9]), to "a small white parcel" ("un petit paquet blanc" [(*N*, 9]), to "deposition" (*déposition*, in the legal sense of the term), to "folio document typed with a typewriter" ("un document folio tapé à la machine" [*N*, 11]), to "report in German" ("rapport en allemand" [*N*, 14]), to "book" ("livre"), to "impossible letter" ("Fred m'a envoyé une lettre impossible" [*N*, 25]), says Ève, to "a book" ("un livre" [*N*, 25]), to, finally, a "report" in German, "Bericht." In a strange scene set after Fred's settlement in Des Moines, Iowa, in 1940, Fred would have sent his "*Bericht*" to Walter Benjamin "in 1941," that is, after Benjamin's suicide in Portbou, Spain, on September 26, 1940: "En 1941, il ouvre les yeux, le temps entre dans sa chambre, il envoie son *Bericht* à Walter Benjamin" (*N*, 62). Furthermore, from 1941 to 1985, the meaning and nature of the *Bericht* has changed:

> Du reste le texte ne tarde pas à être périmé, sa langue se démode, des mots nouveaux apparaissent, [...], à la place circulent de grands noms plus modernes, le *Bericht* devrait se traduire en nouvel allemand européen pour se présenter à ceux qui viennent après son histoire, Fred lui-même n'est plus Fred Buchenwald.
>
> (*N*, 66)[11]

"Fred 1938–1941" had meticulously taken notes without which he would not have been able to "reanimate" (réanimer) "Fred 1985–1986," writes Cixous (*N*, 67). And this is why Dr. Katzmann in Iowa 1985–1986 is able to "speak in the place, in substitution of" (parler à la place de) Siegfried 1938–1941 (*N*, 67). The abyssal structure of the deviation: from Siegfried in 1938–1941, to Fred, to Fred in 1985–1986, to Ève who "forgets" the document on a shelf until Cixous discovers it after Ève's escape in 2013, to Cixous who writes *1938, nuits* in 2019. According to Cixous, Fred had written this "*Bericht*" before putting his luggage down on the ground (in the United States [*N*, 74]). Aside from the fact that this second occurrence of the word *Bericht* on page 74 seems to consolidate the notion of a name with the impossibility to name the object, "*Bericht*" occurs to *immediately* be substituted by another name: "Quand Fred se lance dans le récit d'un *Aktionjude*," writes Cixous (*N*, 75). "Récit," "story," is another new name. This time, it is related to the specific act of telling

---

11 "Moreover the text isn't slow to become out-of-date, its language becomes unfashionable, new words appear, [...], instead, big loaded names circulate, more modern, the Bericht must be translated into new European German in order to introduce itself to those who will come after its history, Fred himself is no longer Fred Buchenwald."

the story, of bearing witness, that Cixous has already deconstructed a few pages earlier. Cixous refers to Walter Benjamin's famous 1935 text on the *Erfahrung* in which Benjamin highlights the fact that during the Great War (1914–1918) soldiers were not coming back "richer" in experiences but poorer, which means that the very notion of "*Erfahrung*," experience, had lost its value (*N*, 67).[12] So even when Cixous poses the word "récit" to qualify the text, it is to remove the term in the footsteps of Benjamin's famous interpretation. From now on, the word by which Fred's text is referred to will be "*Bericht*," as on pages 76, 77, 129 and onward.

Through the countless deviations of the empty-book for which *Bericht* is a substitute word, the only "thing" that seems to remain tangible is the German language. Siegfried Katzmann arrived in Ellis Island, New York, in 1939 (*N*, 62).[13] In the United States, he becomes Fred, which appears to be the name used by Ève to call him back in 1986. Ève, whose name at birth was Eva, Eva Klein. German is the language that Fred—the immigrant who lives in the United States of America—elected to use when he wrote the *Bericht*. It is also what is at stake in this suffocation of the text. German, as a choice, is an answer to the questions that the book-non book named "*Bericht*" raises. In German the *Bericht* becomes and builds the wall that it confronts. German is the wall in which the blank-paper-ashes of the *Bericht* is slipped. The wall is Germany:

—Tu l'as lu? dit mon fils. Je suis debout devant un mur indéchiffrable. Il aurait pu l'écrire en anglais, on l'aurait lu peut-être.

—Ces choses-là on doit les écrire en allemand, dit le texte sans nom et sans auteur. Avec feu et fumée qui s'élève en rouleaux noirs. Sans l'allemand elles n'arriveraient pas, elles ne seraient

---

12 This essay by Walter Benjamin was first published in Prague in the journal *Die Welt im Wort*, no. 10, December 1933, with the title "Erfahrung und Armut" (Experience and Poverty). It is reproduced in the German *Gesammelte Schriften*, vol. 2, *Aufsätze, Essays, Vorträge* (Frankfurt: Suhrkamp, 1991), 213–19.

13 "En 1939, il arrive à Ellis Island. Fin de Siegfried. Il s'appelle Fred" (*N*, 62). The possibility of changing last names is offered by the immigration services in the United States. Siegfried emigrated to the United States on April 15, 1939. He was born on August 15, 1912, in Burgsteinfurt and resided in Osnabrück at the time of his departure for the USA (Stephen P. Morse and Peter Landé, 1933 German Jews Database, "Entries 39551 to 39600," available online: https://stevemorse.org/germanjews/germanjews.php?=&offset=39551 [accessed May 13, 2023]). Siegfried was the son of the head of the Synagogue (Synagogenvorsteher) of Osnabrück.

pas arrivées, il faut les écrire nues, sans refroidissement sans arrêt sans auteur, le feu nu, chaque mot brûlant vif.

(N, 26)[14]

In front of an indecipherable wall, Germany is consumed in the *Bericht*. *Bericht* is another (German) name for *wall*. The *Bericht* is also consumed in itself in the way it is lost and kept, kept-lost in Ève's apartment from 1986, when it was addressed by Fred to Ève after a memorable trip to Osnabrück. *Bericht* is impossible, the impossible letter sent with the instruction that Ève would not read it. Lost-kept and sent to Cixous in a dreamlike glimmer of combustion during the night of July 2018. It is lost-kept, kept-lost in, by, a language tied to the Event. After all, could it be that the Event, which *1938, nuits* tells us is the only subject of the *Bericht*, could be interchangeable with the language with which the *Bericht* is revealed to us? It is German, a familiar language turned entirely estranged, a wall, a "thing" written in a German language consumed by the Event for which German is the consumption. There would be no difference between German and Fire. A German language completely overwhelmed by itself, but still addressed to "us" in an uncanny, legible idiom. "Us" German speakers, "us" Fred and Ève-Eva, us, Cixous's German, Cixous's Germany, Cixous's German-family ... to a certain point. Pif, Cixous's son, cannot read it ("je suis debout devant un mur indéchiffrable" [N, 26] ["I stand facing an indicepherable wall"]) and that is the point: after the *Bericht* this language will be extinct; in fact, the *Bericht* is already written in the language of its own extinction. *Bericht* is the extinction of the German language by the Event it recounts. A language familiar but so far from itself that it has become illegible at the core of its legibility: silence. Omi's silence? Could this be the reason why Ève never read it? Put differently, "elle est contre le couteau dans la plaie" (N, 79), writes Hélène Cixous about her mother: "she is against the knife in the wound." The *Bericht* arrives to "us" like Omi's silence, in a language that is both familiar and heterogeneous to the event of its revelation-wall.

Could "*Bericht*" be the German trope of Cixous's entire œuvre? Not *the Bericht*, but "*Bericht*," as if it was a proper name. *Bericht* as a kind of Χώρα, Plato's Khôra, that receives the form of Fred's "thing" and gives

---

14 "—Have you read it? says my son. I stand facing an indecipherable wall. He could have written it in English, and perhaps we would have read it. / —Those things can only be written in German, says the nameless, authorless text. With fire and smoke that rises in dark spirals. Without German those things would not happen, they would not have happened, they must be written in their nudity, without cooling without interruption without author, the naked fire, every word burning alive."

form to Cixous's book-non book. As if *Bericht* had always been here secretly waiting for its discovery-disappearance that is both deprived of the form while it gives form. Cixous's German turn, Cixous's German twists and turns ("revirements" and "tours" are key terms in Cixous œuvre) carries the structure of everything Cixous expresses about Fred's *Bericht* given to Ève in *1938, nuits*: forgotten, lost, never opened and retrieved by Cixous through a book of *Bericht* in 2019. Key to this structure is the German language as a wall that at once deprives the book of its significance and is the profound significance of *Bericht*. As if *Bericht* had to be written in German, German the trope that operates, again, maybe one last time, as an act of allegiance to a German "event." This also recalls that the true Khôra of *Bericht*, that *Bericht* as Khôra, is the event itself. If an event has an "itself" ... which is what *Bericht* carries as the secret of its deconstruction. The event is deconstruction. November 9, 1938, is deconstruction. German as a language is the language of this deconstruction of November 9, 1938, German being both the point of entry and the word by which Fred exits and constitutes Germany when he writes this text in exile, far from Germany and the German language: "Ces choses-là on doit les écrire en allemand" (*N*, 26), these things should be written in German. This deconstruction at the origin, deconstruction of the origin, is the originary move. At the origin is this default named *Bericht*, a proper name for the book-I-don't-write: *1938, nuits*.

What is the event? We already gave its code-name, its proper name. A date is always the proper name of the event, the code, a crypt: November 9, 1938. Bericht is not a text, nor a book—it is an event, the event named "November 9, 1938." Omi was or was not in Osnabrück on November 9, 1938. And Fred's story of this event is Omi's secret for the Cixous family, for Hélène Cixous. It could be that this event is what holds the family together *in absentia*. In *1938, nuits*, the other name of this structure of absence-silence on which Omi-Ève-Hélène is built is "Etwas."

Eleven "Etwas"

Hélène Cixous's books are deviations of the empty book. While the empty book attests its nonexistence, it is consistent. Among possible consistencies is the date of November 9, 1938, and the silence brought to Oran when Omi arrives in "late 1938" after having been present in Osnabrück on November 9 ... or maybe not. Another consistency is a synagogue in flames. What does not exist but consists here in an empty book and a date is the ashes of the synagogue as they are figured in one photograph (which appears both in *Photos de Racines* and *1938, nuits*, as already mentioned). In *Ruines bien rangées*, the photograph of the absent synagogue, the photograph of the empty spot "replaced" by a "memorial," is the consistent emptiness for which the memory of what was there "before" operates as a trace of disappearance (*RB*, 73). A trace of what Cixous calls the empty book. The empty book consists in allowing the ashes to replace the existing synagogue. It is the book of ashes.

This logic of consistency versus existence is also what gives its undefined nature to the *Bericht* as a writing that consumes the possibilities of a "récit," a "story." What is consistent, finally, is a language, the German language, the language of "ces choses-là," the language of "those things," the language of what can only be written in German ("those things can only be written in German"), the language of the wall, of the fire, of the wall of fire. In a way, what is consistent, here, is what consumes itself in an ignited language, a language set on fire by the Nazis. German is the language of an extinction. Omi's silence in Oran is the memory without a trace of what will ultimately appear as an unnoticed extinction in the memory of the empty book.[1]

This might also explain why *1938, nuits*, Cixous's book of the *Bericht*, calls upon another German word, the language of the night, the night of all concepts, another word that embodies the absence of a signifier to signify the arrival of November 9, 1938: "Etwas."

---

1   A structure that Georges Perec has extensively explored in his œuvre, starting with *La Disparition* (1969) and *W* (1975).

"Etwas" 185

Bericht in the *Bericht*, *Etwas* appears in Hélène Cixous's book in Fred's statement as a way to qualify what arrives as an impossible story-*Récit* in German:

> Nun schien es das Etwas Kommen musste
> Que ce Chose allait arriver, était arrivé, devait arriver, être arrivé, cela semble sûr, oui presque sûr et de plus en plus sûr pas loin de Heger Tor Wall, selon que l'on est dans telle
>
> —et là Récit pourrait
> —ou telle rue, et selon le choriste sur lequel le Récit porte son attention, car chacun tremble et craint différemment.
>
> (N, 21)[2]

It is as if the impossible "Récit" had turned itself into a quasi-character in a Greek tragedy for which "Etwas," "Chose," is a quasi-interlocutor:

> [E]n vérité, vu du balcon du Récit, tout le monde se hâte vers l'Événement-Incroyable, et à chaque coin de rue, l'incroyable diminue, l'Événement nous attend tous, chacun est en train de tomber en lents tourbillons dans l'abîme du Temps.
>
> (N, 21)[3]

This event is a "Chose," "Etwas," seen by Fred's "Récit" from the "balcony" of the "Récit." *Récit* is both a character and a thing, for which the "Event," "l'Événement," takes center stage. Capital letters are assigned to all those words as notions, things and characters. Both proper and improper names. Suddenly, after adding up a number of those words with a capital letter, what erupts in Cixous's text is a single, truncated sentence set in an isolated-line with no capital letter: "—ça aura commencé comme ça—par" (N, 21).[4]

The calcined typography of the sentence is the impression of fire in many typographical creations-cremations of Cixous's *1938, nuits*. These

---

2   "*Nun schien es das Etwas Kommen musste* / That this Thing was to happen, had happened, had to happen, happened, this seems certain, yes, almost certain and more and more certain not far from Heger Tor Wall, depending on whether we are in this / —and there, Narration could / —or in this street, and depending on the chorister upon which the Narration focuses, because each one trembles and fears differently."
3   "[I]n truth, seen from the balcony of the Narration, everyone hastens towards the Incredible-Event, and in each corner of the roads, the incredible diminishes, the Event awaits us all, each one is on the verge of falling in slow whirlwind into the abyss of Time."
4   "—[I]t will have started like this—by."

can also be tracked across her entire œuvre. "Récit" in flames, a cremation within the story, where the sentences are printed by an ignited pen and the cuts are substitute signs for ashes. This is what arrives, what "happens" *in* and *as* an "Événement-Incroyable," an "Incredible-Event" in the text, something that happens *to* the text, and, more importantly, happens *in German to the German text*: *"Nun schien es das Etwas Kommen musste"* (*N*, 21). And: "de toute la suite des Événements-Incroyables dont plus tard Fred fera l'inventaire numéroté" (*N*, 22).

Numbered inventory, digit, code and crypt: this is the Incredible-Event that drives and ruins the Story-*Récit*:

> [P]our eux aussi, à 2 heures du matin, le téléphone sonne. Mon père répond et me réveille.
>
> Il y aurait alors un récit qui commencerait ainsi: À 2 heures de la nuit, *um 2 Uhr nacht schellt das Telephon: ... Fraulein Hurwitz ist am Apparat.* Mlle Hurwitz, à l'appareil, nous annonce que la Synagogue brûle. C'est difficile à croire. Si, si.
>
> (*N*, 23)[5]

If there is no story, it is not only because the event has no decipherable essence in Fred's *Bericht*, but it is also because it is tied to the fact that it has no constructible nature, no nameable existence. This "2 heures du matin" ("2 in the morning") echoes the fall of the *Bericht* sent out to Cixous at night in July of 2018. As if the beginning of the story-*Récit* of the unbelievable had not started yet, "C'est difficile à croire" ("It is hard to believe"). Cixous renders this notion as a word that names without naming, "c'est le mot qui nomme sans nommer," the word-God, "le mot-Dieu":

> L'idée que Dieu est en train de grésiller dans le temple la tue.
> Mais on peut imaginer une version trempée de larmes. Une autre difficulté pour l'auteur: le mot Événement. On ne peut pas plus s'en passer que du mot Dieu. Il advient partout, imprévisible, ouragan, déchaînant des éléments encore inconnus, émissaire de la fin du monde.
> —Sans ce mot on ne pourrait rien dire, dis-je.
> —C'est le mot qui nomme sans nommer, dit ma fille.

---

5   "[F]or them too, at 2 in the morning, the telephone rings. My father answers and wakes me up. / There would then be a narration that would start like this: At 2 in the night, *um 2 Uhr nacht schellt das Telephon: ... Fraulein Hurwitz ist am Apparat.* Ms. Hurwitz speaking, tells us that the Synagogue is burning. It is hard to believe. Yes, yes."

—C'est le mot-Dieu en français, dis-je. C'est pour ce mot que j'écris en français. Dans mes autres langues, en anglais, il n'y a pas d'Événement, en allemand non plus.

—Qui écrit ce livre?
—Est-ce un livre?

(N, 23–4)[6]

---

6   "The idea that God is in the process of sizzling in the temple kills her. / But one can imagine a version soaked in tears. Another difficulty for the author: the word Event. One can't do without it any more than the word God. It takes place everywhere, unpredictable, hurricane, unleashing still unknown elements, emissary of the end of the world. / —Without this word, we could say nothing, I say. / —It is the word that names without naming, says my daughter. / —It's the word God in French, I say. It is for this word that I write in French. In my other languages, in English, there is no Event, not in German either. / —Who writes this book? / —Is it a book?"

Twelve   Epilog

—*Je n'arrive plus à respirer dans ce cauchemar, dit Fred sans aide des mots. C'est la métamorphose de* Etwas *en torche et de la torche en bûcher mondial qui lui donne l'impression d'asphyxie. Dans un instant il n'y aura plus d'air, le monde part en fumée, il n'y a pas Dieu.*

(N, 32)¹

Could it be that Omi knew everything? That *Etwas* had no secret for her? Or is it that *Etwas*, as the point of ignition of everything, had also ignited her consciousness of the "event"? *Etwas* metamorphosized into a torch, into a worldwide stake. *1938, nuits* is the book of Fred's *Bericht* that helps Cixous get closer to the mystery of Omi. The mystery appears in more than one "German" book by Cixous. It reappears toward the end of *1938, nuits*:

> Omi n'écoute pas ma mère, ces larges étendues neutralisées qui entourent le moi d'une bande d'indifférence, même la manifestation de 1935 qui rassemble 30,000 Osnabrücker sur la place Ledenhof, c'est-à-dire *toute* la ville en âge de s'exprimer, ne propage pas jusqu'aux tympans de l'âme son effroyable vacarme de mort, c'est un peu fort, on n'écoute pas les nazis disent certains, on n'écoute pas les Juifs, on n'écoute personne.

(N, 103)²

---

1 "I can't manage to breathe in this nightmare, says Fred without the help of words. It is the metamorphosis of *Etwas* into a torch and of the torch into a worldwide pyre that gives him the impression of asphyxia. In one instant there will be no more air, the world goes up in smoke, there is no God."
2 "Omi doesn't listen to my mother, these wide neutralized expanses that surround the I of a strip of indifference, even the demonstration of 1935 that gathers 30,000 Osnabrückers on the Ledenhof square, that means that *the entire* city of speaking age doesn't spread its terrible din of death to the eardrums of her soul, it's a bit loud, we don't listen to the Nazis some say, we don't listen to the Jews, we don't listen to anyone."

Omi does not listen to her daughter Ève, either. The telephone line of Germany is cut—if it ever existed. Ève takes a trip to Germany in 1936 (Ève had immigrated to France in 1934, and later to Algeria),[3] to talk to Omi, but in vain:

—Ève n'avait pas pu faire sortir Omi. Finalement, c'est l'assassinat de la Synagogue qui l'a délivrée.
Les cas d'envoûtement sont si nombreux, dis-je, il faudrait des milliers de Freud pour les examiner.
—Freud aussi était envoûté, dit mon fils. Il lui aurait fallu un Freud.
—Et il y a aussi la famille Nussbaum, les parents, après une hésitation suisse. Eux non plus n'étaient pas des piliers de la Synagogue.

(N, 56)[4]

Ultimately, at some point, Omi will be freed by the assassination of the synagogue. But right now, in the mid-1930s, she does not see what she sees and refuses to listen to Ève. The next sentence suggests that Omi was "Envoûtée." This word is difficult to render in English. Some translations will say "bewitched." Other common translations are, "enchanted," "captivated," "fascinated." "Envoûter" comes from the Latin *in vultus*, "in the face"; it is the face that hypnotizes through a magical operation of evil charm. As the book progresses, the question of why Omi stayed becomes bigger and bigger. It seems that the more it appears in its clarity, the bigger the mystery. The closer the book gets to Omi's psyche, the farther away Omi is for the narrator. Cixous does not understand. This notion revolves around an impossible concept of what makes the home a home for Omi. After all, she is German. She was born in Germany. She had been married to a decorated German soldier who had died on the front in 1916. Germany is her homeland. But it seems that *Etwas, Etwas* as the coming Kristallnacht, takes a

---

3 "Cette Omi qui-ne-s'est-pas-rendu-compte en 1938 pensais-je et je regardais Selma et Jennie qui ne s'étaient pas rendu compte parce qu'elles étaient déjà un peu parties en 1934 et revenues encore en 1936" (*BM*, 159) ("This Omi who-did-not-realize in 1938, I thought, and I watched Selma and Jennie who did not realize because they were already a bit gone in 1934 and returned back again in 1936").

4 "—Ève was unable to bring Omi out. Finally, it is the assassination of the Synagogue that released her. / The cases of bewitchment are so numerous, I say, we would need thousands of Freud(s) in order to examine them. / —Freud himself was bewitched, says my son. He too would have needed a Freud. / —And also, the Nussbaum family, the parents, after a Swiss hesitation. Neither were they pillars of the Synagogue."

while to appear as a conscious relationship with the home that Omi inhabits:

> [C]eux qui sont rentrés à la maison, alors qu'objectivement on ne pouvait plus rentrer à la maison, je ne cesse de me dire que je ne les comprends pas. Mais pourquoi je ne les comprends pas? Et pourquoi mon esprit revient-il depuis tant d'années cogner à la vitre de cette scène?
>
> ceux qui ont comme *attendu* la *Kristallnacht* pour décider subitement de s'en aller, ceux-là qui n'ont pu vouloir partir que quand on ne pouvait plus partir, les Katzmann par exemple et Omi ma grand-mère
>
> sauf Siegfried qui n'a pu partir quand c'était impossible qu'en passant par Buchenwald afin d'être Aktionné.
>
> Selon moi les Juifs d'Osnabrück fin 1938 ne comprennent pas les Juifs 1940, les Juifs selon les dates s'entrecomprennent de moins en moins, ils se font des signes sur les quais des trains, sur les montagnes, sur les rives, ils s'appellent, ils ne s'entendent pas
>
> ma mère n'a jamais compris comment pourquoi sa mère Rosi Klein née Jonas ne comprenait pas, ce n'était pas à cause de la Synagogue, on ne peut pas dire qu'elle soit partie finalement, je n'arrive pas à entrer à l'intérieur d'Omi,
>
> Nikolaiort 2, par la fenêtre elle donnait sur l'horlogerie-bijouterie Kolkmeyer NSDAP en chef, elle ne voyait pas qu'elle voyait la bannière du Reich pendre depuis la fenêtre jusqu'au sol, elle ne voyait pas qu'elle ne voyait pas ce qu'elle voyait, depuis 1938 elle ne voyait ni 1933 ni 1942, une femme si distinguée, peut-être son mari Michael Klein mort pour l'Allemagne en 1916, croix de fer, lui murmurait-il, ne t'inquiète pas, je suis toujours là pour te protéger
>
> il y a aussi toutes les victimes de la croix de fer, ceux qui ont cru et voulu croire à la croix, malgré les avertissements des *Aktions*.
>
> (*N*, 101–02)⁵

---

5 "[T]hose who came back home despite that they objectively could no longer come back home, I keep telling myself that I do not understand them. But why don't I understand them? And why has my mind been banging on the window of this scene for so many years? / those who *waited* for the Kristallnacht to happen to decide to go away suddenly, those who were only able to want to leave when it was no longer possible to leave, the Katzmanns, for example, and Omi my grandmother / except Siegfried who was only able to leave when it was impossible by passing through Buchenwald in order to be Aktioned. / In my opinion the Jews of Osnabrück ending in 1938 do not understand the Jews of 1940, depending on dates, the Jews understand each other less and less, they

Among all the countless reasons why Omi did not leave, none is understandable. And for Hélène Cixous, who is a playwright, who knows all too well how in theatre, a writer, a troupe, lends its writing powers to characters while slipping inside a character—for Cixous, who has been able to slip inside the character of a dictator, for example, it is impossible to "enter inside Omi" ("je n'arrive pas à entrer à l'intérieur d'Omi" [N, 102] ["I cannot enter inside of Omi"]), her own grandmother. Omi-Moi, her *alter ego*. Omi is a wall. When Omi looks through the windows of her home on Nikolaiort in Osnabrück, she sees the Nazi banner of her neighbor. Her homeland is turning into a prison for the Jews and she still seems to hold on to her sense of belonging to Germany to the point that her "Germanness" seems to supersede her awareness of the threat. Her consciousness of "Etwas" and of the "assassination of the Synagogue" remains a mystery. At least, it seems to be disconnected from practical reality to a certain point. When Ève visited her in 1936, Omi did not want to follow her daughter to Oran, and it seems that exile was still not an option. "Seems": the text is full of "maybes" ("peut-être") and a form of patriotism that we will explore in the following Part:

> [P]eut-être son mari Michael Klein mort pour l'Allemagne en 1916, croix de fer, lui murmurait-il, ne t'inquiète pas, je suis toujours là pour te protéger
> il y a aussi toutes les victimes de la croix de fer, ceux qui ont cru et voulu croire à la croix, malgré les avertissements des *Aktions*.
> (N, 102)[6]

The questions of when to leave and where to go are tied to the deep mysteries of a relationship to the home, the homeland:

---

address signs to each other on the train platforms, in the mountains, on the shores, they call each other, they do not hear each other / my mother never understood why her mother Rosi Klein born Jonas did not understand, it was not because of the Synagogue, we can't say that she finally left, I cannot enter inside of Omi, / Nikolaiort 2, through the window she overlooked the watchmaking-jewelry store Kolkmeyer NSDAP in chief, she did not see that she saw the banner of the Third Reich hanging from the window to the ground, she did not see that she did not see what she saw, since 1938 she did not see, neither 1933 nor 1942, such a distinguished woman, maybe her husband Michael Klein who died for Germany in 1916, iron cross, was whispering to her, do not worry, I am still here to protect you / There are also all the victims of the iron cross, those who believed and wanted to believe in the cross in spite of the warnings of the Aktions."

6 "[M]aybe her husband Michael Klein who died for Germany in 1916, iron cross, was whispering to her, do not worry, I am still here to protect you / there are also all the victims of the iron cross, those who believed and wanted to believe in the cross in spite of the warnings of the *Aktions*."

Il y en a qui partent mais pas assez loin, c'est comme si on se déplaçait soi-même d'un KZ à un KZ, quand Frau Engers va se réfugier à Amsterdam, c'est comme si elle venait cacher ses petits dans la gueule du loup.
    Aucune explication. Je ne comprends pas pourquoi je ne comprends pas. Et si j'avais habité 2 Nikolaiort?

(N, 107)[7]

This is one reason that the mystery's persistence could be tied to the structure of "I do not understand why I do not understand." The absence of explanation is not an event that occurs at the periphery of the capacity to reason. It may be that the very notion of reasoning, of "understanding" and "explaining," has been destroyed by the event; "no explanation" might mean that "explaining" is no longer a strict cognitive concept. It is the very concept of "understanding" that is in crisis. And this crisis' name is the silence kept by a set of crystal glasses that stand on a shelf in Hélène Cixous's Parisian apartment. Crystal glasses brought by Omi to Oran in 1938. Full of silence. Of Omi's silence. They stand still. Which is why the answer to the unsolvable enigma materialized in the strange sentence, "I do not understand why I do not understand," is *poetry*. Poetry is the essence of Cixous's entire œuvre. It may be that Cixous's entire œuvre is tied to Omi's arrival in Oran when Cixous was approximately 18 months old.[8] Perhaps Cixous's entire œuvre is an attempt to answer an unanswerable question, a question contained in a set of ageless crystal glasses. This is also what it means to say "Germany" in the Jonas family.

---

7   "There are some who leave but not far enough away, it is as if we were moving ourselves from one KZ [concentration camp] to one KZ, when Frau Engers takes refuge in Amsterdam, it is as if she was hiding her little ones in the lion's den. / No explanation. I do not understand why I do not understand. And if I had lived on Nikolaiort 2?"
8   At "the end of November 1938," Hélène Cixous was almost 18 months old (she turned one on June 5, 1938).

PART IV

Zugehör
The Jewish-German psyche

Ce qui nous sépare est ce qui nous réunit, dit Isaac, c'est le mot juif. Séparéunis par la complicité qui se garde au secret, à condition de secret, comme si on ne pouvait être juifs ensemble que séparément, comme pour garder en vie le dissemblable, il faut que le désir invente la distance qui maintient en vie le désiré.

(CM, 83)[1]

---

1 "That which separates us and unites us, says Isaac, is the word Jew. Separunited by the complicity that keeps itself secret, under the condition of secrecy, as if we could only be Jews together separately, as if to keep the dissimilar alive, desire must invent the distance that keeps the desired alive."

Thirteen "Envoûté," delirium

Est-elle allemande la voilà juive.

(BM, 199)[1]

Born on June 5, 1937, Hélène Cixous lived contemporaneously to all of her family members from Germany who were persecuted, scattered and murdered in the genocide. Her œuvre is inseparable from what Cixous calls the "hideous death,"[2] and the motif of the German line-lineage carries out the complex construction of the Jewish-German trope in Cixous's œuvre of "Germany."

We have already referenced the word "envoûté" as it appears in a passage from *1938, nuits*. Among the many possible translations of "envoûté" mentioned were "enchanted," "captivated" and "fascinated." It could also be translated as "delirium." "Delirium" is the word that Derrida used extensively when he thematized the "Jewish-German psyche" in a course he taught in the late 1980s. After all, Cixous revolves around the mystery of Omi's psyche—Omi, we recall, was probably in Osnabrück on November 9, 1938, after having seen-not seen so many persecutions and attacks on Jews in Germany.

---

1   "Is she German, there she is, Jewish." Or, as my colleague Dr. Maj-Britt Frenze suggests, "The moment that she's German, she is Jewish."
2   Reference to a text quoted earlier, in which Cixous writes about Helene Jonas geboren Meyer who had a "beautiful life" therefore a "beautiful death": "Quelle belle vie elle a eue, c'est-à-dire quelle belle mort, la dernière belle mort d'Osnabrück, le savait-elle, il y avait le Docteur Pelz qui conduisait l'orchestre recueilli des huit enfants fils et filles, et le docteur Pelz était encore l'honneur et le serviteur des malades et donc des bien portants de toute la ville, le patron de l'hôpital et le protecteur des pauvres, et tout de suite après l'enterrement (il y avait encore le cimetière) la mort violente et hideuse a commencé" (*GO*, 31) ("What a beautiful life she had, that is to say, a beautiful death, the last beautiful death in Osnabrück, did she know that, there was Doctor Pelz who conducted the gathered orchestra of the eight children sons and daughters, and Doctor Pelz was still the honor and the servant of the sick people and thus of the healthy people in the whole city, the head of the hospital and the protector of the poor, and right away after the burial (there was still a cemetery) violent and hideous death began" [*OSJ*, 18]).

The "German Illusion"

As far as psyche is concerned, Freud's psyche was still in Austria after Hitler's triumphant entrance in Vienna on March 12, 1938; Freud, who had to hastily leave Vienna on June 4, 1938, after having been arrested by the Gestapo along with his daughter Anna on March 22, 1938. Freud, like Omi, was "envoûté." It is Hélène Cixous's son who indicates that Omi, like many Germans in her situation, would have needed a Dr. Freud to psychoanalyze her on why she did not see what she saw, why she did not learn what she had learned about the persecution of the Jews in Nazi Germany and Europe (including Austria). Yet Freud himself would have needed a Dr. Freud to psychoanalyze his apparent blindness to what the rise of Nazism meant for him and his family in Austria. Let's reread this segment:

> —Ève n'avait pas pu faire sortir Omi. Finalement, c'est l'assassinat de la Synagogue qui l'a délivrée.
> Les cas d'envoûtement sont si nombreux, dis-je, il faudrait des milliers de Freud pour les examiner.
> —Freud aussi était envoûté, dit mon fils. Il lui aurait fallu un Freud.
> —Et il y a aussi la famille Nussbaum, les parents, après une hésitation suisse. Eux non plus n'étaient pas des piliers de la Synagogue.
>
> (N, 56)[3]

The "grande chronique d'Osnabrück,"[4] often evoked in this study, the great chronicle of Osnabrück told by Hélène Cixous, could also be the chronicle of the "cas d'envoûtement," of a certain *delirium*. A *delirium* so entrenched in the history of "Germany" and "Austria" that even Freud is invoked here as one who, like Omi, could not see what he saw. The chronicle of the relationship to an impossible possible relationship to "Germany" (or Austria) as a relationship to the impossibility of seeing-not seeing that it was past time to leave for Omi, for Freud and beyond. The chronicle of Cixous's radical inability to slip into the character of her grandmother and maybe also of Freud, the "envoûté" in chief. It is the possibility that Germany could be a whole pipe dream, a chimera:

---

3 "—Ève was unable to bring Omi out. Finally, it is the assassination of the Synagogue that released her. / The cases of bewitchment are so numerous, I say, we would need thousands of Freud(s) in order to examine them. / —Freud himself was bewitched, says my son. He too would have needed a Freud. / —And also the Nussbaum family, the parents, after a Swiss hesitation. Neither were they pillars of the Synagogue."

4 *Ever*, 01:34:57.

Les Juifs étaient plus patriotes que les autres, je veux dire les Allemands juifs d'autant plus allemands que juifs. Moi aussi quand j'ai fait ma visite de quinze jours à Dresden en 1934 je suis allée me déclarer moi-même à la police pour quinze jours nous les bons citoyens que nous étions nous allions nous déclarer à la Gestapo d'autant plus ponctuellement. [...] Nous avons habité dans des chimères allemandes.

(*BM*, 166–67)[5]

"We have inhabited German chimeras." "The German Jews were all the more Germans because they were Jews," says Ève in Cixous, the secretary of Ève's litany of the it-must-not-be-said(s). As if a silent, repressed intrinsic distortion, an unsaid essential corruption, an unmentionable principle of divorce, was *constitutive* of what it meant to be German for the German Jews, something that Cixous qualifies as "l'être-allemand mystérieux de la famille Jonas" (*BM*, 160), "the mysterious German-being of the Jonas family." Such a mystery is an unmentionable unifying principle of disunity (or disunion), of division, a constitutive it-must-not-be-said. At the core of this intestine war, of this divorce of the being, the "German-being" of the Jonas family is tied to its Jewish-being, a German-being in which the Jewish-being exponentially augments its German-being. This principle leads Ève's constant German return and the way Germany relentlessly returns to her. She notices the compulsive recall of "Germany" whenever the word "Jewish" appears, and the reverse. When her German self arises, she is all the more Jewish. As soon as "German" arises, it is overflown by "Jew" in a spinning madness of the substitution, a folly of the double ... of the return. This hyperbolic German-being is implemented by its inseparable Jewish-being:

L'Allemagne revient, cela ne veut pas dire qu'elle est revenue. Chaque fois que ma mère l'être-allemande fait retour aussitôt l'être-juive fait retour. Est-elle allemande la voilà juive. Un monde ne resurgit pas des fonds sans l'autre. D'autant plus allemande

---

5 "The German Jews were all the more Germans because they were Jews. Me too when I paid my visit of fifteen days to Dresden in 1934 I went to report myself to the police for fifteen days, we the good citizens that we were we went to report ourselves to the Gestapo all the more punctually. [...] We have inhabited German chimeras."

que juive d'autant plus allemande alors qu'en France elle n'est ni l'une ni l'autre mais quand même.

(*BM*, 199)⁶

This is the void, the silence at the core of "Germany," the it-must-not-be-said that operates as a law of history: when Cixous's family, when Ève and Éri, Cixous's son and daughter, and, of course, Cixous herself, are questioning "Germany," they are questioning an Osnabrück that literally "mistook" and corrupted, twisted and distorted the being, and triggered the return of the substitute as a folly of the double, of the return. Which is why *returning to Osnabrück* for Ève and Éri was a folly. It was caught in a folly of the return; it was returning to a certain folly—which is why it was also the return to a certain figure of the non-return, or of the impossible return to Germany. No wonder they finally decided to go because of the quality of the "large" breakfast buffet at the Hotel Nikolai where the sisters were invited to stay in Osnabrück ...⁷ that, among all kinds of other disputed "trivial" motives. As already emphasized when we analyzed the motifs of the remembrance and of the ruin, Osnabrück sabotaged Ève and Éri—the verb "fausser" is used by Ève and Éri in Cixous's text *Benjamin à Montaigne* (*BM*, 149).⁸ This fact frames the contours of a condition of the soul, of the spirit, that Derrida calls a "psyche" to refine his idea of a "Jewish-German psyche."

During the academic year of 1987/1988, Jacques Derrida taught a seminar at the École des Hautes Études en Sciences Sociales in Paris as part of a series he titled "Nationalité et nationalisme philosophique." The seminar was called "Kant, le Juif, l'Allemand." There is a published version in English of a portion of this seminar.⁹ Among the words Derrida and his translator use to qualify the aforementioned "psyche" is

---

6   "Germany returns, this doesn't mean that it has returned. Every time that my German-being mother returns, immediately her being-Jewish returns. Is she German, there she is, Jewish. One world doesn't erupt from the depths without the other. All the more German that she is Jewish, all the more German whereas in France she is neither one nor the other, but anyway."
7   "Et l'hôtel tu m'as écrit c'est le meilleur, il y a un grand buffet pour le petit déjeuner" (*BM*, 135) ("And the hotel you wrote me it's the best, there is a large buffet for breakfast").
8   "Fausser," is a powerful verb that we have already quoted and obliquely analyzed. "Osnabrück nous a complètement faussés." To an extent, all the developments that I engage in this chapter could be read as a long, impossible, aporetical attempt to translate, or rather to circle around, the impossible translation of this untranslatable "fausser" and what this verb encrypts of the Jewish-German themes in Cixous's œuvre.
9   Jacques Derrida, "Interpretations at War: Kant, the Jew, the German," in "Institutions of Interpretation," special issue, *New Literary History*, vol. 22. no. 1 (Johns Hopkins University Press, winter 1991), 39–95.

the word "distortion." Derrida also talks about a "disjunctive conjunction," a "lack of transition," "a way of connecting without connection in rhetoric and argumentation."[10] Derrida highlights that this tension is displayed by two important German philosophers "who both assumed their Jewishness radically around the war of 1914."[11] Derrida makes it clear at the beginning of his lecture that this is "a retrospective distortion," since neither of the two philosophers, two German and Jewish figures, lived long enough to encounter the Nazis:

> Both are caught up and rooted in that war: in a war, one might say, which neither of the two thinkers has survived—not, in any case, to the extent of reaching the next stage alive, the next stage being the moment when Nazism casts over that whole adventure, over *what I would call the Jewish-German psyche of the war of 1914*, a revealing and at the same time deforming light. The future-in-the-past may lead to *retrospective distortions*, and it may also tear down veils.
>
> (My emphases)[12]

The Jewish-German psyche of the war of 1914 tears down veils, it sheds light on a distortion that retrospectively becomes evident, or flagrant, when Nazism arises on the scene. Derrida's seminar, as well as the long essay-article he published, served as a basis for a lecture he later offered in Israel. It opens a long hermeneutic on the essential texts of the philosophical tradition that Franz Rosenzweig and Hermann Cohen developed in the immediate context of the Great War: Cohen's 1918 text titled *Religion der Vernunft aus den Quellen des Judentums* and Rosenzweig's *Deutschtum und Judentum*, written at the end of 1915 to the beginning of 1916. Here is what Derrida writes about Rosenzweig's text, in which Rosenzweig discusses how he perceived Cohen when he first saw him in person, as he was teaching in Berlin in November of 1913:

> What is thus being revealed to Rosenzweig? A Jew, nothing less than the essence of the Jew, but also of the German Jew. And one

---

10 Derrida, "Interpretations at War," 44.
11 Derrida, "Interpretations at War," 40.
12 Derrida, "Interpretations at War," 41. Here is Derrida's formulation in his notes from the seminar he taught: "D'une guerre à laquelle ni l'un ni l'autre n'ont survécu, en un certain sens, en tout cas survécu au point d'atteindre vivants le moment du nazisme qui jette sur toute cette aventure, sur ce moment de ce que nous appelons ici la psyché judéo-allemande de la guerre de 14, une lumière à la fois déformante et révélatrice." Derrida, notes/tapuscripts of seminar, consulted on July 30, 2019, Langson Library (University of California Irvine), Derrida MS-C01, box 19 folder 17, [1] 76.

cannot very well tell whether he is more purely Jewish because he is a German Jew or essentially Jewish and on top of that, by some accident or otherwise, also a German Jew. The ambiguity is remarkable; for it is with this German Jew, with a particular way of being a German Jew, Jewish *and* German […], that Rosenzweig, like Scholem and Buber in a different way, will eventually break, despite the respect that Cohen still inspired, this great figure of rationalist German Judaism.[13]

"One cannot very well tell whether he is more purely Jewish because he is a German Jew." This sentence could not be much closer to what Cixous-Ève writes when Cixous argues that Ève's German-being simultaneously lets her Jewish-being return. In his close reading of Rosenzweig, but more specifically of Cohen, Derrida highlights the ambiguity that comes with the "and," with the "being" Jew *and* "being" German, and the fact that, at some point, the complex economy of this "and" will break "in different way[s]." This "break," or breach, is not distinguishable from what Derrida calls a "psyche." What is at stake is the artificiality of the "and" and the "delirious forms"[14] that this articulation takes, notably in Cohen's account referenced by Derrida. Derrida asks: "Is not everything artificial or in any case non-natural in what we are calling a psyche?"[15] In the attempt to link or articulate the German and the Jewish, Derrida highlights what he calls a "delirious form" in Cohen's argument, a *delirium* that could very much be understood as an archaic form of the "envoûté" named by Cixous, the skewed, the distorted, the hallucinated. Distortion is a word used by Derrida to render what he also calls the "circuit breaker"[16] of the neo-Kantian philosopher's argument in the way it is seen by Rosenzweig. Derrida writes that the idea of a circuit breaker revolves around "the essence of the conjunction 'and,' which not only defines the relation of the Jew to the German ('let us be Jewish and German') but also determines the Jewish and the German: ruptivity, a dissociative and irruptive power."[17] In this passage Derrida refers to Rosenzweig's famous plea that he wrote in a letter: "Let us then be Germans and Jews. Both at the same time, without worrying about the *and*, without talking about it a great deal, but really both."[18] Derrida adds: "The 'and' of 'Jewish and German' is perhaps a 'syn' or

---

13 Derrida, "Interpretations at War," 43.
14 Derrida, "Interpretations at War," 51.
15 Derrida, "Interpretations at War," 51.
16 Derrida, "Interpretations at War," 44.
17 Derrida, "Interpretations at War," 44.
18 Letter from F. Rosenzweig to H. Sommer, January 16, 1918 (*Briefe* Berlin 35, 279), quoted by Jacques Derrida, Derrida, "Interpretations at War," 43.

a 'with' but without an identifying or a totalizing synthesis. It carries a disjunction as much as it does a conjunction."¹⁹ Derrida expands on this notion, so critical for his idea that this disjunction-conjunction is the core of the *delirium*:

> [O]n the one hand, discontinuity—the abrupt juxtaposition of two heterogenous elements, the relationless relation between two terms with no continuity, no analogy, no resemblance, not susceptible to any genealogical or deductive derivation; but on the other hand, and for the very same reason, the lack of transition produces a sort of immediate continuity which joins one to the other, the same to the same and to the nonsame, the other to the other.²⁰

What Derrida calls a "disjunctive conjunction" is both what defines the Jewish-German psyche and the *delirium*.

Cohen's attempt to expose his argument logically catches Derrida's attention. Derrida shows that Cohen's rendering of the existence of the Jewish-German couple depends on the use of the philosophical logos by Hermann Cohen, who also rationalizes about this logos. Derrida shows that Cohen's "absolute logocentrism"²¹ *is* delirious in its intrinsic logocentric logic: "in order to render an account (*logon didonai*, a Greek and Platonic formula invoked by Cohen on the next page) of the Jewish-German phenomenon (and who will deny the existence of such a 'phenomenon?') *in its often delirious forms*, is it possible not to involve logic, the logos, in this delirium?"²² "In its often delirious forms": this formula by Derrida allows him to point at the double dimension of the Jewish-German psyche. It is a psyche because it is obviously "not at all natural, physical, genetic,"²³ but it is also a psyche because, for Cohen—and who will deny the existence of such a phenomenon—it is inseparable from the "history of the German spirit," quoted by Derrida.²⁴ The notion of Jewish-German psyche obeys the law (logos, logic) of this essential distortion, disjunction; what holds it together is a force that tears it apart. Logically so. Its dissociative nature and irruptive power is its principle of identification, of association. What Derrida demonstrates is that it might not be necessary to attempt to prove that Cohen is "delirious." The apparent delirious nature of his discourse on the

---

19 Derrida, "Interpretations at War," 44.
20 Derrida, "Interpretations at War," 44.
21 Derrida, "Interpretations at War," 51.
22 Derrida, "Interpretations at War," 51.
23 Derrida, "Interpretations at War," 51.
24 Derrida, "Interpretations at War," 50.

Jewish-German psyche might in fact be a way for Cohen to expose, to tell the *truth of the symptom* and about the symptom, to allow the symptom to explore and display its roots, its conscious and unconscious truth revealed by the knowledge in which this symptom is both investigated and exposed. In other words, Cohen might expose what Derrida himself is calling "delirium" and what it is "logically" made of, that is, "the German spirit, within the Jewish-German psyche which constitutes it."[25] Later, Derrida mimics Cohen's voice: "You have the right to consider my discourse as a symptom of the madness it describes."[26]

The "artificiality" (marker of the "psyche") of what Derrida also calls the "rational knowledge as a symptom of an alleged delirium," of a "reflexive delirium,"[27] is not an event that occurs outside of the rationality of the reason as a form of de-reason or any form of departure from the rationality of the logos. It is the *reason itself*, in its logocentric drive, that is delirious.[28] This phallogocentric delirium can now be exposed in greater detail if we refer to the ways that Ève Cixous voices her dissent of the men's rationality of the Jonas family. Two essential quotes by Cixous will allow us to show how Derrida's reading of Cohen (and of Rosenzweig to a certain extent, as well as Rosenzweig's reading of Cohen …) can be enlightening in comprehending Ève's understanding of her father, Michael Klein, the Jewish-German soldier who dies on the Front in 1916. Derrida recalls that Cohen, like Rosenzweig, "never knew Nazism," and that neither were "Zionists, but both of whom had undoubtedly so much to tell us, whether they knew it or not, about what was to follow after their death."[29] Neither Cohen nor Rosenzweig, nor Michael Klein, knew Nazism or were Zionists. The goal of Cohen's text was to affirm his German patriotism while using the Jewish-German motif as the core of his patriotic engagement for his country. As Ève Cixous proclaims, in this delirious logic of the overbid, "Les Juifs étaient plus patriotes que les autres, je veux dire les Allemands juifs d'autant plus allemands que juifs" (*BM*, 166) ("Jews were more patriotic than the others, I mean, German Jews were all the more German because [they were] Jews"):

---

25 Derrida, "Interpretations at War," 52.
26 Derrida, "Interpretations at War," 52.
27 Derrida, "Interpretations at War," 52.
28 "In this region," writes Derrida, "the symptom is knowledge, knowledge is a symptom." Derrida, "Interpretations at War," 52.
29 Derrida, "Interpretations at War," 47. This point is vertiginous if we think about Freud, the *envoûté*, who, like Cohen and Rosenzweig, was not a Zionist but knew Nazism and died after the persecution had started.

Ce qu'ils ont sous le crâne, dit ma mère, et je voyais qu'elle regardait mentalement la photo de son père le Landsman Michael Klein de l'air accusateur et familier avec lequel elle regarde ma tête enragée d'apercevoir la ressemblance secrète avec la tête de mon père, et ce qu'elle fixait avec la fureur retenue de la fille qui adorait son père, c'était le crâne allemand, cette chose en métal qui chaussait le crâne du soldat allemand en 1914 d'un deuxième crâne se terminant par une pointe inutile mais menaçante, ce qu'ils ont sous le crâne mon père et Tonpère, c'est: la gloire. Je hais la gloire, dit ma mère, quelle bêtise! Abandonner sa femme et ses deux enfants, j'appelle ça: la gloire. Qu'est-ce qu'il laisse à sa femme et à ses enfants sur lesquels il ne veille plus sur terre? Une croix de guerre. Est-ce que c'est acceptable, faire son devoir d'Allemand et Tonpère pareillement? Je voyais très bien avec les yeux de ma mère son père, jeune homme de trente-huit ans au front tournant vers l'objectif de l'appareil photographique un visage calme, lisse sans violence, pas une ride, pas un froncement de pensée et par-dessus le front le casque de la mort, la chose inutile et maléfique pour laquelle il trahissait toute la famille. Reste une médaille. Sa famille pour une croix. —C'est compliqué, dis-je. —C'est très simple, dit ma mère. Et toi tu recommences. —Ne recommence pas, dis-je. Je suis vivante, je suis vieille. —Tu as la tête sous les papiers, dit ma mère. Et tu sais où ça mène? Au cimetière.

(OS, 198–99)[30]

---

30 "What they have underneath their skulls, says my mother, and I saw that she was mentally looking at the photo of her father the Landsman Michael Klein with the familiar and accusatory air with which she looks at my enraged face while noticing my secret resemblance to my father's face, and that she fixated on with the restrained furor of the daughter who adored her father, it was the German skull, this metal thing that fitted the skull of the German soldier in 1914 like a second skull complete with a useless but threatening spike, what they all have underneath their skull, my father and Yourfather, I call that: glory. I hate glory, says my mother, what stupidity! Abandon his wife and his two children, I call that: glory. What does he leave to his wife and his children whom he can no longer look after on this earth? An iron cross. Is it acceptable, to do his German duty and be your father like this? I could very well see with the eyes of my mother, her father, young 38-year old man on the front turning a calm face towards the lens of the photographic camera, smooth without violence, not a single wrinkle, not a frown from thought and on top of the helmet of death, the useless evil thing for which he betrayed the whole family. Remains a medal. His family for a cross. —It's complicated, I say. —It's very simple, says my mother. And you are starting over. —Don't start over, I say. I am alive, I am old. —You have your head buried underneath your papers, says my mother. And do you know where it leads? To the cemetery."

Ève's profound awareness—an awareness that goes back to her childhood—of the ties between masculinity and "stupidity" ("bêtise") might have been the reason why she was immediately immune to the dark reality of "glory" ("la gloire"), why she fled Germany as soon as she had perceived the first signs of the rise of Nazism. "Glory" means the abandonment of children, of Michael's two young daughters, and of his wife, in exchange for a cross, a medal. Two orphans and a widow in exchange for a military distinction. These are the chimeras of glory and masculinity mixed with the chimeras of Germany, of Duty and of reputation. After this segment on masculine glory and stupidity comes a long, entirely italicized passage:

> *Toute ma vie j'en ai voulu à mon père d'abord et ensuite à mon mari. Je les considère comme coupables de mort, pense-t-elle, et par-dessus le marché on ne peut pas se plaindre de la mort d'un mort, il y a amnistie, c'est inimaginable. Mon père a trahi sa femme parce qu'il a voulu faire son devoir d'Allemand. C'est là un choix inacceptable que personne ne critique, pense-t-elle, même Omi n'a rien dit quand son mari a voulu faire son devoir d'Allemand, au lieu de faire son devoir de mari, s'engager de lui-même et volontairement dans l'armée allemande c'est inimaginable, et personne ne dit rien, abandonne sa femme avec deux petits enfants, j'y pense ces jours-ci, j'en veux à ce mari. Comment cela s'appelle faire une chose pareille, aller se faire tuer tout seul, madame Klein laissez faire votre mari, il sait quelle cochonnerie faire, est-ce que c'est un mari ce soldat, est-ce que c'est un père ce soldat allemand, je pense que non, mais là-dessus silence, ce qui est fini est fini, j'y pensai ces jours-ci à quoi bon retourner la terre, les pensées non plus, [...]. Mon mari aussi a trahi sa femme.*
>
> (*OS*, 191–92)[31]

The glorification of betrayal, a masculine betrayal, an "inacceptable choice" that no one criticizes (it-must-not-be-said). The German duty,

---

31 "*My whole life I resented my father, first, and then my husband. I consider them guilty of death, she thinks, and on top of that we cannot complain about death to the dead, there's an amnesty, it's unimaginable. My father betrayed his wife because he wanted to fulfill his duty as a German. This is an unacceptable choice that no one criticizes, she thinks, even Omi said nothing when her husband wanted to fulfill his duty as a German instead of fulfilling his duty as a husband, enlisting by his own will in the German military, it is unimaginable, and no one says anything, abandoning his wife with two little children, I've been thinking about it these days, I blame this husband. What do we call doing such a thing, going in order to get killed by his own will, Mrs. Klein, leave it to your husband, he knows, what crap to do, is it a husband this soldier, is it a father this German soldier, I think not, but on that, silence, what is over is over, I thought about it, why move the soil, neither the thoughts, [...]. My husband too, betrayed his wife.*"

the German masculinity, the German manhood, the German man is put above his wife and children. The glory is enhanced by the overbid of putting Germany, the German manhood, above a 32-year-old spouse and two daughters aged 4 and 1. Interestingly enough, although it is always there and always everywhere, never will Ève Cixous's fury—voiced by Hélène Cixous's in *Osnabrück*—explicitly refer to Michael Klein "le Juif, l'Allemand" (the Jew, the German), as Derrida puts it. At the core of Derrida's vertigo when he explores Cohen's fierce patriotism, its "force," its unconditional character, Derrida recalls that Cohen is a socialist, a rationalist, an enlightened, influential neo-Kantian philosopher. A man who seems to be the voice of Michael Klein's generation, including his fierce affirmation of an irreducible logocentrism that Ève Cixous, and Hélène Cixous, highlight as a *phallogocentrism*. Ève's point is that the logic of Michael Klein's move is mad. Phallogocentric folly. It is the madness of Germany and masculinity veiled by the word "glory," by the word "cross." The logic is so fierce that it is not sustainable logically, which only reinforces the logic. Ève is very aware, she knows how to destitute the idols. A whole family and a spouse, Rosi Klein, his wife, Ève (6 years old when Michael Klein was killed in 1916) and Éri Cixous (3 years old in 1916) are worth less than Michael's "Eiserne Kreuz," his Iron Cross, the medal he received on the front that Cixous still has in her possession. That is the logic. The crazy logic of this "German duty," a hallucinated logic (Derrida uses the word "hallucination" more than once about Cohen's patriotic Jewish-German stance) is *wrapped in silence*: "*personne ne dit rien*," "*no one says anything*" screams Ève, "*est-ce que c'est un père ce soldat allemand, je pense que non, mais là-dessus silence*" (*OS*, 191–92), "*is it a father this German soldier, I think not, but on that, silence.*" This silence is also one that explains Omi's silence and her false sense of protection when it is already very, very late, in 1938:

> [P]eut-être son mari Michael Klein mort pour l'Allemagne en 1916, croix de fer, lui murmurait-il, ne t'inquiète pas, je suis toujours là pour te protéger
> il y a aussi toutes les victimes de la croix de fer, ceux qui ont cru et voulu croire à la croix, malgré les avertissements des *Aktions*.
> (*N*, 102)[32]

The story of Michael Klein, her grandfather, is nothing but critical to Hélène Cixous's life and story. Who survives this toxic and lethal

---

32 "[M]aybe her husband Michael Klein who died for Germany in 1916, iron cross, was whispering to her, do not worry, I am still here to protect you / There are also all the victims of the iron cross, those who believed and wanted to believe in the cross in spite of the warnings of the Aktions."

German masculinity? Who is not duped by it? Women (and that ultimately includes Omi). Who tells the story? Cixous. And the idea that this story has to be told is deeply embedded in Ève's proclamation that the silence around the scandalous "glory" of Michael Klein is tenacious. We are dealing with a lineage of women, and it is interesting that it is precisely the philosopher who paid much attention to the alliance of logos and phallus, to the mix of (pseudo) rationality and masculinity, Derrida, who will also expose the *delirious* logic of a certain German patriotism. These structures are profound as they affect the way Cixous's personal narration is shaped; they even affect who she is in the two aforementioned quotes, who she is in the eyes of her mother Ève … could it be that Ève recognizes the need for recognition ("glory"?) in Cixous's own drive to write? "—Tu as la tête sous les papiers, dit ma mère. Et tu sais où ça mène? Au cimetière," says Ève to Hélène (*OS*, 198–99).[33] It-must-not-be-said.

Michael Klein is an intrinsic part of Cixous's being. He is a critical part of what defines Cixous—or at least of how she defines herself. In *Photos de racines*, Cixous gives a photographed copy of the telegram that announced Michael's death to his loved ones on July 27, 1916. She then recopies a portion of the telegram to insert the words into her text. She writes:

> Je recopie et je pleure.
> Pourquoi ce pleur? *Parce que je suis mort*. Je suis si mort. Parce que je suis devenu cette pierre de bois levée qui répète mon nom et ma date de mort à l'air où je ne vécus jamais. La page de bois prévient le vide bois que c'est ici que désormais je demeure, devenu terre et bois étranger. Oh! j'ai besoin de Dieu pour ne pas m'oublier.
> *Je m'appelle Michael Klein.*
>
> (*PR*, 188; my emphases)[34]

"Je m'appelle Michael Klein." "My name is Michael Klein." Cixous also mentions Michael in interviews. *Photos de racines* displays a picture of him in uniform and his "Casque à Pointe," (*PR*, 189) ("the helmet with

---

33 "—You have your head buried in your papers, says my mother. And do you know where that leads? To the cemetery."
34 "I copy and I cry. / Why these tears? Because I am dead. I am so dead. Because I have become this raised wooden stone that repeats my name and my date of death into the air where I never lived. The wooden page informs the empty wood that henceforth it is here that I reside, having become foreign earth and wood. Oh! I need God so as not to forget myself. / My name is Michael Klein" (*R*, 186).

a spike" [R, 187]), the *Pickelhelm* (*Pickelhaube* in German), and Michael Klein appears in this segment by Cixous:

> Et c'est à partir de ce point le plus au Nord que tout mon récit personnel s'est cristallisé : à partir de l'histoire de Michael Klein.
> Michael Klein, qui était alors de nationalité hongroise, a pris la nationalité allemande en 1909 pour épouser ma grand-mère Rosalie Jonas. Ce qui lui a valu d'être enrôlé dans l'armée allemande pendant première guerre. Omi datait encore ses récits de jeunesse du Kaiser. Pour elle, le Kaiser existait.
> Mon grand-père est mort sur le front russe en tant que soldat allemand.
>
> (*PR*, 186–87)[35]

According to Cixous, her personal story "crystallizes" in Michael's. This "Kaizerish," the "Wihelminische" society (from Wilhelm II, the Emperor) as it is called in German, this traditional German society and culture was Rosi and Michael's Germany of which the Emperor Wilhelm II, who reigned from 1888 to 1918, was the sovereign leader. It is also that of Hermann Cohen. Here is what Cixous writes, in *Gare d'Osnabrück à Jérusalem*:

> Et j'ajoute mon silence à celui de ma mère et de ma grand-mère.
> Selon les Jonas puisque Michael Klein est le seul des quatorze Klein qui a été tué sur le front, et de par sa propre responsabilité par-dessus le marché, puisque Michael Klein s'est volontairement

---

35 "And it is from this furthest North point that all my personal narrative was crystallized: from the story of Michael Klein. / Michael Klein, who was then of Hungarian nationality, took German nationality in 1909 so as to marry my grandmother Rosalie Jonas. This cost him getting enrolled in the German army in the First World War. Omi still dated her childhood stories by the Kaiser. For her, the Kaiser still existed. / My grandfather died on the Russian front as a German soldier" (*R*, 185). Born on September 25, 1881, in the city of Trnava (former Austro-Hungarian Empire), Michael Klein probably volunteered to join the army, and especially a combat unit (he was a part of a light infantry unit), given the fact that he was already almost 33 when the war broke in early August of 1914. Today, the city of Trnava is in Slovakia; it is located approximately 90 miles (145 kilometers) east of Vienna and 44 miles (70 kilometers) east of Bratislava. The fact that he might have volunteered is corroborated by Ève Cixous's quoted accounts: "*il a voulu faire son devoir d'Allemand*" (*OS*, 191) ("*he has wanted to fulfill his duty as a German*"); "Michael Klein s'est volontairement engagé dans l'armée allemande" (*GO*, 109) ("Michael Klein voluntarily joined the German Army" [*OSJ*, 83]). David Blank and Gladys Blank, "Michael Klein." *Gladys and David Blanks Genealogy*, available online: http://www.blankgenealogy.com/getperson.php?personID=I2640&tree=Blank1 (accessed July 13, 2020).

engagé dans l'armée allemande, c'est aux autres Klein d'assurer la subsistance de leur petite sœur, c'est-à-dire de leur belle-sœur. Le silence dit la vérité faite par Ève et Omi.

(*GO*, 109)[36]

The trust in Germany that many Jews had, especially those who had fought during the Great War, also allows Cixous to deepen two critical notions that the German-being *and* Jewish-being hold together. Belief and illusion. Belief:

—La seule chose que je sais personnellement dit ma tante c'est qu'Omi voulait nous acheter une machine à coudre et un fer à repasser et mon oncle Max Stern qui était directeur de la Banque allemande en retraite à Essen sur la Ruhr avait placé les biens de ma mère pour la protéger dans son coffre. Quand il est arrivé en 1934 à son *safe* on lui dit vous ne pouvez ouvrir qu'en présence de la Gestapo. Si bien qu'il a renoncé à ouvrir son *safe*—L'argent d'Omi qui était sauf dans le *safe* dit ma mère est toujours dans le *safe*. Je ne peux pas dire ce qu'il y avait dans le *safe* mais comme les Allemands marquent toujours tout exactement le directeur Stern avait sûrement marqué: ceci est à Rosalie Jonas [Omi]. Mon oncle était tellement correct. Il avait un ami un industriel à la retraite qui lui dit en 1935 moi je ne reste pas un jour de plus. Alors mon oncle Max Stern dit se croyant très malin et *se croyant allemand naturellement* dans ce cas vous pouvez me vendre votre concession au cimetière, croyant faire une affaire. Et l'autre qui était très malin lui a vendu sa concession. Mon oncle ne pouvait pas imaginer étant donné ses mérites, sa ressemblance étroite avec le Kaiser pendant la guerre 14 il était officier quand il a été déporté il ne savait pas ce qui arrivait. L'argent d'Omi dort toujours dans son *safe* inconnu et Max Stern n'a jamais dormi dans sa concession qui sait qui dort à sa place. Les Juifs étaient plus patriotes que les autres.

(*BM*, 166–67; my emphasis)[37]

---

36 "And I add my silence to that of my mother and my grandmother / According to the Jonases, since Michael Klein is the only one of the fourteen Kleins to be killed at the front, and by his own fault on top of everything, since Michael Klein voluntarily joined the German Army, it's up to the other Kleins to guarantee the subsistence of their little sister, that is to say their sister-in-law. / The silence says the truth made by Ève and Omi" (*OSJ*, 83).

37 "—The only thing that I know personally my aunt says is that Omi wanted to buy us a sewing machine and an iron and my uncle Max Stern who was the retired director of the German bank in Essen in the Ruhr had placed my mother's

The phrase "se croyant naturellement allemand," "believing" he was himself "naturally" German. Of course, this sense of "naturality" is what Derrida deconstructs when he forges this concept of the psyche, of Jewish-German psyche. Believing, believing in oneself, "Se croyant," "se croire" is an idiomatic form, literally "believing yourself," or "self-believing" meaning the work of building a belief, of making yourself believe, of convincing yourself of something that is obviously all the more natural than it is impossible: mystification. We could have named this "Jewish-German psyche" the Jewish-German mystification, another term for the bewilderment of the "envoûté." Cixous obviously plays with the logical opposition, the oxymoronic nature of the "belief" associated to the locution "naturally German," in the same sentence ("se croyant naturellement allemand") … it is impossible to be "naturally German" and "believe" in it at the same time. This, again, is a symptomatic marker of the *delirium* in Cixous's writing of the "être-allemand mysérieux," the mysterious German-being of the Jonas family, that Derrida would certainly not put in different terms. Such a marker of the belief circulates between the texts through a common signifier: the name "croix" (cross) and the imperative of the verb "croire" (to believe) spelled "crois" ("believe"), with the same pronunciation (croix-crois). Here is "croix":

> Et il y a aussi les anciens combattants, ceux qui font corps avec leur croix de fer, qui ont mal à la poitrine, les encore plus allemands que les Allemands, devoir rendre la croix, la nationalité, la guerre même, comme s'ils étaient des voleurs
> et les veuves de guerre, elles aussi, des voleuses et des femmes de voleurs et de suceurs de sang, des escrocs

---

possessions in his strongbox to protect them. When he arrived at his *safe* in 1934 they told him, you can only open it in the presence of the Gestapo. So that he renounced opening his *safe*—Omi's money, that was saved in the *safe*, says my mother, is still in the *safe*. I can't say what was in the *safe* but since the Germans always write down everything exactly; the director, Stern, had certainly kept the record: this belongs to Rosalie Jonas [Omi]. My uncle was so honest. He had a friend who was a retired industrialist who told him in 1935 I won't stay one more day. So my uncle said, thinking of himself as very clever, and believing in himself as naturally German, in that case you can sell me your plot at the cemetery, thinking that he was making a good deal. The other, who was very clever, sold him his plot. My uncle could not imagine, given his merit, given his close resemblance to the Kaiser during the First War, he was an officer, when he was deported to a camp he did not understand what was happening. Omi's money still sleeps in her unknown *safe* and Max Stern never slept in his plot who knows who sleeps in his place. The Jews were greater patriots than the others."

> Par exemple papa, c'est-à-dire Hermann Katzmann, qui a comme une petite plaie au niveau du cœur là où il y avait toujours la pochette blanche, quand ce n'était pas aux fêtes nationales, la croix de fer. *Nun hier*, il en sent l'absence dans sa poitrine. Mais ce n'est rien.
>
> (N, 59)[38]

The same phoneme "croix de fer" (iron cross), could be heard as "Crois de fer," literally "Believe iron," "iron belief."[39] Here is a development of how the signifier "croyait," from "croire," captures the essence of the articulation between the German-being and the Jewish-being:

> —Sais-tu que Fred n'était pas le nom de Fred? Quand il est né, au temps où on était allemand, citoyen allemand, soldat allemand, savant allemand, on s'appelait Siegfried naturellement, on *croyait être*.
>
> (N, 52; my emphasis)[40]

"Siegfried naturellement," "Siegfried naturally," and not "Fred," naturally German, which meant "German soldier," "German citizen," "German scholar," "on croyait être," "one believed to be," one believed in our pseudo-natural German being and all its associated German roles. The following quote from *Gare d'Osnabrück à Jérusalem* highlights the same structure of the "croyait être":

---

38 "There are also the veterans, those who stand as one with their iron crosses, who had pain in their chests, those ones even more German than the Germans; to be forced to give the cross back, the citizenship, the war even, as if they were thieves / and the war widows, they too, thieves, and wives of thieves and of blood suckers, crooks / For example Dad, that is, Hermann Katzmann, who carries like a little wound at the level of the heart, there, there where the white pocket handkerchief was when there were no national holidays, the place of the iron cross. *Nun hier*, he feels its absence in his chest. But it's nothing." It is probably no accident that these reflections keep taking us back to the time of the Great War (Freud, Michael Klein, Hermann Cohen ...) in the proximity of a great author born in Osnabrück whose name is tied to the Great War, a name that recurs in many of Hélène Cixous's book an author, his sister, a family persecuted by the Nazis: Erich Maria Remarque.

39 We also recall the popular French saying-oath often heard on playgrounds, "Croix de Bois, Croix de Fer, / Si je mens je vais en Enfer," "Wooden Cross, Iron Cross, / If I am lying I will go to Hell." This oath is often considered an equivalent of the expression "Cross my heart and hope to die."

40 "—Do you know that Fred was not Fred's name? When he was born, at the time when one was German, German citizen, German soldier, German scholar, one was named Siegfried, naturally, one thought one was."

Ici j'essaie de répondre à la question: qu'est-ce qui fait que certains n'arrivent pas à se dire qu'ils n'arrivent pas à se résoudre à cesser du jour au lendemain d'être allemand alors qu'ils le sont ou croyaient l'être?

(*GO*, 124)[41]

The idea that Germany could have been a belief is what Derrida would also call a psyche. It is a psyche because "belief" is denied as such in the way Cixous pictures it as a "naturality." This German natural essence is the reality of a belief, of a powerful it-must-not-be-said that holds the mysterious German-being of the Jonas family together. Ève is not fooled. But the belief is so deeply inscribed that it is only when unmasked *as* a belief by Ève Cixous that the *pseudo*-naturality of the phenomenon becomes obvious.

The belief is so deeply entrenched in the German soul (psyche, consciousness, habitus, socius), in the German-being of the Jewish-German psyche, that *it is socially effaced*, it is masked as a belief. Being German is "natural." As natural as "Siegfried" is. "Fred" is the conjuration of the German belief, of "Siegfried naturellement." In Cixous's abyssal vision there would be a believed-Jewish-German psyche. Approaching the Jewish-German psyche would be impossible without believing in the science of beliefs. Cixous is a poet. She knows that there is no such thing as a science of beliefs without a belief in science.

The logos displayed by Cohen to show the intrinsic alliance between the Jew and the German is so "hallucinated" (Derrida) that the only true logic it displays is that of the *delirium*. Derrida argues that it is the logic of Cohen's phallogocentric *delirium* to display this tension as a "true symptom." In Derrida's work, Cohen appears as one who is convinced, who is convincing himself ("self-believing") that it is in the *nature* of the German idealism and of Kantianism to be the German spirit per se as an alliance *with* Judaism. ("This kinship is sealed in the most intimate depth and the most essential interiority," writes Derrida, adding: "This seal is sacred."[42]) This is Fred-Siegfried's (and Omi's ...) cross (croix); this belief (crois) is so strong that being German is naturally resisting the belief that the fire of the Synagogue of Osnabrück on November 9, 1938, could be anything but a criminal act:

---

41 "Here I am trying to answer the question: how to explain that some people cannot manage to say to themselves that they cannot manage to resolve from one day to the next to cease being German, since they are or believed they are?" (*OSJ*, 97).
42 Derrida, "Interpretations at War," 58.

M. Katzmann ne dit rien, père avec fils courent, par Katharinenstrasse, le fils ne *croit* pas qu'il s'agisse d'un incendie volontaire, *la non-croyance résiste encore une centaine de mètres*, mais elle est déjà la proie de son contraire, le père ne *croit* rien du tout, plus le temps de croire ou pas, la cendre est déjà partout sur son cœur sur ses poumons, il ne pense pas, il se précipite pesant vers son désespoir promis, en tant que responsable principal de la Synagogue, il est curieusement pressé de voir sa propre fin en face, pas seulement de souffrir du verdict de Mlle Hurwitz. Par-dessus le vieux bâtiment de l'école le ciel est indéniablement d'un rouge de feu, ce rouge de sang bouillant qui fait si mal à voir. Et aussi les nuages de fumée qui escaladent le ciel, toutes ces couleurs qui hurlent à l'enfer et qui proclament le crime. Naturellement on se met à courir de toutes ses forces. Comme si on avait peur de manquer le dernier instant. Le nôtre. C'est nous qui brûlons, là.

(*N*, 34; my emphasis)[43]

---

43 "Mr. Katzmann says nothing, father and son run, through Katharinenstrasse, the son doesn't believe that it could be arson, the non-belief resists another hundred meters, but it is already the prey of its contrary, the father doesn't believe anything, no more time to believe or not, the ash is already everywhere on his heart on his lungs, he doesn't think, he rushes, heavy, towards his promised despair, as the main head of the Synagogue, he is curiously in haste to look his own end in the face, not only to suffer from the verdict of Mrs. Hurwitz. Above the old building of the school the sky is undeniably fire red, that boiling blood red so painful to see. And also, the clouds of smoke that climb the sky, all these colors that scream to hell and proclaim the crime. Naturally one starts running with all of one's strength. As if one were afraid of missing the last moment. Ours. It's we who are burning, here."

Fourteen "We"

We are burning, "C'est nous qui brûlons, là." The belief is in flames. Which means "We" is in flames, the idea that "we German believers," believers in Germany, are revealed as believers in the exact moment when we are set on fire by Germany. Before developing this aspect, the fire reveals another neighboring form of the "belief": the illusion. The trajectory of this illusion of being-German runs from Michael Klein to Hélène Cixous:

> [D]ans sa rêverie trempée de sang le soldat meurt saintement pour l'Allemagne, il laisse derrière lui femme et enfants à manger pour l'Allemagne, un texte publié en 1916, en 1916 le mari d'Omi est tué sur le front, le sujet: l'*illusion*. Moi aussi je me fais des illusions: parce qu'Omi est ma grand-mère, et la mère d'Ève.
>
> (*N*, 107; my emphasis)[1]

Suddenly, what burns with the synagogue, what gets arrested during the following hours on November 9, 1938, is the German illusion. Siegfried is arrested and becomes one of the *Aktionjuden*. The arrest renders and reveals the illusion. This is the (retroactive and projected)

---

1 "[I]n his daydream soaked with blood the soldier dies in a saintly way for Germany, he leaves wife and children behind to eat for Germany, one text published in 1916, in 1916 Omi's husband is killed on the front, the subject: the illusion. Me too, I create illusions for myself: because Omi is my grandmother, and Ève's mother." "Le dit de la Vie et de la Mort du fantassin Michael Klein. Le soldat est mort. Mort de guerre, mort d'illusions et d'hostilités, mort de fourmi pour la fourmilière, Fourmichael Klein. Tout soldat est en lice pour la mort. Tous s'engagent pour la guerre de Troie. L'âme reste avec les femmes." Cixous, *Mdeilmm*, 55 ("What is said about the Life and Death of infantryman Michael Klein. The soldier is dead. Died of war, died of illusions and hostilities, death of an ant for the anthill, Fourmichael Klein. Every soldier is in line for death. All of them enlist in the Trojan War. The soul remains with the women."). A color photograph of the August 2, 1916 telegram announcing Michael Klein's death on July 27, 1916 is reproduced on page 57 of *Mdeilmm*.

becoming-illusion of "Siegfried." Siegfried the German who was written by Fred in the *Bericht* while in exile in 1941 and 1985. In the days following his arrest, Siegfried is convoyed to Buchenwald, near Weimar, near Goethe's house. In the bus he is guarded by two former high school comrades:

> Siegfried ne comprend pas les deux Polizisten d'Osnabrück. Ils étaient avec lui au lycée. Maintenant, côte à côte, les anciens élèves sont étrangement sur deux continents. Entre les deux, la faille se creuse dans l'Omnibus. Cependant les deux policiers jumeaux en uniforme et, de l'autre côté de la réalité, Siegfried à la tête rasée, contemplent la maison de Goethe. Et de même quand Siegfried est relâché dans les rues de la ville, chaque rue 1939 qui autrefois lui était aussi familière qu'une cousine est maintenant irréparablement étrangère. C'est Siegfried qui a changé: *il est devenu orphelin d'illusions.*
>
> (N, 108; my emphasis)[2]

If the belief is the veil of the illusion, the illusion is also ultimately the veil of a pseudo-naturality. From "nature" to "belief," to "illusion." This is the long trajectory of what happens in the sparkle of an instant when "la Synagogue brûle," the synagogue is burning. The "orphan of illusions," is Siegfried. Siegfried is irremediably changed; the fault, the cliff that suddenly separates the former high school students is abyssal, unsurmountable. Later, when Siegfried is released in 1939, Osnabrück appears to him as estranged, uncanny (which echoes the uncanniness felt by Ève and Éri when they "returned" to Osnabrück in 1985). It is not that the city has changed (in 1939), it is that Siegfried, who is already becoming Fred, has become an orphan of illusions. Fred—who writes the *Bericht*—is the orphan of Siegfried. The nurturing mother of Michael-Rosi-Siegfried has fallen. The *delirium* turns into a display of illusions, which ultimately is a deconstruction of beliefs, of the Jewish-German belief. German chimeras.

---

2 "Siegfried doesn't understand the two Polizisten of Osnabrück. They were with him in high school. Now side by side, the former comrades find themselves strangely on two continents. Between the two the fault is widening in the Omnibus. However, the two twin police officers in uniform and Siegfried with the shaved head on the other side of reality contemplate Goethe's house. And likewise when Siegfried is released in the streets of the city, each street 1939 that once was to him as familiar as a cousin, is now irreparably foreign. It is Siegfried who changed: he has become an orphan of illusions."

German chimeras, German belief, German illusion ....[3] From now on, a proliferation of words, of notions, is the mark of an infinite deconstruction. This proliferation has a name. It is both Cixous's entire œuvre and her being, inseparably. It is another name for her being poet, or poet-being. As she indicates in a passage above, Cixous does not exclude the possibility that she, too, as a granddaughter of Omi, and her mother, the daughter of Omi, could also be immersed in illusions, "Moi aussi je me fais des illusions: parce qu'Omi est ma grand-mère, et la mère d'Ève" (N, 107).[4] This sheds light on all of her texts of Germany, but also on her recent trips to Osnabrück, the City of Peace, in Germany. This also sheds light on Hélène Cixous geboren Hélène Cixous as a "C'est Omi que je peins," or "Je m'appelle Michael Klein." Could it be that she, too, is mystified, hypnotized, hallucinated, *envoûtée* by the German chimeras? Might that poetry, that literature, be for her the ultimate state of the Jewish-German *envoûtement*, the fact that she carries the heavy burden of so many generations through a deconstructive but tenacious resistance of the chimeras of Germany? Michael, Ève, Éri and, finally, what about Cixous herself? Strong literary ties, powerful Romanesque figures, Hélène Cixous included, Cixous, as a Romanesque figure of herself, who is both the writer, the secret-keeper and a powerful literary character in her own texts. The tenacious mysterious German-being remains an abyssal German sorrow, an infinite German burden, an affliction, a German malady from which there is *no* escape:

> —On n'a pas pu faire autrement, les Juifs sont obligés par la maladie de l'Allemagne à l'état d'être-juifs. L'ancienne synagogue a été brûlée il restait juste une pierre comme chaise sur laquelle j'ai empêché Jennie de justesse de s'asseoir devant tout le monde. Au départ ils nous ont donné à chacun un sachet avec quelques petites pierres de cette synagogue brûlée. —C'est très gentil dit Jennie et ma mère reprend sa parole: il restait quelques pierres qu'ils ont gardées à la Mairie. La maladie de l'Allemagne on ne sait plus comment s'en débarrasser: il faudrait savoir qui est malade, qui est le malade, qui est la maladie. Tout à coup nous étions

---

3   "[L]'illusion allemande des Jonas, [...] le coup de l'annulation du sujet, ne plus pouvoir se trouver inscrit dans la liste des vivants, être renvoyé du monde, même pas exilé, décrété non-existant, c'est une maladie brutale qui prend au cerveau," writes Hélène Cixous in a segment quoted from *Ruines bien rangées* in our introduction (*RB*, 65) ("the German illusion of the Jonas, [...] the blow of the cancelation of the subject, no longer being able to find itself registered on the list of the living, being fired from the world, not even exiled, declared non-existent, it is a brutal malady that takes hold of the brain").
4   "Me too, I create illusions for myself: because Omi is my grandmother, and Ève's mother."

traitées comme des malades âgées frappées par leur maladie mentale. Tout à coup nous étions là pour accélérer la guérison de leur maladie. On se passait ces pierres de la synagogue dans les mains, sur le front. Moi je les ai mises au fond de ma valise. Il restait quelques Juifs mais pas des gens d'Osnabrück, des Juifs de l'Est.

(*BM*, 152–53)[5]

This is the account by Ève Cixous of her visit to Osnabrück in 1985; "ils *nous* ont donné à chacun un sachet avec quelques petites pierres de cette synagogue brûlée" (*BM*, 152; my emphasis),[6] says Ève Cixous in this passage. "*Nous* avons vécu dans les chimères allemandes,"[7] she says in another passage (*BM*, 167; my emphasis). "Nous," "we" ... More than once have we seen this "we" pass along the way. "C'est *nous* qui brûlons, là" (*N*, 33; my emphasis),[8] writes Hélène Cixous who voices Siegfried's words when he sees the synagogue burn. Who is this "we"? What does it mean to say "we"? In other words, what is it that remains after the "we Germans," when the German "we" has been revealed as an illusion and reduced to ashes? What part of the German being of the Jewish-German psyche burns with the burning of illusions when the synagogue burns? When the belief has fallen, when it has revealed itself as an illusion, when the *delirium*, the madness, the folly, the fever, the malady of Germany has become deadly and unbearable, it never stops to return to Ève and Éri, to the Jonas family and its mysterious German-being. The belief, the illusion, is reduced to ashes, but yet, it still manifests itself. And not just as a ghost. After all, could it be that a certain "we" Germans is what calls Ève and Éri to "return" to Osnabrück in 1985? This is the question Ève and Éri and their secretary Hélène Cixous are posing. We, the Jonas-Cixous family, is asking the "We

---

5 "—One couldn't do otherwise, the Jews are obliged by the malady of Germany in the state of being-Jews. The old synagogue has been burned, only one stone remained that was like a chair which I barely prevented Jennie to sit on in front of everyone. When we were leaving, they gave each of us a little bag with a few stones of this burnt synagogue. —This is kind, says Jennie and my mother speaks again: there were a few stones that they kept at the City hall. The malady of Germany one never knows how to get rid of it: we should know who is sick, who is the sick one, who is the sickness. All of a sudden, we were treated like sick elderly people stricken with their mental sickness. all of a sudden, we were there to accelerate the healing of their sickness. We passed the stones of the synagogue among ourselves from hands to hands, on the forehead. As for me, I put them In the bottom of my suitcase. There were a few Jews remaining, but not people from Osnabrück, Jews of the East."
6 "They gave to each of us a little bag with a few stones of this burnt synagogue."
7 "We have inhabited German chimeras."
8 "It's we who are burning, here."

Germans" who is calling, and it is no longer the folly of a certain Jewish-German psyche, but, this time—this moment is decisive—the sick "German we" calling, the German malady summons Ève, Éri, Fred and a handful of others to come help them heal: "il faudrait savoir qui est malade, qui est le malade, qui est la maladie. Tout à coup nous étions traitées comme des malades âgées frappées par leur maladie mentale. Tout à coup nous étions là pour accélérer la guérison de leur maladie," says Ève. "*Leur* maladie mentale" (my emphasis), their mental sickness, their *delirium*.

Who is, again, on the hotspot? Ève asks. The Jews. "—On n'a pas pu faire autrement, les Juifs sont obligés par la maladie de l'Allemagne à l'état d'être-juifs." "We" are obliged by the German malady, which also means that "We" is the host, that Ève and Éri are hosted *and* kidnapped, that they are both *guests and hostages* of the German malady, they are hostages *because* they are guests, all the more kidnapped because they are invited, constrained and forced to acknowledge or to be subjected to the German malady.[9] "We," as Jews-of-Osnabrück is invited by the German malady, a malady of the "we." "We," a burnt, destroyed but resisting "we" occurs in Fred's *Bericht* at a critical moment when he and the other Aktion-Jews arrested in Osnabrück find themselves in the cave-prison on November 9, 1938. When "we" has become an illusion, while "we" is burning in the synagogue, the German "we" makes an ultimate return:

> *Nun sind wir hier*
> C'était à lui de prononcer ces paroles, en tant que responsable naturel de cette cave dans laquelle chacun n'avait toujours pas reconnu, avant ces paroles, une imitation de synagogue inversée, au lieu de s'élever vers le ciel s'enfoncer sous la terre.
> (N, 42)[10]

Nun sind wir hier: "We are here now," "Here we are now," *in German*. Hélène Cixous-the-poet, guardian of the "wir." Not "nous" ("we") or "ici" ("here") in Cixous's text, but "wir," "hier," *in German*. "Wir" is

---

9 One implication of Cixous's use of "obliger" is the double meaning of the verb in French. "Obliger" can mean to force someone to do something, while "obliger," often used in a passive sense ("être obligé," "être l'obligé de quelqu'un") means being hospitable, caring, open, attentive, considerate toward someone who helped, supported, cared, etc.

10 "*Nun sind wir hier* / It was up to him to pronounce these words as the natural head of this cellar in which each of them had still not recognized, before these words, an imitation of reversed synagogue that instead of elevating in the sky was sinking underneath the earth."

burning and the language chosen to say, to write it, both in the *Bericht* and in Cixous's text is resolutely German:

> Je ne sais pas pourquoi cette phrase de quatre sous m'émeut tellement, c'est à cause de sa pauvreté, une dépouillée pour dire le dépouillement infini, j'imagine un Job à bout de mots, à la fin de la plainte, il n'y a pas de plainte, Flatauer constate, sa voix est vide aussi, blanche il n'a rien d'autre à dire, toute la pensée du monde se mendie humblement,
>
> et cependant il y a une tiédeur dans le dénuement c'est ce *nous*, cette façon de s'adresser aux autres en leur demandant et leur offrant le *nous*, d'invoquer l'infime parlement de la cave, d'embrasser ces brins d'être, de dire au nom de tous ici nous sommes encore vivants, ici nous sommes foutus. Ici nous sommes, tout notre être est ici, *Hier* est notre pays.
>
> (N, 43)[11]

"Nous," in French, "we," "wir," in German: here, "ici." Here, where this word, "wir," finds its "wir." We, the collective self (Helene, Omi, Michael, Ève, Éri, Andreas, Fred, Marga ...) called-named, recalled and renamed "Hélène Cixous" on the front cover of her books, and beyond, "we" the divided "we," is depicted by its own negation. From this apophatic "we" of the "nous sommes foutus" (we are shot, annihilated) remains the place where the apophatic "we" happens. The spot is reclaimed by the multiple, deconstructed revolutionary writer(s) that speak(s) the impossibility of writing, of not writing, in French in German, in German in French in all of Cixous's texts.[12] Because *hier*-here,

---

[11] "I don't know why this two-bit sentence moves me so much, it's because of its poverty, a privation in speaking of the infinite privation, I imagine a Job spent of words, beyond the complaint, there is no complaint, Flatauer notices, his voice is empty too, an anemic voice, he has nothing to add, the whole thinking of the world humbly begs for itself, / and, nevertheless, there is a tepidity in the deprivation, it is this *us*, this way of invoking the infinitesimal parliament of the cellar, to embrace these stalk of beings, to say on behalf of all, here, we are still alive, here, we are shot. Here we are, our whole being is here, *Hier* is our country."

[12] As Gilles Deleuze and Félix Guattari write of Franz Kafka's June 1921 letter to Max Brod, "impossibilité de ne pas écrire, impossibilité d'écrire en allemand, impossibilité d'écrire autrement," in Gilles Deleuze and Félix Guattari, *Kafka, Pour une littérature mineure* (Paris: Éditions de Minuit, 1975), 29. ("[I]mpossibility of not writing, the impossibility of writing in German, the impossibility of writing otherwise." Gilles Deleuze and Félix Guattari, *Kafka, Toward a Minor Literature*, trans. Dana Polan [Minneapolis: University of Minnesota Press], 1986, 16).

Cixous renames this place *in German*, "Hier." *Hier* is *our* country, on the *Wörterflucht*, the word flight of here-*hier*. This is the performative "we," a revolutionary one, the immobile condition of all mobilities, of the infinite flight that opens the poetic space on the field of ashes and ruins. *Here is we Cixous. Hier is wir Cixous.* We are here, "we" is here, *"wir" ist hier*, *"hier"* is the new "we" separated from Germany, uttered in German, *hier* (here), *hier* is the German word where *wir* (we) is set on fire by Germany, in German, in a story that can only be said in untranslatable German:

> [C]'est dans la Cave qu'aura commencé l'époque du Désarroi, à partir du 9 Novembre 1938, des centaines de milliers de personnes se sont demandé où sommes-nous ici où allons-nous se regardant les uns les autres et se disant nous non plus nous ne savons pas où nous allons où nous sommes les cartes postales tombaient des trains qui étaient comme des caves roulantes les gens qui étaient atteints de cette douleur mentale avaient l'air de ces malades si âgés que dans le couloir de leur chambre ils se sentent perdus, déportés, emportés en pleine maison par le train fatal
> *Hier*. Ici est intraduisible. Sinistre.
>
> (*N*, 44)[13]

Hier is untranslatable, a fragment of a quote we had introduced earlier, like the divided subject of an untranslatable *"wir,"* who becomes a vague, an undefined authorless *"on"* (one) who writes, who still speaks German, German only: "—Ces choses-là on doit les écrire en allemand, dit le texte sans nom et sans auteur" (*N*, 26).

This is what remains. The authorless German language-machine of "these things." *Eine Messe*, says Cixous's mother, a mess. The mess of Germany always *inadvertently* returns as a language, eerie and poetic, here-*hier* are "these things" at the heart of the Jewish-German psyche.

---

13 "[I]t is in the Cellar that the great time of the Disarray will start on November 9, 1938, hundreds of thousands of people asked themselves where are we here where are we going while looking at each other and telling themselves neither do we know where we are going where the postcards are that fell from the trains that were like cellars on wheels the ones who were affected by this mental pain looked like these ill ones so old that in the hallway of their own bedroom they feel that they are lost, deported, taken away in the heart of the home by the fatal train / *Hier*. Here is untranslatable. Sinister."

This is the curse of the psyche, of the German Jews, of the Jewish-German psyche:[14]

> —C'est le malheur des Juifs allemands qu'on ne peut pas se divorcer de la langue allemande. Rendre l'Allemagne et garder l'allemand on ne peut pas. Chaque fois l'Allemagne rentre par l'allemand. J'ai constaté. Dit ma mère. D'ailleurs elles s'y parlent allemand sans le faire exprès. J'entre elles retournent au français j'ai beau leur dire: il n'y a pas de mal allemand, s'il vous plaît parlez allemand pour me faire plaisir, elles n'y arrivent plus. Elles parlent leur ramage de Cuisine. *A mess. Eine Messe.* Elles ont beau lutter. Il y a annexion.
>
> (*BM*, 103)[15]

---

14 Interestingly enough, as far as I can tell, Derrida does not himself embark on an adventurous road. He does not evoke Sigmund Freud, not even once, in his essay or in the notes of his seminar on the Jewish-German psyche, judging by what I was able to consult in the archives. Cixous does. In the aforementioned quote by Cixous, the idea that Freud would be the chief of the *envoûtés* of the Jewish-German psyche has infinite ramifications for the history of the psyche itself as it is explored by Freud.

15 "—It's the misfortune of the German Jews that one cannot be divorced from the German language. One cannot give Germany back while keeping the German language. Every time, Germany comes back through the German language. I noticed. Says my mother. By the way there they speak German unintentionally. I enter they switch back to French, it's no good trying to tell them: there is no German evil, please, speak German to make me happy, they can no longer do it. They speak their Kitchen birdsong. *A mess. Eine Messe.* They may well struggle. There is annexation."

Fifteen Epilog: *Zugehör*

On a besoin d'appartenir à quelque chose dans la vie. C'est bien et ce n'est pas bien. Chez nous on appelle ça le Zugehör. Tu ne peux pas annuler le Zugehör. Tu crois l'annuler et ta façon d'annuler est exactement dans le Zugehör. Comment veux-tu sortir du dedans du Zugehör en entrant par la fenêtre du bijoutier dans le Zugehör.

(BM, 140)[1]

—Mais chez nous ce n'etait pas le genre costaud, il y a eu un déséquilibre du Zugehör et là-dessus toute la famille s'est un peu suicidée mutuellement. Ils étaient tous un peu trop mentalement allemands, alors que les Salamander pensaient aux affaires mon grand-père pensait toujours à la réputation.

(BM, 141)[2]

---

1 "We have to belong to something in life. It's good and it's not good. At our place we call that the *Zugehör*. You can't cancel the *Zugehör*. You seem to believe that you've been able to cancel it and the way you do it is exactly in the *Zugehör*. How do you want to exit from the inside of the *Zugehör* while entering through the window of the jeweler in the *Zugehör*." Some aspects of the meaning of this German name for "belonging" appeared in our introduction.

2 "—But at our place, this was not a sturdy thing, there was an imbalance of the *Zugehör* and with that the whole family kind of mutually killed themselves. They were all a bit too German mentally, when the Salamander thought about the business, my grandfather always thought about the reputation." In her article "La langue véhiculaire—die deutsche Sprache in Hélène Cixous' Poet(h)ik," Brigitte Heymann suggests that Cixous's creative use of German words form an arsenal of Schibboleth ("ein Arsenal an *Schibboleth* bilden." Heymann, "La langue véhiculaire—die deutsche Sprache in Hélène Cixous' Poet(h)ik," in Andrea Grewe and Susanne Schlünder (eds.), "Die ,deutsche Seite' von Hélène Cixous," special issue, *Lendemains*, vol. 42, no. 166/67 [Narr Francke Attempto Verlag GmbH + Co. KG, 2017], 65) when she describes what she calls a "scene of Schibboleth" ("Szene des Schibboleth," Heymann, "La langue véhiculaire," 66) in Cixous's œuvre, Heymann quotes Cixous's "Zugehör" as an example that "is itself Schibboleth" ("das selbst Schibboleth ist," Heymann, "La langue véhiculaire," 66).

Conclusion   Frauenprotest

La beauté ne sera plus interdite.

(RM, 38)¹

*La machine littéraire prend ainsi le relais d'une machine révolutionnaire à venir, non pas du tout pour des raisons idéologiques, mais parce qu'elle seule est déterminée à remplir les conditions d'une énonciation collective qui manquent partout ailleurs dans ce milieu.*²

Naturellement c'est-à-dire littératurellement.

(SP, 40)³

From May 10 to 13 of 2016, I traveled to Berlin with Hélène Cixous. When I was asked by Cixous to suggest a specific location to visit, I immediately thought about the monument at the Rosenstrasse. Rosenstrasse 2-4 is located in Berlin-Mitte, the heart of Berlin, near Alexanderplatz, not far from the Henriette Herz Platz.

Rosenstrasse 2-4 is the site of a collective street protest that took place at the end of February and beginning of March 1943 after the Gestapo had arrested over 8,000 Jews all over Berlin. Among them were about 2,000 Jewish men and "Mischlinge" (the children of so-called "mixed marriages") who were held captive in a building on this street. They had been arrested and targeted for deportation, based on the racial laws of Nazi Germany. Their wives were non-Jewish. For several days and nights, this group of women gathered in front of the building where their loved-ones were detained in anticipation of their deportation to

---

1   "Beauty will no longer be forbidden."
2   Deleuze and Guattari, *Kafka*, 32. "The literary machine thus becomes the relay for a revolutionary machine-to-come, not at all for ideological reasons but because the literary machine alone is determined to fill the conditions of a collective enunciation that is lacking elsewhere in this milieu." Deleuze and Guattari, *Kafka*, 17–18.
3   "Naturally, which is to say literaturally" (SC, 25).

death camps. Although those demonstrators had been threatened to be shot by the armed SS soldiers of the Third Reich, the protests continued. On March 6, 1943, the men being held were released by the Minister of Propaganda of the Third Reich, Joseph Goebbels, who was also the Gauleiter of Berlin. This event is known today as the only public mass demonstration performed by Germans in the Third Reich against the deportation of Jews. Since 1995, this movement is honored by a memorial, the *Block der Frauen* (Block of Women), that was created by the East German sculptor Ingeborg Hunzinger.[4] On the stones, the artist inscribed several sentences that read: "Give us our husbands back" and "The strength of civil disobedience, the vigor of love overcomes the violence of dictatorship / Give us our men back / Women were standing here, defeating death / Jewish men were free."[5]

On May 12, 2016, we visited the monument. As Hélène Cixous was discovering and contemplating Ingeborg Hunzinger's work of art, while she was welcoming the geological energy of the piece and its historical force, stunned by the beauty of the pink faces sculpted in a pink stone (Rosenstrasse, "rose ..."), we noticed that two of the female faces had been profaned. With a dark marker or pen of some sort, someone had drawn Hitler moustaches on the stone. Speechless, we walked back to Hélène Cixous's hotel. As we approached Alexanderplatz, Hélène broke our silent wandering across the city with a simple sentence: "—I know why my mother never wanted to come back to Germany."

This moment is one origin of this book.

The path to Medusa, a Medusa who is not mortal and smiles, was always barred by a war. Cixous's first political and philosophical experience comes to her like the ominous discovery of the Rosenstrasse—a primitive scene. The first political and philosophical experience that Cixous will remember while leaving Montaigne's Tower after having had the Vision of the Roman Charity is a word-prison. A word-prison, word-poison, proffered to her by older kids once she had been allowed to enter the garden, the long desired Garden of the Military Circle of Oran that had always been forbidden until her father had joined the military during the war. She was not even three, yet suddenly she was allowed to enter the garden of paradise. Instead, she was taken to hell.

---

4 Born in Berlin on February 3, 1915, she became a member of the KPD (Communist Party of Germany) in 1932. She had a Jewish mother. She lived in Italy and Germany during the Second World War and then lived in the German Democratic Republic. She died in Berlin on July 19, 2009. Many of her works can be seen in the city of Berlin and are marked by her experience during the war.
5 "1943 Die Kraft des zivilen Ungehorsams / die Kraft der Liebe bezwingen die Gewalt der Diktatur / Gebt uns unsere Männer wieder / Frauen standen hier / Tod besiegen Jüdische Männer waren frei."

The garden became hell when an unknown word, "Jew," was transformed into an insult and spat on her face for the first time. It was 1940. It was the beginning of Cixous's wars, the wars that made Medusa wait for a long time. Always deferred. There has always been a reason to wait, to defer the justice due to Medusa. Then came Cixous's writing; she was 25, the year of the Independence of Algeria. Cixous's own declaration of independence from her Germanalgia, her GermanAlgeria, in the footsteps of a mother, Ève, who had always been a smiling Medusa. Her mother and a few "Résistantes" like the women of the *Frauenprotest*.

This is the other origin of this book. A text Hélène Cixous wrote about her *Medusa* in the 2010 new publication of *Le Rire de la Méduse*, titled "Un effet d'épines de rose" (rose, pink) in French:

> À la fin, j'en eus assez de ces décapitations. J'en voyais tellement, depuis que j'étais venue à penser, quand j'avais trois ans, en Algérie dans un monde dépecé, dépeçant, dé-pensant. Or, il y avait toujours une guerre. À cause d'une guerre, je patientais. Je pensais: "Après la guerre, on va enfin pouvoir rendre justice à Méduse." Mais tout de suite après la seconde guerre mondiale, il y eut la guerre d'Algérie. L'indépendance du peuple d'abord. Méduse et moi nous attendîmes. En 1962, je commençais à écrire et à espérer qu'on allait se pencher sur le corps mutilé de Méduse et lui rendre ses langues vivantes. Et puis non, il y avait du Père de tous les côtés et des foules de fils furieux occupés à l'assiéger. Dans la mêlée, je cherchais des semblables, des femmes avec des yeux et des oreilles au bout des langues, et des corps qui parlaient et riaient. Il n'y en avait vraiment pas beaucoup dans le monde. Souvent, je m'en plaignais à mon ami Jacques Derrida: mais où sont-elles? Les puissantes, les fertiles, les joyeuses, les libres, à part ma mère et quelques résistantes, ces beautés de vies que je rencontrais en littérature, rares et splendides, on ne peut pas dire qu'elles couraient les réalités. Et lui me disait: si elles existent en texte, c'est qu'elles existeront en réalité, "un de ces quatre." "Un de ces quatre" c'est quand?
>
> (*RM*, 23–4)[6]

---

[6] "In the end I got tired of these beheadings. I had seen so many, ever since I came to think, when I was three in Algeria, in a butchered world, butchering, de-thinking. Yet, there was always a war. Because of a war, I waited patiently. I thought: 'After the war, we will finally be able to do justice to Medusa.' But as soon as the Second World War had ended, there was the Algerian War. The people's independence first. Medusa and I waited. In 1962, I began to write and hope that we would be able to care for Medusa's mutilated body and give her back her living tongues. But no, there was always some Father in every corner

Conclusion 225

Figure 26 Hélène Cixous on her way to Osnabrück, October 22, 2019.

and a crowd of furious sons besieging her. In the fray I looked for similar figures, women with eyes and ears at the tip of their tongues, and bodies that spoke and laughed. There were truly not many in the world. Often I would complain to my friend Jacques Derrida: but, where are they? The powerful, the fertile, the joyful, the free, aside from my mother and a few resistors, those beauties of life that I met in literature, rare and splendid, we cannot say that they were running in the streets of realities. And he told me: yes, if they do exist in texts, it means that they will exist in reality, 'one of these days.' 'One of these days' when will it be?" In a passage of *Ruines bien rangées* (October 2020) that revolves around Ève Cixous's exiles from Germany to France, to Algeria, and more specifically around Ève Cixous's imprisonment in Algeria at the time when Hélène Cixous was beginning her own journey as a writer, Cixous writes: "La première fois la prison c'était en 1962, ou peut-être c'était déjà en 1933, ou en 1938, selon les personnages principaux, en 1962 pour moi en tant que personnage secondaire, j'allais justement pour la première fois commencer à écrire un livre, du moins je commençais à être réveillée la nuit par le rêve d'un livre qui chantait à ma fenêtre comme les oiseaux aux barreaux de la cellule de Rosa Luxemburg, c'est-à-dire comme les chantres de la liberté même, et soudain ma mère disparaît je n'avais pas écrit une ligne, seulement senti une joie effrayée au frôlement de la liberté, et soudain, elle n'est plus là, elle n'est plus à La Clinique, au téléphone personne, j'ai l'enveloppe du corps en France, le cerveau en Algérie, tout autour une sensation de mur, finalement elle est retrouvée c'est-à-dire retrouvée perdue

Figure 27 Celebration of the *Instrumentum Pacis Osnabrugensis*, the Treaty of Osnabrück (Peace of Westphalia), signed in October of 1648. The town hall of Osnabrück, built between 1487 and 1512, is the building on the left. Osnabrück, October 25, 2019.

---

bouclée à Barberousse, fin du commencement du livre" (*RB*, 112–13) ("The first time, the jail, that was in 1962, or perhaps already in 1933, or in 1938, depending on the main characters, in 1962 for me, a supporting character, I was just going to begin to write a book for the first time, at least I was starting to be awakened at night by the dream of a book that would sing at my window like the birds at the barrels of Rosa Luxemburg's cell, that is, like the cantors of liberty itself, and suddenly my mother disappears and I had not written one line, had only felt a frightened joy at the gentle brush of liberty, that suddenly, she's no longer here, she's no longer at the Clinic, no one on the phone, I feel the casing of my body in France while my brain is in Algeria, and all around, a feeling of wall, finally she is found, that is, found lost-locked up at Barberousse, the end of the beginning of the book").

Afterword   A filmed-interrupted interview with Hélène Cixous

Conducted in Paris on June 17, 2012, this exclusive filmed interview was a part of the making of the film Ever, Rêve, Hélène Cixous. It happened on the day after an "homage to Hélène Cixous's œuvre" had been organized in Paris at the Bibliothèque Nationale de France (BNF) by Marta Segarra, Bertrand Leclair and Marie-Odile Germain, with the good-heartedness of Daniel Mesguich. This event gathered "around twenty writers and scholars who shared what the experience of reading Cixous's œuvre had been for them, an œuvre placed under the order [une œuvre ordonnée par] of the 'powers of literature'."[1]

Gertrude Baillot was the director of photography whose images (screenshots) are featured in the following pages. Benjamin Bober was the sound recordist. I express my gratitude to them, as well as to Paul Rozenberg and Céline Nusse (producers, Zadig Productions).

It is crucial to understand that this conversation took place while Ève Cixous was resting in a nearby apartment. The texture, the rhythm and the duration of the exchange are inhabited by a theatrical scene that will never leave the room: the session was situated in the anticipation of Ève's arrival, in awaiting the event of her appearance. As we waited and expected her arrival at any moment, more than once we believed that we heard, we felt that we dreamed the probable-improbable ringing of the telephone, of the doorbell, the sound of the keys in the lock to Cixous's apartment ... this psyche of anticipation was and wasn't Ève's arrival. Until Ève finally came in.

Ève's call huddled at the core of Hélène Cixous's poetic words, Ève's voice present and to-come, vivid, for some reason gave me the command to erase most of the questions. Like a breath, a song, the intertitles chant the waiting while binding what they cut. They anticipate and play the waiting. They figure a scene of the call.

---

1   Staff writer, "Lectures amicales d'Hélène Cixous," *Fabula* (Paris: Bibliothèque Nationale de France), June 16, 2012, available online : https://www.fabula.org/actualites/lectures-amicales-d-39-helene-cixous_50740.php (accessed September 17, 2022).

At last, it is Ève's arrival that interrupts the conversation. Just as the dreamed book that ends already contains the one that might call.

Haya means Life: Conversation while waiting for Ève

Who, "she?"

H.C.: It's been a while, not long, maybe three or four weeks, that I've been wondering if she is not immortal. Because it's happened twice now that she crossed the Acheron and came back after having said "goodbye" to me. I have completely changed towards her. Last year I was terrorized. To a certain extent the verdict appeared to me to have been pronounced; I was telling myself that the execution was ineluctable. And now, it is as if I have already crossed to the other side. Precisely. Taking into account that she has crossed the Acheron twice, I'm telling myself, but ... but, why is it that I thought that she would not continue this back and forth? That is, take off with her 101 years, then her 102—she will soon turn 102—with her backpack and grant me with the surprise of her return ... I have completely changed my inner state. Truly! It is a true internal revolution. All of my criteria, all of my fantasies have been pushed aside and new fantasies have replaced them.

Who is this "she?" Who am I talking about? I have no idea ... there is a history of this character. First of all, it used to be my mom from when I was little and for whom I had an adoration that, in a certain way, I have forgotten—let's say that I remember it, but it's become a *memory*. That is, the adoration that I used to have and that was painful when I was little, that was already filled with death, has remained back there in time, in the very, very distant past. I had a fear then, a kind of premonition: I was unable to look at my mother—who, aside from that, absolutely shone, sparkled—without telling myself that she was going to die. And this was when I was very little, I was two or three and I was struck by terror, panic, I was convinced that she was going to die. This was the first blow dealt by fate, it taught me many things because in my early childhood I fixated the fear of death upon my mother—of this I cannot say anything more: was it a death drive? The whole question of mortality was fixated on my mother. And on her face. And it is my father who died.[2] Voilà. In a very brutal manner, unexpected, uncalculated. I believe it was the first great lesson I learned: I told myself, "Oh, one expects death here and then it arrives there." It is true of death and of any event. Namely the fact that in every event that erupts, that hits

---

2   Georges Cixous was born in Oran, Algeria, on May 9, 1908. He died of tuberculosis in Algiers on February 12, 1948, at the age of 39.

us, everything is unpredictable, everything is unexpected, truly unexpected. Every time we place ourselves somewhere in the hope or fear that something *will* happen, it hits elsewhere. This was consequently the first Event, the first moment of my early childhood, and it lasted for quite a long time.

I think that you can hear the sound of the keys, don't you?
H.C.: Afterward, then, I know that I was 10 and that my brother and I were put in summer camps for orphans—since my father had died—and I was also waiting for the sun to rise. I was in the darkness, it was terrible, and once a week my mother came to visit—we were in different locations. I awaited this visit as if I were awaiting life because I was dead when she wasn't around. And then, she would rise like the sun. I saw her coming, I have extraordinarily beautiful visions of this moment. Exactly like in the tale—if I may—of Demeter and Persephone but reversed, I lived for a whole day, the day she was present. In the evening when she left, I died. Etc. This period when she represented life for me was later displaced: I became an adult, and we passed through many chapters and centuries until we finally reached another continent, another universe. On the other side of the times of times, she returned but in a different shape. At first, as a very old woman, the one I featured in some of my books like *Cigüe*, etc.,[3] but a very old woman who was still in flower [*qui était encore en fleurs*]. And now, she appears under another avatar but one difficult to convey. Because ... here I'm talking about things that constantly change from one day to the next, things related to the human adventure, the adventure of life and death as it is altered and transformed every day. It's astonishing. When entering the age of ice floe in what I call Antarctica, in a strange manner, time is extraordinarily slow and as if at a standstill, because one tells oneself that it is impossible to go any further, no matter what. But, at the same time, time is rushed, and everything goes at a crazy pace. There is a reserve of time, and we think "That's it, these are the last days," and it's not true because these last days, ultimately, deepen, wind around themselves and, in the meantime, it's ... let's say that for the past 72 or 73 years, I have known this character who changed a lot. With whom I've had very different relationships. I've talked about my adoration for her but there were also moments of conflict—rather brief as I was able to solve them quickly when I quickly realized what was causing them—ah! I think that you can hear the sound of the keys in the lock, don't you?

---

3   Hélène Cixous, *Cigüe, Vieilles femmes en fleurs* (Paris: Galilée, 2008). See also Hélène Cixous's *Revirements, dans l'antarctique du cœur* [*RV*].

I could follow her with an inner camera

H.C.: So, there was this period when my mother was an absolute mother, was mom, my mother. Then there was a certain era when she was a kind of young man, because she has always been, she has long been a kind of young man, but a young man who was *not* phallic, exactly. Who was, to the contrary, the victim of a phallocentric world. This was the moment when my mother became a widow. She then found herself totally defenseless in an extreme world. At this moment, I became her father and her husband. It lasted for a while. It was in an emergency situation. From the moment I started to write I encountered a kind of resistance. Because, for her, writing never had any value, nor even a reality. This is a kind of mistake that I perpetuate! She resigned herself to this, but ... anyway. At this moment, for a while, instead of being on her side and her on my side in a kind of complex solidarity, she became some sort of an adversary that I had to set aside. Then came this period of resignation.

She became a marvelous midwife. She became one later in life[4] because she had to find her way after the death of my father. She had to understand that she would become a midwife, that she had to study, something I helped with—I made her review her homework—and for a while she truly became this midwife, became the action itself. An action that worked as a defining one for me because it was a beautiful action. A fertile, a marvelous one, one of the rare occupations that produces above all the stuff of life. Indeed, it must be said that she had a kind of luck in the practice of this profession: in front of her and around her there were no catastrophes, no violent things, none of the women died, which is a marvelous and miraculous thing in the history of a midwife ... there was only life! Hundreds and hundreds of lives, beautiful lives.[5] And then with the physical distance, the geographical one,[6] I started to watch her from afar, and I then undertook a whole revolution because I had to start looking from a distance. I truly started to look at her, and there, I found myself at a theatre. And that's how I, in fact, found the ideal link, I saw her onstage, thinking "What an incredible character!"

---

4   When Ève became a widow she was 37, Hélène Cixous was 10 and her brother Pierre, 9 (he was born on November 9, 1938). Ève's husband's investments in his medical practice had caused the family to be seriously in debt.
5   One day, as I was visiting the Cartoucherie, at the Théâtre du Soleil, Hélène Cixous introduced me to a friend of hers, a member of the troupe, who is one of the "babies" delivered by Ève in her clinic in Algiers.
6   Hélène Cixous arrived in Paris to study in 1955, at the age of 18. Her mother worked as a midwife in Algeria until long after the Independence. She left Algiers in the most disturbing and chaotic circumstances after having been put in jail and expelled from the country along with the last French doctors and midwives in the early 1970s.

And how strange! There, she played all the parts. When I found out that she was a theatre character—which took me a while ... I was 32–33—she could ... I could follow her with an inner camera [*une caméra intérieure*] in her innumerable trips. Great traveler. Journeys ... The ones she made and the ones she didn't make. For example, the immense regret that she missed Easter Island, that she found herself just next door but did not have enough time. She has wandered the universe. Truly. There are very few countries where she didn't go. And she's a taster—I don't want to say that she's a pleasure-seeker [*jouir*], because that's not her thing—but tasting, she is a taster of food, of different cuisines from different cultures with a kind of neutrality, because she is not someone who chooses ... well, in fact, she is carrying her double name in an extraordinary manner! So, her name is "Ève." I very lately discovered— maybe, I've got to look for it because it's magnificent!—I very lately discovered that she had a Jewish name, a Hebrew name. No one knew. I'll look for the book.

The Book of Prayers of Michael Klein

II.C.. This is the Book of Prayers of her father, my grandfather [*Michael Klein, September 24, 1881–July 27, 1916; see Figure 28*].[7] Who himself had

---

7   Michael Klein's father, Hélène Cixous's great-grandfather was named Abraham Meir Klein. A rabbi, he was born in Smolenice, Slovakia, on July 17, 1844. He died in Trnava, Slovakia, in 1924. His spouse, was named Rosa (Rivka) Ehrenstein. Born in Skalica, Slovakia, in 1850, Rosa died in Trnava in 1925. From the seventeen known children born to Abraham and Rosa Klein, the great-grandparents of Hélène Cixous, six were murdered as a consequence of the anti-Semite persecutions during the Second World War: Selma (Zelda), in Auschwitz, on May 28, 1944; Sigmund (Asher), in Sobibor on 1942; Leah, in Auschwitz, on November 2, 1944; Schamschi Samson, in the Lubartow ghetto in 1942; Marcus (Mordechai), in Auschwitz in 1944; and Salmi, in Auschwitz in June 1944. Moritz (Maurice) Klein, born in Trnava on August 15, 1875, died in Strasburg on August 17, 1958; he had emigrated to Strasburg in 1908. Six years older than Hélène Cixous's grandfather, Moritz had also, in all likelihood, joined the German army during the First World War. The biographical information attached to his name stipulates: "Still it is our mother [*Rosa Klein née Ehrenstein*] who intervened with the military authorities to obtain the liberation of our father from the Russian front from where he brought back a small prayer book with a blue cover that he found in the trenches from a non-Jewish comrade" ("Interview with Jeanne Rais" indicates the site: Jeanne Rais née Jeanne Klein, third daughter of Moritz, died in Paris on February 9, 2011; she was born in Strasburg on January 19, 1915). Another page of the site, devoted to Michael Klein, reports that Michael was Moritz's business partner. David Blank and Gladys Blank, "Moritz (Maurice) Klein," *Gladys and David Blanks Genealogy*, available online: http://www.blankgenealogy.com/getperson.php?personID=I3761&tree=Blank1 (accessed September 27, 2022). The record also stipulates that Moritz-Maurice spent most of the Second World War in Constantine, Algeria, from 1940 to 1945.

Figure 28 The Book of Prayers of Abraham Meir Klein (1844–1924), Hélène Cixous's grandfather.

inherited it. This is a very old book that is in German and in Hebrew, the book of the family. I finally inherited it, which means that it circulated and came back to me. Basically, I had never deciphered this text and these notes because I was unable to and because nobody could. I discovered that my grandfather, the father of my mother, had written in it something that you'll be able to read.

Read. Because it's written in German. Read.

O.M.: "Unser geliebtes Töchterchen Eva wurde geboren am 14. Oktober 1910 Freitag morgens 8 Uhr. Unser geliebtes Tochter Erika …"[8]
H.C.: Erika, that's his second daughter.
O.M.: "… wurde uns geboren, in der Nacht von 15. July 1913 um 12. Dienstag."[9] The Jewish name appear next to Eva's [*and next to Erika's*].
H.C.: There is the name in Hebrew … This book, I received it rather late, and in fact I noticed … let's say that I did not immediately pay attention to the Hebrew name because I thought that it was very simply the transcription of "Ève" [*Eva*] in Hebrew. When my aunt, my mother's sister, her little daughter, died, the family called me and asked me if I, by chance, did not know if she had a Jewish name.[10]

---

8 "Our beloved baby-daughter Eva was born on Friday, October 14, 1910, at 8:00 am." "Our beloved daughter Erika."
9 "[W]as born to us during the night of July 15, 1913, at midnight. Tuesday."
10 Erika Klein was born on July 15, 1913, in Strasburg. Married to Dr. Bertold Barme, who had fled Nazism in 1933, she died in Manchester on December 31, 2006.

Figure 29 Filmed interview with Hélène Cixous, Paris, June 17, 2012.

Because they themselves, did not know. I looked and I said "yes," I made photocopies that I sent them while being convinced that these were just transcriptions of the German names into Hebrew. When, in fact, it was not quite the case! My mother, in Hebrew, I found out, is named "חָיָה" "Ḥayyâ" "Haya." And Haya means Life. She did not know. She herself doesn't know, she never knew, never paid attention. Her father gave her this name, it was marked in the book, that's all.

O.M.: When did you make this discovery?

H.C.: When my aunt passed away, 5 to 6 years ago, not more.

Leaving Germany, leaving religion

H.C.: She never … this Hebrew name was never used. It is also a family that left … at the same time when they left Germany, they also left their relationship to any religion. That's why, by the way, that's why this book stayed a bit on the sidelines because I discovered, on the one hand, quite early that my family—my paternal family was unbelieving, my father was explicitly an atheist—but I did not know much about my maternal family regarding their faith, for they, on the other hand, were very observant Jews in Germany. The grandfather of Ève was the director of the consistory, etc., anyway, these were families that were very integrated and who were practicing their religion. At some point when I was young, I had a kind of suspicion that, by the way, should have come earlier to me. I was perhaps 25 to 26, and, one day, I was hit by a kind of illumination. I addressed my grandmother, Omi, my German grandmother who used to live with us. All of the sudden, I told her

"Tell me, do you believe in God?" She answered: "—Natürlich nicht!", "—Of course not!" Then I asked: "What do you mean, 'of course not'? It is you who told us the meaning of the Jewish celebrations, who taught us ... —Yes, but that was ..." And there I said, "—But then, why is it that you passed down all those remnants?" "—Well, it was because I wanted to be faithful to my parents who were true believers." I can sense that Judaism or Jewishness [*judéité*]—you know that those terms are very disputed—was never inscribed. Well ... historically, yes, profoundly. But from the perspective of a religious belief, of a belief in God in the family, the idea of a religion had blurred itself. That's why I think that we did not even pay attention to these inscriptions of the Hebrew names ... And, you know, it is I who collected those things! I collected them because I have a relationship to the archive, and also because it is a family that had such a colossal history that I wanted to save it.

A family on the move

H.C.: I think that Ève was born into a series of moves. That's also the history of my family, of her family, that, for me, has metaphorical value for a certain universe that has completely disappeared and that was embodied by this very vibrant world of the Germanophone Jews from which we can track the traces in Kafka and Freud among others.

The father of my mother, Michael Klein, was the tenth of a family of twenty children. He was born in a place called Tyrnau, Trnava, between Bratislava and Prague, so he was born at the time when it was still the Austro-Hungarian Empire. He was the tenth child of a family that had a very special vocation, at least in the history of Judaism. This family had a farm! Typically, the Jews had no farms. They didn't own land. However, there was a time when the Austro-Hungarian Emperor must have granted the Jews the right to farm. It turns out that this family, the Klein family, immediately, either acquired or rented land—but I really think that they acquired it. It became a big farm, and, at this time, there was a kind of division of labor that is quite distinctive: my great-grandfather was a Talmudist, he was busy with books, and the mother of the family was the farmer! She grew crops, rode her horse with her wig on, and raised twenty children. When one has twenty children, one distributes them: the first would take the land, those in the middle would do business, and the rest, I don't know for sure. At least, I know that my grandfather was destined to do business as a career. Therefore he left this land, he was the first traveler. He traveled around the Germanophone countries in search of an ideal spouse. This is why he went to Germany as an Austro-Hungarian subject. In Osnabrück, he found my grandmother, who, as far as she was concerned, belonged to a family that had been German for generations. It was a very ancient German family in which he was told, "If you want our daughter (who was the eighth in the family), you have to be German." Austrian? No way. So he took German citizenship. And he settled in Germany to do business. It was in Germany, in Alsace after the war of 1870. There, he built a factory that is still there today, in Strasburg, and my mother was born in German Strasburg on October 14, 1910. She didn't live in Strasburg for long. My German grandfather enrolled as German in the German military when he was already 34 and had no need to enroll (he already had kids), and he was very quickly killed on the battlefield. I still have, in a drawer, his German Iron Cross [*Eiserne Kreuz*]. He died German. Immediately after the war, my grandmother returned to the German family in Osnabrück. Today, my mother believes herself to have been born in Osnabrück, but she wasn't born in Osnabrück, she spent her youth there with that German family.

So, the move and the voyage were a general dynamic. On my grandfather's side, as well as on my grandmother's side, so on the Austro-Hungarian side as on the Osnabrück side—people from the Hanover region—they moved around a lot. For example, the brothers of my grandmother left to make a fortune in South Africa, that was at the beginning of the twentieth century. Exactly like in *Amerika* by Franz Kafka. People moved around all the time. When my mother turned 19, she took her backpack and left. She told herself, "The first thing I'll do is travel Europe." She had a great European dream. Step by step: she started with England [*in 1929*]; she learned English, she spent a year or two there. After that she thought that she'd go to France and learn French, a language she didn't speak. And Hitler arrived. She made an immediate analysis: Germany, it's over. The symptom, this was my mother's typical fashion: not a great political analysis. It was: "If we are under a regime in which Jews are banned from swimming pools—which was one of the very first laws enforced in Osnabrück—then, it's over." She left. She looked for a job in Paris, her French was still very, very poor at the time. And that's where my father met her. As far as he's concerned, he followed another path. The path of those who belonged to the French colonial empire. Another history. The move: my mother and my aunt had a relationship where I always thought that my mother was the general and my aunt the captain; there was a kind of military organization of things and these were women who had no fear, who always moved around, my mother wandered, as always, with her backpack. I believe she was born with it! Afterward, of course, the backpack became, for me, a kind of substitute belly, the turtle's shell, the portable house. Anyway …

O.M.: A kind of portable *Heimat*.
H.C.: Absolutely. And I believe that, for her, it always worked that way. Without her telling herself …

O.M.: *Heimat*, I say it in German because we don't really have a word for that in French.

H.C.: And it is so much stronger than "Home." Now, "*Heimat*," forget about it: this is a word that my mother never uses. It was charred.

O.M.: It is in Paris that she met your father.

H.C.: In Paris. She was in a Rothschild boarding house. And my father was coming from Algeria in order to defend his doctoral dissertation. Because, at the time, and up until the end of colonization, it was possible to start studies in Algeria but not finish them. Incredible thing. Everything that could constitute a gateway for advancement forced you to go to the *metropole* [*"hexagonal" France, mainland France*]. France was pumping the living forces from Algeria. It was indispensable to return to the mainland for everything that dealt with government certifications and licenses and doctoral degrees. The *agrégation* [*highest teaching diploma in France*], doctoral degrees, the medical doctorate, etc., all that, was delivered in Paris. While he had written his doctorate in Algeria, he had to defend in Paris. For this reason, he came; he visited a friend from Algeria in Paris, and at that moment he met my mother.

O.M.: This is how you were born in Algeria.

H.C.: This is how I was born in Algeria. As far as my mother is concerned it was enchanting because she found adventure ... My father was a man of culture and he was hyper-European. For her, the idea of going to Africa was marvelous. Whereas on my grandmother's side, in Germany, there were clichés, including of racism, that always lingered, in places where they should not have been found.
[...]

I knew that I had already left

H.C.: As soon as I have known how to "read," in the sense that Derrida would talk about it, that is, as soon as I was able to decipher signs and read words, as soon as I had turned three, I knew that I had already left. From then on, it was a matter of time and opportunity. I wondered how to leave this absolutely cursed country that was governed by the worst human predilections, a series of racisms that were overlaid on one another, violence against individuals ... a country that was absolutely devoured by poverty, where the so-called "European" population, the so-called "French," lived on top of ... there was one million pseudo-Europeans and nine million of so-called "indigenous" who found themselves in a devastating poverty. In the streets, there was only poverty. I have only seen its equivalent in India. A dreadful poverty, hunger, people in rags, the mutilated, the amputated, there was also syphilis and all kinds of diseases related to impoverishment that ravaged the people, one would see blind individuals everywhere, it was ... for me it was hell, and I could see where hell was coming from! I saw firsthand what humans do to humans. It was atrocious: it was what France was doing to Algeria, to its colonized peoples.

On top of that, anti-Semitisms came from all parts. The anti-Semitism of the French, anyway, predominantly the Catholics, the anti-Semitism of the Arabs [*in a context where*] the Jews struggled within communitarian systems to which they did not belong, all that, through violence, through permanent brutality. There was also something to which I was very sensitive, that is, cruelty against animals. This drove me completely nuts. Now, I thought the same thing was happening in every country. I told myself, animals are mistreated in the world, in the universe. I still carry the cry of the animals in my chest, of the mangy dogs, the collection of the stray animals by the pound, the cats that perished, the beaten donkeys and horses, emaciated ... things that turned my childhood into a true nightmare. I could not stand it. There was nothing but hatred. The exception was the protected family environment that was mine. My family cocoon was very small, minuscule, it was of a purity, of a depth, a joy, but it was minuscule: we were completely surrounded by violence. So, I told myself right away, it is necessary to leave! This country is not ours—it was stolen. But ... there was no other one! Germany ... I was born with the rise of Nazism. For my family, for my mother, returning to Germany was out of the question—never![11] France ... we didn't know. But I did not care! I told myself, I have to exit! This strip of coast land of North Africa, I had to leave it. I was just awaiting the right moment to do it.

I was there and I was not getting in

H.C.: [...] In fact, Algeria as ... a hidden, a forbidden place—I desired it intensely! I adored it, a bit like I adored my mother. Except that my mother, I could touch her from time to time ... as for Algeria, it was impossible: I was next to it and I could not touch it. There were invisible walls on every side. At night, I could hear the Arab music coming from the terrasses. This was my dream: some, I realized, dream of going to the ball in fairy tales; I wanted to go to an Arab home and share the music with them ... But there was such mistrust on all sides, such great sufferings, that it was impassable. So, in fact, I loved Algeria and the Algerians virtually, but while having given up. It was absolutely ... I can say that it was the Promised Land. I was there and it was the Promised

---

11 After an attempt to convince Omi to emigrate to Algeria in 1936 (which Omi finally does in 1938), Ève only sets foot in Germany again for a brief visit in 1985, at the invitation of the City of Osnabrück (see above).

Land. I was there, and I could not enter. So, I haven't abhorred Algeria. But the place of the murder, of the torture, that, I wanted to leave. What happened is that, when I arrived in France, which was a foreign country to me, and when I later entered into writing—what had been my project forever—I couldn't touch Algeria. I told myself that if there is a thing that I won't do, it is colonize, that means ... [*I won't*] write about Algeria when the Algerians themselves do not have their country—I left [*in 1955*] at the moment when Algeria was about to explode. I could not envision myself [*writing about Algeria*] ... it was an impossible.

A kind of sad happiness
H.C.: Algeria came to me in a completely unexpected manner, I have to say, through a misfortune that was also a kind of sad happiness. The story of Algeria after the War of Independence is a sad story. The Algerians liberated themselves, they became Algerians, something they had not been—they were "Arabs"—and when they became Algerians, they fell under their own blows. From the moment they were free, they started to alienate themselves together through political systems, governments, etc., that robbed them of the freedom they had just won, implementing political regimes and social forms that sadly deprived them from their own good. I could see very well that there was an absolutely extraordinary intellectual wealth in Algeria. I said to myself, are the Algerians, one day, going to have the heartbreaking strength to protest against the fate left to them? All the while, I knew, it was not happening. Exactly as I had seen the Jews entrench themselves—that is, for example, when some Jews were conducting themselves badly—a kind of silence fell inside the community, like "it mustn't be said," because it was forbidden to touch the Jews, the idea that "it will do harm to the Jews" in the arena of outside opinion. And Algerians behaved in a similar way. The idea that if there was a crime committed, or mistakes being made, above all, let's not allow anything to be revealed to the outside world, let's not unveil what's going on that hurts and is shameful inside. So I thought, well, [*the Algerians*] are hostages. I have seen this already, it is starting over, they are hostages of their *amour-propre*, they become one with their own misfortune because it must not be said that an independence was gained in order to lose it again to the profits of embezzlement. From there came this extraordinary moment that, in fact, started in 1991. There was what they themselves called the "Black Decade." This moment when the Algerian elections where interrupted because suddenly it was the Islamists who were winning the elections. This moment where "democracy," in quotation marks, in Algeria, "democracy" defended itself while using antidemocratic means. They interrupted the elections and stopped everything. Evidently, it was the most autoimmune and complicated thing. And, as we know,

this triggered all of a sudden a surge of terrible crimes and massacres across Algeria that targeted the most enlightened people. It started with a massacre of artists, a massacre of teachers, etc., etc. Then came the exodus. Those very enlightened Algerians, though they had been silent until then, hastily fled in order to save their skins, their heads, and I met them immediately. Many of them, by the way, arrived at the Théâtre du Soleil, since they were artists. So, I had the sad happiness of meeting them almost immediately, and it was as if I was reuniting with a family I had never known. We began to fall in each other's arms and they told me "—Write this! Say it!" They told me everything that had just happened to them, everything that was atrocious. I started to take notes and I thought, now I can, it is not impossible anymore, I am not forbidden, and even, it is desired that Algeria enters in my texts.[12]

This supercountry where my father had believed he had a place
H.C.: [...] My father's story is really a different kind of exile story. First of all, there is a unique aspect of it: my family took French citizenship before the Crémieux Decree. In general—and basically, it's true—it is thought that the Jews of Algeria gained French citizenship, that it was granted to them, in 1870. It is Crémieux who granted them French Citizenship in 1870. And it is the French Republic that did this for very complicated political reasons. It is true, except that my family was already French [*before 1870*]. Because before the Republic, there had already been a proposal that is generally forgotten because the Republic doesn't want to remember, a proposal that was much more generous. It was a proposal by Napoleon III to the totality of the Algerian population, Jews and Arabs, to take French citizenship. It did not work at all. Not at all. There were, I believe, about 1,500 families that took French citizenship—out of nine million inhabitants. Including mine. That was 1867. This is how my family, the Cixous family, took French citizenship before the Crémieux Decree. There was an opportunity in more than one respect. The Cixous ancestors[13] were people who had followed

---

12 See, among other texts, *Les rêveries de la Femme Sauvage* (Paris: Galilée, 2000). Hélène Cixous, *Reveries of the Wild Woman: Primal Scenes*, trans. Beverley Bie Brahic (Evanston, IL: Northwestern University Press, 2006) and *Si près* in 2007 [*SP*], translated into English as *So Close* [*SC*].

13 Hélène Cixous's ancestors (who sometimes appear as "Siksou" or "Sicsu" on family records) were already present in the region (Morocco and Algeria) before the time of the French invasion. They most likely arrived in North Africa through their attempt to escape the religious persecutions in Spain following the Alhambra Decree of March 31, 1492. The edict was formally and symbolically revoked on December 16, 1968, following the Second Vatican Council. Here is what Hélène Cixous writes under the chapter titled "Albums et légendes" in

the French colonization and had been interpreters [*truchements*], which means that they had been translators for the French army. The opportunity was also about that, it was about entering as quickly as possible into the world-to-come as French people. There was also a kind of opening to a future that was completely inaccessible to the indigenous people. And so, there was a dream. In my family, there was a French dream. My grandfather, who was a barefoot man, he was poor, he worked at the age of eleven, he had no shoes; however, as soon as he made a little money, he bought all Victor Hugo.[14] In *in folio* formats, the size of the big encyclopedia. I believe that he never read them, but it was as if he had France on his shelves. It was the France of dreams. These were families who wanted to educate themselves: they didn't go to school but practiced piano. Things like that. They studied music, dreamed of becoming French. Later, there were pogroms. All the time. This is also hidden, there were always pogroms in Algeria. And they said "so it is, this is the story of the Jews ..." Then [*the*] Vichy [*regime*]. Where all of the sudden this family that had still been French for quite a while found itself outside of everything! And there, I think, the French dream stopped. That is, for my father, it was over. This is something he did not overcome at all. He died shortly after [*in 1948*]. In my opinion, the ho-, no, it was not even "hope," it was a *belief* ... a dent had already been made in the belief. A very big dent. Because already before the [*Vichy*] anti-Jewish legislation,[15] my father had been drafted in 1939; there, he was on the Tunisian front as a doctor-lieutenant and he was already

---

Hélène Cixous *Photos de Racines*: "la famille paternelle [...] a suivi le trajet classique des Juifs chassés d'Espagne jusqu'au Maroc. Les grands-parents de mon père sont de Tetouan ou de Tanger. Ils voyageaient à dos d'âne. Sans doute suivant l'armée française—comme colporteurs et truchements—ils arrivent à l'orée occidentale de l'Algérie: Oran. Ma ville natale. Une ville très espagnole. Dans la famille de mon père on parle le français et l'espagnol. Le père, Samuel, parle l'arabe également" (*PR*, 183) ("my paternal family [...] followed the classic trajectory of the Jews chased from Spain to Morocco. My father's grandparents are from Tetuán and Tangier. They traveled on donkey-back. No doubt following the French army—as peddlers and interpreters—they arrive at the western edge of Algeria: Oran. My native city. A very Spanish city. In my father's family French and Spanish are spoken. The father, Samuel, also speaks Arabic" [*R*, 182]).

14 Hélène Cixous's paternal grandfather, Samuel Cixous, is mentioned by Hélène Cixous in *Photos de Racines* (*PR*, 183; *R*, 182).
15 This is a fact that Derrida often recalled, a fate that he and his family shared with Cixous's during the war and that applied to the Jews of Algeria: the criminal anti-Jewish legislation was made effective in Algeria by a government of Vichy when not a single German soldier of the Third Reich had set foot on Algerian soil.

facing anti-Semitic insults coming from every direction. Everything stopped in 1940. It was over.[16]

O.M.: It is in this context that you speak about the Algeria of your father as a "supercountry":

> Je vois bien que mes parents ont pu croire être en Algérie, surtout mon père qui y était vraiment né et qui depuis 1908 n'avait pas cessé de progresser dans ce croire être-de et -en, s'élevant par degrés, dans une de ces courbes scolaires et universitaires ascendantes et harmonieuses qui font croire que l'on va vers la Rose Universelle et qu'elle existe. Surtout Ève ma mère qui s'étant tirée elle-même de l'enfer allemand a pu croire en se retrouvant jeune et forte à Oran en être. Tandis que moi dès le début j'ai vu qu'ils étaient poussière et je les ai vus retourner à la poussière, foulés aux semelles de ce surpays où mon père avait cru avoir une place réservée. Tandis que moi j'ai toujours su que j'avais pour toit la voûte d'une cave ou d'un escalier.
>
> (SP, 69)[17]

H.C.: I think that my father's dream, that was a big, ancient and magnificent dream, was interrupted there. And he died. My mother was much more indecisive. Because she did not identify herself. She could not identify herself. She should have ... during her early childhood she was German like German Jews were: believing in it. Then Hitler came. Over. As far as I'm concerned ... I already had that, when I was three, there was *nothing* anymore. I was nothing at all, we were not French, we were told that we were Jews, which was ... anyway, all the doors had already been slammed in our faces. And I believe that I never had the illusions that my parents were able to have when they were young. My mother could believe that she was German, my father could believe

---

16 The October 3, 1940 legislation bans Jews from a number of professions, especially from the French governmental administration. The Crémieux Decree was revoked by the French Interior minister on October 7, 1940.

17 "I realize quite well that my parents were able to believe they were in Algeria, especially my father who was really born there and who since 1908 had not ceased to progress in this belief of being-of and -in, raising himself by degrees, in one of those ascending and harmonious academic arcs that makes one believe one is going toward the Universal Rose and that it exists. Especially Ève my mother who having gotten herself out of the German hell was able to believe she was part of it upon finding herself young and strong again in Oran. Whereas I from the beginning I saw that they were dust and I saw them return to dust, trodden beneath the soles of this supercountry where my father thought he had a place set aside. Whereas I always knew that for roof I had the vault of a cellar or a stairway" (SC, 47).

that he was French, but I never believed anything! *I was born outside. Already outside.*

[...]

A pan-Germanic culture

H.C.: [On my mother's side,] these are people who did not question that they belonged to a pan-Germanic culture. Especially as—it must be said because it is very complicated—the emperors [*of Germany and Austria-Hungary*] had implemented very variable policies towards the Jews. And on occasions, those policies were quite liberal towards the Jews, but sometimes not ... it wavered. I addressed this aspect in *Les Naufragés du Fol Espoir*.[18] Think about someone like Herzl, who, at this time invented Zionism: what swung him into action wasn't the fact that there were Jews accused of ritual crimes, all things that we find in Kafka, everywhere—there was always a Jew accused of a ritual crime somewhere, accused of having murdered a Christian child in order to drink its blood, etc. The big event that changed everything was the Dreyfus Affair. There, Jews of Europe started saying, "But ... what is it that awaits us here?" This leaves a mark. It leaves a mark in Proust, it leaves a mark in Germany, and finally, everywhere. But I think that the Jews were divided, that is, they were profoundly Germans, or Austrians, still during the First World War; there were many who were, I wouldn't say "warmongers," but who voluntarily joined the military during the war while chanting, a lot like people embraced the war in France, that is, in a France where the opposition to the war was scarce with only Jaurès and a few pacifists offering a dissenting view. The dominant culture was pro-war [*in France*], as in Germany and Austria. As a consequence, when my grandfather entered in the war it was ... he was a part of the national effort. And he never thought about what was going to happen to his family in the following few years, that they would be cast out by the country for which he had died. Of course, what fascinates me is that, historically, it's always the story of the nasty surprise. There is only one country in Europe that had a less thorny history with the Jews: England. England, that had very early started to accept the presence of the Jews on its territory while integrating them, as we know they were, to

---

18 Created on February 3, 2010, by the Théâtre du Soleil at the Cartoucherie, this play "half-written by Hélène Cixous through a suggestion by Ariane Mnouchkine" was also adapted into a film by Ariane Mnouchkine in 2013. Staff writer, "Les Naufragés du Fol Espoir," Théâtre du Soleil, 2013, available online: https://www.theatre-du-soleil.fr/fr/librairie-et-editions/les-naufrages-du-fol-espoir-1871 (accessed September 19, 2022).

the point that they had a prime minister during the Imperial era, under Queen Victoria: Benjamin Disraeli.[19]

The tales of Klein, Jonas, Meyer: A general economy of the human memory

H.C.: [...] It is a theory, but I think that, when I was little, since I was not identifiable, I was not identified, but I was not restricted either, that is, there were no boundaries, we were gaping, I did not have the sentiment, precisely, of the *Heimat* [*in German*], or of the *home* [*in French*], or the homeland [*patrie*]. Therefore, this produced a kind of "enlargement" in me. In all the meanings of the word. When I was in a class with little French girls, and I saw to what extent this created a cocoon, a community, I considered it to be very little, because it was just a matter of turning the head to see the *immensity of Algeria*, including its geographical immensity, its immense body that was completely denied. I think that my virtual being, my imagination, was absolutely beyond limits, overflowing. I just needed to turn around on every side to notice the extensions: I was lucky enough to see that my family had already spread out, a true diaspora, the family was already present in twenty, thirty or forty countries in the world. I always told myself, I am here but it's just by chance, I am here when the others are in Australia, Brazil, Argentina, Uruguay, South Africa, England ... as a consequence, there was no reason why I should regroup and be assigned to an inscribed point, planted and rooted on a national territory. Therefore, this kind of denationalization, the "denationalism" that was always there for me, certainly implied that I was in extension. I was inhabited by an intrinsic curiosity. My house was not a tiny little shell, it was humongous, with windows everywhere, we knew, we received, by the way, letters from everywhere and I knew that there were little fellows elsewhere, homologues who were crossing the Australian desert, I knew that there were people in North America, in South America. My surprise was that there were small seeds in France, because there, it was unexpected, rare. It could also be that the sense of destiny was enormous. Having lived through ... for example ... being contemporaneous with the concentration camps, knowing that half of the family had been engulfed, knowing that there was such a colossal loss, that some of my family left Nazi Germany with just a suitcase of what-do-I-know—by the way, this is a thing that my family never lamented: nobody complained of having lost material belongings. However, I told myself, this is the *history of humanity*. And I also saw that this story had to be kept, I saw that it was

---

19 Benjamin Disraeli (1804–1881) served as prime minister on two occasions; in 1868 for a dozen of months, then from 1874 to 1880.

about to disappear. I was already aware of the fact that there were many silences. For example, in my father's family, for reasons that might have been cultural, nothing was being recounted. I don't know why. It is only later that I started to ask questions of my father's side. And everything was already lost. In my mother's family, which was immense but had already begun to be cut into small parts, there were still narratives that circulated that interested me a lot. And then I found it fascinating and funny: I read the tales of Grimm and Andersen, and next to them, I had the tales of the Klein and the tales of the Jonas or the Meyer. I discovered that a cousin of my mother, Horst Jonas, was the mayor of a nearby city of Berlin.[20] That he had been through a concentration camp. Little treasures that can only be found in fairy tales. I collect. And, I could collect them because they were maleficent tales. My mother, my grandmother, my aunt, etc., were depoliticized. Being politicized at this time meant to have an ideology. For example, Horst Jonas had an ideology, he was a communist, which was a rarity in the family. Being politicized requires having a ground: when one leads a struggle, as a Marxist, for example, it is necessary to have a location where it is applied. Now, for most of my family on the move, there was no ground. My father was politicized during his lifetime, he was a socialist. Because he truly believed that we would be able to apply socialism to France. As a consequence for me,

---

20 Horst Jonas (born in Bremerhaven on June 24, 1914, died in Neubrandenburg on June 22, 1967) was a trained machine knitter. A member of the "Sozialistische Arbeiter-Jugend" (SAJ) of the SPD (Socialist Party of the Weimar Republic of Germany) in 1929, he entered the underground Resistance against Fascism when the Nazis took power in 1933. In 1934 he joined the Kommunistischer Jugendverband Deutschlands, the illegal organization of the youth of the KPD, the underground German Communist Party, in Leipzig. Arrested in 1935, he was sentenced to four years and three months in prison for activities of so-called high treason, years that he first spent in the Zwickau prison, then, in the transit camp of Elbe in Dessau/Rosslau, before being detained in the concentration camp of Sachsenhausen, north of Berlin, from where he was deported to Auschwitz. In November 1944, he was transferred to Buchenwald. After the fall of the Third Reich in 1945, he became general secretary of the KPD-KL in Erfurt, before joining the SED (Sozialistische Einheitspartei Deutschlands, the official Communist Party of the German Democratic Republic [GDR]) in 1946. He became a police inspector in East Thuringia in 1947. Adopting dissenting positions from those of the party while being favorable to the insurgents of June 17, 1953 (this popular uprising in East Berlin was the first major insurrection to take place within the Soviet Empire; it was brutally repressed), he was reprimanded for acts of so-called surrender. As a punishment, he was put on probation at the local board of editors of an official paper of the SED, *Freiheit*. From 1956 to 1961, he was the chief editor of the press organ of the district

I started to not forget—that's it—I believe in what I referred to earlier as the point of view, the *history of humanity*. I never thought that I would be in charge of the notebook of the family, I think that I observed the way human beings reject each other, slaughter each other, lose, forget, retain. A general economy of human memory.

[…]

Living in books, where anything can happen
H.C.: Literature, came very, very early for me, in a childish manner. I was lucky that my grandmother, Omi, served as a substitute mother since my mother was trying to work. In order to feed us, to fight against the loss of appetite that struck my brother and me, in order to make us eat, she told us tales. Grimm's fairy tales, etc. She recited poems in German to us, she sang songs in German, and I was charmed by those things. When I was very little, since I wanted to leave the world

Figure 30 Filmed interview with Hélène Cixous, Paris, June 17, 2012.

---

of Neubrandenburg. In 1963, he became the mayor (Oberbürgermeister) of the city of Neubrandenburg, situated north of Berlin, in East Germany, a function he occupied until his death. In 1949, his parents, who had survived in exile in South Africa, settled in Schwerin, a city located at the South of Lübeck, in the GDR (Axel Seitz, *Geduldet und vergessen: Die Jüdische Landesgemeinde Mecklenburg zwischen 1948 und 1990* [Bremen: Edition Temmen, 2001, 154]). Staff writer, "Horst Jonas," Bundesstiftung zur Aufarbeitung der SED-Diktatur (Fondation for the Study of the Dictatorship of the SED; Berlin), n.d., available online: https://www.bundesstiftung-aufarbeitung.de/de/recherche/kataloge-datenbanken/biographische-datenbanken/horst-jonas (accessed September 19, 2022).

as it appeared to me—how bad it was—I told myself that I had to go to another world. Had I been a scientist, I would perhaps have tried to go to the moon, but I wasn't, I was poetical. And so, very quickly, very early, I experienced extraordinary jubilation with books and I decided, it is books that I want to inhabit. I was always trying to figure out how to do it. Very, very early on: it must be, it must be that it is while living in books that everything can happen, the good and the bad. And I was looking for ways [to do it], because I was always telling myself, one has to survive, I have to go to the market, buy food for the children, how is that manageable? When I was teaching in high school [*in Arcachon after H.C. obtained the* agrégation], I was searching, I reminded myself that I had to *make a living* [*in English*] as one says. I was looking for a profession, and I thought that I needed something that would keep me close to books. It was the profession of educator; I did not even know what it was, I was heading there without instructions, without a relay, without my mother's advice—who was the only person close to me who was responsible—she had no idea of what it was, of what studying involved, since she had not studied in France. For me, studying was a way to stay close to the book.

The three tasks of literature
H.C.: [...] When one writes ... you understand the movement that drives me, you'd find it by Proust, by Joyce: Joyce, who, as you know, had this admirable fantasy; I remember my amused wonder when I discovered

Figure 31 Filmed interview with Hélène Cixous, Paris, June 17, 2012.

that he alleged that Dublin could disappear if there was a major earthquake ... but, this wouldn't matter because it exists in *Ulysses*! And I thought, well, that is ambition! And what's more, he realized it! I think that it is an excellent way of translating an impulse. He did that, it's true. I think that I was driven by something analogous without quite knowing what it was. That's why I called my doctoral dissertation "the art of the replacement."[21] It is about replacing what is doomed to disappearance through a kind of projection, through additions, signs, certainly an equivalent, but more specifically a *linguistic equivalent*, with this temerity that consists of claiming that instead of Troy you have Homer. It's true. That is the principle. Collecting: transposing, finding equivalents of what is finished, of what is going to die, of what will disappear. This, is one of the tasks of literature.

The second task is that, when we write, I think that we are also driven by—because there is really loss—something rather paradoxical: it is about saving ... the loss. To make it such that the loss is not lost. Inscribing the loss, inscribing the mourning, responding to what I discovered late while working more closely on Proust: that Proust dreads this above everything, precisely this, that we are also going to *lose the mourning*, lose the loss, lose the grief, the memory itself is erased. Therefore, there is this movement of gathering the loss itself. So, we tell ourselves that we are trying to save, even if the movement of resisting effacement, disappearance, exclusion, etc., is partially a kind of stratagem because, we are replacing. Which is why I quoted this example that amused me when I started to work on Joyce, the idea of replacing a city with a book! But ... after all, it is defendable. After two or three thousand years, it becomes convincing. At this moment, we have Homer while Troy ... Homer gives birth to literature in its totality while Troy was perhaps no more than three hundred people slitting each other's throats on a tiny piece of rock. While writing we save, we don't know for what future. We don't know for what future, nor do we know for whom. But while writing, we are moving away, in the end, we exchange something, we exchange an experience that has such an absolutely unlimited power and that is like a sort of universe deployed before the words, even if this universe is awaited by the words or awaits the words and is dedicated to writing. This infinitum, this unlimited, this multiple, writing will restrict it. It will both give this infinitum another kind of strength because writing is capable of immense resources, polysemies, extraordinary growths of the signifier, but at the same time, writing will cast this infinitum, this unlimited, this multiple, into a kind of form that, in

---

21 Hélène Cixous, *L'exil de James Joyce, ou l'art du remplacement* (Paris: Grasset, 1968). Hélène Cixous, *The Exile of James Joyce*, trans. Sally A.J. Purcell (New York: David Lewis, 1972).

turn, will be a mold, in a certain way. Which marks a kind of decision. It decides. It decides. Now, what I say here also applies to other forms of art. If we sculpt, we allow a shape to appear, that, evidently, as a signifier, seals a forest of signifiers; in the same way, a sculpted form will be the decision of the sculptor's chisel and come instead of a world of images.

But it's not only that. It's also that literature only brings meaning if it is placed under the order of secrecy. It is where secret lays itself. If we lay a secret on a surface, or in a case, it might be saved, but it is saved-lost. For example, yesterday,[22] when I recounted a little story, I did not hesitate, because I never hesitate before doing such things. But I told myself that, if I tell the story, I will lose it, at least to myself. This story will already be frozen in one shape. And in order to find its other hidden resources among the innumerable possible versions of it, a strong dose of forgetting will have to be injected in order for resurrection of its mysteries to occur. So, it is.

[...]

Osnabrück, the name of my mother

H.C.: *Osnabrück*, my book, doesn't claim to replace Osnabrück like *Ulysses* replaces Dublin. Joyce really endeavored to have hundreds and hundreds of Dubliners circulating in the book and then, to register a complete map of the city! That is, we pass through every street, every side, we enter in every pub, every butcher shop, in the ... well ... This is not at all my project in *Osnabrück*. I must say that it was Joyce's project, not mine; I have not written *Osnabrück* like that and I only called it *Osnabrück*, I only named it *Osnabrück* when it was finished. For me, Osnabrück was the name of my mother. It was rather an attempt to ... well, let's say that the city, the location or the scene of Osnabrück, is the theatre of my mother's memory. This is not as totalizing as *Ulysses*.

[...]

The writing doesn't stop

H.C.: We do not write without fear. No matter what. But this is not my worry. Whatever my concern, I recognize that, when writing dreams, when it is the means of transport that dreams of treasures, human treasures, writing is challenged in order to film a few moments, well, a few aspects, etc. I also think that I almost ask myself the question of legitimacy, of aesthetic and ethical legitimacy. When he begins to write,

---

22 At the aforementioned colloquium of the Bibliothèque Nationale de France.

Proust asks himself who he is ... he asks himself who he is to do that! His first letters are about "Am I truly a novelist or not?" Well ... he has asked himself this question for a long time. And this question, he later stages it. The whole *Recherche* ends with the fact that our narrator asks himself and concludes, "Well, no, I am not a writer." And at the moment when he says that, he begins to write. In fact, Proust recorded, in a way that seems necessary to me, the trouble, the *unheimlich* [*uncanny*] feeling that one has when one does a gesture of this type that is not a small gesture, because it's a gesture that lasts for as long as life itself. Because of this, we must tell ourselves that we do not write one book. When one truly writes, it's our whole life. It never stops. We never stop, we will never stop. I always told this to myself ... there's a question often asked to writers with this word, the word "prolific." I always told myself that you have to know nothing about writing to apply this word [*to writing*]. Writing never stops. That's all. It is life itself but differently. There is this affect that accompanies. If we are too fearful, then, we are inhibited, we don't do anything. In fact, when we write, it is precisely that we are beyond fear; at the same time we want to keep writing because that gives us an additional fire, like a fever, like a race, like a power to flee. Because after all, we also flee while writing. We pursue and we are pursued.

[...]

Daughters do not like mothers much

H.C.: The relationship to the death of the other is an infinite mystery. We have to interrogate this substance, we cannot listen to it. This immaterial substance that, at the same time materializes itself, is fear. That is to say, what does it mean to "fear death"? It is an impure feeling, but one that is constitutive of human breathing. Because we are mortals, and it's the proof of our mortality. It is rarely, if I may say ... a generous feeling. It lies at the root of selfishness itself: I fear for myself. To fear death, to fear the death of the mother, it is to fear one's proper death. It is to fear the death of what ensures life. Very disturbing elements can be mixed with this. I think there are no disturbing elements in the fears that accompanied me. I think this, only on the basis on my dreams. Because dreams know everything. If, for example, there had been desire in my fear, if there had been traces of a concealed hope for the death of a loved one, I would have seen it in a dream. But this, I never saw in a dream. I never saw it, precisely, [*I only saw*], only, the same fear. Renewed. But I know that this is a common feeling, especially vis-à-vis the mother, it is an altered feeling. That, I've seen that often, I discovered it rather late, by the way. When I started to work, to attempt to reflect on those scenes, to reflect in a more analytical way on the relationships between parents and children, between the daughter and the mother, the daughters and the mothers, etc., I started to notice, and I was, I should say, very surprised, that nothing was more frequent than a daughter's desire for her mother's death. That, I have encountered very often. Of course, it is an overdetermined sentiment that is caused, but that I've always found disastrous, and that probably also caused—but that's another matter and we now don't have much time left to talk—that is the reason why the liberation of women was delayed for so long ... that is ... daughters do not like mothers much. That's why, if we want to save something and allow the energy of life to pass among women, it starts there.

[*The telephone rings*]

Ah, this, this must be her [*Ève*] coming.

Figure 32 Filmed interview with Hélène Cixous, Paris, June 17, 2012: Ève.

Gratitude

A sense of endless gratitude and affection goes to Hélène Cixous. To Alison Rice, to Rosa and Alexa Morel.

Secret and borderless, a thankful dialogue with Jacques Derrida inhabits this work; Derrida, more than once, encouraged my reading(s) of Cixous.

Professor Imke Meyer, Professor Dr. phil. Andrea Grewe, film editor Matthieu Augustin, film producers Céline Nusse, Paul Rozenberg and Florence Guinaudeau have been decisive allies and influences. Invaluable inspiration came from Adel Abdessemed, Anne and Pierre-François Berger, Michel Delorme, Marie-Odile Germain, Manuel Irniger, Karin Jabs-Kiesler, Jean-Jacques Lemêtre, Eric Prenowitz, Annie-Joëlle Ripoll, Marta Segarra and Claudia Simma.

The "German Illusion" has been made possible thanks to the support of the University of Notre Dame, of the Department of Film, Television, and Theatre, of my colleagues Professor Jim Collins and Professor Pam Wojcik, of the Nanovic Institute for European Studies, of my colleague Professor Clemens Sedmak, of the Institute for Scholarship in the Liberal Arts.

The archivists and employees of the Langson Library of the Special Collections and Archives of the University of California Irvine (USA), especially Krystal Tribbett and Sarah Glover who facilitated my access to the Derrida folders. I thank the employees of the historical Tower Michel de Montaigne for their hospitality. I thank the Éditions Galilée for their constant and generous support.

Madelyn Steurer proofread an early version of the manuscript. Copyeditor Katherine Carney, editorial assistant Hali Han, editorial director Haaris Naqvi, senior production editor Zeba Talkhani, at

Bloomsbury Academic, played a critical role in the pre-production and production phases of the manuscript. Dr. Maj-Britt Frenze verified my translations and edited the final version to accord with idiomatic use of English.

Most parts of this work were composed before sunrise on Gail and Richard Rice's patio in California, a place where I can never distinguish between the act of writing and the cantors of liberty.

Bibliography

Barthes, Roland. *Camera Lucida*. Translated by Richard Howard. New York: Hill and Wang, 1981.
Barthes, Roland. *La chambre claire, Notes sur la photographie*. Paris: Cahiers du Cinéma, Gallimard, Seuil, 1980.
Bazin, André. *Qu'est-ce que le cinéma?* Paris: Cerf, [1951] 2011.
Bazin, André. *What Is Cinema?* vol. 1, trans. Hugh Gray. Berkeley: University of California Press, 2004.
Benjamin, Walter. "Erfahrung und Armut." *Die Welt im Wort*, no. 10 (December 1933); reproduced in *Gesammelte Schriften*, vol. 2, *Aufsätze, Essays, Vorträge*, 213–19. Frankfurt: Suhrkamp, 1991.
Benjamin, Walter. *Selected Writings*, vol. 4, *1938–1940*. Edited by Howard Eiland and Michael W. Jennings. Translated by Edmund Jephcott et al. Cambridge, MA: Harvard University Press, 2006.
Benjamin, Walter. "Sur le concept d'histoire." In *Œuvres*, vol. 3. Translated by Maurice de Gandillac, Rainer Rochlitz and Pierre Rusch, 427–43. Paris: Gallimard, 2000.
Blank, David and Blank, Gladys. *Gladys and David Blank Genealogy*, 2008–2022. Available online: http://www.blankgenealogy.com/getperson.php?personID=I2651&tree=Blank1 (accessed July 20, 2020).
Boulard, Stéphanie and Witt, Catherine. *Ententes—À partir d'Hélène Cixous*. Paris: Presses Sorbonne Nouvelle, 2019.
Calle-Gruber, Mireille and Crevier Goulet, Sarah-Anaïs. "Hélène Cixous's Imaginary Cities: Oran-Osnabrück-Manhattan: Places of Fascination, Places of Fiction." In "Hélène Cixous: When the Word Is a Stage," special issue, *New Literary History*, vol. 37, no. 1 (Johns Hopkins University Press, winter 2006), 135–45.
Cixous, Hélène. *1938, nuits*. Paris: Galilée, 2019. [N]
Cixous, Hélène. *Aïl!* Vincennes: Théâtre de la Tempête, June 2000.
Cixous, Hélène. *Aïl!* Paris: France Culture Radio France, first broadcast December 17, 2000.
Cixous, Hélène. *Angst*. Paris: Des Femmes, [1977] 1998. [A]
Cixous, Hélène. *Benjamin à Montaigne, Il ne faut pas le dire*. Paris: Galilée, 2001. [BM]
Cixous, Hélène. *Ciguë, Vieilles femmes en fleurs*. Paris: Galilée, 2008.
Cixous, Hélène. *Les Commencements*. Paris: Grasset, 1970.
Cixous, Hélène. *Les Commencements*. Paris: Des Femmes, 1999.
Cixous, Hélène. *Correspondance avec le mur*, Accompagné de cinq dessins à la pierre noire d'Adel Abdessemed. Paris: Galilée, 2017. [CM]

254 Bibliography

Cixous, Hélène. *Dedans*. Paris: Des Femmes, 1969. [*D*]
Cixous, Hélène. *Entretien de la blessure*. Paris: Galilée, 2011.
Cixous, Hélène. *Eve Escapes, Ruins and Life*. Translated by Peggy Kamuf. Cambridge, UK: Polity, 2012. [*EES*]
Cixous, Hélène. *Ève s'évade, La Ruine et la Vie*. Paris: Galilée, 2009. [*EEV*]
Cixous, Hélène. *L'exil de James Joyce, ou l'art du remplacement*. Paris: Grasset, 1968.
Cixous, Hélène. *The Exile of James Joyce*. Translated by Sally A. J. Purcell. New York: David Lewis, 1972.
Cixous, Hélène. *La Fiancée juive de la tentation*. Paris: Des Femmes, 1995. [*FJ*]
Cixous, Hélène. *Gare d'Osnabrück à Jérusalem*, Accompagné de sept substantifs dessinés par Pierre Alechinsky. Paris: Galilée, 2016. [*GO*]
Cixous, Hélène. Hegel Lecture, Berlin, Freie Universität (Free University of Berlin), May 11, 2016. Available online: https://www.fu-berlin.de/en/sites/dhc/zVideothek/950hegel-lecture-mit-helene-cixous/index.html (accessed July 27, 2020).
Cixous, Hélène. *Homère est morte….* Paris: Galilée, 2014. [*HM*]
Cixous, Hélène. *Mdeilmm, Parole de taupe*. Paris: Gallimard, 2022.
Cixous, Hélène. *Nacres*, Accompagné de dessins à la pierre noire d'Adel Abdessemed. Paris: Galilée, 2019. [*NC*]
Cixous, Hélène. *Osnabrück*. Paris: Éditions des Femmes Antoinette Fouque, 1999. [*OS*]
Cixous, Hélène. *Osnabrück Station to Jerusalem*, with seven words drawn by Pierre Alechinsky. Translated by Peggy Kamuf. New York: Fordham University Press, 2020. [*OSJ*]
Cixous, Hélène. *Oy!* Directed by Georges Bigot. The Actor's Gang Theatre, Los Angeles, June 2012.
Cixous, Hélène. *Le Prénom de Dieu*. Paris: Grasset, 1967.
Cixous, Hélène. *Les rêveries de la Femme Sauvage*. Paris: Galilée, 2000.
Cixous, Hélène. *Reveries of the Wild Woman: Primal Scenes*. Translated by Beverley Bie Brahic. Evanston, IL: Northwestern University Press, 2006.
Cixous, Hélène. *Revirements dans l'antarctique du cœur*. Paris: Galilée, 2011. [*RV*]
Cixous, Hélène. *Le Rire de la Méduse et autres ironies*. Paris: Galilée, [1975] 2010. [*RM*]
Cixous, Hélène. *Ruines bien rangées*. Paris: Gallimard, 2020. [*RB*]
Cixous, Hélène. *Si près*, Frontispice et culispice de Pierre Alechinsky. Paris: Galilée, 2007. [*SP*]
Cixous, Hélène. *So Close*. Translated by Peggy Kamuf. Cambridge, UK: Polity, 2009. [*SC*]
Cixous, Hélène. *Tombe*. Paris: éditions du Seuil, 1973.
Cixous, Hélène. *Tours promises*. Paris: Galilée, 2004. [*TP*]
Cixous, Hélène. *Twists and Turns in the Heart's Antarctic*. Translated by Beverley Bie Brahic. Cambridge, UK: Polity, 2014. [*TT*]
Cixous, Hélène and Calle-Gruber, Mireille. *Photos de Racines*. Paris: Des Femmes, 1994. [*PR*]
Cixous, Hélène and Calle-Gruber, Mireille. *Rootprints, Memory and Life Writing*. Translated by Eric Prenowitz. New York: Routledge, 1997. [*R*]
Cixous, Hélène and Derrida, Jacques. *Voiles*, Accompagné de six dessins d'Ernest Pignon-Ernest. Paris: Galilée, 1998. [*V*]
Cixous, Hélène with Derrida, Jacques. *Veils*. Translated by Geoffrey Bennington. Artwork by Ernest Pignon-Ernest. Redwood City, CA: Stanford University Press, 2002. [*VL*]

Bibliography 255

Cixous, Hélène and Jeannet, Frédéric-Yves. *Rencontre terrestre*. Paris: Galilée, 2005. [*RT*]
Cixous, Hélène and Wajsbrot, Cécile. *Une autobiographie allemande*. Paris: Bourgois, 2016. [*AA*]
Decout, Maxime. "Standing apart/being a part: Cixous's fictional Jewish identities." *Jewish Culture and History*, vol. 14, no. 2–3 (Taylor and Francis, 2013), 78–86.
Dédéyan, Charles. "Introduction." In Michel de Montaigne, *Œuvres completes*, 7–39. Paris: Les Belles Lettres, 1946.
Deleuze, Gilles. *Cinéma 2, L'image-temps*. Paris: Minuit, 1985.
Deleuze, Gilles. *Cinema 2, The Image-Time*. Translated by Hugh Tomlison and Robert Galeta. Minneapolis: University of Minnesota Press, 1989.
Deleuze, Gilles and Guattari, Félix. *Kafka, Pour une littérature mineure*. Paris: Minuit, 1975.
Deleuze, Gilles and Guattari, Félix. *Kafka, Toward a Minor Literature*. Translated by Dana Polan. Minneapolis: University of Minnesota Press, 1986.
Derrida, Jacques. *Demeure Maurice Blanchot*. Paris: Galilée, 1998.
Derrida, Jacques. *Donner la mort*. Paris: Galilée, 1995.
Derrida, Jacques. *Genèse, généalogie, genres et le génie*. Paris: Galilée, 2003.
Derrida, Jacques. *The Gift of Death & Literature in Secret*. Translated by David Wills Chicago: University of Chicago Press, 2008.
Derrida, Jacques. *Glas*. Paris: Galilée, 1974.
Derrida, Jacques. *H.C. for Life, That Is to Say …*. Edited by Mireille Calle-Grüber. Translated by Laurent Milesi and Stefan Herbrechter. Stanford, CA: Stanford University Press, 2006.
Derrida, Jacques. "H.C. pour la vie c'est-à-dire." In Mireille Calle-Grüber (ed.), *Hélène Cixous croisées d'une œuvre*, 13–140. Paris: Galilée, 2000.
Derrida, Jacques. *Hospitalité*, vol. 1, *Séminaire (1995–1996)*. Paris: Seuil, 2021.
Derrida, Jacques. "Interpretations at War: Kant, the Jew, the German." In "Institutions of Interpretation," special issue, *New Literary History*, vol. 22, no. 1 (Johns Hopkins University Press, winter 1991), 39–95.
Derrida, Jacques. *Nationalité et nationalisme philosophique*. Tapuscripts/notes of Jacques Derrida's seminar. Paris: École des Hautes Études en Sciences Sociales, 1987–1988, second and sixth sessions, Derrida MS-C01, boxes 16, 19 folders 16 and 17, 59, 84, Langson Library, Special Collections (archives), consulted on July 30, 2019, University of California Irvine.
Derrida, Jacques. "Signature, Événement, Contexte." In *Limited Inc*, 15–51. Paris: Galilée, 1990.
Derrida, Jacques. "Signature, Event, Context." In *Limited Inc*, 1–23. Translated by Samuel Weber and Jeffrey Mehlman. Evanston, IL: Northwestern University Press, 1988.
Desan, Philippe. *Montaigne, une biographie politique*. Paris: Odile Jacob, 2014.
Didi-Huberman, Georges. *Devant l'image*. Paris: éditions de Minuit, 1990.
Dufourmantelle, Anne and Derrida, Jacques. *De l'hospitalité, Anne Dufourmantelle invite Jacques Derrida à répondre*. Paris: Calmann-Lévy, 1997.
Dufourmantelle, Anne and Derrida, Jacques. *Of Hospitality, Anne Dufourmantelle invites Jacques Derrida to respond*. Translated by Rachel Bowly. Stanford, CA: Stanford University Press, 2000.
Engelmann, Peter. *Aus Montaignes Koffer, Hélène Cixous im Gespräch mit Peter Engelmann, Passagen Gespräche 7*. Vienna: Passagen Verlag, 2017.

Ever, Rêve, Hélène Cixous ["Nonfiction" Film]. Directed by Olivier Morel[118 minutes]. Paris: Zadig Productions, 2016.

Freud, Sigmund. *L'inquiétante étrangeté*. Translated by Fernand Cambon and J.-B. Pontalis. Paris: Gallimard, 2001.

Freud, Sigmund. "The 'Uncanny'." In *The Standard Edition of the Complete Psychological Works of Sigmund Freud*, vol. 17. Translated from the German by James Strachey, in collaboration with Anna Freud assisted by Alix Strachey and Alan Tyson, 218–53. London: The Hogarth Press and the Institute of Psychoanalysis, 1917–1919.

Freud, Sigmund. *Das Unheimliche*. Paris: Gallimard, 2001.

Grewe, Andrea and Schlünder, Susanne, eds. "Die ‚deutsche Seite' von Hélène Cixous," special issue, *Lendemains*, vol. 42, no. 166/67 (Narr Francke Attempto Verlag GmbH + Co. KG, 2017).

Heymann, Brigitte. "La langue véhiculaire, die deutsche Sprache in Hélène Cixous' Poet(h)ik." In Andrea Grewe and Susanne Schlünder (eds.), "Die ‚deutsche Seite' von Hélène Cixous," special issue, *Lendemains*, vol. 42, no. 166/67 (Narr Francke Attempto Verlag GmbH + Co. KG, 2017), 56–70.

Hilfrich, Carola, Gordinsky, Natasha and Zepp, Susanne. "The Depository of *Zugehör: Ail!* and the Soundscape of Belonging." In Carola Hilfrich, Natasha Gordinsky and Susanne Zepp (eds.), *Passages of Belonging: Interpreting Jewish Literatures*, 48–53. Berlin: De Gruyter, 2019.

Hilfrich, Carola, Gordinsky, Natasha and Zepp, Susanne, eds. *Passages of Belonging: Interpreting Jewish Literatures*. Berlin: De Gruyter, 2019.

Legros, Alain. *Essais sur les poutres, Peintures et inscriptions chez Montaigne*. Paris: Klincksieck, 2000.

Lemêtre, Jean-Jacques. *Ceci est un exercice de rêve*, "Ateliers de création radiophonique." Paris: France Culture Radio France, first broadcast November 20, 2005.

Littré, Émile. *Dictionnaire de la langue française*, vol. 3. Paris: Pauvert-Gallimard-Hachette, 1969.

Littré, Émile. *Dictionnaire de la langue française*, vol. 4. Paris: Pauvert-Gallimard-Hachette, 1969.

Littré, Émile. *Dictionnaire de la langue française*, vol. 6. Paris: Pauvert-Gallimard-Hachette, 1969.

Marder, Elissa. "Birthmarks (Given Names)." *Parallax*, vol. 13, no. 3 (Routlege, 2007), 49–61.

Marin, Louis. *L'écriture de soi*. Paris: Presses Universitaires de France, 1999.

Mayer, Hans. *Outsiders, A study in Life and Letters*. Translated by Denis M. Sweet. Cambridge, MA: MIT Press, [1975] 1982.

McGowan, Margaret. "Contradictory impulses in Montaigne's vision of Rome." *Renaissance Studies*, vol. 4, no. 4 (Wiley, December 1990), 392–409.

Montaigne, Michel de. "De l'amitié." In *Essais*, 1, 27. Paris: Abel L'Angelier, 1604.

Montaigne, Michel de. "De l'exercitation." In *Essais*, 2, 6. Paris: Abel L'Angelier, 1604.

Montaigne, Michel de. "De la vanité." In *Essais*, 9, 3. Paris: Abel L'Angelier, 1604.

Montaigne, Michel de. *Journal de voyage*. Edited by Fausta Garavini. Paris: Gallimard, 1983.

Montaigne, Michel de. *Journal du Voyage de Michel de Montaigne en Italie, par la Suisse et l'Allemagne en 1580 et 1581*, with notes fom M. de Querlon, vol. 3. Paris: Chez Le Jay, 1774.

Bibliography 257

Montaigne, Michel de. *The Journal of Montaigne's Travels in Italy by Way of Switzerland and Germany*, vol. 2. Translated by W.G. Water. London: John Murray, 1903.
Montaigne, Michel de. "Au lecteur." In *Essais*, ii. Paris: Abel L'Angelier, 1604.
Montaigne, Michel de. "Of Friendship." In *The Complete Essays of Montaigne*, 1, 28, Modern Languages Association 9th edition. Translated by Donald Frame. Redwood City, CA: Stanford University Press, 1958.
Montaigne, Michel de. "Of Vanity." In *The Complete Essays*, 3, 9. Translated by M.A. Screech. London: Penguin Books, 2003.
Montaigne, Michel de. "On affectionate relationships." In *The Complete Essays*, 1, 28. Translated by M.A. Screech. London: Penguin Books, 2003.
Montaigne, Michel de. "On practice." In *The Complete Essays*, 2, 6. Translated by M.A. Screech. London: Penguin Books, 2003.
Montaigne, Michel de. "Que philosopher c'est apprendre à mourir." In *Essais*, 1, 20. Adapted in modern French André Lanly. Paris: Gallimard Quarto, 2009.
Montaigne, Michel de. "Sur l'amitié." In *Essais*, 1, 28. Adapted in modern French André Lanly. Paris: Gallimard Quarto, 2009.
Montaigne, Michel de. "Sur la cruauté." In *Essais*, 2, 11. Paris: Abel L'Angelier, 1604.
Montaigne, Michel de. "Sur l'exercice." In *Essais*, 2, 6. Adapted in modern French André Lanly. Paris: Gallimard Quarto, 2009.
Montaigne, Michel de. "Sur la vanité." In *Essais*, 9, 3. Adapted in modern French André Lanly. Paris: Gallimard Quarto, 2009.
Montaigne, Michel de. "To philosophize is to learn how to die." In *The Complete Essays*, 3, 9. Translated by M.A. Screech. London: Penguin Books, 2003.
Montaigne, Michel de. "To the Reader." In *The Complete Essays*, lxiii. Translated by M.A. Screech. London: Penguin Books, 2003.
Morse, Stephen P. and Landé, Peter. *German Jews*, 2012. Available online: https://stevemorse.org/germanjews/germanjews.php?=&offset=39551 (accessed July 20, 2020).
Nancy, Jean-Luc. *Le Partage des* voix. Paris: Galilée, 1982.
Nordholt, Annelies Schulte. "Osnabrück, Berlin: 'villes promises' et villes vécues. Les dessous du dialogue d'Hélène Cixous et Cécile Wajsbrot dans *Une autobiographie allemande*." In Kathleen Gyssels and Christa Stevens (eds.), *Écriture des Origines, Origine de l'écriture Hélène Cixous*, 124–40. Leiden: Brill Rodopi, 2019.
Prenowitz, Eric, ed. "Cracking the Book-Readings of Hélène Cixous." *New Literary History*, vol. 37, no. 1 (Johns Hopkins University Press, winter 2006), R9–R27.
Roussel, Frédérique. "La maison d'écriture d'Hélène Cixous." *Libération* (Paris), December 18, 2020. Available online: https://next.liberation.fr/livres/2020/12/18/la-maison-d-ecriture-d-helene-cixous-parution-de-seminaire-et-ruines-bien-rangees_1809068<%22> (accessed December 31, 2020).
Royle, Nicholas. *Hélène Cixous, Dreamer, Realist, Analyst, Writing*. Manchester: Manchester University Press, 2020.
Seitz, Axel. *Geduldet und vergessen: Die Jüdische Landesgemeinde Mecklenburg zwischen 1948 und 1990*. Bremen: Edition Temmen, 2001.
Sellmeyer, Martina and Junk, Peter. *Stationen auf dem Weg nach Auschwitz*. Bramsche: Rasch Verlag, 2000.
[Sellmeyer, Martina, and Junk, Peter]. *Stadt Osnabrück, Büro für Friedenskultur* Osnabrück. Available online: https://stolpersteine-guide.de/map/biografie/1338/ehepaar-jonas (accessed August 3, 2022).

Sperling, Jutta Gisela. *Roman Charity, Queer Lactations In Early Modern Visual Culture*. Bielefeld: Transcript Verlag, 2016.
Stack, Liam. "An Orangutan Named Hope Was Repeatedly Shot With an Air Rifle. She Was Blinded but Survived." *New York Times* (New York City), March 19, 2019. Available online: https://www.nytimes.com/2019/03/18/world/asia/orangutan-shot-gun.html#:~:text=the%20main%20story-,An%20Orangutan%20Named%20Hope%20Was%20Repeatedly%20Shot%20With%20an%20Air,dozens%20of%20air%20rifle%20wounds (accessed January 4, 2021).
Staff writer. "1400 Schüler erwartet Am 25. Oktober ziehen wieder Steckenpferdreiter durch Osnabrück." *Neue Osnabrücker Zeitung* (Osnabrück), October 19, 2019. Available online: https://www.noz.de/lokales/osnabrueck/artikel/1909922/am-25-oktober-ziehen-wieder-steckenpferdreiter-durch-osnabrueck (accessed June 28, 2020).
Staff writer. "Germany: 75,000th 'Stolperstein' for Holocaust victims laid." *Deutsche Welle* (Bonn), December 29, 2019. Available online: https://www.dw.com/en/germany-75000th-stolperstein-for-holocaust-victims-laid/a-51827506 (accessed May 30, 2020).
Staff writer. "Horst Jonas." *Bundesstiftung zur Aufarbeitung der SED-DiktaturFondation for the Study of the Dictatorship of the SED* (Fondation for the Study of the Dictatorship of the SED; Berlin), n.d. Available online: https://www.bundesstiftung-aufarbeitung.de/de/recherche/kataloge-datenbanken/biographische-datenbanken/horst-jonas, (accessed September 19, 2022).
Staff writer. "Lectures amicales d'Hélène Cixous." *Fabula* (Paris: Bibliothèque Nationale de France), June 16, 2012. Available online: https://www.fabula.org/actualites/lectures-amicales-d-39-helene-cixous_50740.php accessed on September 17, 2022.
Staff writer. "Les Naufragés du Fol Espoir." *Théâtre du Soleil* (Paris), 2013. Available online: https://www.theatre-du-soleil.fr/fr/librairie-et-editions/les-naufrages-du-fol-espoir-1871 (accessed September 19, 2022).
Stevens, Christa. *L'écriture solaire d'Hélène Cixous, Travail du texte et histoire du sujet dans* Portrait du Soleil. Amsterdam: Rodopi, 1999.
Stevens, Christa. "Judéités, à lire dans l'œuvre d'Hélène Cixous." *International Journal of Francophone Studies*, vol. 7, no. 1–2 (Intellect, 2004), 81–93.
Treskow, Isabella von. "Le fleuve sonore, les ouïes extravagantes et le sillon sensuel. Langue, *Muttersprache* et pensée dans *Osnabrück* et *Gare d'Osnabrück à Jérusalem* d'Hélène Cixous." In Andrea Grewe and Susanne Schlünder (eds.), "Die ‚deutsche Seite' von Hélène Cixous," special issue, *Lendemains*, vol. 42, no. 166/67 (Narr Francke Attempto Verlag GmbH + Co. KG, 2017), 71–84.
Wenders, Wim and Zournazi, Mary. *Inventing Peace, A Dialogue on Perception*. London: I.B. Tauris, 2013.
Westphal, Bertrand. *Geocriticism: Real and Fictional Spaces*. Translated by Robert T. Tally Jr. London: Palgrave Macmillan, 2011.
Westphal, Bertrand. *La géocritique, réel, fiction, espace*. Paris: éditions de Minuit, 2007.
Zweig, Stefan. *Montaigne*. Frankfurt: Fisher Verlag, 2012.
Zweig, Stefan. *Montaigne*. Translated by Will Stone. London: Pushkin Press, 2015.
Zweig, Stefan. *Montaigne*. Paris: Librairie Générale Française-Le livre de poche, 2019.

Index

Alechinsky, Pierre 33 n.6, 138, 145–6, 146 n.13, 147–8
Algeria
  Algerian "Black Decade" 238
  Algerians 238–9
  Algerian War of Independence 238
  anti-Jewish legislation in 240
  Barberousse prison (Algiers) 116 n.48
  colonial Algeria, French colonial oppression, French colonial empire 4–5, 91, 236
  Crémieux Decree 239, 241 n.16
  Germany and Algeria. *See under* German
  Jews of 8 n.10, 240 n.15
  malady of 5
  Military Circle (Oran) 223, 105 n.28
  Oran 4–6, 13, 23, 25–6, 28, 48 n.11, 104, 105 n.28, 116, 136, 137 n.1, 138–44, 139 n.5, 152, 159, 163, 164 n.21, 170, 184, 191–2, 223, 228 n.2, 239–40 n.13, 241, 241 n.17
  postcolonial studies 7
alter ego (Montaigne, La Boétie, Omi) 13, 97, 112, 118, 120, 127, 138, 146, 191
anti-Semitism 90, 107, 116, 118, 237

archive, archiving, family archives 75, 84–5, 88, 124, 124 n.8, 135, 155–6, 158, 161, 234
ashes 55, 70, 75–6, 79, 82–3, 88–9, 101, 116, 118, 136, 166, 178, 181, 184, 186, 216, 219
Ashkenazi legacy 14 n.15
Augustus (Roman Emperor) 71 n.29
Austria, Austro-Hungarian empire 22, 90, 196, 207, 234–5, 242
author (theory of), authorship 67, 67 n.15, 75, 155 n.3, 156, 158 n.9, 178–9, 178 n.9, 182 n.14, 187, 210 n.38, 219

Baillot, Gertrude 227
Barthes, Roland 128, 128 n.15, 129, 129 n.16, 17, 157 n.8
Bazin, André 133 n.27, 157 n.8
belief
  and believing 210
  circulation of the 209
  disbelief 159, 164
  fallen 216
  German belief 211–12, 215
  in God 233–4
  and illusion 208, 212
  illusion 1, 9 n.10, 98, 208, 213–17, 214 n.2, 215 n.3–4, 241
  incredible 157, 159 n.12, 164, 185 n.3, 186, 236

is in flames 213
Jewish-German 214
made in the 240
"non-belief" 212
"of being of, of being in Algeria" 5 n.7
and science 211
unbelievable 157, 159, 164, 184
belonging, "Zugehör," 5, 14, 15 n.16, 20 n.4, 35, 191, 221, 256
belongings 26–7, 121, 177, 243
Benjamin, Walter 9, 83, 83 n.12, 89 n.2, 180–1, 181 n.12
Berlin
   Alexanderplatz 222–3
   Block der Frauen, 166 n.27, 222, 223
   Henriette Herz Platz 222
   Rosenstrasse 2–4
Bigot, Georges 34 n.10
Blank, David and Gladys 23 n.9, 207 n.35, 231 n.7
Bober, Benjamin 227
book(s)
   alive in 73
   "*Bericht*" (report, deposition) 172–87, 188, 214, 217–18
   of blindness, camera-book, of impossible photograph 175–6
   as a caller-receiver device, telephone book 50–1, 51 n.19
   empty 155–9, 170, 172, 177–8, 181, 184
   form, 3 n.5, 10–11 n.12, 25 n.13, 27–9, 27 n.15, 36, 39 n.18, 48, 54 n.2, 67 n.15, 100 n.21, 101, 133, 139 n.5, 153 n.1, 175–9, 183, 187 n.6, 245–7
   impossibility of the 22
   of peace 79
   as *Schibboleth* 77
   that is not a 176

that sees the night, of the Night 163
that takes her to Germany 55
Boulard, Stéphanie 91 n.5
Brahic, Beverley Bie 259 n.12
breath, breathless 67, 71, 92 n.7, 93 n.8, 84 n.12, 102, 105 n.28, 154 n.2, 172, 188 n.1, 249
Brod, Max 218 n.12
bruise, scar 3, 3 n.5, 7, 100, 100 n.21, 101
Buchenwald, 27, 44, 172, 173 n.1, 180, 180 n.11, 190, 190 n.5, 214, 244

Caligula (Roman Emperor) 87–8, 88 n.25
Calle-Gruber, Mireille 21 n.5, 48 n.11
Cambon, Fernand 33, 33 n.7
camera
   camera obscura, camera lucida 98 n.16, 175–6
   optical device 91, 111, 128 n.15, 129 n.16, 203 n.30, 230–1
catastrophe(s) 21, 70–1, 83, 83 n.12, 88, 89, 230
cave
   cellar-prison of Osnabrück (*arrests and persecutions of November 1938*) 172, 173, 217, 218, 219
   Plato's cave 96–9, 111
   vault 5, 241
cemetery
   Ève 203, 206
   Montaigne 63 n.6, 70
Charles V (Roman Emperor) 71 n.29, 72, 72 n.30
Choul, Guillaume du 72 n.29
cinema, cinematic, film 71, 98, 111, 122 n.27, 131, 133, 142, 157 n.8
Cixous, Georges 23

Index 261

Cixous, Pierre 230 n.4
Cixous, Samuel 240 n.13, 14
Cohen, Hermann 8 n.10, 199–202, 205, 207, 210 n.38, 211
Cologne (Köln) 142, 144
colonization, colonized 235–7
country
  of Algeria 4, 237–8 *see also* Algeria *and* German
  expelled from (Algeria) 230, 243
  host 3
  left (exile) 120–1
  as legal fiction named "Germany" 12 *see* German
  of military allegiance 202
  as Montaigne, as literature 91
  more than one 6
  of the name "Cixous" 1 n.1
  native 16 n.19
  of persecution (Germany) 218–9
  "supercountry" 5, 239–41
Crevier Goulet, Sarah-Anaïs 48 n.11
cruelty 35–7, 88, 99 n.18, 100, 102, 106 n.28, 106–7, 109 n.34-35-38, 111, 237

Dalaï-Lama 79, 80, 80 n.7
death hideous death, beautiful death 40–1, 40 n.19, 44
deconstruction 61, 85, 88, 135, 177, 183, 214
Decout, Maxime 14 n.15
Dédéyan, Charles 108 n.31
Deleuze, Gilles 58 n.1, 133 n.27, 218 n.12, 222 n.2
deliberation 59, 92 n.8, 93 n.8
Derrida, Jacques 8 n.10, 10 n.12, 11 n.12, 12, 21 n.5, 29, 29 n.17, 40 n.20, 58 n.1, 59 n.1, 69, 69 n.23, 76, 76 n.4, 81 n.9, 138 n.3, 153, 154 n.2, 156, 156 n.6, 158, 161 n.15, 195, 198, 198 n.9, 199, 199 n.10–12, 200, 200 n.13–18, 201, 201 n.19–24, 202, 202 n.25–9, 205, 206, 209, 211, 211 n.42, 220 n.14, 224, 225 n.6, 236, 240 n.15
Desan, Philippe 71 n.28, 109 n.33
diaspora 3, 9, 243
Didi-Huberman, Georges 91 n.5
disfigure, disfigurement, figure, figuration, figurability 38, 55–6, 63 n.6, 66 n.12, 68, 68 n.22, 69 n.25, 77, 88, 90–1, 97, 107, 109–16, 118, 122, 128, 133–8, 141, 147, 148, 184
disgust 108, 110, 111, 146, 148
disjunction 201, 204
dislocation 68, 72, 73, 126
Disraeli, Benjamin 243, 243 n.19
dream(s) 12, 22, 25, 27–8, 30–8, 38 n.15, 41–3, 55, 76, 78, 106, 131, 137–44, 157, 176–7, 182, 196, 213, 226–8, 235, 237, 240–2, 248–50, 257, 264
dream of the prisoner 106
Dreyfus Affair 242
Dubreuil, Laurent 138 n.2
Dufourmantelle, Anne 59 n.1

Eiland, Howard 83 n.12
ekphrasis 91
empty
  blank paper 155–9, 163, 181
  emptiness 155–6, 184
  empty bed(s), 155, 158
  empty book (and empty-book) *see under* book(s)
  nothingness 135
  void 100, 115–16, 118, 123, 134, 136, 142, 146, 147, 155, 157, 159, 163, 198
Engelmann, Peter 6 n.8
erasure 77, 87–8

262 Index

event 12, 20 n.3, 26, 29 n.17, 36, 41,
    48, 50 n.18, 57 n.1, 58 n.1, 59,
    76, 77, 78, 83 n.12, 86, 95–6,
    102 n.26, 126, 128–9, 131,
    132, 133, 170–2, 176, 178 n.9,
    179, 182–3, 185–6, 187 n.6,
    188, 192, 202, 223, 227–9, 242
Ever, Rêve, Hélène Cixous (film) 3,
    23 n.10, 227
execution, death penalty 87–8, 111,
    228
executioner 108–9, 116–17
exile *see* originary exile
extermination, Shoah 21, 123, 134
extinction 132 n.23, 178, 182, 184

Fallersleben, Hoffmann von
    15 n.17
fault, false, "fausser," powers of
    the false, falsifier 12, 57 n.1,
    58, 198, 198 n.8, 208, 214,
    214 n.2
fear 74, 185 n.2, 228–9, 236,
    248–9
feminine writing *see* women
    writing
fiction, fictionalization 3, 3 n.5,
    10 n.11, 12, 21, 48 n.11, 88,
    100 n.21, 139 n.5, 177
film
    filming 39, 49
    photograph 13, 88, 120–2, 125,
        125 n.11, 127
    photographer 40 n.19, 91, 111,
        128
    photography 13, 127 n.14,
        127–9, 129 n.17, 136
fire *see under* Kristallnacht
First World War *(also referred to as
    "Great War")* 4 n.6, 12, 14,
    20, 20 n.2, 22–3, 44, 121, 181,
    199, 207–10, 210 n.38, 223,
    223 n.4, 231 n.7, 242

force (to be forced), enforcement 9,
    73, 76, 92, 92 n.7, 93 n.8, 102,
    102 n.26, 126, 126 n.13, 134,
    137, 137 n.1, 139, 139 n.4,
    141, 141 n.7, 143, 201, 205,
    210 n.38, 217, 217 n.9, 223,
    235, 236
forgiveness, pardon, pardoning 58
    n.1, 69, 69 n.23, 78 n.6
forum ("for") 92 n.8
Frame, Donald 114 n.43
Frenze, Maj-Britt 195
Freud, Anna 32 n.3, 196
Freud, Sigmund 9, 32 n.3, 33 n.4,
    220 n.14, 231 n.7
Freudian slip 156–8, 164
friendship
    Derrida-Cixous 8 n.10, 81 n.9
    Montaigne, Montaigne and
        La Boétie 112, 114 n.43, 127,
        127 n.14, 128

Gandillac, Maurice de 83 n.12
Garavini, Fausta 66 n.12
Gardner, Alexander 128 n.15
Genet, Jean 138 n.3
genocide 3, 83, 84, 134, 143, 146–8,
    195
geocriticism 10 n.11
Germain, Marie-Odile 227
German
    army 13, 22, 207, 208, 231 n.7
    authorless German language-
        machine 219
    -being, mysterious German-
        being 197, 198 n.6, 200,
        208–11, 215
    burden 215
    call, Germany is calling 12,
        17–52, 20–2, 24, 25–7, 27
        n.15, 28–32, 34–9, 40 n.21
    chimera 196, 197, 204, 214–15,
        216 n.7

Index 263

duty 203 n.30, 204, 204 n.31, 205, 207 n.35
evil 189, 203 n.30, 41–5, 45 n.5, 47–56, 74, 77–8, 93 n.8, 161, 176, 216–17, 227–8, 233
fears 24, 185 n.2
figures 4, 7, 9, 12, 159 n.11, 199, 200
German Algeria, Germany in Algeria, Germany and Algeria 4–7, 8, 8 n.10, 13, 14 n.5, 23, 26, 28, 28 n.16, 91, 107, 120, 139, 159, 189, 224–5, 236–7, 243
"Germanalgia" 5, 224
glory 203 n.30, 204, 204 n.31, 205–6
illusion 1, 9 n.10, 208, 213–17, 215 n.3, 4, 241
Kaiser (Emperor) 207, 207 n.35, 208, 209 n.37.
knife 4, 40, 177 n.8, 182
language 3, 6 n.8, 9, 11, 14–15, 20 n.4, 22, 26, 28, 36–8, 38 n.15, 44–6, 54 n.2, 55, 70, 88, 143–4, 146–8, 176, 179–84, 187 n.6, 218–20, 235
Lieder 13
lineage 12, 21 n.5, 40, 121, 206
malady 4, 5, 7, 9 n.10, 85, 215, 215 n.3, 216, 216 n.5, 217 *see also* malady of Germany
masculinity, German manhood, German man 204, 204 n.31, 205–6
maternal language, maternal words 36, 178
mother tongue 15 n.16, 145
naturally German 209, 210, 210 n.40, 211
painted words 118, 142, 146, 146 n.13, 147

patriotism, patriotic Jewish-German stance 191, 202, 205–6
psyche, Omi's psyche 11, 14, 55, 189 *see also* Jewish-German psyche
signifier 10–11, 14 n.15, 46, 138, 142, 145–7, 184
skull 203
soil 4, 204 n.31
soldier, Jewish-German soldier 22, 22 n.7, 181, 189, 202, 203 n.30, 204, 204 n.31, 205, 207, 207 n.35, 210, 210 n.40, 213, 213 n.1, 240 n.15
soul 63, 182, 188, 198, 211
trope 7, 11–13, 63, 182–3, 195
untranslatable German 13, 22, 38 n.15, 44, 198 n.8, 219, 219 n.13
visions 62
"we" 47 n.11, 213–20, 216–19
words 19, 23–4, 30, 33, 36, 38 n.15, 46, 138–9, 143–8, 178, 185, 188 n.1, 217–18
Zugehör (sense of belonging) 14, 15 n.16, 20 n.4, 193–221, 221 n.1–2
ghost(s) 33, 68, 76–8, 85, 131, 131 n.20, 132, 216
God 18 n.1, 21 n.5, 28, 40 n.21, 41, 41 n.22, 43, 48, 106, 108 n.31
Gordinsky, Natasha 15 n.16
Gournay, Marie de 64 n.11, 109, 115
Gray, Hugh 133 n.27, 157 n.8
Grewe, Andrea 15 n.16, 221 n.2
Guattari, Félix 218 n.12, 222 n.2
Gyssels, Kathleen 15 n.16

hallucination, delirium, hallucinated logic, delirious

logic 195–212, 196, 200–2, 205, 211, 215
hauntology 132, 158
Heimat 235–6, 243
hell 5 n.7, 105n. 28, 148, 210 n.39, 212 n.43, 223
Herbrechter, Stefan 21 n.5
Heymann, Brigitte 15 n.16, 221 n.2
Hilfrich, Carola 15 n.16, 20 n.4
Hitler, Adolf 196, 223, 235, 241
Homer 3 n.5, 67, 100 n.21, 136, 140, 141, 247
Horn, Jeannette 34 n.10
hostility and hospitality, "Hostipitality" 58 n.1, 63
Howard, Richard 83 n.12, 128 n.15
Huguenots 66, 66 n.12, 70–1
Hunzinger, Ingeborg 223

idiom 14, 15, 20 n.4, 22, 36, 38 n.15, 91 n.5, 140, 182, 209
image 16, 16 n.19, 20 n.4, 56, 61 n.3, 80, 80 n.7, 84, 84 n.13, 86 n.21, 89–119, 91, 91 n.5, 95–6, 96 n.13, 97, 97 n.15, 98–102, 104, 105 n.28, 106, 109–11, 117, 120, 122, 125 n.11, 126, 128, 133–6, 138, 140, 141 n.7, 142–3, 147–8, 160, 160 n.13, 161, 165, 165 n.24, 248
impression, print 87, 175, 178, 185–6
incarceration 105, 143
  prison, imprisoned, imprisonment, prisoner 64 n.10, 88, 97–9, 99 n.18, 100–1, 101 n.22, 102, 102 n.24, 103, 103 n.27, 105 n.28, 106, 106 n.28, 108, 108 n.31, 111, 115–16, 116 n.48, 117–19, 128, 142, 146, 148, 179, 191, 217, 223, 225 n.6, 244
intertextuality 82

Iron Cross (*Eiserne Kreuz*) 191 n.5, 6, 203 n.30, 205, 205 n.32, 210, 210 n.38–9, 235
Israel 42, 42 n.1, 43 n.1, 44, 199
Italy 61, 66 n.12, 67, 71 n.28, 90, 95 n.12, 108 n.31, 109, 112, 223, 257
iterability, iterable 133

Jennings, Michael W. 83 n.12
Jephcott, Edmund 83 n.12
Jerusalem 42–6, 45 n.5, 49, 49 n.14, 50, 50 n.17, 18, 51 n.20, 55, 156–7, 163, 164 n.21
Jewish-German
  German Jews, Jews in Germany, Jews of Germany, misfortune of the German Jews, Jews of Osnabrück 3, 4, 8 n.10, 26, 63, 90, 116, 126, 126 n.13, 128, 136, 143, 154 n.2, 162 n.16, 179, 179 n.10, 188 n.2, 190 n.5, 191, 195–7, 200, 202, 208–9, 209 n.37, 216, 216 n.5, 217, 220, 222–3, 233–5, 237, 240 n.15, 241 n.16–17, 242
  Germanophone Jews 234
  Jew 3, 4, 8 n.10, 26, 35, 63 n.6, 90, 116, 125, 126 n.13, 128–9, 136, 143, 153 n.1, 154 n.2, 155, 162 n.16, 172, 179 n.10, 188 n.2, 190 n.5, 191, 194 n.1, 195, 196, 197, 198 n.9, 199–200, 202, 205, 208, 209 n.37, 211, 216 n.5, 217, 220, 220 n.15, 222–4, 233–5, 237–40, 240 n.13, 240 n.15, 241 n.16, 242–3
  Jewish 1 n.1, 3, 6 n.8, 7–9, 11–15, 14 n.15, 16, 22, 22 n.7, 23, 26, 28, 34, 40, 40 n.19, 105 n.28, 120, 132 n.23, 159, 193–221, 195, 195 n.1,

197–8, 198 n.6, 8, 199–202, 205, 208–11, 214, 215, 216, 219–20, 222–3, 231, 231 n.7, 232–4, 240, 240 n.15
Jewish-being 197, 200, 208, 210
Jewish-German belief 209, 211, 214–16
Jewish-German mystification 209
Jewish-German Odyssey 6 n.8, 7, 9
Jewish-German psyche, Jewish-German trope 11, 14, 193–221, 195, 198, 198 n.8, 199, 199 n.12, 201–2, 209, 211, 216, 219–20
Jewishness 199, 234
Judaism 200, 211, 234
Kabyle-Jewish 1 n.1
Jonas family *(Hélène Cixous's German family, maternal side: grandmother)*
Carlebach, Marga née Löwenstein *(daughter of Paula Löwenstein née Jonas; Paula is a sister of Omi, Rosi, Hélène Cixous's grandmother, she is Ève Cixous's cousin)* 12, 24, 37, 44–5, 45 n.5–6, 46–7, 47 n.7-10-11, 48, 48 n.11–13, 49, 49 n.14, 50, 50 n.17, 51, 51 n.19–20, 52, 72, 125 n.11, 126, 163, 178 n.9, 218
Jonas, Andreas *(brother of Rosalie Klein)*; Else Jonas née Cohn (spouse) 13, 14, 45 n.6, 121, 124, 124 n.8–9, 125, 125 n.9–10
Jonas, Helene née Meyer *(Hélène Cixous's great-grandmother: Omi's mother is the grandmother of Marga and Eva/Ève; see below)* 39, 39 n.18, 40–1, 44, 45 n.6, 48, 51, 158, 195 n.2, 243, 244
Jonas, Horst *(cousin of Ève Cixous née Klein, daughter of Rosalie Klein née Jonas)* 244, 244 n.20
Klein, Rosalie née Jonas *("Omi," also named Rosi or Rosy: Hélène Cixous's grandmother)* 4, 11, 13, 13 n.14, 14, 23 n.8, 25, 25 n.13, 26, 36, 38 n.15, 45 n.6, 61, 63, 98 n.17, 117 n.52, 118, 120–1, 121 n.2, 126, 136, 139, 141–3, 144, 144 n.10–11, 145 n.12, 146–7, 152, 152 n.1, 153, 153 n.1, 153–71, 158–60, 160 n.13, 161, 161 n.13–14, 162, 162 n.17, 163–4, 164 n.21, 165, 165 n.24, 166, 170–1, 172–3, 173, 173n. 1, 175–6, 182–4, 188, 188 n.2, 189, 189 n.3–4, 190, 190 n.5, 191, 191 n.5, 192, 195–6, 196 n.3, 204, 204 n.31, 205–8, 208 n.36–7, 209 n.37, 211, 213, 213 n.1, 215, 218, 234, 237 n.11, 245
Joyce, James 23, 246–7, 247 n.21, 248
Junk, Peter 125 n.9

Kafka, Franz 9, 25, 26 n.14, 218 n.12, 222 n.2, 234–5, 242
Kamuf, Peggy 146, 146 n.14
Katzmann, Siegfried (friend of Ève Cixous, also referred to as Fred) 25, 26 n.14, 27, 35, 125 n.11, 172, 173 n.1, 177, 177 n.8, 180, 181, 181 n.13, 190, 190 n.5, 210, 210 n.40, 211, 212, 212 n.43, 214, 214 n.2, 216
Klein family *(Hélène Cixous's German family, maternal side: grandfather)*

Klein, Abraham Meir (*Hélène Cixous's great grandfather, grandfather of Ève*) 231 n.7, 232
Klein (née), Erika (Éri) Barme (*sister of Ève Cixous née Klein*) 48, 232, 232 n.10
Klein, Eva (*Ève Cixous née Klein, Hélène Cixous's mother*) 4, 10, 23, 45, 181, 182, 232, 232 n.8
Klein, Leah 231 n.7
Klein, Marcus (Mordechai) 231 n.7
Klein, Michael (*Hélène Cixous's grandfather*) 12, 14, 22, 22 n.7, 23, 202, 204, 204n. 31, 205, 205 n.32, 207, 207 n.35, 210 n.38, 231, 231 n.7, 234
Klein, Moritz (Maurice) 88, 160, 161, 161 n.13, 166, 231 n.7
Klein (née), Rais, Jeanne 231 n.7
Klein, Rosa (Rivka) née Ehrenstein (*Hélène Cixous's great grandmother, grandmother of Ève*)
Klein, Samson (Schamschi) 231 n.7
Klein, Selma (Zelda) 231 n.7
Klein, Sigmund (Asher) 231 n.7
KPD (*Communist Party of Germany*) 223 n.4, 244 n.20
Kristallnacht, November 9, 1938 13, 25, 25 n.13, 26–7, 30, 33, 50, 74, 98 n.17, 126, 126 n.13, 144 n.12, 152, 152 n.1, 163, 164 n.21, 172, 173 n.1, 189, 190
Aktionjuden 153, 172, 213
Kristall 50, 145–6, 148, 152, 152 n.1, 163, 164
night of fire, ignition, ignite, burn 166, 179, 184, 186, 188

La Boétie, Étienne de 56, 77, 97, 112, 113, 114, 115, 117, 117 n.51, 118, 134
Landé, Peter 162 n.16, 181 n.13
Lanly, André 64 n.11, 86 n.21, 115
Larousse, Pierre 24 n.12
law, 36, 37, 40, 41, 68 n.16, 92 n.7, 8, 96 n.13, 135, 171 n.28, 172, 198, 201, 222, 264
racial laws 120, 222, 235
Leclair, Bertrand 227
Legros, Alain 100 n.20
Lemêtre, Jean-Jacques 31, 31 n.1, 35, 42
liberation, liberty 14, 78, 98, 101, 105 n.28, 111, 117–8, 226 n.6
liberation of women 250
literature 1, 9, 10 n.11, 15 n.16, 24, 29, 41, 48, 69, 69 n.23, 76, 82, 85, 91, 93 n.8, 94, 97 n.15, 105 n.28, 136 n.29. 140, 140 n.6, 215, 225 n.6, 245–8
Littré, Émile 59 n.1, 78 n.6
logos 11, 201–2, 206, 211
London 23, 144 n.11
Luxemburg, Rosa 9, 225 n.6, 226 n.6

malady of Germany, 4, 5, 7, 9 n.10, 215, 215 n.3, 216, 216 n.5, 217
suffering (for Germany) 1, 3–5, 7, 11, 14
Germanalgia 5
Marder, Elissa 37 n.15, 38 n.15
Marin, Louis 91 n.5
maternal 14, 24, 63, 67 n.15, 96 n.13, 233
Mauro, Lucio 71 n.29
Maximus, Valerius 106 n.29
Mayer, Hans 1, 1 n.2, 3, 3 n.3–4, 4, 7, 7 n.9, 9, 12
McGowan, Margaret 71 n.29, 72 n.29
Medusa, *Laugh of the Medusa* 223–4

Index   267

Mehlman, Jeffrey 29 n.17
memory 53–149, 13, 23, 24, 54, 54
    n.2, 55–6, 59, 73, 86, 86 n.21,
    87, 98, 99, 101 n.22, 102, 107,
    107 n.30, 110, 111, 117, 135,
    136, 146, 147, 158, 160, 184,
    228, 243, 245, 247, 248
  dismemberment, dismembered
    55, 68, 70, 89, 90, 102, 107,
    108, 109, 109 n.39, 110–14,
    114 n.44, 115–18, 123, 126,
    127, 131, 134, 135, 148
  Erinnerung 146–8
  memorization 81, 110
  oblivion 157–8
  Omi's silence 170–2, 175–6,
    182–4, 192, 205
  omission 162
  recall 28, 41, 49, 90, 100, 101,
    108, 109, 117, 160, 176, 177,
    197, 218
  recollection 88
  recordation 85–7
  remember, "*Remembrer*" 13, 61,
    64 n.10, 73, 89–119, 89 n.1,
    90–1, 97, 101, 101 n.22, 102
    n.24, 107, 110–12, 115–17, 117
    n.51, 119, 147, 154–5 n.2–3,
    155, 158 n.9, 165 n.23, 223,
    228, 240, 247
  remembrance 13, 57–73, 91, 99,
    102, 107, 110–11, 116, 136,
    147, 155 n.3, 158 n.9, 198
Mesguich, Daniel 227
Mess of Germany, curse of the
    Jewish-German psyche
    219–20
Milesi, Laurent 21 n.5
Mnouchkine, Ariane 242 n.18
monstruous bodies 113 n.43, 115
Montaigne, Michel de 4 n.5,
    55–6, 61–3, 63 n.6–8, 64, 64
    n.11, 65–6, 66 n.12, 67–8, 68
    n.16–22, 69, 69 n.23–5, 70,

70 n.26–7, 71, 71 n.28–9, 72,
    72 n.29–30, 73–6, 76 n.3, 77–8,
    78, 78 n.5, 79–82, 82 n.11,
    84–5, 85 n.15–18, 86, 86
    n.19–21, 87, 87 n.22–4, 88, 88
    n.25, 89, 90–1, 91 n.5, 92–3,
    93 n.8–9, 94, 94 n.12, 95, 95
    n.12, 97, 97 n.15, 98 n.16, 99,
    99 n.18, 100, 100 n.20, 101,
    101 n.22, 102–3, 105, 105 n.28,
    106 n.28–9, 107, 107 n.30, 108,
    108 n.29–32, 109, 109 n.33–9,
    110–12, 112 n.40–1, 113
    n.42–3, 114, 114 n.43–4, 115,
    115 n.45–6, 116–17, 117 n.51,
    118, 119, 199 n.54–8, 127–9,
    131, 133–4, 141–2, 146–8, 166
    n.27, 223
  Montaigne, Tower of 13, 89–119,
    90–1, 91 n.5, 92, 92 n.7, 93,
    93 n.8, 10, 94, 94 n.12, 95, 96
    n.13, 97, 97 n.15, 98 n.16, 99,
    100, 100 n.20, 101, 101 n.22,
    102–3, 106 n.28, 29, 111–12,
    114, 115, 117, 117 n.51, 118,
    119, 147–8, 166 n.27, 223
  Arabesque, grotesque 105 n.28,
    113, 113 n.43, 114 n.43, 44,
    115–16, 118, 126, 128, 148
  Librerie (Montaigne's librairie)
    13, 77, 90, 94, 100, 102, 103,
    112, 115, 119
  Nostalgia of the Tower 93 n.10
Morse, Stephen P. 162 n.16, 181
    n.13
mother, 3 n.5–4, 5 n.7, 6 n.8, 8 n.10,
    23, 26 n.14, 28 n.16, 29, 31,
    32 n.2, 35, 35 n.11, 37, 38
    n.15, 39, 42 n.1, 43 n.1, 45,
    45 n.6, 47 n.7, 10, 48 n.11, 49
    n.15, 51 n.19, 58 n.1, 63, 63
    n.6, 67, 67 n.15, 68 n.18, 72,
    72 n.32, 74–6, 80 n.7, 93,
    93 n.8–10, 94, 97, 100 n.21,

268 Index

102 n.26, 118, 121 n.2, 136–7, 137 n.1, 138, 139 n.5, 140–1, 144, 146, 153 n.1, 154 n.2, 158, 158 n.10, 159, 160 n.13, 161, 161 n.13, 162, 163 n.18, 164, 165 n.23, 173 n.1, 175 n.2, 176, 176 n.6, 177, 177 n.8, 178 n.9, 182, 188 n.2, 191 n.7, 198 n.6, 203 n.30, 206, 206 n.33, 208 n.36, 209 n.37, 213 n.1, 214, 215, 215 n.4, 216 n.5, 219, 220 n.15, 223, 223 n.4, 224, 225 n.6, 226 n.6, 228–30, 230 n.6, 232–7, 241, 241 n.17, 244–5, 248
and daughters 249–50

Nancy, Jean-Luc 67, 68 n.16
Nazism, Nazi, Third Reich, NSDAP 1, 4, 8 n.10, 24, 24 n.11, 26, 29, 33–4, 44, 44 n.4, 64, 71, 88, 90, 121 n.2, 123, 146–8, 161, 172–3, 173 n.1, 175, 188, 188 n.2, 190, 191, 191 n.5, 196, 199, 199 n.12, 202, 202 n.29, 204, 210 n.38, 222–3, 232 n.10, 237, 241, 243
anti-Nazi 9
New York City
Ellis Island 181
Ground Zero 117
Twin Towers 117
1968 (May of) 97 n.15
Nussbaum, Felix 125, 125 n.11, 126, 127, 128, 142, 189, 189 n.4, 196, 196 n.3
Nusse, Céline 227

O'Donnell, Mary Eileen 34 n.10
opaque, opacity 110, 134–5
origin 5, 9, 15 n.16, 25, 55, 59, 61, 67 n.15, 85, 92, 107, 110–12, 116, 123, 140, 151–92, 156–8, 172, 175, 183

originary exile 1–16, 1, 7, 9, 183
Osnabrück
Bocksturm (or Bucksturm), Heger Tor, Natruper Tor 106, 108 n.28, 185, 185 n.2
Borken 43 n.2, 124, 124 n.8
cemetery 40 n.19, 195
City-of-Peace 50, 50 n.18
Friedrichstraße 124 n.9, 166
Gemen 43, 43 n.2, 45, 45 n.6, 47, 47 n.7
Hase river 139, 142, 143 n.14
Hauptbahnhof (Central train station) 38 n.15, 132, 144 n.12, 145 n.12
Hexengang 116 n.48
Instrument of peace, *Instrumentum pacis Osnabrugensis*, Peace, peace 50, 59, 60–1, 71, 73, 74–88, 78–9, 81, 85, 215, 226
Ledenhof square 188, 188 n.2
Nikolaiort 20 n.2, 59, 124 n.9, 141, 141 n.8, 142, 172–4, 190–2, 192 n.7
synagogue, remains 26, 27, 44, 62, 63, 63 n.6, 64, 64 n.10, 65, 70–1, 74, 78, 82–4, 87–9, 117, 117 n.52, 149, 165, 165 n.24, 166, 166 n.26, 169–72, 178–9, 181 n.13, 184, 186, 186 n.5, 189, 189 n.4, 190, 191 n.5, 196, 196 n.3, 211–16, 216 n.5, 217, 217 n.10

Panvinius, Onufrius 71 n.29
painting 13, 55–6, 56 n.3, 83, 91 n.5, 100 n.20, 105 n.28, 106 n.29, 112, 113 n.43, 114, 114 n.43–4, 115–21, 126, 127, 127 n.14, 128, 131, 133, 134, 135, 141, 146, 148, 157 n.8, 160 n.13
painter 111–12, 113 n.43, 114, 114 n.43, 44, 115, 128, 141, 142

Palestine 14, 124 n.9, 125–6, 126 n.13, 147–8, 156 n.7
paradise 83 n.12, 84, 116, 148, 223
Payne, Lewis 128 n.15
Perec, Georges 184 n.1
persecution(s) 3, 4, 24, 26, 34–7, 61, 71, 74, 77, 88, 90, 128, 131, 138, 143, 148, 195, 196, 202 n.29, 231 n.7, 239 n.13
phallogocentrism, phallogocentric delirium 202, 205, 211
phantom(s) 76, 99, 132, 139, 147
"Phantomgraph" 129, 129 n.18
philosophy, philosophize 76, 80 n.7, 85 n.18
picture, depiction 55, 61, 61 n.3, 64, 64 n.10, 110–12, 113 n.43, 114 n.43, 44, 117 n.52, 118, 120–36, 122–3, 126–8, 127–8, 131, 133–4, 135–6, 138, 148, 157 n.8, 166, 166 n.26, 175, 206, 211
poetry, poet 9, 10, 10 n.11, 12, 24, 36, 41, 61 n.5, 77, 192, 215
Polan, Dana 218 n.12
Pompeii 72 n.31, 106 n.29
Pontalis, Jean-Bertrand 33, 33 n.7
portrait, self-portrait 61, 61 n.4, 85–6, 86 n.21, 91 n.5, 96, 96 n.13, 112, 117 n.52, 127, 127 n.14, 138
Prenowitz, Eric 10 n.12, 11 n.12
proper name, improper name, name, nameless 11, 111, 133, 161, 161 n.13, 179, 182–3, 182 n.14, 185
Proust, Marcel 242, 246–7
Prunis, Father 66 n.12
Purcell, Sally A. J. 247 n.21

reconciliation 73, 83, 116
reconciliatory process 58 n.1
recording, recording device, tape recorder, recorder, record, *recordation*, cord 13, 28 n.16, 56, 56 n.3, 74–88, 75, 75 n.2, 76–9, 80–1, 80 n.7, 82–6, 86 n.21, 87–8, 95, 109, 127–8, 134
reflection (visual, image) 97–8
reformation 71 n.28
refugee(s) 6 n.8, 7, 143
remainder 52, 161
Remarque, Erich Maria 210 n.38
Rembrandt 91 n.5, 126, 127, 127 n.14, 142
reminiscence 39, 99, 111
response, responsibility, answer 12, 52 n.21, 93 n.8, 136 n.28
Robbins, Tim 34 n.10
Rochlitz, Rainer 83 n.12
Roman Charity 103, 106, 106 n.29, 107, 111, 114–16, 118–9, 138, 141, 146, 148, 223
Rome 55, 61–6, 66 n.12, 68, 68 n.19, 69, 69 n.24, 70, 70 n.27, 71, 71 n.28, 29, 72, 72 n.29, 30, 73, 75, 77, 82 n.11, 94, 105 n.28, 107–11
Rosenzweig, Franz 199–200, 202, 202 n.29
Roussel, Frédérique 56 n.4, 139 n.5
Royle, Nicholas 22 n.6
Rozenberg, Paul 227
ruin(s), debris 13, 56, 56 n.4, 57–73, 62–3, 63 n.6, 64, 64 n.10, 65–6, 66 n.12, 68, 68 n.22, 69, 69 n.24, 25, 70–1, 73–9, 82–3, 85, 87–8, 88 n.26, 89–90, 89–119, 94, 94 n.11, 107, 106, 111, 116–18, 123, 123 n.6, 166, 169–70, 186, 198, 219
Rusch, Pierre 83 n.12

Schlünder, Susanne 15 n.16, 221 n.2
Schulte Nordholt, Annelies 15 n.16
Second World War 143, 223, 223 n.4, 224, 224 n.6, 231 n.7

secret 14–15, 19, 19 n.1, 21, 25, 28, 28 n.16, 43, 62, 68, 68 n.18, 69, 69 n.23, 70, 73, 84, 91, 100–1, 106, 138, 140, 155, 155 n.4, 156–8, 165, 165 n.23, 183, 188, 194, 194 n.1, 203 n.30, 215, 248

Screech, Michael Andrew 65 n.11, 113 n.43

secrecy 68, 68 n.18, 69 n.23, 73, 156, 194 n.1, 248

secretary 64, 65, 67, 68, 68 n.18, 69, 69 n.23, 70, 73, 75, 76, 81, 82 n.11, 85, 108, 128, 197, 216

secretion 68 n.18

Seitz, Axel 245 n.20

Sellmeyer, Martina 125 n.9

Sephardic legacy 14 n.15

Sepulchre 66 n.12, 68 n.19

Shibboleth, *Schibboleth* 22, 77, 221 n.2

shock 3 n.5, 4, 58 n.1, 95, 97, 100 n.21, 131–4

signature, unsigned 29 n.17, 177, 177 n.7, 178

spectacle 66 n.12, 69, 110–11, 179

specter, spectral 77–8, 99

Sperling, Jutta Gisela 106 n.29

Stack, Liam 118 n.54

Stein, Gustav 121–2, 127, 134

Stevens, Christa 14 n.15, 15 n.16, 91 n.5

stolpersteine ("stumbling stone") 122–4, 124 n.8, 125 n.9, 10, 145 n.12, 162

Stone, Will 98 n.16

Strachey, Alix 32 n.3

Strachey, James 32 n.3

Strasbourg 23, 45 n.6, 121, 121 n.2

sublimation 7, 38 n.15, 111, 117

substitution 128, 180, 197

super-ego 93

symptom 14, 82, 83, 166, 202, 202n. 28, 209, 211, 235

telephone, telephony, landline, telephone line 19–30, 6 n.8, 12, 18 n.1, 20, 20 n.2, 3, 21, 21 n.5, 22, 24–5, 28–9, 31, 36–7, 38 n.16, 40, 40 n.21, 41–3, 43 n.1, 44–5, 46–7, 47 n.9, 10, 48–9, 49 n.14, 15, 51, 67, 80 n.7, 81 n.9, 92, 92 n.7, 8, 186 n.5, 189, 227, 250

call *see under* German

recall *see under* memory

Théâtre du Soleil 239, 242, 242 n.18

torture(s) 44, 77, 88, 88 n.26, 100, 102, 106 n.28, 108 n.32, 109, 111, 112, 123 n.6, 148, 238

trace(s) 55, 64, 75, 87–8, 100–1, 123, 135, 160–1, 178, 184, 234, 249

trauma, traumatic 5, 35, 78–9, 83, 110, 111, 131, 143, 147

Treskow, Isabella von 15 n.16

Tyson, Alan 32 n.3

"*unheimlich*," "*unheimlichkeit*," uncanny, uncanniness 32 n.3, 33, 33 n.4, 7, 37, 37 n.14, 55, 145 n.12, 249

untranslatable 15, 22, 38 n.16, 44, 198 n.8, 219, 219 n.13

Vichy (regime) 240, 240 n.15

violence 6, 6 n.8–7, 105, 203, 203 n.30, 236–7

vision 16, 16 n.19, 55–6, 62, 64, 71 n.29, 72 n.29, 73, 76, 91, 91 n.5, 92–106, 95–6, 96 n.13, 14, 97–102, 105, 106, 106 n.28, 29, 107, 111, 114–6, 117 n.52, 118, 118 n.53, 134, 138–9, 141, 143, 147, 211, 223

voice, voices 11, 21 n.5, 27 n.15, 31, 31 n.2, 45, 46, 47, 47 n.10, 48n. 13, 67, 68, 68n. 18, 69,

71–2, 74, 80 n.7, 84 n.14, 90, 95 n.12, 132, 136, 141, 159, 161, 161 n.13, 164, 202, 205, 216, 218 n.11, 227

Wajsbrot, Cécile 6, 15 n.16, 24 n.11
wall(s) 52 n.21, 54, 97, 98, 100, 101, 101 n.22, 102 n.23, 103, 106 n.28, 112, 113 n.43, 114 n.43, 181–2, 182, 182 n.14, 183–5, 185 n.2, 191, 226, 237
wars of religion 24, 59, 61, 71, 77–8, 82 n.11, 87, 87 n.22, 100
war widow (Omi), war widows 121 n.1, 204, 210
"We" 213–20, 47 n.11, 213, 216–9
"we are burning" 212 n.4, 213, 216, 216 n.8, 217–18
Weber, Samuel 29 n.17
Weimar 27, 44, 244 n.20
Wenders, Wim 61 n.3
Western Wall 54 n.2, 55, 156–7, 159, 160–1, 163–4
Westphal, Bertrand 10 n.11
Westphalia 24, 43 n.2, 59, 60–1, 61 n.4, 156, 156 n.7, 226
Wiedergutmachung 36, 36 n.13, 37, 38 n.15
Wilhelm II 207
Witt, Catherine 91 n.5

woman, women (history of) 26 n.14, 54 n.2, 106, 129 n.18, 131 n.19, 145 n.12, 158–9, 159 n.11, 173 n.1, 191 n.5, 206, 213 n.1, 222–5, 225 n.6, 229, 230, 235, 250
women writing 161, 161 n.14, 163
writing and Germany: as filiation, generation, lineage, as writing and painting, as writing and performing 7, 10, 11, 13–14, 21, 24–5, 27–8, 34, 37, 39, 48, 54–6, 56 n.4, 64, 68–75, 77–8, 78 n.5, 79–83, 85, 87, 88, 91 n.5, 92 n.6, 99–100, 100 n.20, 21, 110–12, 113 n.43, 114 n.44, 115, 117–18, 188 n.53, 120, 123–4, 127, 132–6, 141, 144, 146–8, 155 n.4, 156–9, 159 n.11, 160, 161 n.14, 163, 163 n.18, 170, 175–7, 178 n.9, 179, 184, 191, 209, 218, 218 n.12, 224, 230, 238, 246–8

Zepp, Susanne 15 n.16
Zionism 8 n.10, 242
Zournazi, Mary 61 n.3
Zweig, Stephan 98 n.16

Volumes in the series:

Vol. 1. *Improvisation as Art: Conceptual Challenges, Historical Perspectives*
by Edgar Landgraf

Vol. 2. *The German Pícaro and Modernity: Between Underdog and Shape-Shifter*
by Bernhard Malkmus

Vol. 3. *Citation and Precedent: Conjunctions and Disjunctions of German Law and Literature*
by Thomas O. Beebee

Vol. 4. *Beyond Discontent: 'Sublimation' from Goethe to Lacan*
by Eckart Goebel

Vol. 5. *From Kafka to Sebald: Modernism and Narrative Form*
edited by Sabine Wilke

Vol. 6. *Image in Outline: Reading Lou Andreas-Salomé*
by Gisela Brinker-Gabler

Vol. 7. *Out of Place: German Realism, Displacement, and Modernity*
by John B. Lyon

Vol. 8. *Thomas Mann in English: A Study in Literary Translation*
by David Horton

Vol. 9. *The Tragedy of Fatherhood: King Laius and the Politics of Paternity in the West*
by Silke-Maria Weineck

Vol. 10. *The Poet as Phenomenologist: Rilke and the* New Poems
by Luke Fischer

Vol. 11. *The Laughter of the Thracian Woman: A Protohistory of Theory*
by Hans Blumenberg, translated by Spencer Hawkins

Vol. 12. *Roma Voices in the German-Speaking World*
by Lorely French

Vol. 13. *Vienna's Dreams of Europe: Culture and Identity beyond the Nation-State*
by Katherine Arens

Vol. 14. *Thomas Mann and Shakespeare: Something Rich and Strange*
edited by Tobias Döring and Ewan Fernie

Vol. 15. *Goethe's Families of the Heart*
by Susan E. Gustafson

Vol. 16. *German Aesthetics: Fundamental Concepts from Baumgarten to Adorno*
edited by J. D. Mininger and Jason Michael Peck

Vol. 17. *Figures of Natality: Reading the Political in the Age of Goethe*
by Joseph D. O'Neil

Vol. 18. *Readings in the Anthropocene: The Environmental Humanities, German Studies, and Beyond*
edited by Sabine Wilke and Japhet Johnstone

Vol. 19 *Building Socialism: Architecture and Urbanism in East German Literature, 1955–1973*
by Curtis Swope

Vol. 20. *Ghostwriting: W. G. Sebald's Poetics of History*
by Richard T. Gray

Vol. 21. *Stereotype and Destiny in Arthur Schnitzler's Prose: Five Psycho-Sociological Readings*
by Marie Kolkenbrock

Vol. 22. *Sissi's World: The Empress Elisabeth in Memory and Myth*
edited by Maura E. Hametz and Heidi Schlipphacke

Vol. 23. *Posthumanism in the Age of Humanism: Mind, Matter, and the Life Sciences after Kant* edited by Edgar Landgraf, Gabriel Trop, and Leif Weatherby

Vol. 24. *Staging West German Democracy: Governmental PR Films and the Democratic Imaginary, 1953–1963*

by Jan Uelzmann

Vol. 25. *The Lever as Instrument of Reason: Technological Constructions of Knowledge around 1800*

by Jocelyn Holland

Vol. 26. *The Fontane Workshop: Manufacturing Realism in the Industrial Age of Print*

by Petra McGillen

Vol. 27. *Gender, Collaboration, and Authorship in German Culture: Literary Joint Ventures, 1750–1850*

edited by Laura Deiulio and John B. Lyon

Vol. 28. *Kafka's Stereoscopes: The Political Function of a Literary Style*

by Isak Winkel Holm

Vol. 29. *Ambiguous Aggression in German Realism and Beyond: Flirtation, Passive Aggression, Domestic Violence*

by Barbara N. Nagel

Vol. 30. *Thomas Bernhard's Afterlives*

edited by Stephen Dowden, Gregor Thuswaldner, and Olaf Berwald

Vol. 31. *Modernism in Trieste: The Habsburg Mediterranean and the Literary Invention of Europe, 1870–1945*

by Salvatore Pappalardo

Vol. 32. *Grotesque Visions: The Science of Berlin Dada*

by Thomas O. Haakenson

Vol. 33. *Theodor Fontane: Irony and Avowal in a Post-Truth Age*

by Brian Tucker

Vol. 34. *Jane Eyre in German Lands: The Import of Romance, 1848–1918*

by Lynne Tatlock

Vol. 35. *Weimar in Princeton: Thomas Mann and the Kahler Circle*

by Stanley Corngold

Vol. 36. *Authors and the World: Modes and Models of Literary Authorship in 20th and 21st Century Germany*

by Rebecca Braun

Vol. 37. *Germany from the Outside: Rethinking German Cultural History in an Age of Displacement*

edited by Laurie Johnson

Vol. 38. *France/Kafka: An Author in Theory*

by John T. Hamilton

Vol. 39. *Representing Social Precarity in German Literature and Film*

edited by Sophie Duvernoy, Karsten Olson, and Ulrich Plass

Vol. 40. *The "German Illusion": Germany and Jewish-German Motifs in Hélène Cixous's Late Work*

by Olivier Morel

www.ingramcontent.com/pod-product-compliance
Lightning Source LLC
Chambersburg PA
CBHW070021010526
44117CB00011B/1660